THE PSYCHOLOGY OF HUMAN BEHAVIOR

Third Edition

THE PSYCHOLOGY
OF HUMAN BEHAVIOR

Third Edition

RICHARD A. KALISH

Berkeley, California

Brooks/Cole Publishing Company
Monterey, California
A Division of Wadsworth Publishing Company, Inc.

ISBN: 0-8185-0079-4
L.C. Catalog Card No: 72-92710
Printed in the United States of America
  2 3 4 5 6 7 8 9 10—77 76 75 74 73

This book was edited by Micky Lawler and designed by Jane Mitchell. It was typeset, printed, and bound by Kingsport Press, Kingsport, Tennessee.

Preface

Revising a book, I find, is always more complicated than it initially seems. Although numerous new matters are obvious "musts" for inclusion, virtually none of the previous discussions have diminished enough in importance to be eliminated. As a result, I face the prospect of a book that grows with each new edition to the extent that both reading endurance and pocketbook limitations become overwhelmed.

With this revision I was determined to avoid that pitfall. For every page that was added, one page had to be deleted. The environmentalists continue to remind us that growth is not, by definition, good. If true for the environment, the advice is doubly true for textbooks. This edition shows growth, I hope, only in the psychosocial sense—as being a better book. In that fashion it represents the growth of the field of psychology, the greater maturity of students, the greater sophistication and awareness of faculty, and the personal growth that I hope I have had in the years since the last edition.

This third edition is new in many ways. Most of the old photographs have been discarded and replaced by more than 70 new pictures, the majority of them taken specifically for this book by Lehman J. Pinckney. And the format, the cover, and the size are all different.

But the changes are more than skin deep. Only a few years ago, when I felt I was being up-to-date and relevant (and how I have since come to dislike that particular word!), I had not anticipated how rapidly additional changes would come about. The last edition commented on the changing role of women, the increasing impact on the national scene of nonblack minority groups, contemporary trends in sexual behavior, the use of psychedelic drugs, the meaning of the death encounter, the use of crisis intervention. In the present edition each of these topics is greatly expanded. In the last edition I began to reduce the emphasis on dating and going steady; in this edition these materials have been totally revised. In the last edition I avoided the writings about territoriality; in this edition there is an entire chapter on the impact of the physical environment on human behavior. And there are new and renewed controversies: the implications of biofeedback systems, the political ramifications of Arthur Jensen's writings, the thrust of behavior modification, the significance of deprivation, and the entirely new meaning for the expression "my old man." Even in the more traditional areas of psychology—motivation, mental illness, learning theory, perception—new ideas and new research required consideration.

So, when the dust had cleared, the third edition had 102 new references, one totally new chapter, and several thoroughly revised chapters. No chapter escaped unscathed, and not very many pages went intact from the second to the third edition. Even the organization of the book was altered in ways that I felt smoothed out some of the rough spots in the last version.

The orientation is still the same. And the audience is still the same, although both they and I have matured a bit since last time. Yet, despite all the changes in this edition, I feel I can safely quote one paragraph from the previous preface—it still holds true:

> Like the first (two) edition(s), this book has been written for students who come from a wide variety of backgrounds and who may never take another course in psychology. They want to learn about the discipline of psychology, but they also want to learn about human behavior as it applies to them and their world and to their future roles in family and career. I have again attempted to provide a book with a minimum of jargon, one that emphasizes concepts and that uses only the more important psychological terminology. In writing this book, I have aimed at integrating research and theory with concepts and ideas, rather than offering a review of the latest literature; and I have sought to provide a theoretical frame of reference, rather than a totally eclectic approach.

Increasing numbers of four-year schools are dropping the 600-page, double-column texts of the past and turning to briefer books with less traditional coverage—books like this one. Nevertheless, we have continued to depend heavily on junior college faculty for reviewing this book. Those reviewers who were especially helpful were P. James Geiwitz of the University of California, Santa Barbara, Leonard Delury of Portland Community College, John Hoffman of East Los Angeles College, Richard Hageman of Northern Virginia Community College, Marilyn Howe of Quinsigamond Community College, Edward J. Gunderson of Milwaukee Technical College, and Lorna Knokey of Antelope Valley Junior College.

In addition, I must acknowledge those whose efforts have aided so much in the nonverbal aspects of this volume: Ed Fisher, whose cartoons I enjoy as much as ever; photographers Lehman J. Pinckney, P. C. Peri, John G. Warford, Liane Enkelis, Michael Parker, and Mark Davidson; the resources of Braniff International Airlines, the University of California, Davis, and Professor Melvin Ramey, the Institute of Transportation and Traffic Engineering, UCLA, and Dr.

Slade Hulbert, Columbia Broadcasting System, Crippled Children's Society of Los Angeles, Arts and Humanities Division, UCLA Extension, Litton Industries, and Brooks/Cole Publishing Company. Also deserving of thanks is Ann Johnson, who, in addition to being responsible for the Study Guide that accompanies this book, added some of her own ideas to the text itself and who, with Roberta Steiner, handled the cutting, pasting, and typing necessary to turn the second edition into the third edition.

An author is expected to dedicate his book to—or at least acknowledge the importance of—his wife and children. In all candor, I won't. In the spring of 1958 my wife (then not yet my wife) and I had brunch with two members of the Brooks/Cole (then still Wadsworth Publishing Company) staff, and I signed my first contract with them. Since that time my wife and, later, my children have become so accustomed to these publishers' reminding me of deadlines or my reminding them of unanswered letters that I don't think my family would know what to make of me were I not working away on one manuscript or another. (At age 4 one of my children was asked what kind of work her father did, and she calmly responded "He's a typist.")

I dedicate this book, then, to its readers and their families, for whom it is new, rather than to my family, who have lived with it for so long that it has become a part of us.

Richard A. Kalish

Contents

INTRODUCING
PSYCHOLOGY

PART 1

1 Psychology: Its Concerns and Its People

Each person begins his first course in psychology with a different set of preconceived notions about what psychology is. Some individuals assume that they will learn to "psych out" all their friends; some are afraid of what they might learn about themselves; some are positive that psychology is merely common sense. None of these anticipations is likely to be found accurate. Perhaps the wisest course for a student to follow is to be actively curious and to have as few preconceived notions as possible.

Almost nothing fascinates people more than learning about themselves. Today man has opened the vastness of space and the minuteness of the atom for exploration; yet the excitement of the universe is no greater than the excitement of our own thinking and feeling and behaving. Nor is the solar system more complex than a single human being.

People readily accept the idea that it takes a great deal of study to learn about space. After all, space is infinitely vast, and the problems of its study are obviously highly technical. The idea that learning about **behavior*** also requires study is more difficult to accept. "I've lived with myself for 18 (or 30 or 60) years. I should know myself by now, and I should know other people, too."

However, the realization eventually comes that understanding the behavior of others, or of ourselves, is not so simple as it may seem. "Why do I sit watching television when I *know* I have an exam the day after tomorrow?" "Why is it often easier to talk to a girl I don't particularly like than to one I like a lot?" "Why do I

---

* Words or phrases in boldface type are defined in the Glossary.

just smile when he makes nasty comments about my friend, instead of telling him what I really think?" Such examples of everyday behavior are seldom easy to understand. Consider, then, how much more difficult it is to explain phenomena like love and fear, marital success and vocational failure, mental disorder and social adjustment.

Some people claim to have found the key to understanding human behavior in such statements as "Do unto others as you would have them do unto you" or "Man does not live by bread alone." Are these statements true? For the most part they express principles accepted by modern psychologists, but they hardly provide a comprehensive explanation of human behavior.

The purpose of this book is to introduce the world of human behavior as it is explored by psychologists. You will read about things you already know and about things you may never have considered. You will find some of your questions about human behavior answered, and—if you are a perceptive and inquisitive student—you will find many new questions to ask. You may gain a better understanding of yourself and of those around you, and, hopefully, you will find the study of human behavior both exciting and enjoyable.

PSYCHOLOGY: WHAT IS IT?

Psychology is the science that attempts to understand, describe, predict, and influence behavior—particularly human behavior. The **psychologist** may study behavior scientifically, or he may apply the theories and research findings of others to practical problems. Sometimes he does both.

PSYCHOLOGY AS A SCIENCE

Psychology is defined as a science because psychologists make extensive use of the scientific method and attempt to build scientific theories of human behavior. The research psychologist begins by showing curiosity, which some writers feel is the single most important characteristic of a scientist (McCain & Segal, 1969). He is curious about a topic, and he studies existing knowledge concerning that topic. From this knowledge, and occasionally from an accidental occurrence or casual observation, the scientist develops a hunch. After seeking out evidence already available that may support his hunch, he may decide to state the hunch formally as a research **hypothesis.** He must then determine the proper scientific method and procedures for testing the adequacy of his hypothesis.

Once the method and procedures are established, the research psychologist has to translate his ideas into action and collect data. When he has the data, he analyzes them to determine whether they bear out the initial hypothesis. Whether they do or not, they are likely to lead to new hunches and more research.

Since the purpose of a science is not just to collect facts but to develop an understanding of events, psychologists usually try to fit their findings into theories or systems of behavior. These theories or systems generate new ideas and explanations, which are testable through additional research. Most professional psychologists feel obligated to report their findings in a professional journal so that other researchers can use them as stepping-stones for their own research and theory building. Slowly, psychological scientists build, alter, and improve their theories and their understanding.

Psychologists direct a large part of their research efforts at determining relationships between **variables,** or things that vary or change. They also wish to know the conditions under which the change will occur. **Motivation** to succeed in college is one example of a variable. The motivation of any one person will vary or change with time, and the motivations of two or more people are very likely to differ. The psychologist wants to learn what conditions will change the motivation to succeed and what produces the differences among individuals in the motivation to succeed. Is the variable *attitude toward teacher* related to the variable *motivation to succeed?* Does the variable *parental reaction to education* lead to differences among students on the variable *motivation to succeed?*

To select another example: psychologists are interested in learning whether the variable *spanking* has an effect on the variable *obedience.* If the two variables are related — as they appear to be — psychologists will probe further into the problem. How will spanking affect obedience? Is it true that the more spanking a child receives, the more obedient he will become? Is there a point beyond which increased spanking no longer leads to increased obedience but may actually produce an increase in disobedience? Do some children respond favorably to spanking, whereas others indicate little behavior change? What predictions regarding obedience can be made from knowing about spanking? As answers to these questions become established, new variables are added. Under what conditions will spanking lead to obedience? Will it lead to behavior changes other than obedience? Will it produce anger toward the parents? Will it lead to running away from home or pinching baby sister when no one is looking? Piece by piece the puzzle is fitted together as the psychologist's ability to predict and describe improves. (See Chapter 2 for a further discussion of research methodology.)

In conducting research, the psychologist needs to be aware of four important requirements: (1) control of conditions, (2) objectivity of reporting, (3) repeatability of results, and (4) representativeness of sample.

1. The psychologist should control all the conditions of the study. If he learns that children who are frequently spanked get lower-than-average grades in school, it does not necessarily mean that the spankings or the fear of spanking produced the low grades. Perhaps parents who spank their children are less intelligent than parents who don't; perhaps parents who spank are more concerned with obedience at home than with success in school. What other reasons can you think of?

2. The psychologist must take precautions to remain objective, or else he risks permitting his own biases and wishes to influence the investigation. If he feels that children should never be spanked, he might not believe the parent of the school's top pupil who reports giving his child frequent spankings. The psychologist must conduct his research in such a way as to prevent his own feelings from interfering. He can help keep his study objective by collecting data that do not permit his personal judgments to enter.

3. The researcher must conduct and report his study in such a way that another investigator could repeat the project to see if he would obtain similar results.

4. The psychologist must select his **sample** (that is, those people who will be in his study) so that it will be representative of the entire population. To study problem children, he probably should not restrict himself only to children who are willing to stay after school to participate; to study delinquency, he should – if at all possible – work with delinquents both inside and outside penal institutions.

Even the reporting of the study requires a scientific attitude. Obviously all children who get spanked do not get low grades. Psychologists report their findings in terms of tendencies or **probabilities.** In other words, how probable is it or "what are the odds" that a particular event will occur? If you toss a coin, the odds are 50–50 that it will turn up heads. If a child is spanked often, what are the odds that he will get low grades?

Another vital consideration in reporting research is to avoid overgeneralizing. For example, just because a relationship is found between life satisfaction and income among middle-aged men, it does not mean that the same relationship will be found among postcollege women. Similarly, the conclusion that money motivates low-income children to study does not prove that money would have the same effect on high-income children.

Scientists do not expect to find final answers. New information, new understanding, and new hypotheses are always forthcoming. Science progresses through many small steps and few large breakthroughs. A science may be compared with an immense brick house. Each piece of research is one brick that helps the house grow. Some bricks are large, some are small, and some are not made of very good material and demand rapid replacement. Each time one part of the house nears completion, the owners decide they need an additional wing. The work never ends.

PSYCHOLOGY APPLIED

Although many psychologists are primarily concerned with research, some are more interested in applying the research findings and their own informed understanding of human behavior to practical problems.

The psychologist who counsels a student regarding a suitable college is using the findings of others to deal with an immediate problem. From previous research, he knows whether the grades and test scores of his counselee predict success in the college under discussion.

In addition to the *science* of psychology, he has learned the *art* of helping counselees achieve their own goals, instead of trying to impose his goals on them.

Other psychologists are hired by businesses or government agencies to deal with such practical problems as determining whether a new package for breakfast cereal is more likely to entice the buyer than the old one or testing the effectiveness of a **propaganda** program to persuade the Brazilian people that Americans are their friends. By building on the research of others and adding

FIGURE 1–1. Psychological principles are often applied in selling. Technically speaking, however, neither the seller nor the purchaser is therefore a psychologist. Courtesy Braniff International.

research of their own, these psychologists try to come up with the best answers to immediate practical problems.

Psychology, then, is the science that studies behavior in order to understand, describe, predict, and influence that behavior. Psychologists use research for building theories of behavior and for solving immediate problems. They also use the art of psychology to aid in understanding and influencing behavior.

PSYCHOLOGY AND OTHER FIELDS

The next time you look at a painting or statue, ask yourself how it affects you. Does it make you laugh or feel sad? Does it move you to anger, or does it leave you feeling pleased? Art not only expresses the mood of the artist but may also reflect the ways in which people perceive the world. One philosopher has suggested that today's artists depict people as strange and distorted because man no longer has a true sense of who he is or how he relates to the world around him (Barrett, 1958).

The artist wants to understand human behavior, and he may wish to influence it as well. The psychologist and the artist can learn from each other about the influence of color on mood, the effects of space on the focus of attention, the degree to which feelings and attitudes are influenced by works of art, or the significance of communicating through art. Consider, also, the relevance of these topics for the advertising layout artist, the theater technician, the beautician, the hotel manager, or the printer.

Literature also "holds the mirror up to man." A good novelist can communicate the feelings of his fictional characters and make them seem more life-like than the real people whose behavior the psychologist attempts to describe. Plays and films can produce the same result. Writers can use the understanding provided by psychologists to enrich their stories, and psychologists can gain in their understanding of human behavior by drawing from the deep sensitivity of good authors.

The relationship of other social sciences to psychology is readily apparent. Sociology, anthropology, political science, history, and economics all deal with human behavior, although not in the same way that psychology does. Sociology contributes knowledge about the behavior of crowds, the structure of the family, and the functions of institutions such as the church and the school. Anthropology investigates the ways in which people live in various cultures and subcultures, including those of the United States. The political scientist and the political candidate are both interested in predicting the effects of political issues on the behavior of the voter.

The historian seeks an understanding of the behavior of people in past generations. Historians and psychologists alike could profit from discovering what factors enabled Lincoln to rise to such greatness (schoolteachers and parents would certainly appreciate understanding why Lincoln found reading books so exciting). Knowledge of the history of our country and of other countries helps explain the behavior of people today. To learn, for example, that the German army invaded France three times in one century may help explain the attitudes of the French toward Germans; to learn about the history of unions in the United States may help explain why your parents feel as they do about them.

From biology and chemistry, psychologists gain knowledge of the physiology of the sensory and motor apparatus, of the brain, and of the nervous system in order to understand their effects on behavior. At the same time, the medical doctor can use some of the findings of psychologists in treating his patients. Mathematics provides the psychologist with the statistical tools to conduct research. The study of grammar and linguistics suggests that language may affect behavior. Processing data on computers enables the psychologist to enlarge the scope of his research.

Parents, teachers, businessmen, office managers, technicians, policemen, secretaries, government workers, military officers, and innumerable other groups draw upon the data of psychology. They may wish to influence the behavior of children, potential buyers, employees, soldiers, or supervisors; they may want to predict the behavior of the competitor, the enemy, the criminal, or the boss; they may hope to understand the feelings of the spouse, the girl at the next desk, or the commanding officer. And all these people give to and receive from psychologists a deeper understanding of the world.

No field of study or work can exist in a vacuum. Each adds to its own store of understanding and knowledge the results of the efforts of others. What do you feel you can learn from psychology? What do you feel psychologists might learn from those in your chosen vocational field?

PSYCHOLOGISTS: WHO ARE THEY?

Everyone uses the principles of psychology in his work and personal life, just as everyone uses the principles of mathematics and economics. However, the ability to use psychological principles does not make a person a psychologist, any more than computing a batting average or maintaining a family budget makes a person a mathematician or an economist. Professional psychologists usually have a graduate degree—frequently the doctorate, which demands an average of six to eight years of academic training plus the ability to pass lengthy comprehensive examinations and to satisfactorily complete a work of original research.

Most professional psychologists belong to the American Psychological Association, an organization of approximately 33,000 members. Thus one out of every 6350 Americans is a psychologist—certainly a very small proportion of the population.

SPECIALTIES WITHIN PSYCHOLOGY

Although all psychologists share a common body of knowledge, the scientific field of psychology, like other fields, is divided into a number of specialties.

The specialty chosen by most psychologists is clinical psychology. The *clinical psychologist* is primarily concerned with helping others to cope with their problems. He participates in the face-to-face relationship known as **psychotherapy,** a form of counseling that involves helping people with personal and

FIGURE 1–2. Among the topics that interest social psychologists are the relationships among persons of different ethnic groups. Photograph by Liane Enkelis.

emotional adjustment problems. In addition, the clinical psychologist administers and interprets all types of psychological tests. He sometimes does research on tests or on various approaches to psychotherapy. He may have a private practice, or he may work with a government agency, a hospital, or an educational institution.

The *social psychologist* focuses his attention on the behavior of individuals and groups in a social environment. He studies the formation and change of attitudes and beliefs, the effects of society on behavior, and the actions of people in small groups. He is also likely to be interested in how people communicate with each other, since communication is part of a social relationship.

Quite different from the social psychologist is the *physiological psychologist*, who studies the physiology, anatomy, and **biochemistry** of the body as they affect behavior. What changes occur in the human body when the person claims to feel

FIGURE 1–3. The developmental psychologist is concerned with behavior at various stages of development. Photograph by Lehman J. Pinckney.

anger or fear? How do tranquilizer pills alter behavior? Why are some people color-blind? How is memory stored in the brain?

The *developmental psychologist* is primarily concerned with behavior and behavior changes at various stages of development. He tries to discover why some infants learn to walk earlier than others, how adolescent interests change between ages 12 and 18, and why some people seem old at 60 while others are still vigorous at 80.

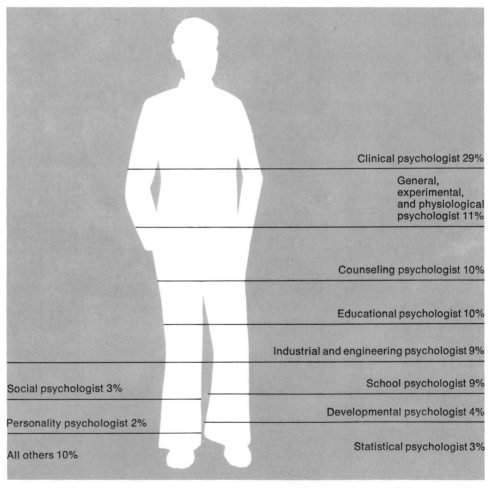

FIGURE 1–4.   The major areas of specialization in psychology and the percentage of American Psychological Association members identifying with each area (Cates, 1970).

Industrial psychologists study a variety of topics, including how to design efficient machines, how to evaluate worker morale (and to improve it, if necessary), how to devise training programs for workers, and how to improve marketing and advertising.

These five specialties were chosen to show what a wide range of human activity is covered by the term *psychology*. Other specialties are cited in Figure 1–4. Overlap, of course, exists among the areas. A clinical psychologist may become interested in the emotional problems of industrial executives, and a social psychologist may find himself studying the effects of friendship on the physical health of the aged.

THE JOB OF THE PSYCHOLOGIST

The largest percentage of psychologists (44%) is associated with colleges, universities, and medical schools, where they teach, conduct research, counsel, and serve as administrators. Various agencies of federal, state, and local governments also employ many psychologists (17%). Others work for public schools (12%), industry (6%), hospitals (7%), and social agencies (4%). Only a very few (6%) are self-employed (Cates, 1970).

Psychologists use both the science and the art of psychology in their work, just as medical doctors use both the science and the art of medicine in theirs. Some psychologists are involved almost completely with research, but most clinical and counseling psychologists try to develop the art of being sensitive to the feelings of those they are trying to help. The industrial psychologist who is responsible for training foremen and managers must achieve a high degree of sensitivity to how others feel. Psychologists who teach in colleges and universities need to develop the art of effectively communicating the content and the methods of psychology to their students.

PSYCHOLOGISTS, PSYCHIATRISTS, AND PSYCHOANALYSTS

Since **clinical psychologists, psychiatrists,** and **psychoanalysts** all perform psychotherapy, much confusion exists regarding the differences among them.

The clinical psychologist usually has a Ph.D. degree with major emphasis in psychology. In addition to his lengthy education, he has spent a year administering psychological tests and practicing psychotherapy under supervision.

The psychiatrist must be, according to law, a medical doctor. His education includes a regular college degree, a medical degree (M.D.), a year of internship, and usually three to five years of medical residency, often in a psychiatric hospital. Until his residency begins, his education is almost completely in medicine, rather than in psychology.

In the United States the psychoanalyst is almost always a psychiatrist who has undertaken additional study and examinations and been formally accepted as an analyst. In Europe it is more common for a nonmedical person to become a psychoanalyst. The psychoanalyst normally adheres to the principles of psychotherapy established by Sigmund Freud or one of his followers.

SUMMARY OF IMPORTANT IDEAS

1. Psychology is the science that attempts to understand, describe, predict, and influence behavior.

2. Psychologists make extensive use of the scientific method in their research, which involves finding relationships among variables.

3. Some psychologists concentrate on applying the psychological understanding of human behavior to practical problems, whereas others focus on performing research.

4. Everyone uses psychological understanding in his daily life, but becoming a professional psychologist requires extensive study.

5. Psychology does not stand in isolation but is interrelated with many other fields of study. At the same time, psychology is divided into numerous interrelated specialties.

6. The work of the clinical psychologist, the psychiatrist, and the psychoanalyst overlaps.

2 The Methods of Psychology

Although every scientist uses the scientific method, each scientific field studies different types of phenomena and thus needs to apply the scientific method in somewhat different ways. A psychologist investigating the relationship between spanking and obedience must use a much different approach from that of a physicist investigating effects of temperature change on spacecraft. The major approaches used by psychologists are tests, including surveys and questionnaires; experiments; and field studies, observations, and case histories.

PSYCHOLOGICAL TESTING

If you were to present a dozen friends with the word *psychological* and ask them to respond with the first word that comes to mind, several would come back with *test*. Tests are one of the major tools of the psychologist, and a vast assortment is available. In his capacity as research scientist and applied scientist, tests help him measure human characteristics; in his capacity as artist, tests provide a better understanding of the individuals he is trying to influence.

Testing has become part of our way of life. For better and for worse, psychological and educational tests have found their way into schools, colleges, businesses, industries, government agencies, welfare agencies, medical centers—everywhere you look.

Because of the importance of testing in psychology, a great deal of effort is expended in determining how good each test is. This determination is made by evaluating the **validity** and the **reliability** of a test. A test is valid to the degree that it really measures what it is designed to measure. It is reliable to the degree that it measures consistently.

Consider your final exam in English last semester. What was it designed to measure? Knowledge of grammar? Ability to write? Understanding of literature? Did it measure what it was designed to measure? If so, it was valid. Now, how consistently did it measure? If you had taken a very similar examination one week later, would you have gotten roughly the same score? If you had received a high score on the first test and then a low score a week later on a similar test, your scores would not have been dependable; that is, they would not have been reliable.

> An Air Force psychologist was approached by a young recruit who was unhappy about being assigned to the motor pool rather than receiving mechanical training to work on an engine crew. The psychologist pointed out that the recruit's test scores showed low mechanical ability, but the recruit objected. He had taken those tests, he explained, at seven in the morning after riding most of the night on a crowded train and arriving in time to get only three hours of sleep and a hurried breakfast. Most of the other recruits taking the tests had gotten to the base in plenty of time for a good night's sleep and a leisurely breakfast. The psychologist agreed to retest the young man, and his scores were considerably higher the second time.

Since school grades are based partly or completely on tests, whatever factors affect the validity of tests also affect the validity of grades. Occasionally a student will believe his grade was not valid. If the grade is too low, he may complain to the professor (although he virtually never complains if the grade is too high).

Some tests make use of national **norms.** In such instances, your score can be compared with the scores of hundreds of other people. You may be told that, nationally, you are in the thirtieth **percentile** (30%ile) in clerical ability or the seventy-third percentile in scientific interest. The score means that you have as much as or more clerical ability than 30% of those who were used for comparison, or you have as much as or more interest in science than 73% of the norm group. (Remember that these percentiles do *not* mean that 30% of your answers were correct or that 73% of your statements showed scientific interest.) To interpret percentile scores adequately, you need to know (1) the nature of the test and (2) the kinds of people with whom you are being compared, since being in the 64%ile on mechanical ability with engineering students as a norm group would mean something quite different from being in the 64%ile on mechanical ability with a general population of high school graduates as a norm group.

Psychological tests measure many kinds of characteristics, including general intelligence and factors of intelligence, aptitudes and achievement, interests, needs, and personality characteristics. Also, many principles of testing hold true for surveys of attitudes, beliefs, and values and for other kinds of psychological and educational measurements.

HOW INTELLIGENCE IS MEASURED

Intelligence cannot be measured directly but must be inferred from performance. The best-known tests of intelligence are probably the Stanford-Binet Intelligence Test, the Wechsler Intelligence Scale for Children (WISC), and the Wechsler Adult Intelligence Scale (WAIS). These three tests attempt to measure general intelligence, and they offer an overall score. They also assume that their results are only minimally influenced by culture and formal education. (Additional discussion of intelligence tests and what they measure will be found in Chapter 7.)

HOW APTITUDE AND ACHIEVEMENT ARE MEASURED

Intelligence tests are used primarily for educational purposes. When the focus is on employment, tests of aptitude and achievement are used more com-

FIGURE 2–1. Your final exam for this course may be an achievement test similar to this one. Photograph by John G. Warford.

monly. **Aptitude** is the capacity to become competent, assuming adequate training; **achievement** refers to a person's present level of competence. Although aptitude and achievement are related, they are not identical.

Countless aptitude tests are available, and some are widely used in employee selection. Many firms use tests to measure verbal, mechanical, numerical, clerical, and sales aptitudes. Achievement tests measure some of the same qualities but are likely to include more factual material than do aptitude tests. Thus a test of mechanical aptitude would present problems that could be answered correctly by a person before he had taken courses in mechanics, and an achievement test of mechanical ability would ask questions that would require previous study or experience. Your final exam for this course will probably be an achievement test, since your instructor will wish to know your level of understanding of the materials studied.

HOW INTERESTS ARE EVALUATED

Many people confuse aptitude tests and interest tests. Students will frequently claim to have taken a test indicating they have a high aptitude for medicine or engineering, but further checking will show that the test actually measured interests.

Two tests of interests are widely used. One, the Kuder Preference Record, is familiar to many students; it requires that the respondent indicate which of three activities he likes most and which he likes least. The second major interest test, the Strong Vocational Interest Blank, gives students letter grades according to how closely their interests compare with those of successful men or women in various careers.

Since a person's interests are highly predictive of what he will enjoy doing vocationally, they also predict vocational success. However, interests can be evaluated through means other than tests. Examine your own activities. What do you enjoy doing? How do you spend your time? What do you stick to? What do you do well? High school and college courses and activities can be evaluated in the same way. If your self-evaluation matches your test scores, you can usually assume you are on the right track. If the test scores disagree with your perceptions of yourself, a careful consideration of what might be causing the differences is in order.

HOW NEEDS AND PERSONALITY CHARACTERISTICS ARE EVALUATED

Students probably find personality tests the most interesting and the most irritating of all psychological tests. Part of the difficulty undoubtedly arises from not understanding why the questions are worded as they are. Sometimes students want to know whether "never" in a questionnaire means "absolutely never—not even once" or whether it implies less restrictiveness. Also, students commonly complain about being forced to check one of five alternatives, even though the real answer may lie somewhere between the alternatives or may not even be offered. Scores on personality tests are often reported in percentiles.

Figure 2–2 shows the categories used in constructing one of the best-known tests of personality and needs, the Edwards Personal Preference Schedule. Although the categories are stated in terms of needs (for example, need for achievement and need for dominance), you will readily see that needs are only one aspect of personality. Other tests measure such varied characteristics as anxiety, sociability, life satisfaction, security/insecurity, self-confidence, and flexibility. Recently tests have been devised to determine how people stand on conservatism, personality conflict, fear of death, subjective moral attitudes, social caution, suspiciousness, novelty seeking, and impulse control (Sarason & Smith, 1971).

1. Achievement—the need to accomplish things well and quickly, to be successful in what is done, to overcome obstacles.
2. Deference—the need to follow someone else, to have a leader.
3. Order—the need to be neat and orderly.
4. Exhibition—the need to attract attention, to be noticed.
5. Autonomy—the need to be independent, to gain freedom, to defy authority.
6. Affiliation—the need to form friendships, to love others, to join groups, to please people.
7. Introception—the need to be imaginative, subjective, to participate in romantic action.
8. Succorance—the need to get help or sympathy, to be dependent.
9. Dominance—the need to influence or control others, to lead, to organize.
10. Abasement—the need to apologize, to accept punishment.
11. Nurturance—the need to help others, to express sympathy.
12. Change—the need to avoid routine, to be involved with change.
13. Endurance—the need to work hard, to avoid distractions.
14. Heterosexuality—the need for relationships with the opposite sex.
15. Aggression—the need to express aggressive feelings, to harm, to punish.

FIGURE 2–2. Personality needs measured by the Edwards Personal Preference Schedule (Edwards, 1954; based on the list of needs developed by Henry A. Murray, 1938).

Counselors use a combination of tests and interviews to help a student evaluate his personality and needs. The validity of personality tests is lower than the validity of aptitude or interest tests, and not enough is known about why or how certain personality attributes fit a person for specific vocational fields. However, objective self-evaluation is very difficult—although many people pride themselves on their self-understanding—and one's personal insights often need to be supplemented by tests and interviews.

Sara came to the counseling center at the urging of her English instructor, who felt she was working far below her capacity. She was not eager to seek counseling and apparently made the appointment to please her instructor, whom she admired, rather than to satisfy herself. When the counselor suggested that she take a battery of tests, she reacted negatively, insisting that tests are artificial devices designed to put people into pigeonholes. The counselor agreed that this was a real danger, especially when tests are used in individual counseling. (The use of tests to measure the educational level of an entire class or to select personnel for industry requires separate consideration.) However, he guaranteed that the tests would be discussed with her and that he was using them only to aid himself, not to categorize her. She consented.

Although Sara completed a number of tests, many of which measured more than one characteristic and provided more than one score, we will touch upon only those results that are meaningful to this particular situation. Sara's basic intelligence was above average for students at her college, but this was due more to her ability to work with numbers, to grasp spatial relations, and to memorize quickly than to her ability to use words effectively. She displayed high clerical and mechanical aptitude and low aptitude for verbal tasks and interpersonal relationships. She indicated a high need for order, for dominance, and for autonomy, with low needs for exhibition, affiliation, nurturance, and aggression. Her interest-test scores were fairly consistent with her aptitudes— that is, high on mechanical and scientific, low on persuasive and verbal. She also showed interest in outdoor work. At that point she and her counselor agreed that further testing was unnecessary.

Sara reacted strongly against accepting her low verbal aptitude and verbal interest scores, as well as against what she felt was the indication that she did not like people. The counselor explained that the tests did not mean she did not enjoy social relationships but that she had more interest in working with things than with people and more ability in dealing with shapes and numbers than with words. Sara did not know whether she agreed, but she did admit that her present major of elementary education held no interest for her.

Later discussion involved her personal life and family relationships, but she appeared to have only a normal number of difficulties, none of which were unusually disruptive. Then the counselor began to explore some other vocational fields. When he mentioned computer operations, Sara began to pay more attention but insisted there was no room for women in that field. The counselor agreed that she would have some difficulty but claimed that doors were not completely closed to her. The counseling ended with Sara looking into the possibility of transferring to a technical school that would permit her to study both programming and computer repair work. She decided she would probably have to satisfy her enjoyment of the outdoors through leisure rather than through work.

Sara's situation was easier than many. She did not have anyone pressuring her into a feminine field; she did not have major health or financial problems; she did not have self-defeating personality conflicts. Once the counselor enabled her to understand that he would approach her as an individual—not as a bunch of numbers—she was willing to consider alternatives. Sara's story is one example of the application of psychological research (the tests were all developed through research) to practical situations, aided by the art of the psychological counselor.

Not all personality tests consist of checking which of several alternatives you prefer; not all tests can be scored by computer. **Projective tests** are open-ended personality tests. For example, in the Thematic Apperception Test (TAT), the individual is shown a series of pictures, most of which depict people in different kinds of interaction. He is then asked to tell a complete, spontaneous story to match each scene. In the House-Tree-Person Test, the person is asked to draw a house, a tree, and a person all in the same picture, and then he discusses or writes about what he has drawn. The examiner later evaluates the stories or the discussions and looks for themes suggesting relationships with others, attitudes toward self, hopes for the future, emotional reactions, or typical modes of behavior. The assumption underlying projective techniques is that the individual will reveal his own feelings in his stories and drawings. For example, in evaluating a story told by a 19-year-old male in response to a picture of an older woman and a younger man, the psychologist will probably look for themes he could relate to a mother-son relationship. Obviously such interpretations must be made with extreme caution and would need to be verified by other TAT stories or by comments made during discussions.

Many other types of projective tests are available. The Rorschach Inkblot Test, a very complex test that is difficult to evaluate, involves a set of ten cards, each containing one inkblot to be interpreted by the subject. The Sentence Completion Test contains the beginnings of sentences, which are to be completed by the respondent as he wishes. The Word Association Test presents a series of words to which the individual responds with the first word that comes to mind.

The justification for projective tests and their scoring is highly complex and need not be further considered here. Research evidence indicates that projective tests have lower validity and reliability than the more objective tests. Nonetheless, clinical psychologists and psychiatrists often claim that the tests are extremely useful for understanding an individual. Because they are not limited to a series of alternatives for checking, projective tests can reveal more subtle and more complex aspects of the personality, which may compensate for the hazards of depending on the subjective interpretations of the examiner.

Tests are subject to numerous kinds of error and have many shortcomings. Some tests, such as those appearing in newspapers and magazines, are fun but may have little or no validity and should not be taken seriously. However, not even the most carefully constructed tests are valid in every instance. Validity of tests of personality and interest is related to the ability and willingness of the individual to respond honestly and without self-deception. When the person taking the test is motivated to distort the results, either to fool someone else or to maintain his own inaccurate self-concept, many tests cease to be valid.

Tests can also be used improperly. For example, they can be employed to make decisions without allowing for exceptions, or they can be administered to persons who are unfamiliar with tests and whose scores therefore will not accurately reflect their actual abilities. Nonetheless, *in combination with other methods of evaluation,* tests are very useful aids in making decisions and in understanding individuals.

USING SURVEYS AND QUESTIONNAIRES

Surveys and **questionnaires** are special forms of tests. Today's newspapers and magazines are filled with the results of public-opinion surveys, attitude and personality questionnaires, and interviews. Statistics show how the Republican voters of California feel about who should be the next governor, how residents of Houston look upon a possible tax increase, or how college students view their future.

However, the surveys you read in the newspapers are only a small portion of those conducted. Businesses and government organizations sponsor thousands of surveys annually. The U. S. Department of State may wish to learn the atti-

"He's telling about how we believe in the Sacred Hippopotamus who created Man out of oyster shells—don't ask me how he keeps a straight face!"

FIGURE 2–3.   Courtesy of Ed Fisher.

tudes of the Spanish people toward American soldiers stationed in Spain; a candidate for the city council may want to know how the voters feel about local issues; a nursing supervisor may want to learn how student nurses feel about their future work.

Questionnaires are used for purposes other than the solution of immediate, practical problems. A psychologist may, for example, hypothesize that attitudes toward education are related to college grades. He could construct a brief attitude questionnaire, administer it to his students, and then check their overall grade-point ratios at the end of the academic year. Or, he may believe that a relationship exists between having emotional problems and being divorced. He could then administer a personality questionnaire for measuring emotional problems to a group of divorced people and to a *comparable* group of married people. His final analysis would show which group had more emotional problems. (The studies described have possible sources of error. Can you decide what they are and suggest ways to eliminate them?)

THE EXPERIMENTAL METHOD

Psychologists use the **experimental method** in their research, since it allows them a great deal of control over all the factors involved. In a typical psychological experiment, one group of subjects (the experimental group) is given special treatment, while a comparable group (the **control group**) is left alone or is given normal treatment. The psychologist then compares the two groups to see what changes, if any, occurred in the experimental group—presumably the outcome of the conditions he arranged.

In one example of the experimental method, college students were given a long word and asked to write as many short words as possible using the letters contained in the long word. One-third of the subjects (group A) were told that the average number of words made by English professors was 31; one-third (group B) were told that college freshmen averaged 31 words; and the final third (group C) were informed that prison inmates averaged 31 words. Interestingly enough, group C made the most short words from the long word, and group A averaged the lowest number. The same procedure was repeated many times, always with the same results.* Apparently the standards people set for themselves are affected by the nature of the group with which they are compared, and these stand-

---

* Based on studies in introductory psychology laboratories at the University of Hawaii, 1955–1959.

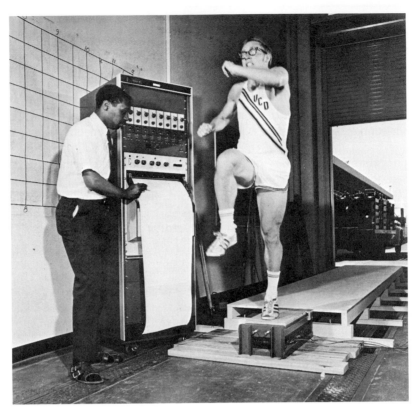

FIGURE 2–4. Many kinds of tests are used to measure many kinds of human performance. Here a machine measures the thrust of a long-distance jumper. The device may aid in the selection and training of track stars. Courtesy Public Affairs Office, University of California, Davis, and Dr. Melvin Ramey.

ards influence level of performance. Consider the implications of this study for success in school or on the job.

In another experiment subjects were told to write down words that were to be flashed very briefly on a screen. One-third of the subjects received a paper telling them that the words would deal with travel; one-third were informed that the words would relate to birds and animals; the remaining third, the control group, were not given specific instructions. Among the "words" flashed on the screen were *sael* and *dack* (Siipola, 1935). What do you think each group wrote down when they saw the above "words"? The results of the experiment indicated that a person's expectations will affect what he "sees." What relevance does this finding have to human behavior outside the experimental situation?

These examples are only two out of thousands of experiments that have been

FIGURE 2–5. Research in the real world can be very difficult to perform. Consider the problems in measuring exactly what happens to an individual as he drives an automobile. In this photograph the girl, the automobile, and the driver are all real, but the scene in front of the driver is a movie film. The equipment monitored by the girl is measuring physiological changes that occur in the driver as he actually drives the car (except that it does not move ahead) along an actual roadway (except that it is on film). The driver's comments and reactions will also be recorded. This is another example of psychological methods being applied to practical problems—in this instance, automobile safety. Courtesy Driving Simulation Laboratory, Institute of Transportation and Traffic Engineering, UCLA.

conducted to learn more about behavior. Some psychologists prefer to use experiments to investigate behavior, but others use observations, case histories, texts, or combinations of all these methods.

OTHER METHODS FOR LEARNING ABOUT PEOPLE

In addition to tests and experiments, psychologists use a variety of other research methods. Among the most important are the field study, the observational method, and the case history.

FIELD STUDIES: RESEARCH IN THE REAL WORLD

Tests and experiments often require a laboratory setting. Surveys and questionnaires also set up an artificial situation. In order to gain greater personal insights into the world as it actually is, many psychologists go into the field (that is, the real world) to see what is going on. Like the anthropologists who developed this method, the psychologist spends a great deal of time with the people he is studying. However, he must be aware that he brings his own biases and preconceived notions into the field with him and that he must be careful that these factors have a minimal influence on his reporting.

One anthropologist, David Reynolds, has participated in three different kinds of field studies that illustrate this method effectively. To study a particular school of psychotherapy practiced only in Japan, he became fluent in Japanese and then spent several months in therapy in Tokyo. On another occasion he spent several hours a day for three weeks in a home for the elderly, working and talking with the residents. In the third instance he wished to learn more about how mental hospitals treat people who have attempted suicide, so he arranged with the director of a psychiatric facility to be signed in as a patient. He remained on the ward two weeks, and no one besides the director knew who he was. (Incidentally, as a matter of ethics, he returned to the hospital after his "discharge" to tell both the staff members and the patients the nature of his visit and to assure them that he would not identify anyone in his report. Research ethics are very controversial matters that you may wish to discuss.)

THE OBSERVATIONAL METHOD

Everyone observes the behavior of others and makes certain assumptions from these observations. For example, have you ever observed what seem to be differences in behavior between commercial art majors and office management majors? Have you ever observed that left-handed baseball pitchers seem to exhibit different off-the-field behavior from that of right-handed pitchers? If so, you have used observations, but probably not in a scientific way. Such casual, uncontrolled observations may add to your understanding, but they are also very likely to be wrong. Whenever you notice an office management major or a left-handed pitcher behaving as you hypothesize, you feel that your beliefs have been confirmed. When you see behavior that contradicts your hypothesis, you may tell yourself that it is only an exception, or you may find some other excuse for the behavior.

You can, however, apply the **observational method** scientifically by imposing careful controls. Commercial art majors, you hypothesize, are more likely to enter into class discussions than are office management majors. By making a careful count of how often each person comments in your class, you can obtain an average class-discussion score for commercial art students and for office management students. You should make certain that you collect your observations in several different classes, since commercial art students may talk more in certain classes and less in others. The final step is to analyze your data to see whether your hypothesis is borne out. (There are many possible pitfalls in this study. Perhaps you can figure out what they are and suggest ways of dealing with them.) Of course, art or management majors in another college may differ from those you have observed, so you need to be cautious in extending the results of your research beyond the group you studied. With such precautions, controlled observations can be a fruitful method of investigation.

THE CASE–HISTORY METHOD

A case history refers to an intensive study of a single individual, utilizing a great variety of information sources, such as school records, vocational evaluations, psychological tests, and interviews with the individual himself and with those who know him. All this material is integrated to provide as complete a picture of the person as possible. Not only does the **case-history method** give an understanding of one individual, but a comparison of several case histories devoted to a specific topic may also generate hypotheses to be tested on a larger scale.

Research in psychology, as in every field, is liable to a variety of errors. Research psychologists must be flexible enough to accept the fact that they cannot predict the future behavior of an individual with the same accuracy with which a chemist can predict the future action of a compound. Nonetheless, if we are to learn more about human behavior, psychological research based on a variety of methodologies must continue.

SUMMARY OF IMPORTANT IDEAS

1. Psychological and educational tests have become virtually a way of life. As a result, considerable effort has been put into developing good tests.

2. A good test must be both valid and reliable.

3. Test results are often reported in percentiles.

4. Aptitude refers to potential ability; achievement denotes a competence already attained.

5. Interests, needs, and personality characteristics are also measured by tests.

6. The use of projective tests assumes that the individual will reveal his own feelings in responding to the materials.

7. Surveys and questionnaires are special forms of tests.

8. The experimental method is used in psychology in an attempt to control as many variables as possible. It is usually applied in a laboratory setting.

9. The field study is research conducted under the conditions of the real world.

10. Additional research methods include observations and case histories.

3 Why People Behave: A Look at Motivation

Among the innumerable things that psychologists study are human wants and needs and how people try to satisfy them. A person must satisfy many needs, such as hunger and thirst, to survive, although at birth he is unable to satisfy these needs without help. Other needs, such as the need for companionship, the need for self-esteem, or the need for safety, are not part of the behavior patterns of infants but develop over the years as a result of experience.

A Book of Verses underneath the Bough,
A Jug of Wine, a Loaf of Bread—and Thou
Beside me singing in the Wilderness—
Oh, Wilderness were Paradise enow!

Apparently Omar Khayyám, the famous poet who wrote these lines, felt that poetry, drink, food, music, and companionship added up to all the satisfactions he might wish for. But most people are motivated by many other **needs.** What needs would you want satisfied to turn a wilderness into a paradise?

MOTIVATION AND ITS MEASUREMENT

Motivated behavior is behavior set into motion by a need. A need indicates that some type of satisfaction is lacking and implies that the organism is activated to reduce the dissatisfaction. Thus a need for food signifies that a person feels the lack of food, and it sets into motion hunger-motivated behavior. The need for money means that a person feels he lacks money, and it sets into motion money-seeking behavior. Needs for affection, for prestige, or for self-respect operate in the same fashion.

> In the middle of studying for an accounting exam, Ned Rose began to feel uncomfortable. He wasn't certain why he was on edge; he just couldn't concentrate. Suddenly he snapped his fingers, jumped up, and dashed to the telephone to call a girl he had been seeing. After he completed the call, he returned to his studying and was then able to concentrate without difficulty.

Ned was motivated to telephone the girl, even though he was temporarily unaware of his need. Nonetheless, the **motivation** was strong enough to activate goal-seeking behavior, which began with agitated feelings and ended with behavior that satisfied his need.

Sometimes people cannot satisfy their needs. A woman on a diet, though perhaps satisfying needs for popularity and self-esteem, may be perpetually hungry; a mediocre songwriter may never satisfy his need for achievement; an irritating and aggressive student may be unable to satisfy his need for companionship. A high proportion of needs can be satisfied, however, and the behavior that leads to need satisfaction is thus rewarded and is more likely to occur on subsequent occasions when the same need arises.

Individuals vary considerably in the degree to which they are motivated by any particular need. John may be highly motivated to attract attention or to express his aggressive feelings, but Jim's greatest social needs are to be neat and orderly and to form friendships with others. Jane, a student nurse, is eager to become a supervisor someday, but her classmate Jean is motivated only enough to slide through and get her certificate.

Motivation and needs are concepts, not things. They cannot be seen or heard or touched; they must be inferred or assumed. By observing Ned's actions, we inferred that he was motivated. The assumption that Ned had a need that motivated his behavior helps explain what he did. Many psychologists believe that *all* human behavior is motivated, even if the person is not necessarily aware of his motives at the time of the behavior.

If psychologists are to study motivation, they must have a method of measuring it. Since it cannot be measured directly, in the way we measure water pressure or speed, indirect measures have been developed. One of the most common of these measures assumes that the more motivated a person is, the harder he will work to satisfy his need. Therefore the individual who expends great effort in his college study is believed to be motivated to achieve academically; the person who spends considerable time solving people's problems is assumed to be motivated to help others.

Psychologists can measure the strength of an individual's motivation through controlled observations, through ratings by friends or teachers or others who know the person being studied, or through self-rating questionnaires. They can study the effects of motivation by using the experimental method to control the degree of need. For example, studies on the effects of the hunger motive have been conducted by depriving subjects of food for a given period of time and then measuring the impact of the deprivation on whatever variable is being considered (for example, work output, ability to concentrate, or irritability).

In making these indirect measurements of motivation and need strength, psychologists realize that their methods are subject to more error than are the methods of the engineer or the chemist. At this point in the development of the science of psychology, highly precise measures are often not available. Therefore psychologists attempt to be careful in their methods and cautious in their interpretations.

Motives are usually categorized as either physiological (basic) or psychological (derived or social). Physiological motives, which are related to the tissue needs of the body, include hunger, thirst, and fatigue. Psychological motives consist of all others; the chart on page 19 lists one group, but many other lists are possible. A totally different approach to motivation is that of Maslow (1970), whose hierarchy of needs will be discussed later in this chapter.

UNCONSCIOUS MOTIVATION

People often behave in a certain way without knowing why — that is, without knowing what their motives are. In this case the behavior results from **unconscious motivation.** The person may become aware of his motives in the future, but, for the moment at least, he is behaving without being conscious of the underlying causes.

Many people like to believe that they always understand their own motives and that they never do anything without knowing why. The idea of unconscious motivation implies that they are not in full control of their own behavior — that forces beyond their willpower are getting them to do something without their even knowing it. However, in the years since Sigmund Freud first introduced the concept and made it a basic part of his theories, most people have come to realize that much human behavior does indeed occur as a result of unconscious motivation.

Consider the following situations:

A slow drizzle has begun, and the sky threatens a real storm. You're going out, and your older sister casually suggests that you take your raincoat with you. You refuse. She becomes more insistent. You become more obstinate. You know she's right, but for some unknown reason you goad her into a silly argument. Then you leave the house. Ten minutes later you're drenched.

You sit in English class biting your nails. The instructor drones on, and you're down to the quick. It hurts. You pull your hand away from your mouth and try to take notes. The instructor drones on. You're biting your nails.

You hate to get water in your face. You avoid swimming; you're even careful in the shower. When you're pressured into swimming, you keep your head above water. Your friends tease you. You joke back. But you don't let water get in your face.

You're spending the evening with an old friend, George, whom you want to call Hank. You don't know why—he just looks like a Hank.

You spill salt during lunch. You immediately laugh about the old superstition of throwing spilled salt over your shoulder. Then you look at the spilled salt. You brush some away. Your hand takes some grains and quickly flicks them over your shoulder. This happens every time you spill salt.

You and A love each other, and you both know it. But A loves you more than you love A. And you hurt A in little ways—like mentioning A's low history grade in front of everyone, or arriving an hour late, or flirting with someone you don't even like at a party. A never hurts you. A whimpers a little but never hurts you. You gripe at A for whimpering. You hate yourself for what you're doing to A. You wonder why A doesn't stop seeing you. You don't know it, but A wonders the same thing. Yet you both claim you love each other.

The motivation for all these behavioral acts is unconscious; that is, the participants are not aware of it. How would you, as an outside observer, interpret the motivation underlying the various actions? Is anything accomplished when a motive is unconscious that cannot be accomplished when motives are conscious? Will unconscious motives help a person avoid feeling guilty? Avoid taking responsibility for his own actions? Express wishes he wants to avoid thinking about? Avoid feelings of inadequacy?

REPRESSION: MOTIVATED FORGETTING

When behavior results from unconscious motivation, it is often said that the basis for the behavior is repressed. **Repression,** like forgetting, is the inability to recall something. Unlike forgetting, however, repression occurs not because of passing time or disuse, but because a person is motivated to be unable to recall. You may quite easily *forget* your dentist's telephone number, but you are not likely to *forget* an appointment made two days earlier. You may have repressed the memory of the appointment, but you have not forgotten it.

A person does not consciously decide to repress something; it happens without his awareness. Why do people repress certain feelings and events? They repress because they have a need to do so—because the incident or feeling is so upsetting or so threatening or disturbing to their self-esteem that they are strongly motivated to be unable to recall what happened. People repress experiences, feelings, wishes, and even thoughts. In our culture sexual and aggressive feelings are especially likely to be repressed, because we are reluctant to accept ourselves as having "those kinds of feelings."

Repressed motives may influence behavior in ways that are not always understood, although people try to make their behavior appear rational.

> When I was still in the primary grades, my parents had a strict rule that I could never hit my younger brother unless he hit me first. So I would tease him into hitting me so I could hit him back. Of course, since I was bigger and stronger, my blows were more painful than his. And, to make things even better, I always felt justified in my actions. It wasn't until I was in college that I realized what I had actually been doing.

This person's unconscious motivation was, of course, the desire to hit his brother. Even a third-grader realizes that hitting a child five years younger is unacceptable, and his self-esteem would suffer if he felt he had picked the fight himself. So, without being aware of why he was doing it, the older boy provoked his brother into attacking. He could thus act out his need to hit the younger boy without losing self-esteem and without bringing his parents' wrath down upon him. However, he repressed the basis for the motivation until a psychology class discussion stimulated his memory. At that time he had much less need to repress his motivation, since the hostility he felt toward his brother had long since disappeared.

Consider the person who tells his friend "I'm only saying this for your own good" and then proceeds to criticize him with considerable vehemence. Is he really motivated by the desire to help the other person? What motives might be repressed? What might be his need to have them repressed?

SELF-ACTUALIZATION AND A HIERARCHY OF NEEDS

When an animal has had enough to eat, it rarely searches for food; when it is warm enough, it rarely seeks new ways of getting warm. The animal's needs seem satisfied when it has, for the moment, all the things necessary to remain alive and to avoid discomfort and pain. Humans, however, seem to have a need for more than this basic level of functioning: they need to grow, to improve, and to make use of their potential capacities.

The young child is eager to learn, to explore, and to have experiences. His parents may encourage his learning, but many children enjoy learning and exploration even when they receive no such encouragement; there appears to be something in learning and in having new experiences that, in itself, excites them.

> Nine-month-old Mike crawled slowly to the couch, reached up, grabbed the cloth, and painfully pulled himself to a standing position. He fell and bruised his chin, but five seconds later he was again pulling himself up so he could stand. His only reward seemed to be the satisfaction—perhaps the excitement—of standing.

> A beautician in Santa Barbara, California, drove into Los Angeles every Monday for ten weeks to take a series of seminars in some recent techniques. Although her shop was so busy that she was turning away customers, she felt that the 200-mile round trip was worth the effort, because what she learned enabled her to do a better job.

In both these instances, the individuals seemed rewarded by the feeling that they had done something to make the most of their abilities. They had responded to their need for **self-actualization.**

What is self-actualization? According to one highly respected psychologist, Abraham H. Maslow (1970), it is the tendency to "become more and more what one uniquely is, to become everything that one is capable of becoming." Also, to self-actualize is to accept one's own real nature for what it is (Maslow, 1955). This concept implies that people have a desire, or a need, to make something of themselves—to do as much as their potential allows.

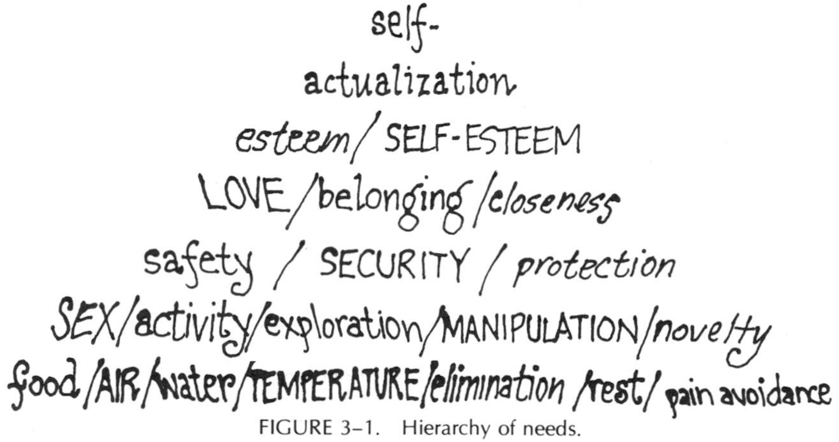

self-
actualization
esteem / SELF-ESTEEM
LOVE / belonging / closeness
safety / SECURITY / protection
SEX / activity / exploration / MANIPULATION / novelty
food / AIR / water / TEMPERATURE / elimination / rest / pain avoidance

FIGURE 3–1. Hierarchy of needs.

One person may self-actualize by doing a good job of framing pictures; another, by maintaining a happy home and bringing up healthy children; a third, by leading the debating squad; a fourth, by taking shorthand rapidly and accurately; a fifth, by writing poetry to express his own feelings.

Before you can do an effective job of self-actualizing, however, other needs must be reasonably well satisfied. These needs, as described by Maslow (1970), form a **hierarchy of needs,** which includes **physiological needs, safety needs, love needs,** and **esteem needs,** in addition to the self-actualizing needs.

PHYSIOLOGICAL NEEDS

The physiological needs can be divided into two categories: (1) survival needs, which must be satisfied or the body processes stop and life ceases; and (2) stimulation needs, whose functions, although not well understood, appear more closely related to the appreciation of life than to the maintenance of life.

SURVIVAL NEEDS

Survival needs include those produced by hunger, thirst, air hunger, elimination pressures, fatigue, temperature regulation demands, and pain avoidance. Relatively few Americans have suffered acutely from being unable to satisfy these needs (except, perhaps, for pain avoidance), but all of us have experienced these needs in milder form.

1. Hunger. For most people in the United States, being hungry means missing lunch and "starving" before dinner. Elsewhere in the world, and even in some American families, hunger is a major motivation—perhaps *the* major motivation—for the behavior of many people. Much of the world's population rarely receives the amount of food that an overweight American is allowed even by a strict diet. The hungry have poor health, their life-span is short, and their infant death rate is high. Consider the overwhelming importance of food as a motivating factor for these people. Consider the motivation caused by hearing your children cry constantly because they do not have enough to eat.

During World War II a group of Americans volunteered to undergo a starvation diet so that the effects of hunger might be studied. After several weeks of intense dieting, they displayed many types of behavior change: their dreams, thoughts, and conversations continually dealt with food; they became irritable; their activity level was reduced; and they became apathetic (Keys, Brožek, Hens-

FIGURE 3–2. The satisfaction of hunger and thirst needs is probably taken for granted by readers of this book, but there are millions of people in the world, including some in the United States, for whom hunger and thirst are daily problems. Here a Hong Kong child carries the family's supply of water, which probably has to last for several days. Photograph by Mark Davidson.

chel, Michelsen, & Taylor, 1950). Thus the stronger the need, the more its impact is felt in all aspects of living.

2. Thirst.   Most Americans have experienced the dry throat and mouth that accompany thirst, but very few have known the extreme discomfort of intense thirst. Those who have will acknowledge that the motivating qualities of acute thirst are overwhelming.

3. Air hunger.   The need to breathe is so obvious and breathing is so automatic that people often forget how essential oxygen is to the body. Even a few seconds without oxygen can produce permanent brain damage, and a few minutes without it will lead to death.

4. Elimination pressures.   The body must rid itself of its waste products in order to survive. Young children relieve the pressure in their bowels and bladder

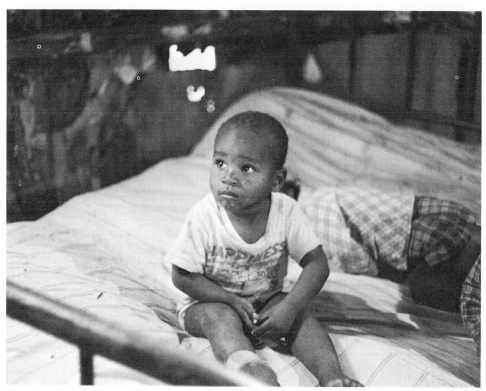

FIGURE 3–3.   This American child has often gone to bed hungry. Photo courtesy of Columbia Broadcasting System.

without hesitating (just ask any parent who is forced to change diapers), but learning reduces this freedom. Teaching children the proper conditions for satisfying the need for elimination consumes much parental energy in the early years of child rearing.

5. Fatigue.   The human organism must have rest and sleep in order to renew its vitality. Occasionally this need becomes so strong that a person will fall asleep in class, on the job, or at the wheel of his automobile.

6. Temperature regulation demands.   People can adjust to variations in heat and cold up to certain limits. However, the need to be in a comfortable temperature can be extremely motivating. As a result, man has gone to great pains to provide himself with clothing, with heating and cooling devices, and with protective shelters. The popularity of southern California, Hawaii, Florida, and Arizona, both for residents and for tourists, is partly based on the comfortable climates in these areas.

7. **Pain avoidance.**   People often do not realize the beneficial role that pain plays in preserving life. If you felt no pain, you would not know when a part of your body was diseased or infected, and the disease or infection could spread and cause severe damage before you realized what was happening. Thus pain avoidance is a survival need — not because pain is discomforting, but because pain is a signal that something has gone wrong with the organism. However, it is the extreme discomfort of pain that makes pain avoidance such a strong motive.

FIGURE 3–4.   Pain avoidance is highly motivating. Often people must accept a lesser pain in order to avoid the potential of greater physical damage. (We wonder how the boy in the background reacted when it was his turn.) Photograph by Liane Enkelis.

The survival needs are the most compelling needs people have. When we are experiencing hunger, pain, or extreme fatigue, we can concentrate on little else except satisfying the need. To obtain food, a starving soldier is likely to surrender to a hostile enemy, even with the knowledge that he may be executed. Under extreme pain, or the threat of extreme pain, people have been known to violate many closely held personal convictions.

STIMULATION NEEDS

The satisfaction of **stimulation needs,** including the need for sex, activity, exploration, manipulation, and novelty, does not appear necessary for personal survival. Nonetheless, a complete lack of environmental stimulation is very distressing, as students in an investigation attested after they were totally shut off from their surroundings for a few days (Bexton, Heron, & Scott, 1954). A series of similar studies conducted some years ago showed that the subjects found it difficult to concentrate, felt they were "going crazy," heard and saw things that did not exist, and often became panicky (reviewed in Janis, Mahl, Kagan, & Holt, 1969). The lack of adequate stimulation for an extended period may affect brain development as well (Bennett, Diamond, Krech, & Rosenzweig, 1964). Children deprived of activity and stimulating human relationships seem to suffer both physically and emotionally.

At one time stimulation needs were thought to develop through learning. Recent observations, however, have shown that animals and young infants respond to **exploratory needs** and manipulation needs without having had an opportunity to learn them (Festinger, 1954; Harlow, Harlow, & Meyer, 1950). Perhaps scientists will find a biochemical basis for all stimulation needs, as they have for the sex needs. A beginning has already been made in this direction: it has been shown that sensory stimulation apparently produces long-range changes in body biochemistry (Lindsley & Riesen, 1968). Although evidence is strong that stimulation needs, both sensory (seeing movement, touching things, and so forth) and social (being with other people), are vitally important for healthy development, we are not yet certain whether their satisfaction is necessary for human survival.

1. Sex. The desire for sex in humans results from biochemical changes within the body, but these changes are set off either by information sent through the sense organs to the brain or by thinking that begins in the brain. Thinking of something with a sexual meaning can lead to stirring up the sex need; seeing, touching, or hearing something with a sexual meaning can also lead to sexual arousal.

2. Activity, exploration, manipulation, novelty. It seems clear that people seek activity and stimulation, not a state of complete rest. Total lack of activity produces boredom, fatigue, and apathy. Complete isolation from stimulation, brought about by placing a person in an apparatus that cuts off all contact with the outside world, has led to such symptoms of mental confusion as fantasies and hallucinations (Heron, 1957).

Given the opportunity, children actively explore their environment. They like to handle objects with their hands and—often to the amusement of older children and adults—to manipulate the objects with their tongues. Observers frequently report that children will bypass a familiar object in order to explore and manipulate a new one, which implies that the need for novelty may be a factor in their behavior. Even monkeys will spend much time and effort manipulating mechanical equipment without receiving any apparent reward (Harlow et al., 1950), which indicates that the act of manipulation is rewarding in itself. However, both infants and monkeys will eventually tire of any given object and will prefer to go on to something else.

You may have observed similar behavior in adults and older children, as when a man receives so much enjoyment from fixing his car that he seems saddened when it is finally in good running order. However, these individuals have had the opportunity to learn by having been rewarded for performing such actions. Infants have not had the same opportunities for learning, and their responses to stimulation needs probably result from inborn characteristics. The degree to which stimulation needs may be inherited is still under debate.

FIGURE 3–5. People need activity and stimulation. Photographs by Lehman J. Pinckney.

Adults would rarely try to restrict a child's efforts to satisfy his survival needs; yet many adults appear unaware that the satisfaction of stimulation needs is similarly very important. Limiting the opportunity for a child to explore his environment and to be physically active may actually harm the child's normal process of development. The hunger need cannot be ignored without risking the death of the child; punishing the child for expressing his needs for activity and exploration may also turn out to be harmful.

Stimulation motives support the contention that people have the need to make the most of their talents and capacities. In other words, one way in which people desire to make the most of their environment is by manipulating and exploring it and by being active and having new experiences.

SOCIAL ASPECTS OF PHYSIOLOGICAL NEEDS

The satisfaction of survival and stimulation needs involves more than biological responses. Such social factors as rituals, restrictions, traditions, personal tastes, and laws all play a role in determining how a person will go about satisfying physiological needs. People eat certain foods and refuse others because of early learning experiences, not because of their food value. Eating in a clean environment, preferably with pleasant companions, seems to foster the enjoyment of food. A person who enters a smelly restaurant and notices lipstick smudges on his water glass and dried bits of food caked on his fork is very likely to lose his appetite.

"Man Does Not Live by Bread Alone."

The history of the world is filled with examples of people who gave up the satisfaction of a physiological motive in order to satisfy a motive higher on Maslow's hierarchy of needs.

In wartime Europe, starving parents gave their only food to their children. Their love and sense of duty and responsibility were stronger than their hunger.

A music student lived in near poverty, without adequate food or warmth, to save money to pay for lessons.

Early in World War II, three military chaplains drowned after giving their life jackets to others.

Prison inmates risked abuse, beatings, and even death to demand that they be treated with more dignity.

Food also has great symbolic meaning. To "break bread" with someone is an indication of friendship. Wine or grape juice and wafers are vital to the Christian celebration of Communion; Orthodox Jews adhere to kosher laws that forbid them to eat any meat from pigs, goats, or shellfish; Moslems refuse to eat pig meat; and devout Hindus will not eat any part or product of the cow.

Food preferences vary greatly. In Japan, raw fish (*sashimi*) is very popular, but oysters are eaten cooked; in the United States, oysters are eaten raw, but never fish. Many people enjoy rabbit meat, but others become sick at the thought of eating such a lovely, furry creature (although they may not hesitate to eat a young chicken).

The intensity with which a physiological need is felt may also vary as a result of the social or external situation. Research into the effects of fatigue has been complicated by the close relationship between fatigue and boredom. You have undoubtedly found yourself wide awake, despite having been up all night, because you were so involved in what you were doing. The experience of feeling very tired, even after sufficient sleep, is a common result of boredom.

Social relationships can also affect the strength of a physiological need. Intensely felt hunger needs and subsequent overeating have been known to result from feelings of social rejection. These observations have been confirmed by laboratory experiments. In one study circumstances were contrived so that the subjects felt they were being personally rejected in a social relationship; as a result, these subjects reported increased feelings of hunger (Spence, Gordon, & Rabkin, 1966).

Pain is similarly affected by social factors. One physician reported that a **placebo** (a fake pill or other kind of treatment that does not actually influence body physiology) reduced the pain of surgical wounds in a third of the cases he studied and eliminated severe seasickness within 30 minutes in half of his cases (Beecher, 1969). Reports of pain, especially intense pain, are more common among certain ethnic groups than among others (Zborowski, 1969). The ability to withstand pain is often a sign of pride, particularly in men.

The list of social influences on physiological needs could be continued indefinitely. What examples can you think of?

SAFETY AND SECURITY NEEDS

If you are deeply involved with satisfying your hunger need or your need to avoid pain, you will have little time or energy for anything else. However, once you are able to satisfy these needs, at least at a minimally adequate level, and can feel reasonably confident that the need will not return to disturb you for a period of time, you can turn your attention to satisfying safety and security needs.

Everyone needs to feel safe from such harm as meeting with physical violence, having things he values taken away, or losing the care of parents or other protectors. People in countries where the Secret Police might suddenly burst in and arrest them certainly will find it difficult to concentrate on satisfying any except the basic physiological needs. The child whose parents are constantly arguing and threatening divorce will have unfulfilled safety needs, and his behavior may be strongly influenced by attempts to assure himself that his parents or some substitute will continue to protect him. What is the effect of the threat of nuclear war on your own safety needs?

FIGURE 3–6. The safety needs of many people are protected by guns and police. However, whether police and weapons satisfy safety needs or disrupt safety needs often depends on where you are standing at the moment. Left: courtesy Columbia Broadcasting System; right: photograph by P. C. Peri.

Yet people with physiological and safety needs sometimes will satisfy needs higher on the hierarchy in preference to those lower. Determining the reasons for this kind of preference involves the study of values, which are discussed in Chapter 18. Does anything motivate you so much that you would risk survival or safety to achieve it?

LOVE AND BELONGING NEEDS

No doubt exists about the motivating power of the need for love and for a sense of belonging. Some evidence shows that, at least for infants, love may be necessary for the maintenance of good health. Babies who lack the love of a mother or mother-substitute have been observed to become depressed (Spitz, 1949), apathetic, and physically and emotionally retarded (Ribble, 1943). But since such infants usually are also deprived of normal satisfaction of stimulation needs, we cannot be certain whether the ill effects resulted from the lack of love or the lack of opportunity for stimulation. (See Chapter 11 for further discussion.)

In any event, the need for love and belonging is important. People with an unsatisfied need for love or for the feeling of belonging to a group may go to great lengths to satisfy this need—even at the cost of their self-esteem.

In his childhood Steve Rogell had lived in a series of foster homes. At age 16 he ran away from a particularly unpleasant situation and, lying about his age, joined the Navy. Steve had no memory of his parents, both of whom had died before he was 3. Perhaps equally important, he had no memory of ever being loved in any of the homes where he stayed.

Shortly after leaving the Navy, Steve met and married an 18-year-old girl who greatly admired his knowledge and sophistication. Steve felt that she loved him, and he was very happy with the relationship. However, over the next few years, his wife matured and developed her capacities in many ways, whereas Steve remained very much the person he always was. He became tense and uncomfortable with his wife, and he began to resent her. On the one hand, she represented the love that he badly needed; on the other hand, her growing competence reminded him of how little he had matured.

His wife became increasingly irritated with Steve, and, in time, she began to express this irritation. Steve, frightened of losing the one person who had loved him and whom he had been able to love, was unable to show any anger. He became submissive and constantly found ways to seek approval from her. Now more sophisticated than he, his wife was disgusted by the meek behavior of the man she had once looked up to, and her reactions to Steve became more and more overtly rejecting. The more she attacked him, however, the more Steve reminded her of how much they loved each other and how much he wanted to do for her.

Love needs are not restricted to romantic love and parent-child love. They include the feeling of closeness between two good friends, the feeling of neighborliness that exists in some communities, or the feeling of good fellowship that occurs in some social groups. People who feel friendless and unloved exert great efforts to satisfy their love needs.

Although love needs and belonging needs are related, they are far from identical. In recent years, awareness of the importance of belonging needs has increased. People who do not feel they belong to their community or who feel that they cannot relate to a group have been described as experiencing **alienation.** That is, they are strangers or unrelated persons. Since they feel unrelated to both individuals and groups, they may lack the kinds of motivation that normal social relationships lead to. Often they feel goalless and uncertain of themselves. Not being able to turn to others, they may turn increasingly inward.

Three interrelated meanings have been suggested for alienation (Gold, 1969). First, it implies isolation. Alienated people may not feel a part of any system. They live in the world, in a country, in a community, but they are not part of this world, country, or community. Since they do not belong anywhere, they feel no responsibility to any group.

Second, alienation reflects a feeling of powerlessness—a frustration over not having any influence. There was a time when most young people believed they could change the system and make the world a better place to live. Today many fewer people maintain this belief.

Third, alienation refers to an identity crisis, as when a person asks "Who am I?" or "Why am I here?" or "What is it all about?" but does not get a satisfying answer. People look for meaningful work, for meaningful human relationships, for meaningful political movements; but they are not exactly certain what "meaningful" even means. This kind of alienation is extremely difficult to explain or understand, unless you have experienced it yourself or have at least had a close friend who has.

You may hear people apply the term *alienated* to almost any kind of behavior or attitude they do not understand. Nor is it unusual to hear someone talk about himself as alienated, although he probably means that he is irritated or frustrated or bitter, or perhaps lazy or ineffective. When the word is used, it helps to know which of the three meanings is intended, whether perhaps they are all intended, or whether the user is trying to justify behavior that has relatively little relationship to alienation.

Fortunately most (but certainly not all) alienated people do gain a sense of belonging within a small group. They may feel alienated from the community or powerless or confused about their own identity and purpose; but they find warmth, love, friendship, influence, and meaning among a small group to compensate for their lack of relationship to the larger community.

ESTEEM AND SELF-ESTEEM NEEDS

Once physiological, safety, and love needs have been satisfied, the individual can turn his attention toward gaining the respect of others and having respect for himself. Steve Rogell sacrificed this opportunity when his unsatisfied love needs became so demanding that he had to beg his wife for her love.

As humans we all feel we have the right to be treated as people of worth. Perhaps the strongest insult one 3-year-old can hurl on another is "baby," because this label implies a lesser level of competence and worth (at least in the eyes of a 3-year-old). The person who feels inadequate may channel his energy into proving his adequacy to *himself*. He may also wish to establish his adequacy in the eyes of others, but he needs most to convince himself.

The self-esteem needs include "the desire for strength, for achievement, for adequacy, for mastery and competence, for confidence in the face of the world, and for independence and freedom" (Maslow, 1970, p. 45). The relative importance of each motive differs from person to person, and even the definition of each may differ. For example, "strength" signifies the ability to withstand pain to one person and the ability to remain emotionally stable under great stress to another; "achievement" to one person refers to artistic creativity and, to another person, to piling up money.

Esteem needs interact with self-esteem needs. That is, your feelings about yourself depend to a large measure on how you believe other people, especially people very important to you, such as your parents, esteem you. Among the esteem needs are "the desire for reputation or prestige (defining it as respect or esteem from other people), status, fame and glory, dominance, recognition, attention, importance, dignity, (and) appreciation" (Maslow, 1970, p. 45).

People who respect themselves and are respected by others rarely need to proclaim their own capabilities. Perhaps they are pleased, and even proud, of what they have done and how others regard them, but they do not require constant compliments (although they probably enjoy compliments) or demand constant attention (although they may enjoy attention also). They are less likely to be withdrawn or fearful and more likely to have faith in their own judgments as well as in those of other people. Also, they do not need to expend time and energy worrying about their inadequacies (Jessor & Richardson, 1968). Is it possible for a person to have self-esteem but lack the esteem of others? Or vice versa?

SELF-ACTUALIZATION NEEDS

Only when the more basic needs have been at least minimally met can the individual turn to satisfying his needs for self-actualization. Self-actualization, as explained earlier, refers to the process of making maximum use of your abilities, of developing your talents, and of being the sort of person you really are, rather than the sort of person you believe others would like you to be.

Just as the young infant seems to need to explore his environment, and just as the monkey seems to need the challenge of manipulating puzzles, mature humans also seem to wish to develop their capacities. No one is constantly self-actualizing, just as no one is constantly in the process of satisfying any one other need. But each individual has the potential to feel the need to self-actualize and to satisfy this need. A few examples may help clarify this complex concept.

LeRoy Hawthorne spent two years at the state college before he and the dean had their final argument. He left campus and moved into a nearby old house that was serving as a commune. After several weeks of moping around, he decided that he was doing too much of the work, and he tried another house. This one was better, but LeRoy quickly became restless. When a friend at a farm commune invited him to join, he did, although he had never had much regard for farmers. Three years later, LeRoy feels happy and involved. He has never worked harder in his life—60 and 70 hours almost every week—but everyone on the farm works hard. He feels that farming enables him to use his strength, his imagination, and his love of the outdoors; the commune requires that he use his capacity to get along with others; and his ability to participate in making things grow is more exciting than he had ever imagined.

Vinnie Hopkins disliked her hometown, her home, and, especially, her parents. At college she majored in elementary education, because her father refused to pay for any other program and because she figured that even studying a field she didn't like was better than returning home. After finishing college, she taught for three years, saved her money, and studied geology on the side. She is now working with the National Parks Service at Death Valley. When she looks around at the desert and the distant mountains, she feels that the job, the climate, and the desolation just "seem to fit me."

Miller Fulton was a successful sales manager for a large urban new-car dealer, but he suddenly quit his job and bought a small paint-supply shop from a friend. "I had had it with taking orders from people who knew less than I did. I wanted to be my own boss. I want that freedom." He worked longer hours with more headaches for less money, but he felt that he was meeting an exciting challenge. "Anyone can sell cars, but not very many people can run their own show without going bankrupt."

An English professor told the following story: "At the small town college where I teach, older people rarely take daytime courses, so I was surprised to notice a shiny, bald head among the more youthful ones, and I was doubly surprised when I realized this head belonged to the owner of the nearest thing to a department store our town had. He later explained that, by the time he was 45, he had made all the money he needed and had proved to himself he could run a business. But all his life he felt he could be an excellent furniture designer, and now he was returning to college to learn both the techniques and the artistic background, so that he could develop this capacity. The truth is that he didn't have much talent, but he certainly had fun."

All these people were motivated by the need to develop their capacities and to be "themselves." Each one was fulfilling his need for self-actualization, regardless of what the rest of the world thought.

Because self-actualization is not sharply defined, it is difficult to apply the concept properly. How can you tell whether or not you are self-actualizing? Four situations occur when a person self-actualizes:

1. The self-actualizing individual raises his standards and demands more of himself. By so doing, he also demands more of life and expects greater rewards from the things he does.

2. Self-improvement becomes continuous. This improvement may occur through a course in Chinese cooking, through reading books and magazines, or through a summer camping trip to the national parks. If the end result of a person's activity is that he gains in his understanding of the world or of himself, or if he becomes better able to do something, then he has been self-actualizing.

3. The individual increases his self-understanding and becomes more the kind of person he wants to be. It may seem strange to say that many people do not really like themselves, but it is true. People are ashamed of certain things they have done or wish to do or have not done or are afraid to do. The self-actualizing person behaves so that he can respect himself.

4. The self-actualizing person makes the fullest use of the abilities he has and also tries to develop new ones. Most people will attempt only a small proportion of the many things they have the potential to do. People self-actualize when they develop present competencies and investigate new and untried areas (Coleman, 1960).

The need to self-actualize motivates people to grow and to develop their talents. However, some needs produce behavior that merely compensates for deficiencies, rather than leads to growth.

DEFICIENCY MOTIVATION AND GROWTH MOTIVATION

Behavior motivated by hunger or by fear of physical punishment results from **deficiency motivation;** that is, it is motivated by things the organism lacks. You sense an uncomfortable inner tension, you wish to reduce this tension, and so you seek food or escape.

A starving man does not worry about how his food is seasoned. A child, frightened because his parents have left him alone at night without warning, would probably welcome a spanking if that were the price of his parents' return. Such individuals are deficiency-motivated. When they satisfy their hunger or safety needs, they have not attained any degree of personal growth; they have merely reduced a deficit.

On the other hand, when you are motivated by the possibility of truly enjoying a meal or by the pleasure of warmth and security in being with those you love, your behavior is based on **growth motivation.** The opportunity for personal growth and pleasure, not tension reduction, provides the motivation. You may even create mild tension on purpose, such as eating a very light lunch when anticipating an excellent dinner in order to heighten the enjoyment of the later meal.

Thus behavior occurring in response to a need may lead either to the reduction of a deficit or to some form of personal growth. Satisfying the hunger need may merely reduce hunger, or it may be an enjoyable process taking place in good company and pleasant surroundings. Satisfying the esteem need may merely compensate for lack of self-esteem, or it may be a wonderful experience that leaves you with a warm glow of pleasure, as when your employer commends you for having done an excellent job with a task on which you worked particularly hard.

Here, then, is the hierarchy of needs: physiological needs, safety and security needs, love and belonging needs, esteem and self-esteem needs, and self-actualizing needs. In order to focus on the higher needs, you must first adequately satisfy the more basic ones. In satisfying each need, you may be motivated either by deficiency and tension reduction or by growth and enhancement. The hierarchy is not a rigid one but must be considered in light of the specific background and values of each individual.

We shall return to the concept of self-actualization at many points in this book. At present, consider a few of the implications of this idea:

1. Everyone has potential capacities and talents.

2. These capacities and talents are often never developed.

3. Before you can develop them effectively, you usually must first satisfy physiological, safety, love, and esteem needs.

4. You are wasting a part of yourself if you leave your potential capacities and talents undeveloped.

5. Developing these capacities and talents is enjoyable and natural, not dull or strained.

6. If you try to influence others to be what *you* want them to be, you may be limiting their possibilities of developing themselves as *they* want.

Each individual has a unique personality. When he is able to satisfy his physiological, safety, love, and esteem needs adequately, he can attempt to develop his unique personality to the limits that his capacities allow.

SUMMARY OF IMPORTANT IDEAS

1. Motivated behavior is behavior set into motion by a need, which indicates that some satisfaction is lacking. A need implies that the organism is activated to obtain the satisfaction.

2. Motivation and needs are concepts, not things. To measure them, indirect measures have been developed. Psychologists measure motivation through controlled observations, ratings by others, self-ratings, and laboratory experiments.

3. Much behavior occurs because of unconscious motivation, or motivation that the person himself is not aware of.

4. When behavior results from unconscious motivation, the basis for the behavior may be repressed. Repression occurs when a person does not recall something because he is motivated to be unable to recall, not because the matter was too trivial to recall (as in forgetting).

5. A hierarchy of needs implies that the individual has to find adequate satisfaction for the more basic needs before he can turn his attention to needs higher on the scale.

6. The most basic needs are the physiological needs, which include the survival needs (such as hunger, thirst, and fatigue) and the stimulation needs (such as exploration and manipulation). When the former are not adequately satisfied, the organism dies. The stimulation needs develop partly as a result of learning but may have a biochemical basis.

7. People usually satisfy the physiological needs in keeping with certain customs, traditions, personal tastes, and habits.

8. The second most basic needs are the safety and security needs. Next in the hierarchy of needs are the love and belonging needs, the esteem needs, and —after all the previous needs are reasonably well satisfied—the self-actualizing needs.

9. A self-actualizing person makes maximum use of his abilities, develops his talents and potentialities, and becomes the sort of person he really is.

10. Some behavior is motivated by deficiencies, or things the organism lacks; some behavior is motivated by growth, or the desire to be better or do things in a better way.

4 What Is Personality?

The human personality can be studied and discussed in terms of processes, sections, characteristics, and pieces, but the human being behaves as a total entity. More-over, he behaves as an organism interacting with his social environment and culture. The previous chapter discussed human behavior in terms of what motivates it; the present chapter discusses human behavior in terms of who the person is and why. Later chapters will discuss the basic processes that underlie behavior. We begin with motivation and personality because, once you have encountered the entire person, you will find that learning about the parts makes more sense.

When psychologists look at people, what do they see? Do they see living beings whose behavior is beyond their own control, who are helpless in the face of the pressures of their environment? Or organisms that will harm others unless kept in careful check? Or animals that differ from other animals only because they can walk upright and talk?

Different psychologists look at people differently. My particular orientation involves certain assumptions that will be presented repeatedly throughout this book: first, people will try to make use of their capacities, if given the opportunity; second, people can become successful in using these capacities in spite of great environmental pressures; third, most, and perhaps almost all, behavior called "good" and "evil" is learned; finally, the factors distinguishing humans from lower forms of animal life are numerous and extremely meaningful.

AN INTRODUCTION TO PERSONALITY

The theme of this book is human behavior and, therefore, the human **personality:** its nature and development, the way it adjusts to the world, its feelings, its values, its problems, and the ways in which it deals with these problems. Although you all have an idea what the term *personality* implies, the psychologist's definition may differ from yours in several ways.

Personality can be defined as the **dynamic** organization of characteristic attributes leading to behavior and distinguishing one individual from other individuals. It refers to the total individual and includes (but is not limited to) needs, motives, methods of adjusting, temperament qualities, self-concepts, role behaviors, attitudes, values, and abilities. The term covers behavior the individual himself is aware of and behavior he is not aware of, behavior evident to others and behavior evident only to himself. This definition is extremely broad and requires some additional explanation of the terms used.

Dynamic.   A dynamic person is forceful, always moving, filled with energy. In psychology, to refer to personality as dynamic is to say that the human is constantly changing and that each change affects the entire personality in such a way that the original change may itself be affected, thus setting off another series of changes. No element of personality is isolated from any other element; nothing operates independently, as in a vacuum.

Organization.   Personality is neither a single entity nor a combination of entities but an organization or a "whole." An automobile is not a shell; neither is it merely an assortment of separate parts. In order to work, an automobile must be an organization of individual parts into a whole automobile. Personality also is organized into a whole.

Characteristic.   An example of behavior that is fairly typical of an individual is said to be characteristic of him. If a man is consistently kind and gentle but will strike anyone who threatens to strike him first, we would still call him kind and gentle, because such behavior is more typical of him.

Behavior.   Any observable action is behavior. Eating a ham sandwich is behavior; so is each separate step in eating it, such as making it, raising it to the lips, biting it, chewing it, and swallowing it. Two people may both eat ham sandwiches frequently, but each will make, bite, and chew the sandwich in different ways.

Thinking is also behaving, since thinking involves brain-cell activity, which is indirectly observable through a device such as the electroencephalograph. Any expression of an attitude or a need, even if only in thought, is thus a behavior. Other examples of behavior include deciding whether you received the correct change at a store, wondering whom to vote for in the next campus election, becoming angry when you hear someone tell a lie about your friend, and trying to listen to the professor who speaks so quietly that you can barely hear him.

To repeat the initial definition of personality in other terms: personality is the *changing and interacting organization of typical qualities into a whole that leads a man to behave as he does and that makes him different from other people.*

POINTS OF VIEW ABOUT BEHAVIOR AND PERSONALITY

Newcomers to the study of a field are often amused, and sometimes irritated, by the inability of the experts to agree. Yet this situation may be viewed as a strength rather than a weakness, since disagreement can lead to productive research and exciting new ideas. (Of course, it can also lead to meaningless arguments, but that may be the price of free scientific expression.)

Among the many controversies in psychology, I have selected five that I feel are most important to discuss. There is no need for you to take a stand on these issues now, but understanding their significance will help you to relate the discussions in this book and in your class to one another and to the world outside the classroom. The five issues concern whether personality should be viewed as: (1) enduring and stable or based primarily on a specific situation, (2) a number of different elements grouped together or a total integrated entity; (3) having the potential for growth or always coming to rest; (4) primarily the outcome of genetic and biochemical factors or primarily the outcome of learned and environmental factors; and (5) totally controlled by heredity and environment or under the free will of the individual.

Enduring or situational? Some psychologists focus on social setting or environmental pressures to understand behavior. Since your behavior varies so much as a result of a specific situation, these psychologists are concerned primarily with how each situation affects behavior. For example, you behave differently with people your own age than with those younger or older; your reactions to your instructor change when you walk with him from the classroom to the coffee shop; you respond differently to the fear of having a tooth pulled than to the fear of having an injection.

The other side of the coin is to emphasize those relatively enduring characteristics that you bring to each situation. Although you do react differently to people as a function of their age, you are basically considerate, friendly, and respectful, no matter whom you are with; although you are more relaxed with your instructor in the coffee shop, you are always a bit guarded in any interaction with faculty members; although you overreact to inoculations and react only normally to a tooth extraction, you respond to any anticipated pain with dread.

This, like other controversies, need not be an either-or issue. But ask yourself, as you try to understand behavior, how much attention you pay to the situation and how much to what the individual brings to it.

Part or whole?   The recent history of psychology is filled with systems for dividing personality into parts (Sanford, 1970). One such approach involves the use of personality **traits,** or behavior characteristics that differentiate people from one another. Examples of traits are thriftiness, boastfulness, and friendliness. To describe an individual in terms of a trait implies that the trait is fairly typical of his behavior.

We talk in terms of traits all the time. "John seems to be a happy guy." "Jeanne isn't as thoughtful as she used to be." "Greg is too shy to be a good salesman." Traits are obviously oversimplifications, since personality is both unique and dynamic. John is not always happy; Jeanne is still thoughtful in some ways; Greg may find the right kind of selling job.

The question is not whether using traits (or other kinds of divisions) is useful. Rather, it is whether we can really understand people — or one person — by bringing together a large number of different traits. Or is our understanding enhanced only by trying to deal with the entire person all at once? Should we try to break down personality into as many parts as possible so we can put it together again more sensibly? Or should we accept the opinion that combining all the parts can never describe the true essence of an individual?

Growth or rest?   Is the goal of human behavior to reduce tension and to come to rest? You are hungry; you feel a need to eat; you eat; the need disappears. You are lonely; you feel a need to be with someone; you get together with a friend; the need disappears. Can all behavior be explained by this approach?

Or is there more? Is there something within you that requires you to demand more of yourself? When the tension caused by hunger or loneliness is gone, do you seek excitement and activity? Or do you happily accept your tension-free state? When you apply stress to a rubber band, its nature is to return to its previous state, which it does when the tension is released. Can the nature of humans be explained in the same way? In essence, do people have the potential for self-actualization, or do they respond primarily to the push and pull of the environment? In other words, are people actors or reactors?

Biological or learned?   The very first moment of being occurs in the womb, when the sperm from the father unites with the ovum from the mother. The cell that emerges from this joining and eventually matures into the human fetus is called a **zygote.** At the time the zygote is formed, the individual inherits certain characteristics from each of his parents through microscopic bits of life called genes and chromosomes. These inherited characteristics are referred to as **genetic,** or **hereditary,** in origin.

FIGURE 4–1. Shopping is carried out in marketplaces all over the world. People in the two environments shown here behave differently in some ways and similarly in other ways. How important do you feel genetic factors are to these similarities and differences? How about the influences of early learning? Of the immediate environment? Top photograph by Lehman J. Pinckney; bottom photograph by Richard A. Kalish.

Behavior genetics is the area of study that concerns itself with hereditary (genetic) and environmental aspects of behavior. A question that has long plagued psychologists is the degree to which heredity and environment contribute to various human characteristics. Debate over this question has traditionally been known as the *nature-nurture controversy*. However, many people now feel that biological and learned factors are both so important that they should be considered simultaneously and regarded as being in dynamic interaction.

When the infant is born, he is different in appearance from all other infants — unless he has an identical twin. There is little doubt that such characteristics as eye color, hair color, bone structure, and facial features are inherited, which accounts for why children resemble their parents.

Other characteristics are believed to be heavily influenced by genetic factors but also affected by the environment. Your height and weight, for example, depend both on your gene structure at conception and on your health, nutrition, and eating habits in later life. Your *potential* intellectual capacity may be inherited, but your ability to make use of this intelligence is influenced by the environment.

The newborn infant differs from other infants in ways that go beyond physical appearance. He displays patterns of activity, irritability, and mood that seem to be inherited; at least, the possibility that they have been learned is definitely limited. These patterns are expressed through differing amounts of movement, crying, sucking behavior, and sleep. Some psychologists claim that these behavior and temperament differences developed during the nine months in the womb; others contend that heredity is by far the major influence.

People often make statements such as "He has his father's temper" or "He cries easily, like his mother." The implication is that temper and readiness to cry are genetically inherited. Geneticists and psychologists are not at all certain how important heredity is in determining these kinds of behavior. Both heredity and environment interact dynamically in causing a person to develop a hot temper or a tendency to cry; but it is not necessary to assume that heredity and environment contribute in the same proportion to the temperamental or crying behavior of every individual.

Some characteristics are only minimally and indirectly affected by heredity. Political attitudes, religious values, enjoyment of television shows, and interest in watching or playing baseball are virtually completely the result of previous learning; yet heredity may play an indirect role. People who are, for genetic reasons, very intelligent, irritable, or emotional may, because of their inherited characteristics, find a particular political viewpoint or type of entertainment more or less appealing than would people with different inherited characteristics.

Basically, heredity provides a boundary to your behavior that you cannot exceed. You cannot fly by flapping your arms, no matter how hard you try or how much you learn. Heredity also affects other kinds of behavior, since your size, race, physical appearance, and sex are all largely or completely the result of heredity, although the environment determines how people react to you because of these characteristics. The genetic fact of your size interacts with the perception people have of you and you have of yourself because of your size. This interaction influences your personality and behavior.

Less certain is the degree to which heredity influences your intellectual capacity (and therefore your schoolwork and job capabilities) and your emotional behavior (and therefore your reactions to other people and your responses to stress). Even at birth each person has a distinctive brain, nervous system, and body biochemistry, and the individual differences are enormous (Williams, 1960). Mood, temperament, and intelligence appear to be related to differences in the physiology of the brain and the nervous system; thus it seems reasonable to assume that people are born with tendencies to behave and think in different ways. In addition, evidence is overwhelming that later learning and social environment also have a substantial influence on mood, temperament, and intellectual capacities—and related behavior. What we still know little about is the degree to which different kinds of behavior are affected by heredity and by environment.

In view of this evidence for genetic differences in behavior tendencies, parents who treat all their children exactly alike may be making an error, since the needs and desires of each child differ. An older sister may require more sleep than her younger brother, which would cause total confusion at bedtime; a teacher can afford to be stricter with Jill than with Jack, since Jack is very moody and will burst into tears when criticized. (Heredity may or may not have an effect on these examples of behavior.) Some politically explosive issues arising from this controversy involve the assumption that males and females or members of different racial groups are, on the average, genetically different. (See Chapter 19 for a related discussion.)

Careful observations of patients suffering from certain medical problems have led scientists to talk about **inherited predispositions.** Two people who lead the same sort of life and are equally healthy both become ill with a strep throat; person A contracts rheumatic fever, but person B does not. Person A, therefore, may have genetically inherited a predisposition or weakness toward rheumatic fever. He did not inherit rheumatic fever, but he inherited a susceptibility to contract the disease, whereas person B inherited a strong resistance to the illness. Considerable evidence shows that one person may have a greater inherited predisposition to become mentally disturbed than another, even though they both lead similar lives and face equally stressful situations (Kallmann, 1953).

Many studies, including the one just mentioned, have investigated differences between **identical twins** and **fraternal twins.** Since identical twins come from the division of a single fertilized egg, they share an almost identical heredity;

they are nearly identical to each other in appearance and are inevitably of the same sex. Fraternal twins result from the fertilization of two separate eggs; their heredity is no more the same than that of any two children of the same parents, and they may not look alike or be of the same sex.

Fraternal twins share a highly similar environment, just as identical twins do, but they share a much less similar heredity than do identical twins. As a result, in behavior presumed to have some genetic basis, identical twins should resemble each other more than fraternal twins resemble each other. Research results bear this conclusion out. Identical twins have been found more similar than fraternal twins on measures of intelligence, interests, and personality (Nichols, 1968); on the length of time it takes to react to stimuli and on other tasks involving sensory and motor responses (Osborne & Gregory, 1966); and on the likelihood of becoming mentally disturbed (Kallmann, 1953). Even when identical twins are reared in different homes, their intelligence-test scores are almost the same (Burt, 1966).

Other studies have shown that the intelligence of foster children is more closely related to that of their biological parents than to that of their foster parents (Honzik, 1957), even though a good foster home appears to increase the IQs of foster children beyond scores otherwise expected (Skodak & Skeels, 1949).

Determined or free?   In 1971 psychologist B. F. Skinner published a highly controversial book entitled *Beyond Freedom and Dignity*. In it he proclaimed that freedom is a delusion and that people should accept the idea that everything they do and think and feel is the result of an interaction between their genetic inheritance and their later learning. He was referring not to political or religious freedom but to the freedom to choose one's own fate. Skinner insists that people do not really have choice—that what they think is free choice actually results from genetics and from learning, over which they have no control. Furthermore, genetics is the outcome of the accidental meeting between sperm and ovum at the moment of conception, and later learning stems from factors in the environment.

This extreme position leads to some thought-provoking considerations. For example, if everything you do is determined by forces over which you have no power, then you are responsible neither for your vices nor for your virtues. It is not *you* who is accomplishing something good or evil but the accumulation of forces over which you have no control.

The opposite point of view contends that the individual is very much responsible for his own behavior, that he is free to select among alternatives, that he can take part in shaping his own destiny, that he can resist the influences of the environment and be himself. (Skinner would probably reply that "being yourself" is merely being what heredity and environment shape you to be.) The **humanistic**

psychologists, who are among the most outspoken advocates of the opposing theory, believe that people *need* to be true to themselves.

Followers of Skinner use such terms as **behavior modification** and *shaping* to describe their methods in changing behavior. The assumption is that, to change behavior, one must control appropriate aspects of the environment. Since the environment is almost all-powerful in determining behavior, when you control the environment, you control behavior.

FIGURE 4–2. Are these men doing what they are because they were so influenced by their environment that this course of action was virtually inevitable? Or are they responding to freedom of choice and selecting among alternatives? Photos courtesy of Columbia Broadcasting System.

Humanistic psychologists try to alter behavior by encouraging people to have a variety of experiences, to explore the world. They use terms like *authentic* and *encounter* and *becoming* to imply honesty, integrity, openness, and personal growth. Skinner assumes that you are what you are made to be by outside people and events; the humanistic psychologists assume that you have the potential to become much more than you are.

We will return to these themes later. In the meantime, remember that, although the humanistic position may be more appealing, since most of us like to feel we are in control of what we do, this appeal does not prove that the humanists are correct.

THE BEHAVIOR OF HUMANS AND LOWER ANIMALS

The human is considered the highest form of animal life. Although by definition he is an animal and shares many characteristics with other animal species, the human differs from lower animals in distinct ways. Obviously, humans have higher intelligence, the ability to walk upright, and the ability to use tools. You can easily add many other examples. More relevant to the study of human behavior are seven major bases for differentiating humans from lower animals:

1. People develop more slowly.   As a result, the effects of the environment have more time to operate. Since infancy and childhood last longer for the human than for other forms of animal life, human experiences during these periods may have more lasting effects.

2. People study themselves.   No other creatures study themselves. As a matter of fact, no other creatures seem aware that they exist and thus *can* be studied.

3. People develop interests that have nothing to do with keeping alive. Many animals enjoy play, new experiences, and companionship, but only at a relatively primitive level. People become interested in such activities as reading, traveling, watching television, participating in sports, talking, collecting matchbooks, studying ancient civilizations, and playing poker.

4. People use symbols in thinking and communicating.   The symbolic language of animals is very limited, but people have developed a great variety of symbols, including words, gestures, and numbers, which open whole new worlds for them.

5. People can govern their behavior by occurrences far away in time or in space.   A man may act in a certain way because he wishes future generations to think well of him. A student can learn what happened in 1492 or in 1933, or he can anticipate what may happen in 1984 or 2001. People can alter their behavior by learning what is happening in Bogor, Indonesia, or Indianapolis, Indiana (points 1–5 adapted from Diamond, 1957).

6. People change the environment of each generation.   You are living in a world much different from the one your grandparents knew when they were your age. Most of the changes are the result of human accomplishments. A dog or a horse, on the other hand, lives in the same sort of world in which its grand-parents lived, except for the changes produced by humans. Humans can acquire, accumulate, alter, and transmit values, ideas, and material goods (adapted from Sanford & Wrightsman, 1970).

7. People can anticipate future changes in themselves. The length of time you will be a student is finite; the length of time you will be young is finite; the length of time you will be alive is finite. Today, whatever age you happen to be, you are aware of these facts, and, in varying degrees, you plan your life around them. You anticipate future changes in yourself that, to the best of our knowledge, other forms of animal life cannot anticipate.

These differences between human and animal behavior allow the human wonderful opportunities for personal growth, for controlling his environment,

FIGURE 4–3. Although humans differ greatly from lower animals, we often do research with the latter and then see if we can relate what is observed to humans. We do so because the behavior of lower animals is less complex, because animals have little or no ability to deal with symbols—and because they don't complain much or expect to be paid when we study them. Photograph by Lehman J. Pinckney.

for using his abilities, and for enjoying his life. They also offer him great destructive potential and great potential for anxiety and fear regarding his future. How well do you think the human has used his abilities and opportunities?

To emphasize, as we have, the differences between humans and animals does not mean that similarities do not exist also. Humans and most other forms of animals have the potential for learning, the ability to adapt to new situations, the need to take in some form of nourishment, the ability to reproduce young, a dependency on receiving sensory stimulation from the environment, and the capacity to move through the environment. Humans and higher levels of animals also share the capacity to seek food, sex, and shelter; to care for their young; to exhibit aggression and fear; and to enter into relationships with other individuals and with groups. Can you think of other examples?

THE SELF-CONCEPT: WHAT YOU MEAN TO YOU

A very useful way to understand the human personality is through consideration of the **self-concept.** The definition of self-concept is deceivingly simple: self-concept is your picture or image of yourself. Like personality, self-concept is a dynamic organization of characteristic qualities; but, unlike personality, self-concept is a picture of those qualities *as seen by the individual himself.* Your self-concept includes *your* picture of your abilities, of your effect on others, of your temperament and other elements of personality, and of your physical qualities, such as health and appearance.

Self refers to what you really are. Self-concept refers to what you think you are — your picture or image of yourself. Most people have a fairly realistic self-concept, perhaps being a little too generous about themselves in certain ways and a little too self-critical in other instances. Undoubtedly each of us develops major distortions in self-concept on occasion, but such distortions are corrected as we interact with other people and with events.

Ron Vance saw himself as a loser. His mother had walked out when he was 7, leaving his father, a prison guard, to care for three young children. Caught between the stress of his work and the pressures of his family responsibilities, Mr. Vance was equally short of temper and of cash. Ron's childhood memories of him consist of shouts, slaps, and complaints about "the lousy government that lets prices go up, coddles criminals, and won't pay prison guards a decent wage." Ron's father also worried a great deal about "not having my kids go bad," and he was suspicious of every friend Ron brought home. Once, when he was 10, Ron and two friends were caught stealing gas-tank caps from automobiles, and their parents were notified. From then on Mr. Vance's suspicions of Ron intensified.

Ron finished high school, despite several suspensions for truancy and a poor record, largely because he was afraid — realistically — that his father would beat him if he tried to drop out. By this time his self-concept as an unworthy person was well established. After all, his mother hadn't loved him enough to stay with him, his father didn't trust him, his teachers, for the most part, didn't care whether he finished or not, he was a financial drain on the limited resources of his father, and he couldn't even succeed in stealing! And when he had tried out for the school football team, he had his leg broken in the first serious scrimmage. He was skinny, he had pimples, and one ear stuck out from his head while the other one was plastered back almost flat.

In young adulthood Ron began to recognize that he was not the only loser, and he developed considerable sympathy and understanding for others who also felt that the world was against them. In his bitterness and anger he found the words to make other losers want to fight back, and he began to organize a group that met to plan action regarding their complaints. A local politician, trying to oust a city councilman who had held his post for nearly 30 years, brought Ron into his office to help him.

Slowly Ron's self-concept changed; with improved feelings of belonging and of esteem and self-esteem, he could be more objective about himself. He realized that his mother had deserted him only because she was a weak and immature woman, that his father did feel a strong affection for him but just wasn't capable of dealing with so much pressure, and that he had been so unpleasant to his teachers that they left him alone because they felt he wanted to be alone. Most important, he realized that he had worth. He had the ability to lead others, to plan action, and to work for a possible future city councilman. His bitterness regarding "the system" remained, but it was directed at the injustices suffered by others, rather than at the injustices he felt he had suffered.

His new feelings about himself affected the way he reacted to others. Instead of expecting people to put him down, he was more relaxed, enabling them to be relaxed with him. This dynamic interaction led to Ron's first close friendships.

Ron's self-concept changed in relationship to both changes in his circumstances and changes within himself. Although his self-concept was never too far from his actual self, it took a long time before he could understand that he had the potential to be much different from what he was. He was never able to fully overcome his early concept of himself as unworthy, but he did diminish the self-destructive aspect sufficiently so that he could function effectively and enjoy life.

The self-concept, like any feeling or attitude, may be partially unconscious or based on unconscious needs. You are likely to have elements in your self-concept that you are not fully able to recognize. Many people find ways to avoid dealing with their feelings about themselves.

One look at Patricia Tratner's academic record would leave most people confused. It consisted of approximately one-third As and Bs, one-third Ds and Fs, and one-third Incompletes. The explanation was, on the surface, simple: whenever Pat found herself in a difficult course, she would cut out and not show up for the final. The underlying reason was more difficult to comprehend. In talking with Pat, you would quickly get the impression that she was extremely confident of her academic abilities and that only boredom caused her to drop a course. But if you had some way of knowing her unconscious feelings, you would realize that her unconscious self-concept was of being academically inferior. To repress this awareness, she avoided difficult courses; if she wasn't confident of at least a B, she'd leave the class and justify her low grade on the basis of not showing up for the final. Therefore her conscious self-concept of being bright was never seriously questioned.

Many forms of behavior that appear inconsistent or irrational on the surface begin to make sense if you can learn about the self-concept of the person involved. For example, a 14-year-old girl became furious during Christmas dinner because she was seated, as she had been for years, with the children. Her self-concept was that she had attained sufficient age and status to eat with the adults, and being seated with the younger children disturbed that self-concept.

The self-concept has been extensively investigated. The results of one study (summarized in Figure 4–4) suggest that an individual's self-concept, in combination with his attitudes toward others, can tell a lot about his behavior. Research has shown that people whose self-concepts are unpleasant are more likely than average to be poorly adjusted (Calvin & Holtzman, 1953).

Acceptance of self	Acceptance of others	Personality traits exhibited
Good	Good	Healthy self-confidence, accepts responsibility, has faith in mankind, optimistic.
Good	Poor	Critical of others, overestimates own acceptability.
Poor	Good	Timid, modest, popular, feels open to attack.
Poor	Poor	Dissatisfied, dependent, frightened, great need for security, impulsive.

FIGURE 4–4. Relationship of acceptance of self and acceptance of others to certain personality variables (adapted from Fey, 1957).

SELF-FULFILLING PROPHECIES

Sometimes an individual makes an assumption about the future and then, without realizing it, behaves in such a fashion that his assumption is confirmed. Afterward he says, in essence, "Aha, I told you so." This phenomenon is known as the **self-fulfilling prophecy.**

A child enters school believing that he will have trouble. He views his teachers with suspicion, he is fearful and agitated in class, he pays little attention and lets his imagination wander, and he pokes the girl in front of him. The teacher becomes increasingly irritated and impatient and, eventually, critical. And the child's initial anticipations are confirmed.

After the remarriage of her mother, a young girl wanted desperately to love her father, even though he showed little interest in her. However, she reacted to him with such warmth and trust, interpreting any little favor he did as very meaningful, that he eventually became fond of her. As he enjoyed her more, she felt increasingly secure and was even more capable of offering her love to him.

Many leaders in ethnic communities, particularly those with a history of suffering from discrimination, have encouraged ethnic pride as a legitimate stepping-stone to gaining the respect of others. A healthy pride leads to self-esteem; a person who esteems himself is more likely to behave as though he expects others to esteem him, not because he demands esteem but because his behavior is worthy of esteem. Conversely, a person who lacks pride and self-esteem treats others in such a way that they may resent him and respond abusively, thereby diminishing his feelings of pride even more.

THE BODY-IMAGE

Your self-concept is also influenced by your **body-image** — that is, the picture you have of your physical being. The body-image extends beyond outward physical appearance and includes physical health and handicaps that cannot be seen. Being color-blind, having a rheumatic heart, and losing a front tooth all affect the body-image.

During the early years of life the body-image must change quite rapidly to remain accurate in light of the actual physical changes that occur. Like all facets of the self-concept, your body-image is largely a reflection of how you feel others perceive you. If you are considered physically attractive, you are likely to have a corresponding body-image.

A person with a healthy self-concept will not be overly disturbed by not being considered physically attractive, since he accepts himself as a worthy individual. However, the individual whose self-concept causes him to feel insecure may place too much emphasis on the need to be thought physically attractive. You can make some interesting guesses about people's self-concepts and body-images by observing what they do to their physical appearance; notice clothing, hairstyle, cleanliness, use of makeup and jewelry, style of eyeglasses, posture, walk, smile, and so forth.

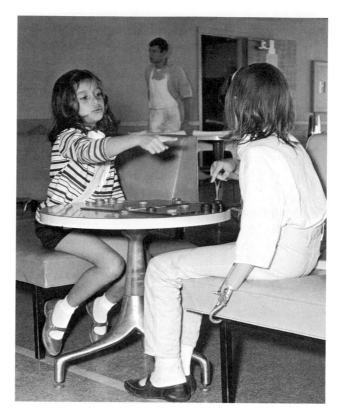

FIGURE 4–5.   What hypotheses would you make concerning the body-images of these two girls? Courtesy Crippled Children's Society of Los Angeles.

Charlotte was an extremely pretty 17-year-old high school senior. Although she was very popular with both boys and girls, her parents noticed that she seemed to avoid making close friendships. They paid little attention, however, until her grades began to drop and she became increasingly moody and depressed. One morning, during a particularly bitter bickering session, her 14-year-old sister shouted "Oh, go to hell, you flat-chested pig!" A moment later a milk glass sailed past her head and smashed against the refrigerator.

That evening Charlotte's mother finally got the story. Charlotte was not merely flat-chested; she was among that 1 percent of adolescents who had still not reached puberty by 17. Unable to talk about it with her parents—they were warm and loving but uncomfortable about discussing the human body—Charlotte recognized that her body was unusual and interpreted it as meaning that she was "queer" and would never be a woman. Unfortunately, her parents, who had had no idea that she was concerned, understood it less than she did. A trip to the family doctor was required for all three to learn some basic facts of human development.

LEVELS OF ASPIRATION: HOW HIGH DO YOU REACH?

Your **level of aspiration,** which refers to the goals you anticipate achieving, is a direct outgrowth of your self-concept. The person who intends to be a straight-B student has a higher level of academic aspiration (not necessarily financial or social or vocational) than someone working to attain a straight-C average.

Life satisfaction and happiness are closely related to the gap between actual accomplishments and level of aspiration. The farther an individual falls below his level of aspiration, the less happy he is — *even if his achievement is objectively high* (Block & Thomas, 1955; Rosenberg, 1962). When a person's achievement level begins to approach his aspiration level, he will usually raise his sights; if he finds himself unable to succeed, his goals may become less ambitious.

Aspiration is affected by one's **reference group,** or the people with whom he compares himself. If you attended a high school in which 80% of the graduates went on to college, your reference group would most likely have been a college-preparatory group, and you would probably aspire to higher educational achievement than would your friend who went to a high school that sent very few graduates to college.

Other factors that influence the person's level of aspiration are his maximum potential ability, the degree to which parents and others in the environment encourage success, personality factors such as feelings of security or anxiety (which may work for or against success), early-childhood experiences, and his unique history of attempts to realize a particular aspiration. Some people set a level of aspiration beyond their abilities to achieve and then refuse to change it. Others set their level so low that it is easily achieved, but they never fully develop their talents, since they need to use only a small portion of their abilities to reach their goals.

THE IDEAL SELF

The self-concept is an individual's image of himself as he thinks he is. The **ideal self** is his image of himself as he would like to be. The ideal self of a young child is usually a parent; older children tend to idealize glamorous or historical figures; adolescents and adults select a combination of several people or an imaginary or hypothetical person for their ideal self (Havighurst, Robinson, & Dorr, 1946). Thus, as we mature, the ideal self becomes more complex.

People try to live up to their ideal self, but they usually fall short. When a person's self-concept falls far short of his ideal self, he is likely to show maladjustment (Rosenberg, 1962) and confusion (Block & Thomas, 1955). He is dissatisfied with himself and feels that he has failed to become the sort of person he wants to become.

At the same time, people who claim that their self-concept and ideal self are almost identical may also be unstable. Research has shown that these individuals have an unusually great need to be liked and accepted by others and that they dislike expressing their emotions (Block & Thomas, 1955). All in all, the self-concept of the healthy personality is close—but not too close—to the ideal self.

Ideal self and level of aspiration are, of course, related. Both represent goals that people establish for themselves. However, the level of aspiration is something that the individual is actively moving toward, whereas the ideal self is that ultimate goal, the almost perfect self, that occurs more in dreams than in reality.

ROLES

Any given society has many positions, such as male and female, leader and follower, minister and doctor, or teacher and student. In each society a certain pattern of behavior is expected of the individual who occupies a given position. This anticipated behavior pattern forms the **role** associated with that position. Thus the role of the minister is to be concerned with spiritual matters; many people become upset when a minister seems to be trying hard to make a lot of money for himself, since that behavior appears inconsistent with his role. The role of the adolescent male in the United States is much different from that of the adolescent male in many other countries. In what ways do you suppose these roles differ?

The roles that command the most attention include age roles, sex roles, vocational roles, ethnic roles, leadership roles, family roles, and educational roles. Consider yourself in terms of what is expected of you because of these factors. Also consider what happens when two or three of these elements are combined. Role expectations of a middle-aged unmarried male teacher are quite different from those of a middle-aged unmarried male basketball coach. And if you learned that the teacher was once a union organizer, the role expectations shift considerably.

Sometimes behavior is inconsistent with a role, as in the case of a classroom teacher who breaks down and cries when the children get beyond control or a policeman or clergyman who operates a crime ring. We recognize that not all teachers can retain classroom control and that not all law officers and clergymen are honest; but these behaviors are so out of keeping with what we expect from their roles that they seem disturbing or, sometimes, humorous.

You may have had the experience of observing someone (perhaps yourself) move from one position into another through testing out role behavior in advance.

The high school senior, ready to enter college, begins to behave as he thinks the college student behaves; a pair of newlyweds may attempt to act as they believe more experienced married people act. Such anticipatory role behavior permits experimenting with new ways of behaving, so that, when people eventually move into the practiced-for position, they have more understanding of what they are doing.

Role conflict is not uncommon. Since we all find ourselves in numerous positions, the behavior expected for one position may conflict with that expected for another. For example, a man may have a conflict between his role as son and his role as husband; a businesswoman may be torn between the demands placed on her as a woman to be passive and dependent and the demands placed on her as a business person to be aggressive and achieving; a black lawyer may simultaneously wish to move his office to a high-income neighborhood (in his role as a money earner) and to continue to serve the low-income black community (in his role as a black).

SUMMARY OF IMPORTANT IDEAS

1. Personality is the dynamic organization of characteristic attributes leading to behavior and distinguishing one individual from other individuals.

2. The human personality may be viewed in a variety of ways. You may see it as either enduring or arising from a specific situation, as either an integration of segments or a whole entity, as being motivated to come to rest or being motivated to grow and develop, as stemming predominantly from heredity or predominantly from the environment or varying combinations of the two, as being totally determined by heredity and environment or as having freedom and choice.

3. The behavior of humans and of lower animals differs in many highly significant ways.

4. The self-concept is the picture an individual has of himself. The conscious self-concept and the unconscious self-concept are usually similar but not necessarily identical.

5. The body-image is that aspect of the self-concept that pertains to physical health and appearance.

6. Your level of aspiration is the goal you anticipate achieving; your ideal self reflects the image you have of yourself as you would most like to be.

7. A role is the pattern of behavior expected of a person with a given position in society. Roles include such categories as male, female, physician, student, leader, or teenager.

BASIC
PRINCIPLES
OF HUMAN
BEHAVIOR

PART 2

5 Sensing and Perceiving: Windows to the World

Psychologists have always been deeply interested in how man determines what is going on in his environment. This interest was carried over from philosophy and can be traced far back into history. Much of the early research in psychology, dating back about 100 years, involved the relationship between what is actually, objectively, in the environment and how man interprets and analyzes it. Psychologists, in conjunction with physiologists and physicists, have studied this question in many ways, and they are still interested in it, although at a much higher level of sophistication than in the nineteenth century. The awareness that man could develop research methods to evaluate his own behavior came partly through the study of sensation and perception.

Have you ever been without the use of your eyes? Of your ears? If you have, or if you can imagine what it would be like, you will understand why we refer to the senses as our windows to the world. The human organism is highly sensitive to its environment because of these senses. Through the sense organs comes awareness of colors, shapes, sounds, tastes, pressures, odors, temperature change, and other environmental stimuli. Without your sense organs you would not be able to receive any information from your environment.

Everything that enters through these "windows" is transmitted to the brain, where the information is interpreted, largely in light of previous experiences. As the individual matures and has more experiences, he is better able to understand the significance of this information.

Each sense is represented by **receptor** organs that receive the "message" from whatever in the environment is presenting a stimulus. **Visual** receptors are in the eye; **auditory** receptors are inside the ear; taste receptors are on the tongue. After it is received by the receptor, the "message" is transmitted through the nerves to the brain, where it is interpreted and its significance is communicated to the appropriate part of the body; then the organism can take some form of action.

    Sensation is the term applied to what occurs each time a receptor organ is stimulated. **Perception** is the process through which the various sensations are interpreted and organized into meaningful patterns.

SENSATION

    Traditional thought states that man has five senses: sight, hearing, taste, touch, and smell. Psychologists have changed the list somewhat, adding the **kinesthetic sense** (sense of body movement, posture, and weight), the **vestibular sense** (sense of balance), and the **internal** (or interoceptor) **senses** (sense of hunger, thirst, and so forth).

    Thus sensory stimulation takes many forms. You are constantly being barraged with stimuli. However, your receptors are selective; that is, they respond only to certain kinds of stimulation. For example, your ear contains receptors for sound only and is not sensitive to odors or light. The receptors at the surface of the body that react when stimulated by the skin sensations are similarly highly specialized. The receptors for pressure respond only to the sensation of pressure, and the receptors for cold respond only to the sensation of cold. When you rub your eyes, you not only feel pressure, but you also see shapes and colors, because the visual receptors have been stimulated and the corresponding nerves conduct only those impulses that communicate visual stimuli.

    In addition to being selective to stimuli, receptors require a certain intensity of stimulation before they will respond. Some sounds, sights, and smells are too weak to cause the receptor to respond. Thus the sound of an ant walking can be recorded by a highly sensitive instrument, but without magnification it remains below man's sensory **threshold.** Bloodhounds can sniff their way along a trail, hawks are very sensitive to movement (Sanford & Wrightsman, 1970), and dogs can hear specially constructed whistles; but these odors, movements, and sounds are outside the range of human perception. Also, many stimuli, such as X rays, atoms, or extremely high-pitched sounds, are recognized by neither man nor animal. Man responds to only a small portion of all possible environmental stimuli.

    We can illustrate the role of sensation in perception by showing what happens when a driver approaches a red light. When the light waves (stimuli) from the traffic light strike the eye (receptor for vision), impulses representing the colors and shapes of the light are established (response), and these impulses travel through pathways in the nervous system to the visual center of the brain, where the meaning of the stimuli is interpreted. The entire process takes only a fraction of a second. The action response (in this case, depressing the brake) may take a little longer.

Frequently, sensory **adaptation** will occur. This process takes place in two different, although related, ways. The first kind of adaptation refers to becoming accustomed to changes in the environment so that your senses remain effective. For example, when you enter a dark movie theater, you are initially unable to see anything, but your visual receptors quickly adapt to the darkness. The second kind of adaptation refers to the reduction in effectiveness of your senses after you have been exposed to the stimulus for a period of time. When you first step into a hot bath, it will seem hotter than it will after you have been in for a few minutes; odors, after you have been around them for a while, may seem to diminish or disappear altogether, because you have adapted to them.

SPECIFIC SENSE ORGANS: WHAT ARE THE WINDOWS?

Vision has probably received more attention than any other sensory process. Psychologists study the anatomy of the eye and its neural connections with the brain; they investigate how we perceive color (or, in the case of people who are color defective, why color perception differs in some people); and they try to learn more about depth perception, or how the individual knows that one object is closer to him than another.

If there were no color at all, you would make out shapes and forms only because of the relative **brightness** of the objects you were seeing. Since you undoubtedly see color (only an extremely small percentage of people are completely color-blind), you will recognize not only brightness but also **hue** and **saturation.** Hue is the color of what you see, such as red or green or, perhaps, reddish-green. Objects that are black or white have no hue. Saturation refers to how much white is mixed in with the hue. Light green (green mixed with white) and pink (red mixed with white) have less saturation than green and red.

Although complete color blindness is extremely rare, partial color blindness is more common. That is, many people are unable to distinguish between certain colors, usually red and green. These individuals, almost all of them male, range in color deficiency from being totally unable to differentiate red from green (unless there are other clues in the environment) to having only a little trouble in their judgment.

In hearing, the two major dimensions are **pitch** and **loudness.** Pitch refers to whether the sound is high or low, squeaky or deep. Loudness, of course, is volume. If you have a good radio, tape deck, or stereo, you will be familiar with these concepts. There are several kinds of hearing defects. Some people hear all sounds as being less loud than they actually are; others have difficulty in hearing certain pitches, perhaps high-pitched sounds.

A similar analysis could be made of the other senses. For example, taste has been broken down into sweet, sour, salty, and bitter, each having receptors on a different part of the tongue. Touch (the **skin senses**) can be divided into pressure, pain, warm, and cold.

SENSITIVITY ENHANCED/SENSITIVITY DIMINISHED

Humans, if they wish, can develop their sensitivity to sensory stimuli for their own enjoyment and satisfaction. A forest ranger develops his ability to see movement; a wine connoisseur develops his ability to distinguish wine bottled in 1957 from wine bottled in 1958; an opera lover learns to recognize when the tenor is the slightest bit flat. What sensitivities are developed by a safe cracker? A perfume tester? An art historian?

This cultivation of the senses can also aid in self-actualization. The idea that you need not accept all your limitations but can expand your potential for pleasure and satisfaction is basic to self-actualization. Expanding your sensitivity requires some effort, just as playing ball or painting or dancing does. Some of the effort involves practice and experience. What is also required of you is that you pay attention, remain alert, and be receptive to new stimuli and to shades of difference in old stimuli. For example, to learn to distinguish bird calls, you not only have to learn about birds and their calls, but you need to focus your attention on a bird call even though others with you may not be aware of the call. Or, if bird calls are not intriguing, being able to identify automobile makes and models and years at a distance or being able to identify recording artists after two bars might suit you better.

Because we are completely dependent on our senses for contacts with the world, any reduction in sensory accuracy will reduce knowledge of what is happening in the environment. When one sense is not able to function at all, the individual is deprived of one aspect of knowledge about the world. Consider the added barriers to need satisfaction when someone is unable to see or hear. Ironically, even the sensation of pain is necessary. Without pain, you would not know that your tooth was infected or that your toe was sprained, and the ailment could become much more serious, perhaps causing grave illness or death.

Fortunately, people have learned ways to overcome the disadvantages produced by sensory handicaps. Eyeglasses and special Braille books have been developed for those with visual handicaps; hearing aids and sign language enable those with auditory defects to communicate. Nonetheless, personal determination, rather than mechanical devices, often seems to be the major factor in compensating for sensory handicaps. Many handicapped individuals can fulfill their needs for self-actualizing as well as, or better than, people who are not handicapped.

Yet even blind or deaf people retain several "windows to the world." What happens when an individual is *completely* isolated from his environment? Investigations have been conducted with people placed in an apparatus that deprives them of all contact with their environment and all stimulation of their senses. Such isolation means that they could not participate in *any* sort of activity. After a period of time the subjects become upset and temporarily displayed symptoms commonly associated with mental disturbance (Heron, 1957).

Many societies, through some of their customs, acknowledge the importance of stimulation and the difficulties of sensory deprivation. Isolation is one of the most severe punishments that can be dealt out, whether it involves placing a prisoner in solitary confinement or ordering a pupil to stand in the corner of the classroom or out in the hall.

Sensation plays a vital part in your life. When stimuli are absent, serious emotional problems may occur; when stimuli are restricted, the individual may attempt to adjust to his condition or to find ways to compensate. But an adequate amount of sensory stimulation provides pleasure, satisfaction, and help in self-actualizing.

PERCEPTION

Perception is the process of organizing and interpreting sensory stimuli into meaningful patterns. It involves "becoming aware of objects, qualities, or relations by way of the sense organs" (Hilgard & Atkinson, 1967). The stimuli received by your visual receptors (eyes) when you look at the cover of this book do not tell you that you are looking at a book; they merely communicate a pattern of colors and shapes. The brain, as a result of previous learning, interprets this pattern as a book. The auditory receptors receive spoken words as sounds without meanings, and the brain interprets these sounds as words. People who suddenly gain their sight after having been blind all their lives report that the patterns of color and shape are meaningless until they learn to distinguish what they represent.

To some extent, certain types of perception seem to occur inevitably, as a result of **maturation.** Some infants as young as 6 or 7 months of age will crawl to the edge of a bed but will not venture beyond or even put their hand out to see if they can continue—even though they may have had no opportunity to learn through experience that the end of the bed indicates a sudden drop (Gibson & Walk, 1960). By and large, however, perception entails some learning. In early infancy, it is hypothesized, the individual perceives his environment as a mass of shapes, colors, and sounds, along with miscellaneous pressures, temperature sensations, pains, smells, and tastes. Order slowly develops out of this chaos. One set of colors and shapes becomes identified with food or warmth; another set, which appears less frequently, may add an uncomfortable scratchy sensation to that of warmth and wetness (that is, when Daddy kisses him). The infant explores his world by touching, biting, and moving through it, and he is continuously testing to learn what it all means. Gradually he learns to identify people and objects, to locate sounds, to anticipate tastes and pressures, and to recognize relationships among the various stimuli.

The infant learns not only to identify people and objects but to think of them in ways that have little to do with their physical-stimulus value. After an initial meeting with someone, you would probably describe him to a friend in terms of physical appearance. After you get to know the person, however, you would focus on nonphysical aspects. The physical appearance has undergone no significant change, but your perceptions have changed with learning. The very homely girl seems to have average or even above-average good looks when you get to know her and like her; if you love her, she may appear beautiful.

Perception, then, suggests an emotional component. It refers not only to the organizing and interpreting of sensory stimuli but also to social and emotional responses. When a stimulus becomes familiar, you are increasingly likely to perceive it in terms of its meaning to you, rather than in terms of the way it strikes the receptors.

Consider the importance of this meaning of perception for understanding human relationships, including those with persons of a different ethnic or racial group. Reactions to such persons are based on the previous meaning these individuals had for you—often a reflection of the group to which they belong—rather than on the objective characteristics they display. Thus, on first meeting a person of a different group (the group might be distinguished by race, religion, sex, school, vocation, or some other feature), you tend to interpret his behavior in light of your notions regarding his group.

Perceptions are influenced both by the objective characteristics of the stimuli and by the perceiver's characteristics, such as needs, experiences, set, and personal rigidity. Because of these characteristics, all people do not notice the same stimuli; neither do they perceive and interpret the same objective stimuli in identical ways.

STIMULUS CHARACTERISTICS

Stimulus characteristics, such as size, color, shape, movement, contrast, uniqueness, and repetition, obviously play a major role in perception. They stimulate the receptors, and their message is then transmitted to the brain. Not only do they determine the sensory stimuli, but they also influence **attention,** a familiar term used here in a more technical fashion to refer to the process of responding to only a portion of the stimuli in the immediate environment.

People do not attend (that is, give their attention) to every environmental stimulus equally but select certain things for increased attention. Consider some stimulus characteristics as they influence your perception of and attention to advertisements.

FIGURE 5–1.   What captures your attention in this picture? Why? Photograph by Lehman J. Pinckney.

1. Size.   Large pictures and loud noises receive more attention than small pictures and soft sounds. An immense billboard, a gigantic neon sign, and the crash of drums are all attention-getters.

2. Contrast. Two sounds or two colors that contrast with each other may attract more attention than two that are similar. A lone neon sign contrasts dramatically with a black night but is less likely to receive attention if it is just one of many such signs all near one another.

3. Color. Certain colors and color combinations attract more notice than others. Research is conducted with food packaging to determine what kinds of colors can be used to compete effectively for the attention of the supermarket shopper. How do you think television advertisements make use of color?

4. Movement. A moving object is more likely to be noticed than a still object. Because of apparent movement, flashing neon signs will capture your attention more than still signs of similar color and size. When you look at a number of people standing together, your eyes will shift to the one who is moving. Can you apply this principle to perception of sounds?

5. Uniqueness and novelty. The new and unusual gain attention. When African "natural" hairstyles were new, the first few you saw probably captured your attention. When someone with a natural suddenly appeared with a more traditional (or less traditional) style, this also captured your attention — at least initially. Uniqueness and novelty often, but not always, work together. A new person in a small class is noticed, even if he is not unusual in appearance. Similarly, an extremely obese person may always get attention, even after others become accustomed to him. Advertisers try to blend the old and familiar with the new and unique.

6. Repetition. Radio jingles, television commercials, newspaper advertisements — each appear over and over again, sometimes until you think you will go crazy. Nonetheless, repetition attracts attention, even if the stimulus has little attention-getting value when it is presented only once. Keep in mind, however, that getting attention in an advertisement may not pay off if the attention produces a negative reaction.

PERCEIVER CHARACTERISTICS

Perception and attention are also related to conditions within the individual, such as physiological and other needs, personal experiences, set, and personal rigidity.

1. Needs. A hungry person may notice, for the first time, a restaurant he has walked past on a hundred previous occasions when he was not hungry. Research has shown that hungry subjects are more likely than nonhungry subjects to "see" food in a highly blurred picture (Levine, Chein, & Murphy, 1942). The physiological need "hunger" has an influence on both *which* stimuli are attended to and *how* these sensory stimuli are perceived and integrated into meaningful patterns.

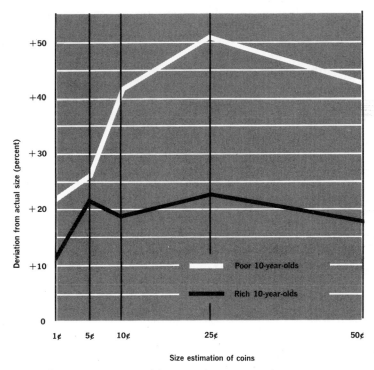

FIGURE 5–2. Motivational factors and perception. The top curve represents the size estimation of coins made by poor 10-year-old boys asked to adjust a circle of light so that it was the same size as a designated coin. The bottom curve shows the estimates of rich boys. Although all the boys tended to overestimate the size of the coins, the poor boys overestimated more than the rich boys (Bruner & Goodman, 1947).

Love needs may function in a similar fashion. You vaguely notice a group of six people talking together, and suddenly you realize that one of them is a person for whom you have strong affection. A few moments later you are able to give a complete description of the clothes, posture, and mood of the loved person, but you are not even certain who the other five were, because you did not attend to them.

Psychological needs affect not only attention but also perception itself. One investigation showed that the need for self-respect and for the respect of others affected the perceptions of some subjects.

A group of students were placed in a half-circle facing a pair of posters. One of the posters contained three lines of different heights, while the other contained one line identical to one of the three lines on the first poster. Each student called out, in turn, the line on poster A that was the same as the one on poster B. Then another pair of posters was presented, and the procedure was repeated. On the third pair of posters, all the students but one called out the *wrong* line (since all but one had been trained by the experimenter to do so). The student who was not "in" on the study sometimes called off the correct line and sometimes called off the same line as all the others, even though it was obviously incorrect to the objective observer. Then the procedure was repeated with other naïve subjects.

When later asked why they responded incorrectly, the subjects gave several reasons: (1) "I figured the group was wrong, but I thought I'd better go along"; (2) "I saw them differently than the others, but I felt something was wrong with me"; (3) "I saw them the same way the group called them" [Asch, 1951].

Thus, in the first instance, group pressure won out; in the second, the personal insecurity and uncertainty of the student caused him to answer against his better judgment; in the third, the student stated that he actually perceived the lines as being of a length they were not! If the perception of the length of a line can be so much affected by the need to go along with the group, many other perceptions must be similarly affected. If one boxer is strongly favored by the crowd, will the referee and judges be affected in their decisions? "I know it happened because I saw it with my own two eyes." Is that always sufficient proof?

2. Experiences.   Previous experience also affects attention and perception.

A 4-year-old American child, living in Paris while his father was assigned there by his company, was playing in a sandbox at a large park. A French child of the same age approached and, holding his shovel above his head, called out in French "Do you want to play with me?" The American boy was unable to understand the words, but he responded in light of his previous experience with children who held shovels over their heads: he slugged the French boy in the stomach.

People necessarily interpret the environment in terms of their own background. If your experiences are such that a raised shovel means "fight," you respond accordingly.

When you observe two Japanese men bowing and smiling to each other, you perceive them as being friendly; however, their culture demands that they show such behavior, even when they do not like each other. An American observer may have no idea which of the two bowing men is the manager and which is his assistant; but a Japanese observer could easily tell by the depth and frequency of the bowing, because *his* experiences have taught him what cues to attend to for such information.

3. Set. Because of previous experiences and learning, we often anticipate that certain things will occur before they actually happen. That is, we have a **set,**

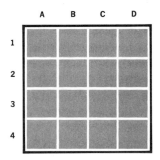

1. Buzzing insects
2. Organs of vision
3. What older brothers do to younger sisters
4. Without difficulty; with _____
A. Lions do it
B. Mosquitoes do it
C. Dogs do it
D. Snakes do it

FIGURE 5–3. Can you overcome a set and complete this crossword puzzle? The answer is at the end of the chapter.

or expectation, that they will occur. The basketball referee knows that the visiting team's center has fouled out in three successive games, and he develops a set that this man is likely to foul. With this set he is more likely to interpret the center's actions as a foul than to interpret the same actions by another player as a foul.

Even a simple suggestion can produce a set that will lead to inaccurate perceptions.

> Professor Blanchard, a friend of mine, told me of this demonstration. First he set a bottle of yellowish liquid on the table in front of him, and then he turned to his large class and said: "I want to test your power of smell today. This bottle contains a very bad-smelling chemical. When I take the stopper out, the odor will slowly drift back, and it should be strong enough to reach even the back rows. Please raise your hand when you first smell the chemical." Professor Blanchard then removed the stopper. First a few hands in the front of the room went up; within a few minutes most of the students had raised their hands.

The chemical solution in the bottle was colored water—without any odor at all. Yet well over half the students believed they smelled something, or at least raised their hands to indicate that they did.

4. Personal rigidity. Some people display the personality characteristic of being rigid or inflexible. This quality appears to affect perception. In one well-known study subjects were shown a series of simple drawings of a dog; in each successive drawing the dog looked a little more like a cat, until the dog was obviously no longer a dog but a cat. Those indicating a high degree of racial prejudice were more likely than the average subject to continue to insist that the animal was still a dog, whereas the more flexible subjects recognized the change more rapidly (Frenkel-Brunswik, 1949). This is an excellent example of the close relationship that exists between perceptual processes and personality.

Although everyone is susceptible to the sorts of perceptual distortions just described, frequent or extreme distortions are probably not often made by individuals who are successful in self-actualizing. The self-actualizing person can see the world more nearly as it really is, rather than as he wants it to be. Conversely, misinterpretation of sensory stimuli produces errors in judgment along with errors in perception and thus reduces a person's chances to make maximum use of his abilities.

PERCEIVING DEPTH

When you sit in a classroom, you know that the head of the person in front of you is closer to you than the instructor is. Why? What are the cues that enable us to understand relative distance or depth? Some of the cues require the use of both eyes. Since the image of the world differs slightly as seen by each eye, the combined images provide more than a flat surface. To test this yourself, place your finger about 10 inches from your eyes and close one eye and then the other. (Have you ever used a stereopticon viewer?) Also, as you move your gaze from something close to something far away, your eye muscles change, and this muscular action may provide cues for depth perception.

However, even a person lacking vision in one eye can perceive depth. He does so by learning the meaning of shadows, of size, of how distinct the outline is, of changes in color that occur with distance, of one object getting in front of another, and so forth.

FIGURE 5–4.   What clues inform you that the pillar on the right is closer to the camera than the last one down the line? Photograph by John G. Warford. (Return to Figure 5–1. What are the clues for depth in that illustration?)

PERCEPTUAL CONSTANCY

To make better sense of the world, we often interpret sensations quite differently from what the actual objective stimuli suggest. This misinterpretation occurs particularly with respect to perceptual constancy. Place a coin flat in your hand and put your hand in front of you, a little below eye level: does the coin look round? Probably it does, even though the visual sensation you are receiving is not that of roundness. If you were to draw that coin to look exactly as it now appears, the drawn coin would be far from round. When you look at an automobile a couple of hundred feet away, it looks as big as the one only 20 feet away, although once again the objective visual sensations you are receiving must be reinterpreted to communicate the size quality. The process of perceptual constancy causes us to perceive objects as appearing to be what we think of as normal, regardless of objective sensory stimuli. The two examples just given illustrate shape constancy and size constancy, respectively. Perceptual constancy also occurs for color and brightness.

DISTORTED PERCEPTION

Perceptions can be distorted because of qualities of the stimulus or because of qualities of the perceiver. The best-known examples of the former are **illusions.** An illusion is a mistaken perception. You think you see or hear or feel something, but the circumstances have fooled you. When you look at a stick half immersed in water, the stick appears broken, even though you know it is straight. The road

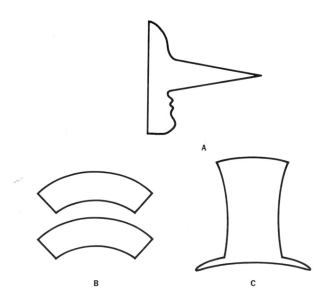

FIGURE 5–5.   Distances are not necessarily what they seem. In A, the nose is as long as the figure is high; in B, the two arcs are identical; in C, the brim of the hat is as long as the hat is high.

ahead of you reflects the sun in such a way as to give the illusion of a puddle of water.

One form of illusion is the optical illusion, several examples of which are shown in Figure 5–5. Another form of illusion is the illusion of movement. A moving red neon arrow, on closer inspection, turns out to be several different red arrows blinking on and off at a precise speed and sequence. A motion-picture film is nothing more than a rapidly changing sequence of stills that gives the impression of motion. Characters in films from the 1920s appeared to walk with jerky movements because fewer individual stills were used and the film moved less rapidly through the camera.

Qualities of the perceiver may also distort perception. From time to time someone reports hearing voices or seeing visual stimuli when no stimulus is present. These perceptions are **hallucinations,** or perceptions that occur without stimuli. Although hallucinations are most commonly associated with severely mentally ill or alcoholic individuals, they can occur in normal persons under extreme circumstances. Sometimes a dream or even a daydream will seem so real that it feels like a hallucination. (See Chapter 7 for a discussion of dreams.)

Hallucinations and illusions are often confused with each other and with **delusions.** The differences are vitally important. An illusion causes a person to confuse or distort existing stimuli, usually because of the qualities of the sensation. A hallucination is a perception *without* external stimuli; a delusion is a false belief.

With so much emphasis on the factors that alter and distort perception, there is danger of underestimating the accuracy with which we perceive. In spite of inevitable subjectivity and lack of 100% accuracy, distorted or inaccurate perceptions only occasionally have a meaningful influence on the lives of normal people.

SUMMARY OF IMPORTANT IDEAS

1. The human organism becomes aware of the world through the senses. These senses include vision, hearing, smell, taste, the skin senses, and others, such as the sense of body movement and the sense of balance.

2. Sensation is the term applied to what occurs each time a receptor organ is stimulated.

3. Perception is the process of interpreting the sensory stimuli received from the environment by the receptors and communicated to the brain through impulses in the nervous system.

4. Some sensations are too weak to activate the receptors.

5. Although partial reduction of sensation, as through blindness, can be compensated for, people who are completely deprived of sensory stimulation may become emotionally upset.

6. The infant explores his world through his senses. Gradually he learns to identify people and objects by their stimulus patterns.

7. The term *attention,* when used technically, refers to the process of responding to only a portion of the stimuli in the immediate environment.

8. Attention and perception are influenced by stimulus characteristics, such as size, contrast, and movement. They are also affected by perceiver characteristics, such as needs, experiences, set, and personal rigidity.

9. Perceptual constancy refers to a process by which we interpret sensations to coincide with what is normal, rather than perceiving them as objective sensations.

10. Distorted perceptions include illusions and hallucinations.

	A	B	C	D
1	B	B	B	B
2	I	I	I	I
3	T	T	T	T
4	E	E	E	E

Here is the answer to the crossword puzzle in Figure 5–3. Did you figure it out?

6 How People Learn

Once the psychologist becomes interested in how humans are stimulated by objects in the environment, he wishes to know about the processes of learning and forgetting. Learning affects the interpretation of stimuli; thus perceptual processes and learning processes are closely related. Interest in learning principles descended from philosophers of centuries ago and led to the development of techniques for the study of behavior. Sensation, perception, learning, thinking, memory, motivation, and emotions are often considered to be the basic processes of human behavior.

Throughout history man has been curious about the processes of **learning.** How do people learn language, values, motor skills, social behavior? Very little behavior is totally uninfluenced by learning, and much behavior would be impossible without a great deal of learning. As a result, the study of learning principles has become basic to the study of the psychology of human behavior.

Learning takes place whenever a relatively permanent change in behavior results from experience or practice. Like motivation, learning cannot be measured directly but must be assumed to occur when a change in performance is observed. When you see a 1-year-old walk, you know that he has learned this behavior, since he was not able to walk three months earlier. However, you are not observing the actual learning process; rather, you are observing the learner's performance, which is overt behavior. Similarly, your instructor in this course will probably grade you on your examination scores and other evaluations of performance, since he assumes that these performances represent learning.

The measurement of learning is further complicated by the fact that performance, although strongly influenced by learning, is also affected by such factors as fatigue, motivation, and health. Thus the psychologist's ability to measure learning is far from perfect. Only when he can introduce accurate measuring devices into the brain will the psychologist be likely to overcome these sources of inaccuracy.

The importance of learning cannot be overestimated, since virtually all behavior involves some learning. You learn to talk, eat, be interested in politics, feel insulted, want money, thread a needle, love your parents, plan a budget, drive an automobile, respect or dislike yourself, and satisfy your physiological, safety, love, esteem, and self-actualizing needs. Without the ability to learn, people would be little more than vegetables and would need constant care to continue to exist.

Organisms, of course, are not merely a collection of assorted processes such as sensing, perceiving, learning, and thinking. A person must be looked on as a unified whole rather than as a series of parts. Thus, although perception and learning are discussed in different chapters for the sake of convenience, try to keep in mind the continual interplay between these and all other behavior processes. Your perceptions are based on what you have learned through previous experiences; your learning is strongly influenced by what you perceive.

In developing principles of learning, psychologists must account for both simple learning, such as an infant's learning that he can stop crying for his bottle when he sees his mother enter the room, and complex learning, such as a student's learning how to design the plans for a skyscraper. The present discussion will focus on two forms of simple learning: classical conditioning and operant learning. The latter part of the chapter will deal with more complex forms of learning, and Chapter 7 will discuss thought, including problem solving, concept formation, and language.

CLASSICAL CONDITIONING

The Russian physiologist Ivan Pavlov conducted the first systematic studies of **classical conditioning** more than 60 years ago. After observing dogs salivate when their food was brought to them, Pavlov demonstrated that they could learn to salivate to a previously neutral **stimulus,** such as a bell, sounded a moment before the arrival of the food (Pavlov, 1927). Originally the stimulus *food* produced the **response** *salivation*. After many trials during which the buzzer was sounded prior to the presentation of food, the buzzer became the stimulus for salivation. The salivation response occurred involuntarily—the dog could not control it. This process, in essence, is classical conditioning.

You can try out a little demonstration yourself. The next time you are with a group of friends, yawn. A great big soulful yawn! Make it realistic! Then watch the way the others begin to yawn—or try not to yawn. When you were a very young child, the stimulus of another person yawning would not have led to your responding with a yawn, but you have since been conditioned to yawn when you observe others do so. (By the way, do you feel like yawning now? If not, try reading this paragraph once again, slowly, and think about yawning.)

CLASSICAL CONDITIONING APPLIED TO SOCIAL BEHAVIOR

Classical conditioning helps explain more than such simple behaviors as yawning and salivating. Let's begin with a reasonably well-accepted statement: year-old infants enjoy being cuddled by their parents. That is, the stimulus of warm physical contact with the parent will produce in the infant a response indicating pleasure, such as gurgling and smiling. Assume that this year-old infant has had many such experiences with both his mother and his father. He has, by now, come to associate the presence of his parents with the warm, pleasant, physical contact that produces the gurgling and smiling. What happens? He now responds to the sight, perhaps even to the sound of the footsteps, of his parents with gurgling and smiling. His response occurs virtually inevitably to the approach of his mother or father. Gurgling and smiling did not originally occur in response to his parents; but through the constant association of *warmth and affection* with *parent nearby,* the infant has become conditioned to respond in this fashion.

The original stimulus *warm human contact* produced the response *gurgling and smiling;* after many experiences with the parent, the stimulus *sight of parent* produced the response. Thus it can be said that the infant is conditioned to gurgle and smile at the sight of the mother or father; that is, he has learned to give this response virtually automatically.

After a while the infant responds with gurgling and smiling to all adults. This process is called **stimulus generalization,** since the infant's response to his parents has been generalized to other adults. Then his older brother, who is jealous of him, enters the picture. Whenever the brother comes by, the baby is likely to get a pinch or a squeeze. The baby then learns **discrimination** between adults and older brother. If his brother's friends are pleasant to him, the baby may learn further discrimination, this time between his older brother and other boys of the same age.

Each time the stimulus-response sequence occurs, **reinforcement** of learning takes place. That is, each time the sight of the parent is followed by cuddling, reinforcement occurs. The more reinforcements, the more thoroughly the infant learns to respond to his parents with pleasure and the longer it would take for his responses to stop if his parents ceased their cuddling.

The response, however, may not follow the stimulus forever. A process called **extinction** can occur. For example, when Pavlov stopped feeding the dogs following the sound of the buzzer, they eventually ceased to salivate when they heard the stimulus. If the infant's parents stop giving him love and warmth, he will stop his smiling and gurgling.

Or will he? Human behavior is complex. Although classical conditioning is a very useful model, like other models for understanding human behavior, it has shortcomings. There was a time when many psychologists felt that classical conditioning could explain virtually all learning and that all human behavior could be controlled as easily as the salivation of dogs or the yawns of your friends. This belief no longer holds, and classical conditioning is usually seen as only one form of human learning.

OPERANT LEARNING

In classical conditioning, the original stimulus-response sequence is part of the person's potential behavior. That is, the infant gurgled and smiled in response to being cuddled without having to learn to smile. Much learning, however, is of a different nature; it involves rewarding the learner for the proper response and either not rewarding him or punishing him for improper responses. Eventually the individual learns the correct response.

Four conditions are necessary for **operant learning** to take place: (1) the learner must have the motivation to do something, to behave in some fashion; (2) he must have the potential for producing the correct response; (3) when he gives the correct response, he must receive some kind of **reward** or reinforcement; and (4) if he does not give the correct response, he must be motivated to continue to respond until he does.

Each time the correct response occurs and is followed by reinforcement, learning has taken place. On each successive occasion, the correct response should occur sooner and the number of incorrect responses should diminish until, finally, the correct response will regularly follow the stimulus.

Sometimes the person does not produce the correct response but does respond in the proper general direction. He is reinforced for that approximate response until he gives it regularly; then the reinforcement is stopped until he again behaves a little more in the correct general direction. Consider a young child learning to catch a ball; you do not reinforce his behavior only when he makes a perfect catch but also every time he comes a little closer to making a perfect catch. You continue this process until he has learned how to catch a ball correctly.

A young girl wants to thread a needle. She knows generally what to do but cannot do it properly. Each time she fails to get the thread through the hole, her response is not reinforced. Finally she responds correctly and is successful. The next time she tries to thread a needle, she succeeds more quickly.

A clumsy student wants to learn to make lay-ups on the basketball court. He makes attempt after attempt, most of them failures. However, his occasional success is reinforcing, and he begins to repeat those responses that lead to baskets. Slowly he learns, through success and failure, to sink a high percentage of his shots.

A man receives a brand-new, expensive camera. He reads the directions and then goes out to take pictures. He tries to adjust the camera to account for light, glare, distance, and so forth, but his early photographs are either too blurry or too dark. Eventually he learns to judge the conditions properly, by remembering what he did when his pictures turned out well. The correct responses – that is, camera adjustments – are reinforced; they tend to be repeated, and, as a result, his pictures improve greatly.

FIGURE 6–1. These geese have learned that swimming toward this child will be rewarded with food. Have you noticed how often, at parks and zoos, birds and animals will flock to people who carry food – and sometimes to those who do not? Photograph by Lehman J. Pinckney.

In classical conditioning, the initial response is made involuntarily—the dogs salivated and you yawned, not because of decisions but because the conditions led almost inevitably to the responses. Eventually the response—again almost inevitably—occurs following a previously neutral stimulus, such as the buzzer. In operant learning, the individual does something to the environment—he makes many voluntary responses until one is reinforced. As B. F. Skinner, a major pioneer in this field, has said, "the behavior operates upon the environment to generate consequences" (1963). When the consequences are rewarding, the behavior is reinforced and is more likely to occur again when the circumstances are repeated.

Each attempt by the individual to respond correctly to a stimulus is termed a **trial;** each rewarding of a correct response is termed a reinforcement. The more rapidly and the more frequently a person's trials are reinforced, the faster he will learn. We must be very cautious in using the concept of reward, however, and some people avoid using it altogether in these circumstances. This is because a reward is interpreted through the eyes of the recipient: you may feel that a child is rewarded when his teacher pats him on the head, but the child may hate it. Sometimes a punishment—or what seems like a punishment—can serve as a reinforcement. Although reward and reinforcement are, in practice, very often identical, they differ in meaning and they are not *necessarily* identical.

Extinction also occurs with operant learning. When a previously successful response is no longer rewarded or reinforced, the person will eventually stop making that response under the given circumstances. When the photographer decides that his pictures are not good enough or the basketball player finds that his shooting success has reached a standstill, he alters his previous behavior and emits new responses.

Extinction is not the only way to get people to stop doing what they have been doing. Punishment may also be used. The child who sucks his thumb is punished for his action in a variety of ways until he eventually stops. Or at least he seems to stop—when anyone is watching him. Using punishment to stop behavior is not always successful, as anyone who has tried to stop a thumbsucker has found out. Sometimes the attention that punishment provides is more rewarding than the penalty of the punishment itself; on other occasions, punishment only gives the person more strength to fight back. Also, punishment may mark that behavior as something special, so that the person recalls—and perhaps repeats—his response on subsequent occasions.

Operant-learning methods have been widely applied in working with schoolchildren. One 4-year-old child cried after the slightest frustration. His teachers tried to help him but achieved little success. Finally, when they began to ignore him, so that his crying was not rewarded, his tears came no more often than any other child's (Harris, Wolf, & Baer, 1964).

Another example was that of a nursery-school child who always played by himself. To alter this behavior, his teacher gave him extra attention every time he approached another child, regardless of the reason, but ignored him as long as he played by himself. Initially the teacher provided the reinforcement whenever the child merely stood next to another child; later she rewarded him only when he played next to another child; finally she rewarded him only when he played with another child (Harris et al., 1964). This careful use of operant-learning methods in encouraging social relationships has been repeated in a variety of settings.

FIGURE 6–2.   Has this animal learned through imitation or through trial-and-error based on reinforcement? Or, perhaps, some of both? Courtesy Columbia Broadcasting System.

LEARNING THROUGH IMITATION

Children learn a great deal by observing others and imitating them. Imitation seems to occur without any obvious reinforcement—some people think that it is innate, although we do not know for certain. Often, however, being able to imitate someone successfully would be rewarding in and of itself; doing something "just like Mommy" could be satisfying and thus reinforcing. Whatever the basis, much of our behavior is based on what we see others do. Sex-role behavior, for example, is the result not only of direct reinforcement, but of observing how others of our own sex behave and trying to appear like them.

The young teenager observes his father smoking a cigarette, notices how he lights it and how he inhales, and then tries to imitate his father. He may not succeed the first time—he may need to go through some trial-and-error learning and having correct responses reinforced—but he will certainly save many steps in the learning process as the result of imitating the model. Imitation can also occur by observing what happens to someone else—that is, whether his behavior is successful or not—and then following the behavior of people who appear to succeed or be approved. There is some evidence that the violent hero on television provides a model for impressionable children (and perhaps not only children) (Bandura, 1969).

REMEMBERING AND FORGETTING

Learning is very closely related to remembering. If no learning occurs, there is nothing to remember. Conversely, if no remembering occurs, learning is without value. Learning refers primarily to acquiring the capacity for behavior change, whereas remembering implies the continued capacity to act on the learning. When you say that you have learned to ride a bicycle, you mean that you have acquired the skill to ride; if, ten years later, you claim that you still remember how to ride a bicycle, you mean that you are still capable of acting on the earlier learning. Stating this another way, the ability to ride a bicycle is stored in your memory and is available on recall.

KINDS OF REMEMBERING

The three major ways in which remembering is exhibited are *recall, recognition,* and *relearning.* Recall refers to the act of bringing to your thoughts an image or representation of what has occurred earlier. Recall is tested by asking the person a question or asking him to perform a task. What does your best friend look like? What foot do you use to press the brake? Show exactly how you set up accounting books for your company. When did you last have an ice-cream cone? These responses all require recall. Your instructor measures your recall of the course content when he gives you an essay exam.

Recognition refers to your awareness that something is familiar — that you have experienced or perceived it previously. You recognize people from their photographs, or you recognize the new Chevrolet from its familiar trademark. A multiple-choice exam is a measure of recognition, since the alternatives are presented to you and you select the one that you recognize as correct. You do not need to recall — that is, bring the answer to mind — because the answer is in front of you.

Relearning is a less frequent indication of remembering. Relearning merely means that a second, usually much later, attempt at learning something will take less time and effort than the initial attempt, because something of the original learning stayed with you. If you were brought up until the age of 4 in a home in which Spanish was spoken, at 18 you might no longer be able to speak the language. However, it would take you less time to learn Spanish than it would take someone who had never had the early contacts. The increased rapidity of learning in a relearning situation implies the existence of some memory.

THE NATURE OF FORGETTING

You may have heard that everything you have ever perceived or experienced in any fashion is stored somewhere in your brain and that, given the proper circumstances, could be remembered. If such were the case, nothing would ever be truly forgotten: we could only say that some perceptions and events are extremely difficult to recall.

Psychologists have not been able to prove or disprove this hypothesis, but much contemporary evidence points to a three-stage theory of memory. The first stage is *sensory store*, in which sensations are retained for a fleeting second and are then usually lost. Some of this information goes into the *short-term store*, but the rest decays or fades away. Only a limited amount can be held in short-term store. Have someone recite ten unrelated words to you, slowly and one after the other without expression — then see how many you can repeat right back to him. A portion of the information in the short-term store then goes into the *long-term store*, where it is relatively permanent, although you cannot always retrieve it from this storage because of interference or motivated forgetting (see below). The basis for this storage is a biochemical change that occurs in the brain. In some recent experiments with lower animals, psychologists have been able to alter long-term and short-term memory independently of each other by altering the body chemistry. In related research, investigators have found that rats that had been brought up in a stimulating and varied environment and had been exposed to many experiences developed brains that could be distinguished by chemical analysis from those of rats that had been reared in isolation (Krech, 1968).

Thus the nature of remembering and its opposite, **forgetting,** may be twofold. For some experiences the memory time span is very brief or even nonexistent, the result of inadequate impact of the event. For other experiences the long-term variety of memory makes forgetting more complicated. It may occur because of *disuse, interference,* or *motivated forgetting.*

To state that forgetting takes place because of disuse implies that the chemical base in the brain deteriorates. Since our own experience suggests that we have greater difficulty recalling events of the distant past or events that we are not reminded of, the disuse approach has appeal. However, you may also have had the opposite experience—you suddenly recalled the name and face of a person you had not thought of in 15 years. People often report dreaming of events that had not crossed their thoughts for 30 or 40 years. Other evidence has been supplied through recall under hypnosis.

Interference implies that something has gotten in the way of remembering. The interference may be retroactive; that is, later learning interferes with the ability to recall earlier events. In a sense, the recent events squeeze the earlier events from your memory. Or, interference may be proactive, in which case early learning makes it more difficult to recall what you have learned afterward. If both proactive and retroactive interferences operate, you should be able to memorize the first part and the last part of a poem or a list of terms more easily than the middle part. Indeed, that result is just what both personal experiences and numerous research studies have shown.

In Chapter 3 the term *repression* was introduced to describe what happens when a person is unable to remember something because he is motivated to be unable to remember. (The concepts of repression and unconscious motivation will be used several times in this book.) Obviously repression provides an additional explanation of why we are unable to remember.

It is not necessary to debate the three factors that adversely affect recall of long-term memories, since all three may operate simultaneously. As with many problems, the evidence on forgetting is far from complete, and the immediate future is likely to bring some exciting developments.

Another unknown in the psychology of remembering is the point at which forgetting takes place. For memory to occur, three things must happen: (1) you must be aware that the event has taken place; (2) you must be able to store that material; and (3) you must be able to bring that information into focus when you need it. In the three-stage theory of memory, short-term memory is only briefly stored; long-term memory implies both storage and retrieval from storage. But at what point in that sequence does forgetting usually occur? When psychologists can answer that question, they will have made a major step in understanding the dynamics of memory.

LEARNING APPLIED TO STUDY

Given the thousands of studies of human and animal learning that have been conducted by psychologists, educators, and others, what can be said to help a college student improve his performance? We can tell him, of course, that learning—at least academic learning—rarely occurs in the absence of motivation, but we are less successful in making suggestions to help him improve his motivation. We can remind him that he will need to pay attention to what he is reading, to what others are saying, and to what is being done and said around him, but we are not especially clever in offering a program to overcome his inability to attend.

Nonetheless, psychologists are not helpless in providing aid to students. They have learned, in part through experience and in part through their research, some specific approaches and some general guidelines. A particular approach depends on the individual student:

- A sophomore was persuaded that notes taken with a thick, dark, smudgy pencil in a small notebook were impossible to return to for later study.
- A recently married woman carrying a full course load completed her degree only after she was helped to sit down at the beginning of the semester and set up a rigid schedule.
- Another woman, recently divorced, was helped to change from a rigid time schedule to a more flexible one, which was required because she had three young children who demanded her time and attention.
- A freshman, on the verge of flunking out, was shown how to reorganize his notes at the end of each week, so that he was simultaneously reviewing the class lectures and giving himself better study materials.
- A more mature student was taught how to take notes effectively in class, thereby avoiding the need to reorganize them later.

Other students learn that their academic difficulties result from personal or social problems, from being in the wrong program or the wrong college, or from physical health problems. Although specific approaches must be tailored to the needs of the individual student, there are some general guidelines based on research.

RESEARCH CONTRIBUTIONS TO STUDY GUIDELINES

The following principles are not magic formulas for success, and they cannot be substituted for self-discipline, individual competence, or motivation and attention. Nor should they be followed inflexibly. Nevertheless, they can help students make maximum use of their abilities.

The first important principle is **warm-up.** Just as a pitcher warms up in the bullpen before coming in to relieve, each study period requires a little warm-up. You rarely sit down, pick up your text, turn to page 137, and start to read. Normally you look the material over, read a few picture captions, see how many pages the assignment contains, and estimate how long it will take you. All this is a type of warm-up, which gets you ready to begin. For some tasks, such as working on an accounting problem or putting an automobile engine together, warm-up can take several minutes — especially if you are interrupted in the middle. In planning study, you need to take warm-up time into consideration.

Once you have warmed up, how do you decide how long to study at a time? If you spend too much time at one stretch on a course (*too much* is defined by you), boredom and fatigue may decrease your learning and performance. Both retroactive and proactive interference increase when you study the same material for a long period of time. Such prolonged study is termed **massed practice** and is exemplified by cramming for an exam.

Distributed practice, or spaced practice, tends to be more effective than massed practice, both for recalling the material a few hours later and for recalling it many months later (Anderson, 1967). However, distributed practice loses much of its force when the sessions are too brief or are separated by too long a period of time. The more frequently adequate practice sessions are held, the less forgetting occurs — which suggests the value of periodic reviews.

Research and experience with **overlearning** suggest that many tasks should be studied well beyond the point at which they are "just understood." For the student as well as for the football team or the stage actor, repetitious drill serves to improve learning and to retard forgetting.

Perhaps you learned in high school that distributed practice and whole learning (that is, going over the material in its entirety rather than part by part) are better than massed practice and part learning. The research says "maybe." You cannot establish rigid standards for yourself — you need to find the kind of scheduling and the size of unit of material that are best for you (Hovland, 1951). In other words, move in the direction of distributed practice and whole learning, but not to the point of losing flexibility.

Knowledge of previous results, or **feedback,** is definitely helpful in studying, because it enables you to correct previous errors and learn your weaknesses (Anderson, 1967). Imagine shooting a rifle at a target but never knowing whether you hit it or not! How much learning would take place? How much would your performance improve? Teaching machines (see below) make good use of feedback.

Similarly, meaningfulness permits you to learn more rapidly and remember longer (McGeoch & Irion, 1952). Looking for relationships, applying what you are learning to your own life, relating the ideas you are studying in your various courses — all these approaches improve meaningfulness. To some degree, meaningfulness is to the psychologist what the term *relevance* was to the students of the late 1960s and early 1970s. A major difficulty in using these terms is the problem of *who* determines what is meaningful or relevant: the instructor, the college administrators, the textbook authors, the student? Since meaningfulness is so significant in human learning, this is not merely a theoretical question.

Transfer of training is an extremely important principle in learning. *Positive transfer* occurs when learning one type of task facilitates learning another task. In *negative transfer,* learning one task interferes with learning another. An example of the former is learning to use an electric typewriter after learning to use a manual one. The latter would be exemplified in a child's attempts to stop calling a substitute teacher by the name of his regular teacher. Learning both the principles and the techniques of a task broadens the extent of transfer that will be possible. Learning only the routine of your job will only permit you to transfer to a very similar job; learning both the routine and the principles underlying it will enable you to apply your knowledge in a much greater variety of settings.

DEVELOPING AN ACTIVE SET FOR LEARNING

The words *active, attention, motivation,* and *goal* constantly come up in discussions of effective learning, because they appear to be highly predictive of success in both educational and vocational settings. Ask yourself how often you have needed to reread the same paragraph four or five times because none of the ideas seemed to stick. You were not attending to your reading; you did not have an active set to learn. A method for studying textbooks has been developed that helps establish an active set and, simultaneously, enables you to follow other principles of effective learning, such as familiarizing yourself with what you are about to read, making reading meaningful, and responding immediately.

This method of textbook study is called **SQ3R,** and it consists of five steps. First, *survey* the book or section you are going to read by skimming the materials and reading the summary carefully. Second, turn each major (only major) heading into a *question* and write the question down. Third, with the question in the back of your mind, *read* actively to answer the question. Fourth, *recite* the answer to the question aloud, and then jot it down under the question in your notes. Fifth, *review* your notes and reread the summary (Robinson, 1961).

Proper use of SQ3R will not only produce an active set for learning, but will also supply you with a brief chapter outline, enable you to recall the material longer, and reduce daydreaming. As with all techniques, you will need to adapt it to your own maximum effectiveness.

PROGRAMMED INSTRUCTION AND TEACHING MACHINES

Teaching machines and other forms of programmed instruction make use of the principles of SQ3R, especially the *question* and *recite* steps, but they are based more directly on operant-learning principles. Teaching machines are merely mechanized devices for the presentation of programmed instructional materials. Programmed instruction usually operates in the following sequence:

1. *Input,* which usually consists of a series of small steps that take you from what you already understand to the new concepts you are learning.
2. *Stimulus presentation,* or the way in which you are presented with the steps (for example, through the device of a teaching machine).
3. Your answer to the question presented in Step 2 should be the *desired response,* since with programmed instruction a serious effort is made to have the learner give the correct response.
4. When the learner does respond, whether it is correct or not, he receives *immediate feedback* (that is, he learns immediately whether his response was correct).
5. *Reinforcement* for correct responses and *nonreinforcement* (but not punishment) for incorrect responses are also necessary. Often the immediate feedback provides reinforcement, but a child may also be given candy or some other more material reward (after Sanford & Wrightsman, 1970).

Programmed instruction is a method of self-instruction, not just another way of getting you to review your coursework. Some of the most impressive uses of programmed instruction have been made in industry and the military. For example, programs to instruct individuals in the fundamentals of insurance, salesmanship, and basic electronics have all been tested and found to be about as good as or better than other kinds of instruction, such as classroom or traditional booklets (Campbell, 1971). Attempts to use programmed instruction with high school and college students have worked quite well also, even in introductory psychology (Holland, 1960), probably because they provide the opportunity for each student to work at his own pace and to check immediately whether his response was correct; also the programmed instruction lets the individual figure out the answers by himself, without someone lecturing to him. On the other hand, most programmed instruction depends on fill-in questions to encourage the student to learn. Do you feel this is the most appropriate way to learn in a course?

Programmed instruction and teaching machines appear very helpful in teaching certain kinds of skills and in providing self-instruction; they also permit the teacher to spend more time with individual students (Sanford & Wrightsman, 1970). But—at least for the present—they cannot substitute for a competent teacher or a well-written textbook in areas that are not closely related to specific skills.

COMPLEX LEARNING

Much human learning involves seeking relationships and working out new solutions. Sometimes problems are solved largely by *trial and error*. Thomas Edison is said to have made several thousand attempts, each time trying a different method or material, before he produced the electric light. Of course, his efforts were far from random, since there had been considerable previous thought, but there was also much trial and error. A personal experience of mine also illustrates **problem solving** by trial and error, which, in this instance, turned out to be more successful than careful thought and planning:

> Our newly purchased French automobile seemed to intrigue and baffle all American mechanics who were entrusted to repair it. As long as we remained in Los Angeles, we had little difficulty, but one summer we decided to take a cross-country camping trip, and the car's water pump fell off 20 miles from Kansas City. The local dealer was reassuring, but his mechanics were less so. They put on three successive water pumps, none of which lasted more than a few miles. A total of five man-hours went unsuccessfully into what should have been a one-hour task. Finally, just before closing time, the head mechanic came back over for the upteenth time, leaned over to face the water pump, touched and twisted and yanked and pushed every conceivable contrivance. Then I noticed that he began turning a bolt that had been partly hidden and completely unnoticed. As he turned it, he began to grin. Then he got up, said "Try 'er," and walked away. The water pump lasted the remaining two years we owned the car.

The *step-by-step* method is usually used in solving algebra problems or in figuring out what is causing your faucet to leak. Although the step-by-step process in problem solving is often obvious, at other times the solution of a problem may seem to happen all at once. Such experiences may result from some step-by-step process that has gone on without our knowing it, but we end up with the feeling that the solution came suddenly.

In these instances the solution is often referred to as resulting from **insight learning. Insight** has been differentiated from other kinds of problem solving in several ways: (1) it comes suddenly; (2) it occurs smoothly and without hesitation; (3) it may come before the person actually tackles the task of solving the problem; and (4) it may reveal a novel solution (Osgood, 1953), or at least a solution that is original for that person. In terms of these characteristics, the auto mechanic who fixed my car was not using insight. Three-year-old Danny, however, did use insight:

> After a hard morning of playing on the monkey bars at his school, Danny arrived home to demand a cookie "Right now!" His mother reminded him that lunch would be ready in ten minutes and said he could have a cookie for dessert. Mother's logic was not persuasive, but the fact that the cookies were on the kitchen counter about two feet out of his reach was persuasive — or at least it had been on previous occasions. This time, with his climbing of monkey bars fresh in his mind, Danny pulled out two of the kitchen drawers to form steps and quickly clambered up to the counter and the cookies.
>
> Danny saw the relationship between two previously unconnected acts — climbing on monkey bars and getting a cookie — whereupon a sudden insight occurred.

Not all persons go about solving problems in the same way. For a given problem, one person may apply trial-and-error techniques, another may try to solve it logically step by step, and a third may experience a sudden insight.

Learning occurs in all humans. It ranges from the painful and difficult learning involved in being able to understand human behavior or the political process or atomic theory to the simplest forms of learning, such as an infant's turning his head in response to his mother's greeting. Learning is essential for human existence.

SUMMARY OF IMPORTANT IDEAS

1. Learning is the process that takes place whenever a relatively permanent change in behavior results from experience or practice.

2. Learning cannot be measured directly but must be inferred from observation of performance.

3. In classical conditioning, a stimulus is presented a moment before a second stimulus. If the second stimulus elicits a response, the first stimulus will eventually elicit the same response, assuming the procedure is repeated often enough.

4. Additional learning takes place through generalization and discrimination. Extinction weakens the bond between stimulus and response; reinforcement strengthens the bond.

5. Operant learning requires the motivation to respond, the possibility of producing the correct response, and a reward for producing the correct response.

When the correct response is not emitted spontaneously, operant learning can be guided by eliciting the correct response through a series of approximations.

6. Some learning occurs through imitation.

7. Learning and memory are closely related. If no learning occurs, there is nothing to remember; without memory, learning is valueless.

8. Evidence for memory occurs through recall, recognition, and relearning.

9. A two-factor theory of remembering has been proposed. The factors are long-term memory and short-term memory.

10. Memory has a biochemical base. When the relevant body chemistry is altered, memory is affected.

11. Forgetting may occur through disuse, interference, or motivation to forget.

12. Principles of learning and memory may be applied to study. Application of these principles includes making proper use of warm-up, using the optimum number of study sessions spaced in optimum fashion, making proper use of whole and part learning, obtaining knowledge of results, making material meaningful, using transfer of training principles, and applying SQ3R.

13. Programmed instruction and teaching machines also use principles of learning applied to effective study.

14. Much human learning involves problem solving, which may occur through trial and error, through step-by-step logical considerations, or through a sudden insight.

7 Thought, Language, and Intelligence

Learning and remembering provide the base from which more complex aspects of intellectual capacities can be considered. Humans must learn to solve problems, to gain insights, and to form concepts. In brief, they must learn to think. Since language is such a basic part of the thought processes of humans, thought and language will be discussed here in the same context. The nature of intelligence emerges from a consideration of thought and language. Thus Chapters 6 and 7 examine learning from its simplest to its most sophisticated forms.

Our society places a very high value on intellectual competence, especially the kinds of competence represented by abstract thinking and the ability to work with symbols such as words and numbers. Although other forms of animals do think, make decisions, and act intelligently, a wide gap exists between the capacities of the most intelligent of lower animals and those of the average man. Writers of science fiction sometimes create characters whose intelligence is as far beyond that of humans as ours is beyond that of lower animals; yet the science, technology, and social institutions of these wonder-creatures are often not beyond the potential of man. Hopefully man will use his thinking ability to save the future of the human race from the effects of the destructive potential this same ability to think has permitted him to evolve.

THINKING

Humans are able to combine the many symbols, concepts, and other results of learning into **thinking.** Imagining the future or trying to make sense of the past is thinking. Creating a comic strip, designing the body of a new sportscar, and solving a problem in algebra all involve thinking. Criticizing a movie and deciding to break off a relationship are forms of thinking. Whether the thinking leads to good or poor results is not the point—the point is that thinking takes place. Animals show a form of behavior that can be called thinking, but the difference between thinking by man and "thinking" by animals is very great.

Thinking has been described as "any process or activity not predominantly perceptual . . . . Judging, abstracting, conceiving, reasoning, and . . . imagining, remembering, and anticipating are forms of thinking" (English & English, 1958).

Thinking may work under our control, or it may be partly or completely outside our awareness. In working out an accounting problem or in trying to figure out the identity of the criminal in a murder mystery, we use controlled thinking—that is, we try to guide our thought processes to gain a particular goal. Thinking for school or for work is frequently controlled thinking.

Some thinking is based on images—usually visual images but sometimes ones involving hearing or even touch, balance, smell, taste, or the internal senses. As you think about a friend, you receive a picture of him in your "mind's eye." In

FIGURE 7–1. Complex learning, trial and error, thinking, problem solving, insight—all are required in playing chess. Photograph by Liane Enkelis.

trying to decide which pair of shoes to buy, how to follow the dress pattern in your sewing, or where you left your notebook, you tend to create visual images. But thinking is obviously more than images: it encompasses concepts and language or other symbols as well.

FORMING CONCEPTS

The question of how humans develop their understanding of concepts is undergoing extensive investigation by psychologists. How do you learn what is meant by the terms *democracy, manly, three, total, blue, opposite,* or *Swedish?*

FIGURE 7–2.   Concept formation consists of learning that one response describes a number of related things. Courtesy Fillmore H. Sanford.

One way in which concepts develop is through abstracting from experiences with the concept in a number of different settings. The young child hears the word *blue* applied to a blue coat, the blue sky, his sister's blue eyes, and his blue blanket; slowly he recognizes that blue refers to the color. If he has previously formed an understanding of the concept *color,* he could merely be told that blue was the color of the coat, sky, and so on. Once the child has learned what common quality of the coat, the sky, his sister's eyes, and his blanket is encompassed by *blue,* he can generalize blueness to other objects. Through the responses of others he will gain an understanding of the outer limits of blueness: when does blue become black or white or purple or green? And, if he hears his father ask his mother why she is so blue, he may become confused all over again.

Very young children tend to develop concepts through concrete features shared by various items: for example, automobiles and trains are similar because they are both hard, fast, and big. A later step in **concept formation** is to respond to the function of the items; for example, automobiles and trains are similar because we ride in them. The most mature phase of concept formation is to recognize the similarity between trains and automobiles because both belong to the abstract concept *vehicle* (Reichard & Rapaport, 1943).

Some concepts are very difficult to grasp—not only for young children but also for adults—particularly when the concept is abstract and there is nothing physical to point to. Sometimes abstract concepts mean different things to different people. Thus concepts such as *democracy, religion, love,* and *independence* are understood only through varied experiences with situations in which the words are applied.

THE USE OF SYMBOLS IN THINKING

People learn to do things for immediate satisfaction, but they also learn to do things for symbolic rewards, such as money, which has no value in and of itself but acquires value in terms of what it can purchase. Chimpanzees can learn to work for poker chips that can be exchanged for food a day later (Wolfe, 1936), which indicates that they can learn a relatively sophisticated symbolic relationship. People also work for money to buy things, but—for some people at least—money eventually becomes important in its own right, perhaps because of its association with previous satisfaction of needs. When the chimps found that their poker chips would no longer get them food, the response that they emitted to obtain the chips (that is, work) met with extinction, and they stopped working. People, on the other hand, will work hard to obtain far more money than is needed to purchase the goods and services they desire. The accumulation of wealth for its own sake seems to become autonomous, or independent, of other need satisfactions.

Both humans and some lower animals learn to respond to symbols with as much fervor as they respond to what the symbol stands for. A smile, a word of encouragement, and a raised fist are all symbols that we learn to associate with other stimuli, until the symbol becomes as meaningful and as motivating as the initial stimulus.

FANTASIES AND DREAMS

Since ancient times fantasies and dreams have excited, inspired, irritated, and exasperated mankind. Joseph, in the Old Testament, rose from slavery to power because he used dreams to predict the future. Although for many centuries dreams were believed to represent the voice of gods, Sigmund Freud pointed out that our sleeping visions represent our own voice saying the things we do not permit it to say during the waking day.

Dreams and fantasies, or daydreams, are examples of thought processes that occur with little or no conscious control. Although the external environment may trigger a fantasy or dream, the images that form usually have little relationship to what is going on outside the person. Dreams and fantasies are related to hallucinations only to the extent that all three refer to apparent perceptions that take place without any external sensation (see Chapter 3).

FANTASIES

Humans have the ability to recall a situation in "their mind's eye" or to create a situation that has never occurred. Such creations are called daydreams or **fantasies.** Before calling a girl for a date, a college freshman rehearses the event through fantasy; a student in police science "pictures" what he will say when he catches one of his professors speeding—especially if that professor has flunked him; an unpopular girl fantasizes dating the most popular boys at the college.

Fantasies and daydreams can be helpful in achieving self-actualization. You rehearse the future to see "how it fits"; you anticipate, through fantasy, things that may happen, and you are better able to cope with them when they do occur; you blow off steam harmlessly by yelling at your professor, arguing with the boss who fired you, or making your rival in romance look foolish—all through fantasy. Fantasy can also help in other ways. Have you ever created, through fantasy, a short-story plot, a new office procedure, or an improvement on the dress pattern you recently purchased?

However, fantasy can be carried too far. When you begin to find daydreams easier than making an effort, or when your fantasies become so interesting that real life seems dull, then fantasies can become harmful. People who are severely emotionally disturbed confuse fantasy with reality, so that their fantasies seem real to them.

FIGURE 7–3. Humans have the ability to recall a situation in their mind's eye. Photograph by Lehman J. Pinckney.

DREAMS

Everyone dreams every night. Strong evidence has accumulated to indicate that people dream four or five times each night, for an average of 20 minutes per dream (Dement, 1960). This evidence is based on (1) reports by dreamers, (2) measures of brain-wave changes by the electroencephalograph (EEG), and (3) measures of rapid eye movements during sleep. Modern technology has been effectively utilized in studying this ancient mystery.

You may not remember your dreams; indeed, you may even insist that you don't dream. But the weight of scientific research has reasonably well established that dreaming is a normal, usual, and probably necessary process. Recent studies show that not being allowed to dream is very upsetting. If dreams are interrupted one night, the number of dreams will increase the following night; if dreams are interrupted several nights in a row, anxiety and irritation result (Dement, 1960).

The content of dreams appears to be a continuation of the dreamer's daytime concerns, except that in sleep his ideas can drift, rather than be focused by the demands of the environment. To some extent dreams may be a way of expressing the feelings, desires, and fears that the dreamer cannot admit, even to himself. Dreams may also be an attempt to cope with pressing personal problems (Foulkes, 1964). Often the content that we "see" makes no immediate sense, and we need to interpret it through an understanding of our own feelings and experiences. Frequently dream symbols occur that are difficult to interpret, although the following dream should provide few problems:

> "All the guys I knew had been making out pretty good, but I was kind of scared. Yet I wanted to make out too, maybe just to show them that I could. Or maybe to show *me* that I could. I was playing a lot of basketball then, and I had a dream that was so vivid I still remember it, about my basketball — only it wasn't really about basketball — or maybe it was. Anyhow, I was dribbling down the court, and everybody was cheering, my teammates and everybody, and I shot the ball through the basket, and people went really wild. And then I woke up and found that I'd had a wet dream."

This dream can be interpreted as (1) a continuation of the student's daytime concerns, (2) a way of expressing feelings he could not otherwise express, or (3) a way of working out demanding personal problems. Or it may have served all three functions. Although it contains symbolism, it is also very realistic. What do you think it meant?

The next dream example does not depend on symbols at all.

> Penny Joseph, a lively and attractive graduating senior, entered my office close to tears. She had been having the same dream off and on for about four weeks, and she always awoke from it in a state of panic. The dream setting was the family dinner table, where Penny, her parents, her two brothers, and her fiance were eating Sunday brunch. But, Penny insisted, someone else was at the table, although no one could see him and only she seemed aware of his presence. This "presence" came closer and closer to Penny, until she woke up drenched with perspiration, her heart pounding.
>
> After about 30 minutes of discussion, I asked whether anyone in her family disapproved of the wedding. She shook her head, but then her hands began to clench. "Now I know," she said.
>
> It turned out that Penny had been married when she was 18, but the marriage was annulled soon afterward. Since the marriage had occurred in a distant state and few people knew about it, she and her family had agreed not to tell anyone about it. (Her ex-husband had subsequently been imprisoned on

several counts of robbery, and the entire incident was a very painful one.) When she fell in love with Robert, her fiance, she had intended to tell him, but "the moment was never right." Robert's family was known to be "stuffy" in their concern about reputation, and Penny feared that they would not approve of the marriage if they learned of her past. By the time wedding plans were begun, Penny totally lacked the courage to talk to Robert about her past. Yet she felt guilty about not telling him and was fearful that her first husband would find her.

Consider Lorrie's dream, which occurred during her freshman year at college.

> "I dreamed I was running after a little pig. I chased the pig through the town, in and out of houses, across streets, to the edge of town, and back to our house. I finally caught the ugly little thing, picked it up, and started to carry it to the butcher — when it suddenly turned into my baby sister."

When Lorrie was 16 and deeply involved in dating, cheerleading, and high school dramatics, her mother gave birth to a baby girl. Lorrie's brothers were both in college at the time. You can interpret this dream yourself.

Very few dreams, however, lend themselves to interpretation as easily as these. Each dream must be considered in light of the unique personality and life circumstances of the dreamer. Penny's dream, for example, could never have been understood without a full knowledge of her background. For this and other reasons, psychologists consider most dream-interpretation books to be without merit.

LANGUAGE

The child's capacity to develop an understanding of concepts is closely bound up with his ability to comprehend language. Language, in its broadest sense, is any communication between two or more individuals. Concepts represent communication largely through verbal symbols, but gestures, facial expressions, body movements, diagrams, and mathematical formulas also communicate and are a type of language.

Every known human society has a spoken language, and every spoken language is organized around rules of grammar. In addition, every spoken language has: (1) pronouns; (2) ways of communicating concepts of time, space, and number; and (3) words meaning true and false (Miller, 1964). Although animals can communicate, only man has a true language.

You may have heard the claim that residents of some ghetto areas do not use rules of grammar or of vocabulary. However, evidence indicates that such persons, although they may not use generally accepted rules, do indeed follow an accepted grammar and accepted definitions that are well understood within their own community. When there is a need to communicate with people outside the community, the lack of similar grammatical rules and word definitions can be confusing, particularly when people from both groups believe they are speaking the same language.

FIGURE 7–4. Language is used to communicate many phenomena, including expressions of feelings and attitudes. Photograph by Lehman J. Pinckney.

Language is used to communicate many phenomena, including descriptions of physical things and events, expressions of feelings and attitudes, and abstract concepts. Thus people can learn to use language properly only to the extent that they have also learned about the world and have come to understand concepts. Words, like concepts, are learned through abstracting and generalizing. Can you explain how the principles of operant learning might be applied to the process through which a young child learns the meanings of new words?

Languages differ not only in vocabulary and grammar but also in classification of phenomena. In English the word *aunt* refers to your father's sister, your mother's sister, your father's brother's wife, and your mother's brother's wife.

However, other societies use four different terms to describe these four different people (Murdock, 1949). Residents of Yap, a small mid-Pacific island that is part of Micronesia, have more than 30 distinctly different words to describe kinds of water (for example, ocean water, bay water, stream water, fresh water). Living on a small island, the Yapese find water a very important element in their lives.

Words describe physical realities, and they also attach implied values to physical realities. I am slim; you are thin; he is skinny. *Nigger, Negro,* and *black* all refer to the same physical reality, but their meanings are very different. The same is true of *broad, woman,* and *lady* or *fuzz, cop,* and *police officer.* The meanings and implications of words are studied by the science of semantics.

COMMUNICATION WITHOUT WORDS

Words are not the only means of communication. Raising an eyebrow, coughing, blushing, spitting, taking a girl's hand, crying, sending a gift, or kicking someone in the shins can all communicate feelings, ideas, beliefs, and intentions.

Folklore has it that a hearty handshake and a firm glance mean that a man is honest. The truth is that the salesman who is trying to persuade you to buy an encyclopedia or a new car you do not need is also aware of this folk belief. **Nonverbal communication** can easily be as complex as verbal communication.

> A college freshman takes a blind date to the movies and tries to hold hands. What does this mean? Is he showing honest affection? Is this the lead-up to "making out"? Does he just enjoy holding hands? Then his date slips her hand away from his. What is she communicating? Is she trying to get rid of him? Does she want him to think she's a "nice girl"? Do her hands perspire and embarrass her?

Nonverbal communication can also produce misunderstandings between people of different cultures who have established differing patterns of expected behavior.

> A very sociable American doing business in Manila came to like one of the Filipino businessmen with whom he was dealing. They met for dinner that evening, and the American, who was feeling the effects of two martinis, slapped the Asian across the back. The Asian looked at him in amazement, then realized that the American had meant it to be a friendly gesture. However, the deal fell through, and the two companies did no further business.

Frequently the actual words of a conversation contradict the other forms of communication. Thus you may continue to say "Yes, that's very interesting," but your eyes move around the room and you slump back in your chair—communicating that you hardly find the speaker's statements interesting. Even in the verbal part of communication, the words themselves carry only part of the meaning. Your tone of voice may communicate something quite different from the words. Sometimes the speaker will produce this disparity on purpose, but often he does not realize that what he is saying contradicts what he is communicating. Your words say "I had a very nice time this evening"; your voice says "It was really rather dull"; and your movements say "I'm very eager to get out of here."

Whether we communicate through words, through actions, through tone of voice, or through physiological change, communication is vitally important. To make the most of your abilities, you need to be able to communicate effectively to others and to receive the real meaning of what others are communicating to you.

THE NATURE OF INTELLIGENCE

The 1968 science-fiction film *Planet of the Apes* proposed that man, through his destructiveness, would reverse the present flow of evolution and revert to being a less intelligent being, whereas apes would develop into higher beings and eventually take over the planet. The prospect, although farfetched, is not completely impossible. For the foreseeable future, however, no animal—not even the relatively intelligent monkey or porpoise—is likely to approach a normal human in intelligence.

Without his superior intelligence, the human would lack the self-awareness to study himself, to attempt to self-actualize, or to transmit his values, ideas, and material goods across time and space. He would be unable to build on the knowledge and products of past generations and to plan for future generations. He would not be able to prolong life through science and medicine or to destroy life through wars and other forms of destruction. Man's intelligence even enables him to search for ways to improve his intelligence.

DEFINING INTELLIGENCE

Intelligence refers to the ability to grasp abstract concepts and symbols (such as language), to learn, and to cope with new situations (English & English, 1958). It also involves the ability to profit from experience and to solve problems. This definition is necessarily broad, since a great variety of specific acts may be termed intelligent.

It is intelligent behavior to ride a bicycle, recognize a person you met last week, and know the difference between a bush and a tree; it is intelligent behavior to count, to read a blueprint, and to spell; it is intelligent behavior to learn the meaning of concepts such as *afternoon, love, round,* and *democracy;* it is intelligent behavior to know what to do when your best friend is in trouble, when you see an automobile accident, and when you have a fight with your brother. In the following argument, Pete and Mike are in a hopeless deadlock because each is referring to a different type of intelligent behavior.

Pete: My kid brother is really bright. He can take his bike apart and put it back together all by himself, and he gets along great with the other kids. He's a real leader.

Mike: Yeah? That's pretty good, but my sister is a *real* whiz. She cracks top grades in her class, and she won an award in Sunday School.

Pete: She may be bright, but she isn't *that* bright. She doesn't have more than one or two friends. Besides, she still thinks Santa Claus is a real person.

Mike: Well, your brother isn't so smart either. He forgot his lines in the school Christmas play, and he was a semester behind in his reading for a long time.

Numerous difficulties can occur when we talk about an "intelligent person." An individual may exhibit a high degree of intelligence in his verbal behavior, yet display very limited intelligence in acts that demand an understanding of mechanics. For this reason psychologists have become interested in "factors of intelligence." Some of the most commonly described factors include the following:

— the ability to use words effectively (verbal ability)
— the ability to reason effectively
— the ability to memorize easily
— the ability to know how to behave effectively in social situations
— the ability to work well with numbers (numerical ability)
— the ability to act quickly when necessary
— the ability to perceive spatial relationships
— the ability to work effectively with the hands (motor ability)
— the ability to understand principles of mechanics

A person who is above average in one factor of intelligence is likely to be above average in others. A child with a good memory is also likely to be good in handling numerical concepts, in reasoning, and in adjusting to new social relationships. Nonetheless, although the various kinds of intelligence are related to one another, many exceptions exist, and the relationships are far from perfect.

Most psychologists and educators believe that intelligence is influenced by both heredity and environment — by both what we are born with and what happens to us after birth. Psychologists are not certain, however, *how* important heredity is and *how* important environment is. They know, for example, that the measured intelligence of a child is noticeably related to the measured intelligence of both his mother and his father (Conrad & Jones, 1940). Does this mean that the child inherited his intelligence genetically? Or does it mean that intelligent parents help a child learn more than do less intelligent parents? Both elements enter into the situation. (See Chapter 4.) Many people have come to feel that there is too much emphasis on genetics versus environment, since a child is clearly the product of a constant, dynamic interaction between his genetic inheritance and his social environment. The issue is much more complex than it initially appears.

THE MEASUREMENT OF INTELLIGENCE

The most successful and most commonly used individual tests of intelligence, the Stanford-Binet Intelligence Scale and the two Wechsler tests (WAIS and WISC), strongly emphasize the kinds of abilities that predict success in the present school programs. As a result, they have been amazingly valid in predicting school success. However, these tests (and the school systems) have been accused of being highly biased in favor of the verbally capable, already motivated middle-class child. They assume a moderate amount of interest in exploring the environment, as well as an adequate attention span and a willingness to sit and listen.

Many children do not fit this description. For a variety of social, psychological, and physiological reasons, they are not as verbally fluent, not as well motivated, and not as able to sit still and listen. These children usually get low scores on intelligence tests *and* low grades in school. Therefore they are considered stupid, and they are either ignored or placed in special classes with others like themselves.

The IQ tests have many limitations. First, they assume a good knowledge of English, so that any child brought up in a home in which English is either not spoken or not spoken well has a disadvantage. Second, the child may react negatively to the person giving the test. Third, he may have a health problem or be emotionally upset by some recent incident (including being required to take the IQ test). Fourth, although psychologists have tried to construct an IQ test that is not influenced by culture or previous learning, they have not succeeded. Fifth, the test only infers intelligence by measuring performance.

On the one hand, the IQ test has been useful in predicting success in academic work, in vocational achievement, and even in leadership (Anastasi, 1958; Mann, 1959). On the other hand, its use has caused some children to be unfairly labeled as unintelligent. More important, its very success in predicting performance for healthy, middle-class children has taken attention away from some exceedingly meaningful questions: Is what the IQ test measures what we really should be measuring? What happens if we ignore IQ-test labels and treat *all* children as if they had at least average intelligence? Can we provide interventions (for example, through improved nutrition or better child care) that will raise IQ scores? The IQ test is only a measure. Like any measure, it is often unsuccessful, and parents and teachers need to be alert to some of the harmful effects that can arise from its failures. Some opponents have demanded that it cease to be used; others insist that psychologists and educators develop tests that are free of previous learning or that compensate for the initial handicaps of the child from the "disadvantaged" home.

Intelligence is one aspect of the total personality, and it inevitably interacts in dynamic fashion with other personality attributes. Self-esteem, for example, affects performance on IQ tests, and performance on IQ tests affects self-esteem. The case of Eddie illustrates many of the principles discussed in this section.

Eddie: A Case History

At the time of testing, Eddie was finishing second grade. He was reported to the principal because he was totally unable to read, he could not draw even the simplest house or person, he constantly daydreamed, he paid little attention to the teacher, and he did not get along well with the other children. His teacher believed he was well below normal in intelligence and might need special treatment.

The first test Eddie took consisted of drawing a person (described in Goodenough, 1926). The maturity level of his drawing, compared with others of his age, showed Eddie to be in the upper 5% — an amazing performance for a child whose teacher stated he could not draw a man that even remotely resembled a man. He then took the Stanford-Binet Intelligence Scale and scored in the upper 10%. Eddie scored in the top 10% on every test, except one that demanded reading, which he could not do.

Eddie was obviously a child of high ability. Why was he doing so poorly? The answer was found mainly in his family relationships. His father, frustrated in his work, constantly criticized the teachers and the school system and sometimes even made fun of the entire process of education, claiming it was a waste of time; at the same time, he demanded that Eddie study hard and get good grades. His mother, a weak person who worried more about her imaginary illnesses than she did about her children, both feared and resented her husband and gave Eddie neither affection nor discipline. Eddie admired his father but did not know how to please him, so he withdrew by becoming apathetic.

DEPRIVATION/ENRICHMENT

Some families do much to encourage their children to develop intellectual abilities; others do nothing. Parents who take time to talk intelligently to their children, even when the children are very young, aid in the children's use and development of intelligence. The attitudes of parents toward learning, books, and school are also important: children whose parents ignore or make fun of education and books are less likely to be successful in intellectual tasks related to school progress.

Parents influence their children's intellectual competence not only by their attitudes but also by their use of language. A person whose language ability is poor will not do well on intelligence tests or in school. When children are reared in an environment in which parents seldom talk to them, the children do not learn much language in the home. Since they are inadequately prepared for schoolwork, they quickly fall behind. As a result, they come to dislike school and pay even less attention to language, which further reduces their test scores. A vicious circle is set up. This situation is particularly prevalent regarding children from socially and economically poor homes.

Some children are faced with another problem: the language spoken in their home is different from that spoken in the community. Living in a home in which English either is not spoken or is poorly spoken, the child uses English less frequently and may have some difficulty thinking in English. He will probably not speak English as well as others of his age (Soffietti, 1955), which may lead to poorer performance on intelligence tests and in classroom work.

The parent-child relationship can have an effect on intelligence that extends beyond language and verbal symbols. The willingness of parents to encourage, rather than stifle, the child's needs to explore and manipulate his environment may affect many of the factors of intelligence. Can you suggest ways in which parents might influence a child's mechanical ability or social ability?

The home also influences potential ability indirectly by affecting the physical health of the individual. For example, when diet is poor, intelligence suffers (Birren & Hess, 1968); when the expectant mother has inadequate nutrition, her baby may suffer later health and intellectual deficits. One geneticist remarked to me that infants whose mothers had severe dietary deficiencies during their pregnancy "are probably already irreversibly brain-damaged."

Middle-class children succeed in school partly because the values internalized in the home are similar to those that guide the school. In addition, their family life has probably prepared them for school. Just the opposite is often the case with disadvantaged children.

> The lower-class child . . . tends to have a poor attention span and to have great difficulty following the teacher's orders . . . he generally comes from a nonverbal household: adults speak in short sentences, if indeed they speak at all. . . . The child has never been obliged to listen to several lengthy sentences spoken consecutively.
>
> In school, the middle-class teacher who rambles on for several sentences might just as well be talking another language . . . lower-class children have a limited perception of the world about them: they do not know that objects

have names . . . or that the same object may have several names. . . . They also have very little concept of size or time.

The lower-class youngsters are poorly motivated, because they have had little experience in receiving approval for success in a task or disapproval for failure; but school is organized on the assumption that children expect approval for success. And since the parents . . . do not ask the youngsters about school, the children have no way of knowing that the parents *do* very much want and expect success [Silberman, 1964].

The parents of these children usually wish to help their youngsters, but they may lack the necessary financial resources or the awareness of what to do and how to do it. Since many belong to ethnic minority groups, their attempts at helping themselves are often rebuffed by the rest of society because of racial prejudice. As the children grow up and have families, they pass their disadvantages on to their own children, in much the same way as the educated person will pass on his understanding of the world to his children. Of course, some children from disadvantaged homes do break the pattern and escape from the problems they grew up with. (This breaking away is not the same as leaving their ethnic community, which is an entirely different matter.) Perhaps they were influenced by a parent or other relative, a teacher, a social worker or policeman, or by some inner resource not fully understood.

Here is a word picture of the obstacles faced by one hypothetical student from a disadvantaged home; it is by no means an extreme example.

He comes from a home that is physically crowded, permitting him little privacy and no space of his own. His father has not been around the home for many years, and he has to take care of his younger brothers and sisters — not a serious matter except that it drains considerable time and energy and requires taking on adult worries. His mother works, so he has to prepare many of the meals; most of them end up being cereal or sandwiches. He knows nothing of nutrition and has no way of getting enough food, even if he did know. Because of his inadequate diet, he functions at a low energy level and with limited alertness. Economic uncertainty is constant.

Because the use of language in the home is often restricted to one-syllable words or nods and grunts, he is behind his age group in language development. Also, since his early environment lacked stimulation, his memory and learning skills have rarely been challenged. He has not learned middle-class concepts of time or middle-class notions of reward and punishment, so he finds the demands of his middle-class teachers strange and unrealistic. Since he knows many people who have failed, failure in school is neither unanticipated nor terrifying. And, once he begins to fall behind, the chances are that he will fall farther and farther behind [based on Powledge, 1967].

A very thorough study of the achievement of 600,000 American students in 4000 schools, grades 1 through 12, was completed in 1966. Results indicated that differences in achievement were due largely to home background, type of age-peer associations, and teacher characteristics, rather than to the school itself. This finding suggests that the disadvantaged child who is surrounded by other disadvantaged children is in a worse situation than he would be if he were part of a school population of more varied backgrounds (Coleman, Mood, Campbell, et al., 1966).

The behavior of teachers toward their students should not be underestimated as a factor in the intellectual growth of children from low-income homes. Like everyone else, teachers respond to others in terms of their prior expectations, which are often based on stereotypes. In one study teachers were told that certain of their pupils were considerably more intelligent than their classmates. Although the teachers did not realize it, these pupils had been selected at random and were neither more nor less intelligent than their classmates. Nonetheless, by the end of the school year these children, previously known to be comparable to the other pupils in intelligence, had apparently improved more than average, as reflected by various measures of ability. The investigators concluded that the teachers treated these children as superior and expected greater achievement from them, and the children responded to this treatment by actually improving (Rosenthal & Jacobson, 1968). However, several follow-up studies by other authors did not consistently obtain similar results (Dahlstrom, 1970).

Recently a combination of federal and local programming has been established to help the children who are most likely to face the difficulties that arise in disadvantaged homes. These programs, focused on very young children, particularly preschoolers, attempt to expand the children's worlds both socially and intellectually. The former is achieved through discussions and through visits to places where the children would not ordinarily go. The latter is accomplished in two related ways: first, by attempting to improve the children's ability to use the English language, and, second, by giving them experience in handling objects and in exploring their physical and social environment. Some programs have encouraged or even demanded that mothers participate in the project, in the hope that the mothers can reinforce the learning outside of class (Tyler, 1972).

As more experience with these programs is reported, the need for follow-up becomes increasingly apparent. The children who as 3-year-olds receive help through a program such as Operation Head Start will in later years continue to need extra help. Research suggests that these children do indeed have a head start, but that differences between them and other children are greatly diminished several years later (Tyler, 1972).

The complaint may arise: "Why succeed in school? After all, look at all the problems those middle-class, academically successful people have. And look at the way they chase the buck, rather than pay attention to the things that would help humanity." Do you feel this point has merit? How would you respond to this attitude?

BECOMING CREATIVE

In recent years the nature and measurement of creativity have been of much concern to psychologists. Creativity is not the same thing as intelligence. People with extremely high IQ scores may show little creativity, and those with average or even below-average intelligence may exhibit highly creative behavior at times. On the whole, though, various measures of creativity do show relationships to various measures of intelligence; that is, people who do well on tests of creativity tend to do well on tests of intelligence.

Creativity is defined as the "ability to find new solutions to a problem or new modes of artistic expression" (English & English, 1958). Novelty and originality are also implied by creativity, and the creative person is frequently assumed to be making some form of contribution to the community (Piers, 1968). In some ways creativity is the opposite of rigidity. The creative person can see new and unusual relationships or find new and unusual uses for things.

A businessman may be creative in finding a way to enter a previously untouched market; an artist who turns out one basic type of painting with many slight variations is not creative, although he may be a competent craftsman. A housewife who creates her own recipes for homemade soup and bread is more creative than an author who writes only "formula stuff."

There is real danger in discussing who or what is creative, since psychologists are far from agreeing among themselves how to judge creativity. However, one investigator (Piers, 1968) found that 15 characteristics are most often cited by psychologists in describing creative people: (1) strong motivation, (2) involvement in what happens, (3) curiosity, (4) persistence, (5) dissatisfaction with things as they are, (6) self-sufficiency, (7) autonomy, (8) independence of judgment, (9) self-confidence, (10) self-acceptance, (11) sense of humor, (12) intuition, (13) tolerance for ambiguity, (14) desire to deal with complex ideas, and (15) flexibility. The similarity between these characteristics and Maslow's description of the self-actualizing personality is striking (see Chapters 3 and 16).

Research has compared highly creative students with highly intelligent (but not especially creative) students. The former were less well liked by their teachers, placed more importance on a sense of humor, and were more likely to choose unusual vocations. Perhaps of more importance, the highly creative students were much less interested in working toward what most of us consider to be success; they preferred to wander off in their own directions, doing what they wished (Getzels & Jackson, 1962).

Every society has many pressures against creativity and in favor of conformity. Creative people do things differently, and people who do things differently are often a bit frightening to others. Sometimes creative people have ideas that seem to oppose the accepted way of thinking and living. Sigmund Freud and James Joyce are examples of men who have been attacked for their creative ideas. Modern art has also been widely attacked by people who make no attempt to understand it.

FIGURE 7–5. One kind of creative activity. Photograph courtesy of Columbia Broadcasting System.

To differentiate the truly creative from the merely clever or the crackpot is not always easy. However, some people are so fearful of new ideas and new ways of doing things that they regard all change as dangerous or peculiar.

What can parents, teachers, and others do to encourage creativity in children and young people? What can you do to help yourself be more creative? First, of course, you need to decide which definition or definitions of creativity you are talking about. To help develop creativity in art or music is quite different from encouraging creativity in business, which is in turn different from enabling a person to be innovative in thinking about social reform or political values. Your second consideration is whether you really wish to encourage creativity at all, since creative people are likely to question authority, ask embarrassing questions, behave in offbeat and unusual ways, and behave impulsively (Cropley, 1967).

One study suggests that, if you wish to encourage creativity, you should get people to examine their environment with all their senses, instead of just looking at things around them (Goodnow, 1969). According to other studies, creativity could be stimulated through (1) not requiring children to respond rigidly or insisting that neatness and orderliness prevail, (2) stimulating the enjoyment of new experiences and discouraging strict routine, (3) rewarding flexible thinking, (4) not trying to make children be like everyone else but rewarding them for being different, and (5) permitting children to accept their own "irrational impulses" (based on Berelson & Steiner, 1964).

Since creative thinking often requires seeing new relationships, many people believe that people should be more relaxed about "just letting things happen" instead of trying to control their thought processes rigidly. In a sense, the underlying theory is that you have all the elements necessary for creativity and innovativeness, but, by trying too hard, you continue to follow the same old paths to the same old destinations. The ability to be receptive to ideas that come spontaneously is important.

Educating people to be creative is not an impossibility. A few attempts toward such education have shown some hope for the future. Even public schools might do a better job of encouraging creativity if they could gear their programs to permit students to discover principles and ideas on their own, rather than emphasize the kind of presentation in which the teacher does the work (Piers, 1968).

The following individuals fit my criteria for being creative. Though you may not approve of what each of these individuals has done with his creative abilities, consider the creative and innovative nature of their accomplishments. Whom would you add to the list? Whom would you eliminate? Why?

Some Representative Creative People

Beatles (singers, composers)
Martin Buber (philosopher)
George Washington Carver (scientist)
Charlie Chaplin (actor)
Cesar Chavez (union organizer)
Charles Darwin (scientist)
Walt Disney (artist-businessman)
Thomas Edison (inventor)
Albert Einstein (scientist)
Henry Ford (businessman)
Benjamin Franklin (inventor, writer, political figure)
Sigmund Freud (psychiatrist)
Mahatma Gandhi (political figure)

Helen Hayes (actress)
James Joyce (author)
Gustav Mahler (composer)
Horace Mann (educator)
Karl Marx (political theorist)
Pablo Picasso (artist)
Margaret Sanger (social planner)
Charles Schulz (cartoonist)
Frank Lloyd Wright (architect)

SUMMARY OF IMPORTANT IDEAS

1. The understanding of a concept develops at least in part through abstracting from experiences with the concept in several different settings. More abstract concepts are more difficult to grasp.

2. Thinking may remain under conscious control or may occur outside a person's awareness. Fantasies and dreams are examples of the latter.

3. Fantasies, when not carried too far, have an important and useful function in problem solving and creativity.

4. Everyone dreams frequently. Without the opportunity to dream, emotional upsets may occur.

5. Language is any communication between two or more individuals. All societies have a spoken language with a recognized grammar and recognized word definitions.

6. Nonverbal methods of communication are as important as verbal methods. To receive communication accurately, one must be sensitive to nonverbal communication.

7. Intelligence refers to the ability to grasp abstract concepts and symbols, including language; the ability to learn; the ability to solve problems; and the ability to cope with new situations.

8. There are many factors of intelligence. The individual who is high in one factor will probably be above average in others, but the relationship does not always hold.

9. Heredity and environment are both thought to have an influence on intelligence.

10. The standard IQ tests have many valid uses, but great care is required to make certain they are not used in inappropriate settings.

11. The home, the school, and the community all contribute to the enrichment or the deprivation of any child. Good nutrition and health care are also important in enabling children to perform at their best levels.

12. Creativity implies novelty and innovation. Although it is related to general intelligence, creativity can occur when intelligence is not pronounced.

13. Creativity can be fostered by parents and teachers through the right kinds of attitudes.

8 Understanding Emotions and Stress

Among the basic principles of human behavior are those that involve emotions and stress. Although previous chapters have, of necessity, touched on emotions, we have not yet explored the topic. We cannot feel an emotion without prior perception, learning, thought, and intelligence. We need to perceive the stimuli that we have learned to respond to emotionally; through thought and intelligence we may modify our emotional response to these stimuli.

From the greatest glee and happiness to the most miserable sorrow and depression, from extreme contentment to extreme agitation, from the tension of jealousy and suspicion to the security of love and trust, humans are capable of feeling and expressing a wide variety of emotions. Without the ability to feel emotions, we would find the world a much duller, although probably more peaceful, place.

An **emotion** may be thought of as a feeling or state of arousal that stirs a person to observable action or to internal change. The similarity between the words *emotion* and *motivation* is obvious—they are both evolved from the same Latin word meaning "to move." Both emotion and motivation move us to action; both are represented by biochemical changes within the body and by psychological feelings, either conscious or unconscious or both.

Try to recall the last person who spoke to you. What emotions was he feeling at the time? How do you know? Determining whether a particular person is feeling a particular emotion at a particular time can be very difficult—perhaps even impossible. However, we usually accept the idea that an emotional state exists if one or more of the following criteria can be applied: (1) certain physiological changes have taken place that indicate an emotional state, (2) the person reports that he is feeling an emotion, or (3) observers report that the person is displaying behavior commonly believed to be caused by an emotion. Although psychologists assume that physiological changes underlie all emotional responses, it is rarely possible to investigate such an assumption; therefore we must rely on the report of the person himself or of an observer.

When you are feeling the emotion of anger, your heart is beating faster, your breathing has changed, your mouth may be dry, your pupils might have enlarged, your system is infused with adrenaline and noradrenaline (hormones secreted during anger), and you may feel a pounding in your stomach. Your body has assumed an alert posture in an effort to meet the stressful stimuli. Beyond these observable bodily changes, you are experiencing a subjective feeling that you yourself identify as anger. What is *anger?* It is a word, a learned label, for certain physical and psychological sensations that occur in certain kinds of social situations—it is something you perceive. Aside from the obvious physical changes

FIGURE 8-1. Physiological changes underlie all emotional responses. Photograph by Lehman J. Pinckney.

and your subjective understanding of them, the emotion called anger also involves very complex chemical and electrochemical processes in your brain and body.

Certain physiological changes that accompany anger also accompany fear. However, evidence exists that different emotions are related to different physiological change patterns (Ax, 1953). These change patterns may serve to motivate the organism into behavior, or they may produce an emergency store of energy to facilitate such actions as fighting or running away.

Examples of emotions that motivate behavior are numerous. Mild fear of failure, for example, may cause a student to study harder; moderate anger may induce a policeman to run faster when chasing a suspect. Extreme emotional states have been known to make possible amazing acts of strength and endurance, such as the instance reported several years ago of a small woman who lifted an automobile that had fallen on her son. Normally, she probably would have had trouble lifting a tire. But under emergency conditions her emotions not only motivated her to lift the car but also produced the bodily changes that enabled her to do so.

Intense emotional feelings may not always motivate or facilitate behavior. Blushing and fainting result from physiological changes brought about by emotion, but they certainly do not facilitate behavior; anger or fear can cause stuttering when verbal fluency is needed or "freezing" when quick action is necessary. Strong feelings can also motivate impulsive, rather than appropriate, behavior. The fear that leads to driving away from the scene of an accident or the anger that causes an employee to shout his resignation at the boss are two examples.

DEVELOPMENT AND EXPRESSION OF EMOTIONS

The range of emotional behavior that a person is capable of displaying is extremely great during maturity, and even during childhood, but observers report that very young infants respond in a similar fashion to all emotion-arousing stimuli. Thus at birth the only emotion shown is excitement or arousal. Before the infant is 2 months old, a pleasant state of excitement (delight) and an unpleasant state of excitement (distress) can be distinguished. A few weeks later, anger, disgust, fear, and elation emerge, followed by most of the remaining emotions, all of which appear within the first 18 months (Bridges, 1932).

Both learning and maturation influence emotional development. Some emotional responses occur with no opportunity for learning to take place. For example, an infant does not learn to smile when he is pleased — it happens inevitably. But he does learn to smile at the sight of his mother standing in the doorway with his bottle in her hand. He learns that this picture is soon followed by the opportunity to drink milk; using technical terms, we might describe his smile as a conditioned response to the stimulus of the image of his mother holding his bottle. (See Chapter 4.)

Other emotional responses are learned. People learn to love their parents (although a few learn to hate their parents). Children learn to fear snakes, the dark, and the bully down the street. Later, fear may be aroused by the sight of a motorcycle policeman in the rearview mirror, by the news that surgery is needed, or by hearing some politician claim that war will begin within the year. Human emotions can be aroused by anticipation of the future or recollection of the past.

EXPRESSING EMOTIONS

Sometimes it is simple to recognize the emotion another person is feeling. He may laugh or cry or show his feelings by the expression on his face. But facial expression alone can be misleading. Determining the emotion is helped by know-

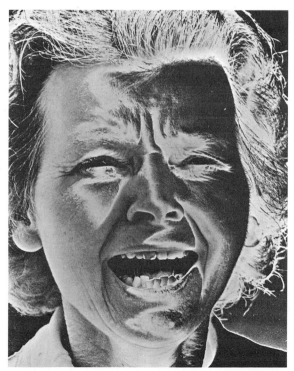

FIGURE 8–2. Can you tell from facial expressions what a person is feeling? Photograph by Lehman J. Pinckney.

ing the entire situation. In general, the more you know about the situation, the better you can judge what emotion is actually felt.

In every society people learn what emotions may properly be expressed under what conditions. Little boys are repeatedly told "Don't cry or be afraid—be a man," until they feel that being afraid and being masculine are contradictory. Thus they may become reluctant to show any signs of fear and may also believe they have failed as men if they even feel fear. Sometimes such people make a great show of bravery in order to prove to themselves that they are not afraid.

Children are also discouraged from expressing anger, especially anger toward adults. Children will often shout "I hate you!" at their parents long before they have any accurate idea what "hate" means. If their display of anger is punished, they learn not to express their anger directly; however, they cannot be stopped from feeling anger, which may then be expressed indirectly. There are many emotions that our society does not allow to be expressed directly.

Anger that cannot be directed toward parents may be redirected toward some handy object. After getting an undeserved scolding from his father, a student stormed out of the house, drove off in the family car, and—for the first time in his four years of driving—drove well over the speed limit and was ticketed. Through **displacement,** he redirected his anger to the automobile.

Many people who feel anger because of some frustration take out their feelings on minorities, such as blacks, Mexican Americans, Indians, Jews, Catholics, or Southerners. They are displacing their aggressions on a **scapegoat.**

> During the early 1930s the German economy was suffering badly. The country had to repay massive debts for the war it had lost; the money system was so unstable that people did not know from one day to the next what the prices would be; international esteem for the country was very low. Hitler, recognizing that the German people could not make effective use of their capabilities in the absence of national self-esteem, found a scapegoat in the Jews. Instead of directing their anger at themselves for having lost World War I and for being unable to control their own economy, the Germans readily displaced their aggressions away from themselves and onto the Jews, who were thereby held responsible for all of Germany's ill fortune.

> In major-league baseball, when a team does not do well for a year or two, the owners often fire the manager. Although the team's inability to win may actually result from the unwillingness of the owners to obtain good players, it is easier and cheaper for the owners to use the manager as a scapegoat.

When feelings of anger or fear are not expressed directly or displaced in some fashion, they may be repressed. Everyone has feelings he is unable to admit, even to himself (for example, you may be so furious with your parents that you

may, for a moment, wish to do them harm), and these feelings become unconscious. However, even though you are not consciously aware of them, such feelings still influence behavior. Can you think of examples?

Different societies teach different forms of emotional expression. Affection
between an adult man and his father may be expressed by kissing and hugging in
France, Italy, Israel, or Iran, but Americans usually just shake hands. In Japan
a son would rarely talk back in anger to his father, but such behavior is not uncommon in the United States. Englishmen have the reputation of showing their
enthusiasm at athletic contests by clapping their hands; Americans at a baseball
game may shout, cheer, threaten the umpire, or even tear their programs and
throw them onto the field; in Latin American countries the response may be
much more violent.

Emotional restraint, although certainly necessary in many instances, can be
carried too far. Americans are probably more likely to inhibit the expression of
their emotions than are people in most other countries. "Play it cool" is an attitude encouraged among many Americans of all ages.

TWO EXAMPLES OF EMOTIONS: FEAR AND ANXIETY

Two familiar emotional states are fear and **anxiety.** Fear is a response to an
actual stimulus. A person may feel fear if he stumbles across a rattlesnake, if he
sees a snarling dog racing toward him, or if a drunk approaches him with threats
of violence.

Anxiety, an emotional state closely related to fear, occurs when a person
worries about what *might* happen in the future or when he is fearful about some
vague or unknown thing that he cannot explain.

Watch airplane passengers when the plane begins to take off. Notice their
variety of reactions, such as gripping their armrests, closing their eyes tightly, or
staring straight ahead. These are signs of normal anxiety, of people anticipating
future possibilities. Here are some other examples of anxiety-provoking situations.

Your professor asks you to drop in to see him after class. You have no
idea what he wants, but you did copy part of your term paper directly from an
encyclopedia.

You have been driving about 20 miles an hour over the speed limit on a
deserted country road, and you see automobile headlights flashing on and off
in your rearview mirror.

About three weeks after applying for a job with a Chicago company,
you find a note in your mailbox stating that the post office has a certified letter

from Chicago for you. Unfortunately, it is Saturday, and the post office won't be open again until Monday.

You have just been informed that you will need an operation early next month. The operation is a routine one, resulting in complete success 97% of the time, and only 1 person in 200 dies as a result of it. But there is that 3% failure rate and that one death. . . .

When you feel anxious, you are strongly motivated to reduce the source of your tension. Sometimes the reduction of anxiety is so rewarding that you would rather know the worst than remain uncertain. Doctors report that patients who have been anxious about whether they will need an operation are relieved when the decision is made, even when the decision is that the operation will be necessary. Anxiety tends to be deficiency-motivating rather than growth-motivating.

Sometimes it is difficult to relieve anxieties. Some people seem constantly anxious, in which case their anxiety stems from their own feelings of inadequacy, not from what is happening in their environment. You frequently meet students who are constantly anxious about their grades, even though they do well in all their classes. In one such instance the student's anxiety resulted from his being compared to an older brother who was always at the top of his class; no performance of the younger brother could surpass that of the older, and parental praise was reserved for the older boy.

Tension-reducing behavior is very reinforcing, and a person may repeat such behavior on later occasions when he feels anxiety. Thus, if a freshman's anxiety concerning dating is relieved by avoiding dates (and assuming this solution does not produce even greater problems), he is likely to continue to avoid dating, even if it means missing some fun and making up some strange excuses.

Because feelings of fear produce discomfort, many people do their best to reduce fear in others. At times these attempts are misdirected, since fear, like other emotions, will often motivate adjustive behavior. In one study hospital patients about to undergo an operation were asked whether they were afraid; the degree of fear they expressed was found to relate to postoperative difficulties. Those who indicated very high *or* very low fear displayed more trouble in subsequent adjustment than those in between. In a follow-up study, some patients were told exactly what to fear in a forthcoming operation, but others were told very little. The former not only were better off psychologically, but their medical condition improved more rapidly (Janis, 1968). Patients who lack normal fear may be unprepared for the pain and subsequent discomfort of operations. They also lack the opportunity to anticipate and thus rehearse for the future. In a way, objective fear may serve as an inoculation to prevent worse fear, disappointment, and frustration after the event (Janis, 1968).

Fear and anxiety are constantly being discussed and written about by psychologists and psychiatrists; anger also gets a good bit of attention. Strangely enough, the more positive emotions (such as happiness, serenity, pity, elation) receive very little study (Maslow, 1970). Are these feelings less important? More difficult to study? Perhaps psychologists and psychiatrists are not yet able to escape their history of concern with helping the unhappy.

THE NATURE OF STRESS

Stress is a strong, unpleasant emotional force or pressure that produces feelings of **tension** or strain. The term *stress* is frequently used in physics and biology to refer to pressure, such as the stress of a weight resting on an iron bar or the stress of a bone pressing on cartilage. Stress in physics and biology implies that the resulting tension is accompanied by the possibility of distortion.

The term is used in a similar fashion in psychology. We talk about stress associated with academic pressure to succeed, which causes tension and perhaps distortion in the person's normal functioning. Driving on a crowded freeway while trying to get to an appointment on time is a stressful situation that leads to strain, distortion of normal driving habits, and possibly a traffic ticket.

Stress is inevitable in our daily living. Even young children meet frequent stress in their interactions with adults, with other children, and with their physical environment. Experience in meeting and dealing with normal, day-to-day stressful situations is not unhealthy for young children, assuming the stress is neither too great nor too frequent. As children learn to cope with mild stress, they gain in ability to cope with greater stress and are able to develop a self-concept of being competent and potentially independent. In the same way that a physically strong person can recuperate more rapidly from flu than a physically weak person, the mentally healthy person can withstand emotional stress better than a mentally unstable person.

Stress is definitely motivating, and the resulting behavior is directed largely at reducing the stressful conditions and the accompanying tension. The greater the stress, the stronger the motivation for its reduction. Stress may take the form of frustration, conflict, anxiety, or guilt.

FRUSTRATION

Have you ever gotten a flat tire while trying to get to a very important exam on time? This is an excellent example of a situation that may produce **frustration.** When a person cannot reach the goal he desires, or when the demands placed

FIGURE 8–3. A man-made frustration. Photograph by Lehman J. Pinckney.

on him are greater than his ability, frustration occurs. Frustrations may be caused by personal limitations, natural conditions, or man-made conditions.

Personal limitations. Most girls are never going to win a beauty contest, even if they are intelligent, charming, and clever at dressing and using makeup. If a girl is strongly motivated to win a beauty contest, she will probably be doomed to frustration.

Fortunately, winning a beauty contest is so irrelevant that it is not frustrating to many people, but other personal limitations are. Limited intelligence can keep a person from entering college; limited height can keep a competent soldier from being an officer; limited knowledge of English may cost a person the chance to get a good job. Limited social skills, limited business experience, limited funds, limited technical skills, limited strength — all these and many more can lead to mild or extreme frustrations.

Natural conditions. Conditions beyond our control can keep us from achieving a desired goal. A long period without rain will lead to limited food and water, destruction of farmland, and, often, the death of animals; a fire started by lightning can destroy hundreds of acres of timberland and homes; fog can delay the return home of thousands of airline passengers. A delayed flight may not be so critical as the destruction of a home; however, both can frustrate people.

Man-made conditions. Man is often his own worst enemy. He creates wars that result in death, pain, and frustration. Professors create frustrations for students, who in turn create frustrations for professors. Parents can provide great frustrations for children, who may not realize the frustrations they bring to their parents.

Not all man-made frustrations are bad. The man-made law against my stealing your car may frustrate me, but it is very much in your interest. Restrictions on hitting a person when you get angry with him may be frustrating, but not to the person about to be hit. Some drivers are frustrated by speeding laws, but this is no reason to discard the laws.

CONFLICT

Conflict occurs when an individual is motivated by two or more needs, and the satisfaction of one causes the denial of the other. A conflict will occur only if the alternative goals are fairly equal in importance. Confronted with the choice between a delicious hamburger and a $20 bill, you would rarely be in conflict, no matter how much you loved hamburgers. However, if you had not eaten anything for two days and the hamburger was the only food available, a conflict might well exist.

There are four categories of conflict: **approach-approach, avoidance-avoidance, approach-avoidance,** and **multiple approach-avoidance.**

Approach-approach. Two desirable and mutually exclusive goals create an approach-approach conflict. Examples of an approach-approach conflict would be deciding between two good jobs, choosing between buying a new suit and taking an exciting three-day trip, and debating whether to vote for a close friend or for someone else who is much more competent.

Avoidance-avoidance. Being forced to choose between two unpleasant alternatives leads to an avoidance-avoidance conflict. A few examples are getting a painful tooth pulled or having it continue to hurt, going on a date with a dull escort or staying home, and studying a very difficult and tedious textbook or risking an F.

Approach-avoidance.   Often one goal involves both pleasant and unpleasant features. A part-time job provides necessary spending money but cuts into free time and social life; joining the Navy for four years is patriotic and will enable you to visit exciting places, but it might do little for your career.

Multiple approach-avoidance.   Most real situations involve a complex combination of pleasant and unpleasant factors, as exemplified in the following hypothetical case.

> George is a college student who doesn't enjoy college, and he isn't doing especially well either. If he leaves school, he'll be drafted immediately, and he doesn't want to go into the Army. College will increase his lifetime income, give him a better understanding of the world, offer him enjoyable social activities, and perhaps allow him to escape the draft altogether. On the other hand, he's likely to flunk out, he's bored with his courses, and he can take over his father's hardware store whenever he wants. In addition, he's not so certain he wants to marry his steady girlfriend, although her father owns a chain of hardware stores and has no son to take into the business. Joining the service would be an easy way to get away from his girl, but it wouldn't help him in the hardware business. Besides, he hates marching and gets irritated when people give him orders.

George will have a difficult time making a decision. Settling conflicts becomes even more difficult because of the influence of unconscious motives. Part of George's motive for not wanting to get married is that the girl reminds him too much of his mother, who has made life miserable for his father by pushing him to be successful. Taking orders in the Army is too much like taking orders from his mother. Working in a hardware store symbolizes the life his father led, which frightens George because he does not wish to live like his father. However, George is not aware of these feelings, even though they do influence his behavior.

A study of real-life conflict resulted from a series of disastrous explosions that rocked the town of Texas City. People were caught in the conflict between wanting to see what happened to their families and wanting to do what they could to stem the terrible destruction, between wanting to save their own lives and property and wanting to help others (Killian, 1952).

Some people find making a decision very difficult. They cannot decide which movie to see, and so they end up missing the beginning; they cannot decide which job to accept and finally find that both have been filled; they cannot decide where to vacation and then learn that there are no more reservations. Such people may have weak self-concepts and be very frightened of making an error. They do not feel adequate in making decisions and are unwilling to accept the consequences of making the wrong decision.

ANXIETY AND GUILT

The discomfort caused by anxiety about the future and the discomfort caused by guilt over the violation of **internalized** standards of behavior in the past are both forms of stress. The tension that results from anxiety is particularly disconcerting because the specific source is vague and therefore difficult to deal with or to dismiss. Some people suffer from varying degrees of anxiety all the time. Termed **chronic anxiety,** this condition causes a continuing tension that constantly interferes with effective behavior. Guilt tends to be associated with a particular situation. However, a few people do seem to experience a chronic sense of guilt, so that virtually any occurrence will elicit guilt feelings.

> Joseph McArthur had internalized his father's value that any form of disobedience of parental authority was evil. When he was 16, all his friends were actively dating, but Joe's father would not allow him to date or to attend house parties. One morning he felt so frustrated that—for the first time in his life—he argued with his father. The discussion became increasingly heated, until Joe finally yelled "Oh, drop dead!" and stormed out of the house. That afternoon Mr. McArthur was killed in an automobile accident.
>
> Joe felt that the accident was God's way of punishing him for his disobedience, even though he knew that logically this was impossible. He began to have frightening nightmares in which his father came back as a ghost to threaten to kill him in revenge. For weeks he was unable to sleep until thoroughly exhausted, because he had a fear (which he again recognized as illogical) that he would die in his sleep. His guilt and his anxiety were slowly destroying his physical health and his emotional stability, until he finally sought help through a psychologist associated with his school.

Internalized values become very much a part of us, and when our behavior violates these values, guilt and anxiety are common responses. Joe had internalized the value that disobedience was improper, and when it seemed to him that his disobedience and his hostile statement were related to his father's death, he felt very guilty. No matter how hard he tried to persuade himself that there was no cause-effect relationship between his outburst and his father's death, he continued to feel that his sin was going to be punished, and his dreams were an expression of the fear that the punishment would be his death. Guilt and anxiety worked simultaneously.

Frustration, conflict, anxiety, and guilt occur constantly in the lives of all people. Sometimes stress becomes too great for the self-concept to maintain itself in the face of this stress. Then the individual, instead of being able to work toward utilizing his abilities to the fullest, consumes his time and energy in dealing with the stress.

FACTORS CAUSING STRESS

Innumerable situations, incidents, relationships, and conditions are stressful. Those that affect children are not necessarily the same as those that trouble college students, and those that disturb college students may differ from those that concern middle-aged people. Some types of situations, however, may be stressful for most age groups.

Family relationships. Even in emotionally well-adjusted families, stressful situations frequently occur. Frustration results when the parents have established such high standards for academic achievement that their children cannot possibly live up to them; conflict is felt when students develop religious beliefs and church-attendance patterns that their parents oppose; guilt and anxiety occur when parents begin to think their teenage daughter is having a sexual affair.

Some families attempt to work out their conflicts and frustrations together, perhaps through sitting down and discussing the problem and working out a solution agreeable to all. Other parents put their foot down and demand complete and immediate obedience—which they may or may not get. The reactions of most families fall between these extremes.

In a few families stress seems to be present all the time. Perhaps the parents fight with each other, placing the children in conflict; perhaps the father has such a great need to assert his own power that he constantly criticizes the children; perhaps the older brother has been so successful that other children are pushed to do as well, despite their interests and abilities.

Love and affection. Marriage, going steady, dating, and good friendships are all sources of great satisfaction and great potential stress. They can create anxiety (Does he really love me?) or guilt (I shouldn't have spent the night with him) or frustration (I love her so much, but she says I'm like a brother to her) or conflict (I wish he'd ask me out, but I can't flirt too much because he's dating my best friend).

Some individuals refuse to risk the possible unhappy consequences of love and affection. To receive full satisfaction from a human relationship, you have to take a chance that it will culminate in an unhappy separation. Any true affection means that you become dependent on the other individual and on the continuation of the relationship. In loving, you open yourself up to possible emotional pain, and—because of previous unhappy experiences or because of an inadequate self-concept—certain people are not willing to take this risk. They prefer giving little to a relationship, even if they get little in return, because they feel safer that way.

Opposing group standards. The ability to adhere to what you think is right when the entire group opposes your position is not only very difficult but also very stressful. Everyone has defied certain groups on minor matters—perhaps you have stood up for a friend the others were disparaging, expressed your admiration for a movie the others disliked, or defended a political candidate no one else voted for—and each of these little acts caused a certain amount of stress.

Opposing group standards on important issues opens a person up to more extreme stress. He may endanger his status in the group; he may be threatened with property loss and even bodily injury or death; he may be isolated from all his friends. At the very least he must face the conflict between remaining faithful to his values and making a major sacrifice.

Consider the stress and other forms of pressure that the following individuals face:

> —the dedicated political activist who identifies for the police the member of his organization who threw the rock that injured a riot squad officer.
> —the clergyman in an all-white suburb who actively advocates state laws that would result in integrating his community's schools with those of an adjacent, primarily black, area.
> —the professor who gives testimony to the state legislature that faculty teaching loads could be increased without loss of effectiveness.
> —the successful business executive who resigns his position with a strong verbal attack on the ethics of businessmen and corporation executives.
> —the young artist who readily admits he cares much more for money than for creativity or artistic values.

Sex-role demands.   Every society has forms of behavior that are acceptable for members of one sex but not the other. In our culture women are expected to take care of the home and the children while men produce income and perform heavy physical labor; women are supposedly talkative and indecisive, whereas men are silent and able to make decisions; women like romantic movies, and men prefer westerns. Men are expected to be more aggressive, better educated, and more interested in "things" as opposed to people.

Stress can occur when one's actual behavior is in contradiction to one's **sex role.** Men are more likely than women to feel frustrated when their parents pay for their college education. A girl who is known to make obvious sexual advances may find that many men are ambivalent or even negative about being with her, although comparable behavior in a man would have much less impact. Both husband and wife may feel uncomfortable if the wife is more successful in her job than the husband is in his, and the discomfort is intensified if they are both in the same field.

Expression of sexual and hostile-aggressive behavior.   Most Americans have internalized the values that sexual behavior and hostile-aggressive behavior should not be expressed openly. Hitting someone when you get angry or "making a pass" when your sexual needs are aroused is certainly forbidden by custom, and often by law. Even the thought of sexual or hostile-aggressive behavior may be considered improper (recall the story of Joseph McArthur).

But, even though you cannot express these feelings, you continue to have them, and the frustrations caused by not being able to act according to your feelings can be very stressful. After being teased by his younger sister for failing English, Jerry exclaimed "I wanted to hit her so much I could feel my fist tingling."

When sexual or hostile-aggressive feelings are expressed in a socially or personally unacceptable fashion, guilt and anxiety ensue. If Jerry had hit his sister, his guilt and anxiety would have caused more stress than expressing his feelings would have settled.

Problems with authority figures. Ask any policeman, teacher, minister, or parent about the resentment some people have toward authority. We have all had to work toward becoming independent, and most adults have succeeded. However, some people find themselves unable to accept any authority or sign of not being independent. Usually those who fight authority the hardest have either had unpleasant experiences or are unable to feel secure in their independence.

Academic and vocational success. Even though definitions of "success" may vary, most people consider academic and vocational success important. Pressures to succeed come from all around. One's family, friends, general community, and, often, one's self-concept all encourage a high level of academic and vocational achievement. Frustrations are acutely felt by those who do not measure up to their own standards of success. Perhaps even more stressful are fears and anxieties like "I may not make it." Such anxieties are likely to be stronger in the United States, which might be termed an achievement-oriented society, than in countries where greater importance is attached to success in having many children or in being recognized as a good wife and mother, a valiant warrior, or a cooperative member of the community.

Financial pressures. No matter how wealthy a person appears, he may not have enough money to satisfy himself. As income and financial worth increase, the level of aspiration tends to rise proportionately. Ask someone who has been working for ten years whether he could get along on what he was earning seven years ago. Then ask him whether he had fewer financial problems seven years ago or today. People all over the world envy the material possessions and financial opportunities of Americans, but Americans themselves are not necessarily satisfied.

Money is a source of stress between husband and wife, parent and child, employer and employee, and, occasionally, college and student. Cheating, stealing, lying, and killing have often been the results of pressure to obtain money.

The love of money may not be the root of all evil, but it is undoubtedly the root of some.

If having money can cause conflict and anxiety, imagine the frustration that results from having no money, especially if the economically deprived individual sees others around him living much better. The misery of poverty is bearable until the impoverished suddenly decides that lots of people are much better off than he and that he deserves to have a better life than he has been living. This is an example of what has been called the law of **relative deprivation.**

Think of the stress caused by not having enough to eat, not being able to keep warm, not having the skills necessary for a job, not being able to live without worrying how you and your family will eat or where they will sleep tomorrow or next week, or not being able to have occasional entertainment. These instances illustrate absolute poverty, not relative deprivation.

Health problems. As long as health is good, people seldom think about it. When health is poor or as people grow older, health worries increase. Poor health or physical defects or limitations can cause great stress.

DEATH AND LOSS

When the prospect of death appears, other causes of stress seem to shrink in importance. This is true whether it is your own death or that of someone close and important to you. Evidence that the stress is great is shown by the number of words and expressions we use to discuss death — without ever saying *dead:* passing away, going west, no longer with us, beyond the Great Divide, in heaven, life insurance (rather than death insurance).

Many people dislike talking about death and dying, except in a very abstract way. They feel "it isn't nice." As a matter of fact, so many similarities have been observed between the topics of death and sex that death has been called the new pornography (Gorer, 1965). But in the past few years death — perhaps also like sex — has been discussed with much greater freedom.

OUR OWN DEATH

Can you conceive of a time when there will be no more you? Is it possible to deal with such a thought? Or is it just impossibly unreal? Many people cannot accept the idea of their own death, even though they plan for it in such ways as taking out insurance and making wills. If you ask people whether they are afraid

FIGURE 8–4. Many symbolic acts, events, and things are involved in death. Photograph by Lehman J. Pinckney.

of death, most of them will say they are not. However, younger people admit to more fear of death, whereas older people indicate that they think of death more often (Kalish & Reynolds, unpublished data). More than 400 persons in Los Angeles, roughly equally divided among blacks, Japanese, Mexicans, and Anglo Americans, were asked how strongly they felt about what their dying would mean. Their reactions are shown in Table 8–1.

When we die, we suffer from several kinds of loss. First, we suffer from losing the people and the things that we love and enjoy; second, we lose our own identity, since we are uncertain about who (or even if) we will be after death; third, we lose control of the body and, indeed, the body itself (although some religions compensate for this); fourth, we suffer because our family and friends will lose us.

People tend to go through psychological stages as they die. The first stage is *denial*—the feeling that "It can't be me. I can't die." Slowly the person accepts that he is going to die and enters the second stage, *anger* for having been chosen. Anger is followed by *bargaining:* "I'll pray every day if I don't die." "I won't care if it hurts a lot, as long as I can live." Next is *depression*, at which point the dying person recognizes that he cannot hold death off. And finally comes *acceptance*, when the individual comes to peace with the inevitable and begins to plan

TABLE 8–1.   Importance of reasons for not wanting to die, as given to interviewers by 434 black, Japanese American, Mexican American, and Anglo American respondents in the Greater Los Angeles area (Kalish & Reynolds, unpublished data).

	Very Important	Important	Not Important
	(Percent of all respondents)		
I am afraid of what might happen to my body after death.	5	9	86
I could no longer care for my dependents.	40	29	31
I am uncertain as to what might happen to me.	11	19	70
I could no longer have any experiences.	7	21	72
My death would cause grief to my relatives and friends.	25	48	27
All my plans and projects would come to an end.	13	31	56
The process of dying might be painful.	20	35	45

to use his remaining time for the things that are most important to him (Kübler-Ross, 1969). These stages do not always take place in this exact order; not everyone goes through each stage; and it is not unusual to move back and forth between stages. But the stages do show some general trends.

THE DEATH OF OTHERS

When a death occurs, the social structure of the family, of the work setting, and of other situations is disrupted. Either a replacement is found, or else the tasks done by that person are taken over by several other people or are left undone. When old people or very young babies die, the tragedy is not considered so great (Kalish & Reynolds, unpublished data), since others are not dependent on them and the death is less disruptive than that of a young mother or teenage son.

A major controversy has developed regarding whether a dying person should be told that he is dying. Can he be shielded from the knowledge of his death, when he receives cues both from the pain and discomfort within his body and from the changing attitudes of his family and the attending medical personnel? I feel that most people, including children, have the right to know that they are dying, provided that they show signs of wanting to know. This does not necessarily mean that someone must sit down and tell them they are dying—only that their questions should be answered honestly and fully. How do you feel about this?

Loss is very painful for the survivors, and the dying person often is more concerned about their emotional pain than about himself. It is not unusual for a dying person to pretend he does not know he is dying, so that his loved ones are not required to share his sorrow. In the meantime his family members and physician are trying to hide the truth from him. This is called a mutual pretense situation (Glaser & Strauss, 1965).

Since the dying process is both emotionally and physically painful for all concerned, dying persons are sometimes avoided both by the medical staff and by relatives and friends. Human kindness is replaced by medicines and life-sustaining machines, and sometimes death is postponed, but at the sacrifice of meaningful life. A great deal of discussion has recently centered around helping people die with dignity, and a British physician has established a hospice near London to care for patients whose physicians feel nothing more can medically be done to help them.

Is there such a thing as a will-to-live or a will-to-die that can make a difference between life and death? Much disagreement centers around this issue also, but many physicians and others believe that people's attitudes about living and dying can make a difference in their resistance to illness. Perhaps some of the physiological responses that accompany emotional reactions will eventually be used to explain will-to-live and will-to-die.

BEREAVEMENT

When someone you feel close to dies, you are sad because of the loss of friendship, companionship, and love; but sadness is not the only way to respond to grief. You may also feel guilty for the arguments you had, for not having been nicer than you were, or for having been neglectful. You may find that the image of the dead person is constantly in your mind's eye and that you continue to think of him, even when you wish to do other things. You may even show physical symptoms, such as loss of appetite, an empty feeling in the stomach, or a lack of your usual muscle power (Lindemann, 1944).

The mentally healthy response to the stress caused by bereavement is complex. People who try not to show grief or who try to avoid thinking of the deceased person often take longer to recuperate from the loss. Crying and unhappiness are normal grief reactions, and tension is often caused by trying too hard to avoid displaying emotions (Lindemann, 1944). Once the grief is expressed, the person can begin to adjust to a life without the deceased and can begin to enter into new relationships.

SUMMARY OF IMPORTANT IDEAS

1. Humans are capable of feeling and displaying a great range of emotions.

2. An emotion is a feeling or state of arousal that stirs an organism to observable action or to internal change.

3. When an emotional state occurs, the body undergoes certain internal physiological changes; since these changes are usually difficult to observe, we often need to accept the report of the individual that he is feeling an emotion.

4. Emotions can be motivating. On occasion, emotions can reduce the effectiveness of behavior, but they are more likely to increase the effectiveness of behavior.

5. At birth the only emotion expressed is excitement or arousal.

6. Some emotional responses occur almost inevitably; others occur as the result of learning.

7. In every society people learn which emotions may properly be expressed under which conditions.

8. Anger and other emotions may be displaced on scapegoats.

9. Emotional restraint, although often necessary, can be carried too far.

10. Anxiety, an emotional state similar to fear, results from worried anticipation of the future or concern over some vague or unknown and unexplainable possibility.

11. Stressful conditions include conflict, frustration, anxiety, and guilt. Stress is inevitable in day-to-day living, but not all individuals have an equivalent ability to cope with stress.

12. Specific factors leading to stress include family relationships, love and affection, opposing group standards, sex-role demands, sex behavior and hostile-aggressive behavior, problems with authority figures, academic and vocational demands, financial pressures, health problems, and death and bereavement.

13. When death occurs, other causes of stress seem less important. This is true whether it is your own death or that of someone close to you.

9 Reacting to Stress

You have just finished reading about the nature and causes of stress. This chapter discusses the variety of responses that stress elicits. Since every individual finds himself having to cope with stress throughout his life, many of the behavior patterns mentioned in this chapter will be familiar to you. You may even have noticed some of them in yourself—which is, of course, to be expected.

The architects who planned the Egyptian pyramids designed them with a strong, solid base, and the structures have withstood the punishment of many centuries. Men who design today's long-span bridges allow for some swaying in strong wind, because bridges with "bend" are less likely to break. If psychologists could design personalities as engineers and architects design structures, they would specify a strong, solid base and enough flexibility to prevent breaking.

The impact of stress on humans, like the impact of stress on buildings, is small if a firm base exists. For humans the base would be the strength of the self-concept, which is directly related to the **stress tolerance** of a particular individual.

Flexibility, or adaptability, is also needed to withstand stress. Rigid people, who are unable to modify their behavior in the face of stress, are very likely to be harmed by the stress. In a violent storm a thin bush with deep roots will neither break nor blow away, but a tall rigid tree may break, and a bush with shallow roots may be pulled out by the force of the wind. (However, a bush that is too flexible bends and twists in the slightest breeze, and no one ever knows its real form.)

The specific response to stress of any given individual depends on his self-concept, stress tolerance (or frustration tolerance), and methods of adjustment, as well as on his previous experiences, the specific nature of the stress, and the immediate situation. Some major categories of response include bodily changes; rigidity, withdrawal, aggression, and disorganization; defense mechanisms; violence; and coping and new growth motivations.

BODILY CHANGES IN RESPONSE TO STRESS

Every change in behavior involves a pattern of physiological changes. The brain, the **nervous system,** the **receptor** and **effector organs,** the voice box, and many other parts of the body must work together when you touch a hot stove, yell "Ouch!" and pull your hand away. More complicated forms of behavior involve more complex patterns of bodily change.

According to one theory, the body undergoes three stages of physiological change in response to stress. At the initial sign of stress, the *alarm reaction* occurs, at which point the body rapidly organizes itself to get ready to cope with the stress. The second stage, *resistance,* describes the continued attempt to cope with the problem. The final stage, *exhaustion,* comes after the body has used its resources in fighting the stress. This pattern of responses, termed the **general-adaptation syndrome,** describes the physiological workings of the body, which in turn determine much observable human behavior (Selyé, 1956).

PSYCHOSOMATIC PROBLEMS

If the tension produced by stress continues for a long period of time, the resulting bodily changes will continue also. Unfortunately, these bodily changes, which initially protect the individual against stress, may have a harmful effect if extended too long and may contribute to such physical disorders as ulcers, asthma, and skin problems.

Physical disorders arising from stress are termed **psychosomatic** disorders. They are real physical problems (not imaginary, as some people think), but, instead of resulting from germs or from a blow to the body, they result from physiological changes induced by stress. A psychosomatic headache is very painful; a psychosomatic asthma attack causes real danger.

Ulcers may be caused by emotional tension that leads to an unusually heavy and long-term flow of chemical secretions produced by the body. Under normal circumstances these chemicals are manufactured for only a short time, and the body's defenses can cope with them. With certain types of emotion (for example, chronic resentment) or as the result of extremely intense emotions, the chemicals are produced over a longer period of time or in greater quantity, and the body cannot maintain its defenses. Eventually the chemicals overwhelm these defenses and cause sores, or ulcers, on the inner walls of the stomach (Sanford & Wrightsman, 1970).

Unlike conversion reactions (discussed in Chapter 10), psychosomatic disorders produce recognizable **organic** symptoms that may require medical treatment if they become incapacitating. Like other reactions to stress, these disorders appear in both mild and severe forms.

One young college couple encountered a psychosomatic problem that finally ended their relationship:

> Ed Bradford and Rita Alonzo met during tennis class, spent that evening together, and were inseparable by the end of the week. They responded perfectly to each other. After a few weeks of an increasingly warm and exciting relationship, Rita became a little worried. She felt that any possible marriage was far in her future, and Ed had begun to talk as though they were a permanent couple. She debated breaking off with Ed but finally decided to continue to see him.
>
> On the way home from a party one night, Rita's eyes began to tear, her nose got extremely red and runny, and she sneezed and sneezed and sneezed. She excused herself as soon as she arrived home, leaving Ed mildly frustrated and unhappy.
>
> Their next evening together ended the same way. The time after that Ed was on guard, and he arranged to get to Rita's early, supposedly to watch television. A young married couple from next door was there, and Rita showed no signs of a cold. When the neighbors commented that they would be leaving after the news, Rita's eyes began to cloud, and she started to sniffle. By the time the weather report came on, her cold was going full blast.

Many other psychosomatic symptoms come to mind: the headache the night before a difficult examination, the nausea after seeing the mutilated victim of an automobile accident, or the rash that develops during especially anxious periods. But these are not particularly damaging psychosomatic disorders compared with ulcers and asthma, which build up over a long period of time and produce serious medical symptoms.

That stress is associated with the onset of disease is well established, but the mechanism through which the stress operates is not fully understood. Studies have shown that the death of a spouse can cause an increase in illness (Parkes, 1964) and that an accumulation of life crises (for example, divorce, loss of job, or being imprisoned) may be followed by much more frequent illness than would be anticipated by chance (Rahe & Arthur, 1968). Since the body is known to respond to physical stress with physiological change, and since it has been shown that the body can also build physiological defenses against social stress, it seems logical that social stress could lead to tissue damage and to the development of psychosomatic illnesses or the worsening of illnesses already in progress (Mechanic, 1968). On the other hand, the crises might have brought about a change in behavior patterns and personal care. A woman whose husband has just died and a man who is suddenly unemployed may alter their way of living so that their health deteriorates. Psychosomatic change and behavior-pattern change very likely interact dynamically with each other to produce the increase in stress-caused illness.

OTHER BODILY REACTIONS TO STRESS

Psychosomatic disorders are not the only bodily reactions to stress. Fatigue and bed-wetting are other frequently observed occurrences. Emotional tension over an extended period of time can be very tiring. Three hours of a difficult examination may be more fatiguing than three hours of physical labor; driving a dynamite truck is usually more tiring than driving the same truck loaded with wooden crates. The body mobilizes its energies to cope with stress, but the expended energies must be renewed through sleep or rest.

Fatigue and the resulting sleep can also be a form of escape. How often have you had the following,type of experience?

8:00 P.M.	You sit down to study. Tomorrow you have an examination, and, even though you are not fond of the textbook, you feel hopeful and almost enthusiastic.
9:00 P.M.	You have read one chapter and now feel impossibly sleepy.
10:00 P.M.	You cannot keep your eyes open any longer. You have read only a few pages during the past hour, and you remember little of what you read because of the brief naps you took between sections. You decide to watch television, since you are not getting any real work done.
11:00 P.M.	After an hour of television, during which you are not in the least sleepy, you return to your studies.
11:10 P.M.	You decide that, since you are too sleepy to study, you may as well get a good night's sleep before the examination. So you go to bed.
1:00 A.M.	You are still tossing and turning in bed. You have not been at all sleepy since you put your book down.

Fatigue has served to remove you from the unpleasant or stressful situation of studying for a course you do not like or for an examination that causes you to feel anxious.

Some physiological responses to stress are so commonplace that we often do not think about them seriously. You have probably had the experience of waking up in the middle of the night to find your teeth clenched tightly together. Your hands perspire, or you feel your heart pounding, or you know your stomach muscles are tight. Although these experiences are not likely to produce a long-term effect on your health, they can easily disrupt your activities for the moment.

Other kinds of physiological responses to stress often take place without our awareness. For example, the secretion of one biochemical substance by the body in response to psychological stress makes the skin more difficult to penetrate, decreases bleeding, and increases muscular output; another chemical affects energy levels; a third influences alertness. In most instances these automatic physiological responses aid in survival (DiGiusto, Cairncross, & King, 1971).

RIGIDITY, AGGRESSION, WITHDRAWAL, AND DISORGANIZATION

Stress produces not only biochemical changes but also many overt behavioral changes. Some of the more familiar patterns of stress-induced behavior include rigidity, aggressive behavior, **withdrawal,** and disorganized behavior.

RIGIDITY

People, like bridges and bushes, need some flexibility in the face of stress. They need to be able to re-evaluate their behavior and their beliefs — not at the slightest pressure, but when the situation is appropriate. However, certain individuals become extremely rigid when faced by stress. When the situation causes them to feel anxious or confused, they fall back on previous forms of behavior, rather than investigate new possibilities.

Some people appear to behave in a rigid fashion much of the time. They may see only black or white, rather than shades of gray; they may prefer being told what to do, rather than have to decide their actions for themselves. The world of today is a fantastically complex place, and some of its problems seem almost impossible to solve; but rigid individuals continue to believe in simple, clear-cut solutions.

Because rigid people need something definite to cling to, they are said to have **intolerance of ambiguity** — that is, they cannot accept or cope with vagueness and uncertainty but require rules and guidelines. They feel cheated by the psychology professor who cannot give them exact rules for psyching out their friends; they resent the artist whose painting can be interpreted in numerous ways; they become suspicious of the mechanic who cannot guarantee whether regular or premium gasoline is better for their car; they distrust the minister who feels that different religious views might be equally truthful. When they go on vacation, they need to know exactly where they are going, when they will arrive, how long they will be there, and what they will be doing.

AGGRESSIVE BEHAVIOR

Stress, especially frustration, elicits feelings and expressions of anger and aggression. You may direct the aggression toward the cause of the frustration, toward another source (displacement), or toward yourself; or, you may attempt to ignore the feelings and not act on them at all. Have you ever become so frustrated by pounding a nail crookedly that you smashed at it with your hammer, missing the nail but not your thumb? Have you ever forgotten that you parked your car in a tow-away zone and then cursed yourself out for being so stupid?

Later in this chapter violence is discussed as a response to emotion-arousing stimuli. Such violence is a form of aggressive behavior and often arises from frustration. Whatever other causes may have contributed to the prison and ghetto riots of recent years, the high level of frustration in the minority communities has certainly been a—and perhaps *the*—major source of aggressive behavior. Have you ever felt so frustrated that you were ready to turn your aggression into violence? Have you ever actually become violent as the result of frustration?

WITHDRAWAL

Withdrawal as a response to stress can be either physical or psychological, although the two are related. Physical withdrawal occurs when a student fails to appear for an examination because he is poorly prepared; the soldier who deserts when he is ordered into a combat zone is also withdrawing physically. Psychological withdrawal can occur even in the presence of other people. When someone embarrasses you, you can withdraw into silence; if you learn that someone you thought was a close friend has been slandering you, you may respond very coldly next time you see him (that is, you are withdrawing from the relationship).

Drugs and alcohol can also be used to withdraw psychologically. You take a few drinks or ingest some mood-elevating drug, and the world seems a more pleasant place again. The self-concept, which might have suffered because of guilt or frustration due to failure, is temporarily adequate and the threatening future looks cheerful again. After the effects of the drug or drink wear off, the problems return, so that being high becomes more rewarding than not being high —and back to the drug/drink. Heavy use of liquor or drugs for escape does nothing to change the outside environment but only temporarily changes the outlook on the environment. To make matters worse, few people do anything to change their circumstances when they are drinking or taking drugs, so that the problems are likely to intensify, leading to more highs, and a circular frustration pattern of drinking/taking drugs → withdrawal → more liquor or drugs → more withdrawal is established.

FIGURE 9–1. Sleep is a way of withdrawing temporarily from stress.
Photograph by Lehman J. Pinckney.

Tranquilizers and sleep are two other ways of withdrawing temporarily from stress. Physicians may recommend tranquilizers to help a person feel better during a particularly tense situation. A person may retreat into sleep but then wake up feeling better equipped to deal with his problems. (In Russia, sleep is used as a form of psychotherapy.) Both types of withdrawal can be useful but are sometimes abused through overuse, and neither deals directly with the tension-inducing problem.

People can even use recreation, hobbies, television, schoolwork, sports, or their jobs as ways to withdraw from the demands of the world around them. Have you ever known anyone who withdrew into a world of "things," such as mechanical activities or books, in order to escape from the world of people?

DISORGANIZED BEHAVIOR

You may have heard the expression "He got on his horse and went galloping off in all directions." The implication is that the person described has become disorganized, a common reaction to stress. Frustrations, conflicts, and anxieties can become so great that an individual is no longer able to function effectively. He vacillates back and forth between one decision and another; he makes foolish errors on simple tasks; he forgets to do things that he normally never forgets. These are all forms of disorganization resulting from stress.

Rigidity, withdrawal, aggressive behavior, and disorganized behavior are all basic reactions to stress. Such reactions may also be expressed through defense mechanisms.

DEFENDING THE SELF-CONCEPT

The need for self-esteem—and a resulting healthy self-concept—is very important. If you do not respect yourself, your energies are expended in justifying your own behavior to yourself, and little effort can be channeled into developing your potential capabilities. When frustration, conflict, anxiety, or guilt threatens your self-concept, you tend to defend yourself and try to retain a satisfying self-concept.

Each individual, in his attempts to maintain and improve his self-concept, especially in the face of stress, utilizes certain types of behavior, termed **defense mechanisms.** These mechanisms operate unconsciously and automatically, so that he is not aware he is using them (Coleman, 1964). For example, the fox who could not reach the grapes decided they were sour. He defended his self-concept against having to accept failure. If he had said to himself "I'll pretend they're sour," he might have fooled others, but he would not have been able to fool himself and thus could not have defended his self-concept.

Probably the most basic of all defense mechanisms is **repression.** Repression occurs when an individual is unable to recall or recognize something because of unconscious needs to deny the awareness. The concept of repression is at the core of the psychoanalytic theory of personality, as described by Sigmund Freud.

> Sid Janson was an effective campus politician. He managed to win every time he ran for office, except for the time he lost the election for vice-president of the senior class. Many years later, when he bumped into an old friend he had not seen since graduation, Sid's politicking career was brought up. "I wasn't too bad," Sid said. "I never lost an election." His friend mentioned that he had lost his campaign for vice-president of the senior class, but Sid shook his head. He was able to name six or seven offices he had won, including that of treasurer of the German Club, but he could not recall losing any.

If Sid was able to recall winning the relatively unimportant German Club office, it is unlikely that losing the senior class vice-presidency would have been forgotten. Rather, he had repressed this blow to his self-esteem.

Not only memories but also ideas and feelings unacceptable to the self-concept are repressed. A child who is deeply resentful of some parental behavior may repress his resentment, since to recognize it would cause him to direct anger against the parent, an act unacceptable to his self-concept. The entire process, of course, is unconscious.

A conscious attempt at forgetting or ignoring something is called **suppression.** When a favorite uncle of yours is very sick, you may try to forget about his illness by going to a movie; when you are very angry with your closest friend, you may decide to work your anger off through a hard game of tennis. In these instances you are not fooling yourself, but you are making an effort to ignore the anxiety you feel; perhaps you will find it easier to hide your worry from your uncle when you visit him or your anger from your friend when you see him next (assuming, of course, that you want to hide your feelings from them). Suppression, according to the definition used in this book, is not a defense mechanism.

Many sorts of defense mechanisms have been observed. Some mechanisms redirect responsibility from yourself to other people or things; some allow you to withdraw either psychologically or emotionally; still others enable you to gain support for your self-concept by affiliating with those recognized as more capable. The following discussion covers only a portion of the possible categories of defense mechanisms.

REDIRECTING MECHANISMS

Sometimes a person seems to be trying to say "Not me. I didn't do it. I couldn't. I'm not that type. It must have been some other guy." He does not actually make such statements, but his behavior implies that, unconsciously, he wants to redirect responsibility away from himself.

A very common redirecting defense mechanism is **rationalization,** which is the attempt to make behavior or feelings seem rational, sensible, and consistent with the self-concept, when they really are not. Here are some common rationalizations for a low examination grade. Remember that the students expressing these ideas actually believe their statements to be true.

"There were too many tricky questions." (That may be true, but it does not explain why the other students were not tricked.)

"All the questions came from the one chapter I didn't read." (This also may be true, but a careful check usually shows it is not.)

"You never knew what the professor really wanted to know." (But the other students apparently did.)

"I'm not interested in the course—the teacher is boring." (This may be true, or it may be a rationalization by a student who is afraid he will fail.)

"I didn't study." (Why? Is this a rationalization by a student who unconsciously felt he did not understand the course well enough? Was he afraid to try, because if he did try and then failed, he would have no excuse left?)

Each of these rationalizations explains failure in such a way as to protect the self-concept. It redirects the cause of failure to sources outside the self.

Projection is another way of redirecting responsibility. Two types of projection occur: first, denying your own thoughts and feelings and attributing them to someone else; and, second, justifying your own behavior by claiming that others feel the same way.

> A 5-year-old had just been bawled out by his teacher for socking another child.
> "I had to do it," he sniffled.
> "Why?" asked the teacher.
> " 'Cause he wanted to hit me, so I hit him."
> "How do you know he wanted to hit you? He was playing with the blocks."
> "I just knew."
>
> In talking to his 16-year-old son, a father said "All men want money and power. Those are the only real goals in life."

The 5-year-old is transparent in his use of projection (although nations have used the same defense mechanism for going to war), but the father's statement is less obvious as a projection. Whether or not he is correct, he is probably projecting his own attitudes toward money and power onto "all men."

Sometimes people feel so guilty or anxious about their unconscious feelings and motives that they lean over backward to deny them. They say, in essence, "I'm not the one you mean. Look—I'm just the opposite." This is an example of **reaction formation.** The self-concept is protected by an exaggerated display of behavior indicating feelings opposite to those actually felt.

> Jay Laub was the most aggressive, girl-hungry fellow on campus. He went out three or four nights a week and talked freely, although vaguely, about his supposedly active sex life. Still, he had a reputation among girls as being easy to handle. His conscious self-concept was a reflection of his behavior: popular, aggressive, debonair. Unconsciously, however, Jay was afraid of girls, but he could not admit this fear to anyone, especially to himself. He was saying, unconsciously, "I'm the fastest, most popular, most aggressive guy around —it's obviously impossible even to consider that I'm afraid of girls." Jay had been engaged five times, but had not married, by the time he was 36.

Movie and book censors, who reserve for themselves the right to see or read what they forbid others to see or read, may be using reaction formation. They seem to be saying "Look how moral I am—I not only oppose seeing such terrible movies, but I keep other people from seeing them. Of course, I have to see them myself, but don't get me wrong—I don't really enjoy it."

Often people have feelings and needs, especially of an aggressive or sexual nature, that cannot be expressed directly. When you feel extreme anger toward authority figures, such as policemen, parents, or teachers, you are often frustrated in your attempts to show anger. Since in all likelihood you would be punished for expressing your feelings, you redirect the anger through the defense mechanism of **displacement.** Instead of expressing anger toward the person or thing responsible, you direct it at someone or something else. You cannot kick the teacher or yell at the traffic policeman; so you kick the wastebasket and yell at the clerk in the store —they are your scapegoats.

Rationalization, projection, reaction formation, or displacement occurs without your realizing that something other than objective perception and appropriate motives elicits your behavior.

WITHDRAWAL MECHANISMS

Rather than face a threat to the self-concept and its resulting discomfort, people may withdraw. Some people withdraw into **fantasy,** the defense mechanism through which they create their own world rather than face the conflicts, frustrations, and anxieties of the real world. Although the content of the fantasy is conscious, the ways in which the fantasy protects the self-concept are not conscious.

> Myrna Toland had never affiliated with any political group, but she did have vague feelings that women's rights were being ignored. When a young male professor made several negative comments about the intellectual and emotional capacities of women, Myrna started to answer him back. But she became flustered and finally sat down, amid the giggles of other students. As the professor's lecture droned on, Myrna re-enacted the confrontation—but in her fantasy she made the professor look very foolish.

Fantasy is not the only type of withdrawal. Rather than retreat into a dream world when the present is too filled with anxiety and frustration, you can unconsciously withdraw into the past. An older child may demand to drink from a bottle and begin to wet his pants when his baby brother is born, even though he had been weaned and toilet-trained two years earlier. He is using the defense mechanism of **regression** to return to an earlier form of behavior. In the face of frustration, adults will often regress to name calling, threats of violence, and other forms of childish behavior. When people long for the good old days, they are, in a way, expressing a desire to regress from the stress of the modern world.

People also withdraw from the emotional impact of frustration or anxiety through **intellectualization.** One student with a religious conflict undertook a study of religion and tried to bury his conflict in an intellectual explanation. Another student, whose fiancée broke off their engagement just three weeks before the scheduled wedding, developed a lengthy explanation, using all sorts of psychological terms, for his ex-girlfriend's behavior.

When a person is apathetic, we usually assume that he is just not interested. However, **apathy** can be a defense mechanism used unconsciously when frustrations or conflicts are too great. Removing oneself completely from the situation reduces the threat to the self-concept. "I don't really care if I make the team or not" protects the speaker's self-concept. If he does not make the team, his self-concept is not greatly damaged; if he does make the team, it is all to the good. Some students claim they are bored or apathetic about college when they are unconsciously trying to withdraw from a tension-provoking situation.

AFFILIATING MECHANISMS

Identification is the unconscious act of taking for oneself the attitudes, values, and behavior of some person or group. As such, it is very important in the socialization process, and parents are often very much concerned about those with whom their children identify. A boy will identify with his father, and perhaps with a popular television hero as well. Such identification adds to the boy's self-adequacy, because he feels, to some extent, that *their* abilities and positive traits are now *his*. The young child is expected to identify with the parent of the same sex and behave like that person, at least in regard to sex role. The concept of identification is very similar to internalization, which refers more specifically to values and attitudes.

DEFENSE MECHANISMS AS CRUTCHES

We use most defense mechanisms to fool ourselves about ourselves. They function much like a psychological crutch to support an anxious self-concept. Like every crutch, they are necessary at certain times. You do not remove a person's crutch until he can walk without it; if you try to do so, he will either reject your offer or will fall and hurt himself.

To carry the analogy further, when a person on crutches reaches a certain point in his recovery, he can begin to walk for short distances without them. However, premature removal of the crutch will cause the patient to fall and will perhaps worsen his condition.

FIGURE 9–2. A boy will identify with his father. Photograph by Lehman J. Pinckney.

If the doctor forces the patient to discard the crutch before he is ready, the patient may find a cane that is lying around the house, he may become angry and get another doctor, or he may not use the crutch when the doctor is around but continue to use it at other times. Sometimes, when the patient is nearly ready to walk without the crutch, the encouragement from the physician is just what is needed to get him back on his feet, especially if the first trial steps are firm and not painful.

The parallels between the physical crutch and the psychological crutch become more apparent through the experiences of Loren Kane.

Loren Kane was working part-time, attending college part-time, having a reasonable social life, and scraping through his courses with just enough decent grades to keep from flunking out. During the two years he had been doing this, he explained to everyone that he knew that he could improve his performance if he could only go to school full-time, but his widowed mother was too ill to work, and he was needed to support her and himself. Just before he began his third year, his mother's illness worsened and she died, leaving Loren an unexpected $10,000 from her insurance policy. Loren's fiancée immediately insisted that he quit his job and take classes full-time. This provoked him into an argument, which resulted in his breaking their engagement. Loren soon became involved with another girl, who was less concerned about his education and more concerned about his income. He now told his friends that he could not take classes full-time because he had to save money to get married.

Loren needed the rationalization crutch of having to work in order to avoid facing the possibility that his academic capacities were not sufficient to do better than he was doing. When he was threatened with losing his crutch, he clung to it. When the "doctor" (his girlfriend) tried to get him to take a few steps without the crutch, he got rid of her. He then found another "doctor" who believed in crutches. What could happen to give this story a "happy ending"? What ending do you assume the story actually had?

Professionals in psychology, psychiatry, and social work are extremely cautious in their attempts to get people to throw their crutches away, and they prefer to try to reduce the need for the crutch in other ways. Eventually, when the self-concept no longer needs defending, the crutch is given up without resistance.

Defense mechanisms of many varieties are evident in normal (as well as non-normal) behavior. All of them are alike in that they occur automatically, are used unconsciously, cause us to look good in our own eyes, and make our behavior appear consistent with our self-concept. These mechanisms serve an important purpose for the individual using them, and mental health goals are not served by premature attempts to persuade people not to use them.

VIOLENCE AND THE EMOTIONS

"Violence," claimed a leading militant of the 1960s, "is as American as cherry pie." Is this true? Does the violence of assassinations and street riots stem from American traditions, from the actions of a few disturbed people, or from chance circumstances? To what extent can violence be prevented? Can this prevention be brought about through the crackdown of power, through psychiatric treatment, or through biological changes?

The rage that leads to violence is undoubtedly associated with frustration, but not all highly frustrated people become violent and not all violent people are visibly frustrated. Violence seems to run in families, but, again, we cannot determine the degree to which it is transmitted to children through the genes or instilled through learning experiences in the environment (Rosenfeld, 1968).

Rage and violent behavior have been produced in animals by electrical or chemical stimulation; they have been controlled by drugs or radio signals. "The doctor can, by pushing a button and sending a radio signal, induce a peaceful monkey to go into a rage and attack other monkeys. When he releases the button, the monkey is peaceful again" (Rosenfeld, 1968). This evidence certainly suggests that the potential for violence resides in human physiology, and very possibly this potential differs from person to person as a result of genetic factors. Maslow (1970) even suggests that a psychological need for violence may exist — that fighting and conflict may be, in part, a natural occurrence. However, if this were the case, socially acceptable channels for the direct and indirect expression of violence are available.

Does the evidence mean that environmental influences have little to do with violence? The answer is most definitely "No." Violence occurs only when it is aroused by environmental conditions, usually through anger and frustration, although other forms of stress may be involved. The individual's ability to cope effectively with stress is also related to his ability to deal with the motivation to become violent.

If you agree with one sociologist (Wolfgang, 1970) that violence is "physical injury to persons and damage or destruction of property," then you will very likely also agree with him that violence is not always inappropriate. Whether or not you feel violence is called for depends on how you feel about the person who is being violent, the victim of the violence, the goals of the violence, and the situation in which it occurs (Wolfgang, 1970). Your opinion is based on your personality, upbringing, and value system. Violence occurs in boxing matches and bullfights, in spankings and child abuse, in the commission of crimes and the punishment of suspected and convicted criminals, in wars of aggression and defenses against wars of aggression, and in revolutionary wars presumably waged in the cause of freedom.

Although it is debatable whether people are born with substantial differences in predisposition to violence, it is not debatable that immense cultural and social differences exist regarding the frustrations that lead to violence. The ABC of the *subculture of violence* consists of: (A) the high urban crime rate and the immense numbers of people who carry or keep guns and other weapons, combined with (B) feelings of anger and aggressiveness and a readiness to violence, and (C) a value system that encourages violent behavior to establish masculinity or to gain revenge. You may want to make the case that (D) is the mass media, since movies, television, and even newspaper articles may provoke people with a predisposition to violence, although without these sources of excitation they would remain relatively calm. Even the sight of a gun can increase the tendency to act out violent and angry behavior (Berkowitz, 1968).

The history of the world details the history of violence: wars, assassinations, suicides, revolutions, burnings, and bombings. One side's hero is the other side's

FIGURE 9–3. Violence or threat of violence elicits feelings of fear or anger. Photograph courtesy Columbia Broadcasting System.

villain, and the winning side gets to write the history books so that future generations know whom to honor. (Very different descriptions of the American Revolution often appear in texts in the United States, Canada, and England.) In recent years the violence in both Southeast Asia and the urban United States has received great attention. The Report of the National Advisory Commission on Civil Disorders (1968) stated that the basic causes of urban American riots were: (1) pervasive discrimination and segregation, (2) black migration into urban areas and white migration out, (3) conditions of poverty in the black ghettos and the observation of relative prosperity among blacks living outside the ghettos, (4) rising expectations that were not fulfilled, (5) observation of violence, (6) the frustration of powerlessness, (7) encouragement to violence by the verbal abuse of whites who hate blacks and by the rhetoric of those black militants who responded in kind, and (8) the police, who symbolize white power to many blacks.

These causes were listed in 1968. Do you feel they were valid then? Are they valid in regard to the prison riots that occurred a few years later? Are they valid for the urban tension and violence that exist today?

None of us are immune to rage and violent behavior. Overcrowded living conditions may reduce the *threshold* for violent behavior. Constant exposure to violence in entertainment, in the news, and in political speeches may also reduce the threshold. The minor frustrations of everyday life probably contribute. Given sufficient cause, almost anyone might feel rage (Rosenfeld, 1968). Violent behavior appears to result from the dynamic interaction between human physiology, the individual's background and general environment, and the arousal properties of the specific situation. In consideration of these factors, how do you feel about the claim that a political assassination or a war is the responsibility of an entire population?

COPING STRATEGIES AND GROWTH RESPONSES

Perhaps our discussion thus far has left you with the feeling that human response to stress is essentially a holding action—that is, people can only defend themselves against the impact of stress. Fortunately, this is not the case. Your reaction to stress can be extremely effective, and, under some circumstances, you will end up the better for having had the experience.

You are not a passive entity, to be buffeted around by stress with only defense mechanisms to aid you. You can cope directly with stress in a number of ways. Coping, as Maslow (1970) shows, means getting something done; it means causing change. It is a kind of behavior that you decide to undertake. Three direct-action forms of coping have been suggested (Lazarus, 1969). First, you can prepare against the potential of stress; second, you can make a direct attack on the causes of stress; third, you can decide to retreat from or avoid the sources of stress.

Effective coping with stress often involves growth responses. Part of your preparation, attack, or avoidance can involve increased motivation to learn and self-actualize, new insights and new levels of aspiration, and new approaches to old problems. You could also decide to learn to live with the stress if you feel it is unavoidable.

INCREASED MOTIVATION TO LEARN AND TO SELF-ACTUALIZE

Stress is often caused by a lack of learning or lack of accomplishments. Therefore a stressful situation may motivate new efforts and new learning, which lead to increased self-esteem and the opportunity to use available talents. If your frustration stems from being unable to dance, you can learn to dance; if you feel anxious about talking in groups because your vocabulary is limited, you can find numerous sources of help; if you feel guilty because you have not written to your grandparents in nearly a year, you could write to them.

Classroom exams provide stress that motivates learning; competition for an award motivates greater effort; suffering a great personal tragedy may cause time and life to seem more precious and more worth exploiting for your personal satisfaction. In each of these instances the resulting behavior may be deficiency-motivated or growth-motivated, depending on the specifics of the situation and on the individual.

NEW INSIGHTS AND NEW LEVELS OF ASPIRATION

Patrolman Hazarian had just been promoted to sergeant and placed in charge of the department's drug-education program. Feeling confident that he knew all about drugs and all about young people, he launched a series of speeches at local schools and youth centers. Students were required to attend in the schools but not in the youth centers. The officer began to notice that his school audiences seemed increasingly restless, and his youth-center audiences had dwindled to almost nothing. At first he blamed the teachers and parents. But he finally realized that his task was not merely to give talks but to reduce drug usage—and there was no doubt he was failing. From this acceptance of his own responsibility for failure came a willingness to talk with—instead of at—his audiences and to listen to all views, not just those he agreed with. His new insights led to reduced, but more realistic, aspirations.

Sometimes the insight produced by stress may require a new level of aspiration. A politician is subjected to so much stress after losing the nomination for mayor three times straight that he decides to run for another, less important, post. A student who tackles an advanced mathematics course and does poorly decides to take a refresher course at a more elementary level. A salesman becomes frustrated because he is bored with his work and finally recognizes that he needs a different sort of challenge in his occupation.

If stress provides you with a better understanding of yourself or with a new, more appropriate, level of aspiration, it has served a useful purpose.

NEW APPROACHES TO OLD PROBLEMS

A situation may become sufficiently stressful that you are motivated to seek a more effective way to deal with the matter. Thus the second time you arrive 15 minutes late for class, your instructor waits in silence as you walk nervously to your seat, all eyes on you; that evening you set the alarm 15 minutes earlier. Responding to a different kind of stress, a physician devotes considerable time and energy to finding an effective treatment for a disease after years of frustration because he was unable to help his suffering patients. A supervisory secretary, frustrated after spending too much time looking for a letter in the files, reorganizes the filing system for the entire company.

LEARNING TO LIVE WITH STRESS

Sometimes there is nothing you can do to eliminate stress. For example, you have an ill parent, or the draft board is going to re-evaluate your deferment, or you have had a recent traffic accident and the hearing is next Monday. Such stressful situations do occur, and you are powerless to eliminate them. Thus all you can do is try to deal with your reactions to the stress. Perhaps talking to a professional counselor or close family friend or personal friend will help. Sometimes you can only try to ignore the stress or live with the stress and put additional effort into the tasks that the anxiety has disrupted.

SUMMARY OF IMPORTANT IDEAS

1. The degree of stress tolerance is related to the strength of the self-concept and the flexibility of the individual.
2. Physiological changes occur in response to stress.
3. A psychosomatic disorder is an organic problem induced by stress.
4. Other bodily reactions to stress include fatigue and bed-wetting.
5. Overt behavioral reactions to stress include rigid behavior and intolerance of ambiguity, withdrawal, aggressive behavior, and disorganized behavior.
6. Defense mechanisms are unconscious reactions that serve to protect the individual's self-concept and enable him to interpret his behavior as being consistent with his values and self-concept.
7. Defense mechanisms may redirect responsibility (rationalization, projection, reaction formation, displacement), allow for withdrawal (fantasy, regression, intellectualization, apathy), and produce feelings of affiliation (identification).
8. Defense mechanisms often function as psychological crutches. There is danger in using them longer than necessary, but removing them too quickly can also be dangerous.

9. Violence is an ancient problem that has had major repercussions recently in this country. Some kinds of violence are encouraged by the culture, whereas other kinds are discouraged.

10. Responses to stress may produce growth (for example, increased motivation, new insights and new levels of aspiration, and new approaches to old problems). Sometimes the individual must learn to live with the stress in his life.

10 When Defenses Fail

When stress becomes so great that the individual can no longer cope with it through normal defense mechanisms and other response patterns, the result may be faulty or disordered behavior. The degree of disturbance may become so extreme that the person requires professional help or even hospitalization. On the other hand, the behavior disorder may be such that he can care for himself and continue a relatively normal life, even though certain aspects of that life may appear strange or self-defeating.

Nuts, loony, crazy, out of your mind, psychotic, mentally ill, emotionally disturbed, cracked, insane, mentally deranged, screwy, daft, batty, bats in the belfry, mad—the more different words we use to describe something, the more important it is to us. Obviously much effort, energy, time, and money are expended in working with and caring for the emotionally disturbed; similarly, much effort, energy, time, and money, as well as emotional pain, family and social disruption, and lost potential are the costs of severe emotional disturbance to the disturbed individuals themselves and to their friends, families, co-workers, and others in their environments.

WHO IS NORMAL?

Have you ever been worried that you "weren't all there"? Did you ever do something "a little nutty"? Is it possible that you are not normal? What is *normal* behavior?

This last question is not easy to answer. First, keep in mind that "normal"

FIGURE 10-1.   Did you ever feel that you weren't "all there"? Photograph by Lehman J. Pinckney.

and "average" are different concepts. For example, average height for adult American males is about 5 feet 10 inches, but normal height would probably range from about 5 feet 3 inches to 6 feet 4 inches. Student grades may average a little above a straight C, but normal people receive grades of straight F and straight A, although both of these extremes are unusual. The average person does not play chess, but chess players are certainly normal. Normality, then, is a wide range of possible behavior, not just an average.

Second, what is normal in one society or in one time period is not normal in another society or another time period. In 1750 it was normal to believe that witches could destroy your cattle by putting a curse on them; today we would not consider such a belief normal in our culture. In Nepal many citizens believe that smallpox is the "kiss of the gods," but that idea would not be considered normal in our country. So, to some extent, normal behavior depends on the time and the place in which it occurs.

Third, the concept of normality is usually expanded to include values and morality. According to some persons, it is not normal to disbelieve in God, to feel that wars can be justified, to engage in sex without love, or to join a commune. Thus in some ways normality refers to patterns of behavior and values that are considered morally defensible by whatever individual or group is defining what it is to be normal.

This book will use another definition of normality: a normal person is one who knows the difference between what is real and what is not, who does not use defense mechanisms to excess, who is able to get along satisfactorily outside an institution, and whose day-to-day behavior is not dominated by *excessively* rigid, irrational, or self-defeating actions. According to this definition, a person may be far from average yet still be normal.

SYMPTOMS OF THE NON-NORMAL

There is no particular point at which a person moves from normal to non-normal. Certain types of behavior are, at least in our society, clearly normal; certain types are clearly non-normal; certain types are borderline. Consider a simple rationalization for not getting a job, as expressed by four different people:

"I didn't get the job, even though I'm qualified, because I don't have a college degree." (Probably normal rationalization; perhaps true statement.)

"I didn't get the job, even though I'm qualified, because the supervisor is afraid to hire someone smarter than he is." (Probably normal rationalization; probably not true statement.)

"I didn't get the job, even though I'm qualified, because the personnel director is part of a secret ring of scientists who are trying to get control of the company, and they know I will expose them." (Probably no longer normal; probably not true statement; person may be mentally ill.)

"I didn't get the job, even though I'm qualified, because the president of the company is under the control of the devil, who has eaten away his brain and now wants to take over the plant to control the world." (No comment necessary.)

Many deeply disturbed people behave normally most of the time, and almost all normal people show some mannerisms, ideas, or behavior that might be considered non-normal. A cold shares certain symptoms with pneumonia; a student who has drunk one bottle of beer shares certain characteristics with an alcoholic. Yet no one would claim that a cold *is* pneumonia or that taking one drink *is* alcoholism.

Emotional disturbance is not an all-or-nothing condition—it is a matter of degree. The following symptoms of emotional disturbance are often found in normal people but may occur in exaggerated form in deeply disturbed individuals:

Depression: feeling that everything is going wrong, that nothing matters.

Inappropriate worry and fear: constantly worrying or being afraid of one thing or another, far out of proportion to the actual cause; suffering chronic anxiety.

Suspicion: being unable to trust others; feeling that others are deceitful.

Inadequate emotional control: crying, being frightened, getting angry far out of proportion to actual stimuli.

Depersonalization: feeling unreal, not belonging to one's body, not really a person.

Overly strict emotional control: not showing emotions, even when appropriate circumstances occur.

Fantasy: daydreaming so much that little gets done.

Rigidity: having difficulty in behaving or thinking in new ways; having a tendency to follow rituals in behavior.

Organic symptoms: suffering from fatigue, illnesses, and ailments that occur without medical basis.

Hostility: being unduly ready to fight, argue, or verbally attack others.

Ineffectiveness: being unable to make decisions; disliking responsibility for one's own behavior; behaving in an immature fashion.

Unhappiness and tension: seeing the world as a difficult, tense place.

Inadequate interpersonal relations: having contacts with other people marked by hostility, arguments, tension, suspicion, overdependence, and other signs of inadequacy.

From time to time everyone exhibits behavior patterns like those just described, and exaggerated worry about them may be labeled *symptomitis*, a disorder common among college students.

Webley R. Confused had a classic case of symptomitis during his freshman year. When his psychology professor talked about rationalization, Webley knew he himself rationalized all the time; when he heard about sibling rivalry, he recalled how much he disliked his brothers; when he studied religious values, he realized that he had a religious conflict. When the professor lectured on mental disturbances, Webley panicked—he had every symptom the professor described, and the more he heard, the worse they became.

People who overestimate the importance of some insignificant example of unusual behavior are creating unnecessary stress. People who underestimate the importance of consistently unusual behavior are ignoring a potentially real problem.

The final evaluation should be left to professionally trained individuals. Very few untrained people consider themselves competent to diagnose cancer, to construct a skyscraper, or to program a computer. Unfortunately, many untrained people feel competent to diagnose and even treat serious emotional problems. Trying to determine who has received adequate training is a more difficult matter. Teachers, ministers, lawyers, policemen, and physicians are constantly placed in the position of being asked to help people with emotional problems. How should they respond in such situations? The validity of advice rendered through newspaper and magazine columns appears especially open to question. It is implausible that even the most capable individual can learn enough about the writer of a brief letter to offer him valuable advice. These columns probably do no harm, however, as long as they are read for fun.

"I don't know exactly why, but people always seem to come to me with their problems. I guess I'm that sort of person." No doubt you have heard someone say something like that, or perhaps you have made the comment yourself. What are your responsibilities when people bring their problems to you? How should you respond?

BEHAVIOR UNDER SEVERE STRESS

The person under severe stress is in a bind. As feelings of frustration, conflict, guilt, or anxiety build up, he finds it more and more difficult to respond effectively and within the range of normal behavior. He may need to turn to highly exaggerated forms of behavior or, eventually, to behavior considered non-normal. The situation forces him to adapt to extreme stress, and he learns ways of doing so. However, the behavior he learns is likely to disrupt other aspects of his life. When he does find a way of behaving that enables him to avoid the stress-produced feelings, this behavior is reinforced because it reduces his discomfort, even though it may be destructive in the long run. A person learns that living in a world of fantasy is less painful than facing reality; he learns that attributing his own sexual impulses to the forces of Satan is less painful than accepting himself as he is. And just as a student learns a correct response when a teaching machine reinforces his answer with the word "Correct," the person suffering greatly from stress learns the "correct" response through being reinforced by tension reduction.

As the stress continues to build up, the faulty adjustment becomes more obvious, and the resulting behavior becomes more rigid, more irrational (from the observer's point of view), more confused and disorganized, and less in touch with reality. If the stresses are moderately severe, the person will find great difficulty in being successful or happy in certain phases of his life but will be able to function in the day-to-day world. If the stresses are very severe, the person may need protective services or hospitalization, since he can no longer care for himself or be responsible for some of his actions.

FIGURE 10–2.   People who can withstand stress probably had early family relationships that provided support and love in times of frustration. Photograph by Liane Enkelis.

Why are some people able to withstand stress better than others? Psychologists believe that those who can satisfy their physiological, safety, love, and self-esteem needs are better able to withstand stress than those who cannot. Such persons have established a strong and secure base, so that the world is not interpreted as threatening or disturbing. These people tend to come from homes in which the family relationships enabled them to feel loved and wanted, and they have developed a concept of themselves as individuals of value and worth. They feel that they are likable because they have been liked; they feel respected because they have been shown respect; they feel secure because they have been given security. In essence, normal, effective, and perhaps self-actualizing behavior has been possible, and it has been rewarded. Since they do not need to direct their efforts at warding off anxiety and other outcomes of stress, these people approach their problems realistically, and the world seems a relatively understandable and friendly place.

Like everyone else, the emotionally disturbed try to find ways to cope with the stress in their environment. However, because of the interaction between their own unique, often faulty, personality structure and the intense stress that occurs, their method of coping does not enable them to lead a satisfactory life. Rather than consider them abnormal people, you might think of them as people under abnormal stress. Keep in mind that the stress is abnormal *for them* because of their background and personality—it might impress you as being rather mild stress if you do not understand their experiences and feelings.

ORIGINS OF EMOTIONALLY DISTURBED BEHAVIOR

Perhaps by now you have asked yourself "But what is it that's disturbed? Is it behavior or feelings or body chemistry or what?" The answer is complex. We talk about disturbed *behavior,* because we recognize that it is faulty and non-adjustive; we talk about disturbed *feelings* or *emotions,* because we assume that underlying the behavior is the subjective feeling of great discomfort; we talk about disturbed *body chemistry,* because we have learned that biochemical changes influence the subjective feelings and the behavior (see the section on violence in Chapter 9). And sometimes we refer to the disturbed or disordered *personality,* a term that encompasses a variety of aspects. When we want to alter the disturbed condition, we can attack it through behavior, through the underlying emotions, or through body chemistry. Each approach has its proponents and its opponents.

How, exactly, do genetic inheritance and biological changes work to influence resistance to stress? The answer is necessarily incomplete, but many psychologists would agree with one authority (Coleman, 1960) who says that genetic factors can operate in two ways. First, people have differing degrees of stress tolerance at birth. Thus some persons, because of inherited (or, perhaps, because of later biochemically changed) brain chemistry, would show severely disturbed behavior in response to relatively little environmental stress, whereas others would remain free of symptoms unless their life history and present environment were extremely stressful. Second, inherited differences may help determine the particular type of personality disorder that occurs. We would not state that a person has inherited a particular mental disorder, but we would say that he might have inherited a predisposition or a reduced resistance to that disorder. Combining the two assumptions, if three different individuals were subjected to exactly the same life history and exactly the same present stress, one might develop a personality disturbance of one type and severity; the second might develop a disorder of another type and severity; and the third might show no signs of behavior disturbance whatsoever.

Although the evidence for this point of view is far from complete (see Chapter 4), if it turns out to be the case, all serious mental disorders will be shown to have some biochemical basis. It is also possible, of course, that only certain kinds of disturbed behavior will be traced to brain chemistry, or that the same symptoms will be shown to occur with a biological basis for one person and with a psychosocial or faulty learning basis for another.

Frequently newspapers announce that a biochemical basis for some mental disturbance has been found and that the disorder will soon be under medical control. Unfortunately, these early reports usually are not verified by follow-up studies, or the proposed treatment does not have a long-range effect. One recent report, however, does show promise. The investigators are studying children from the age of 8 on. Results after eight years of follow-up indicate that medical difficulties during pregnancy and at birth are predictive of later emotional disorder (Mednick, 1971). For the time being, however, we need to approach these results with great caution.

DIFFERENTIATING NEUROSES AND PSYCHOSES

The two major classifications of severe emotional disturbances are **neurosis** and **psychosis.** Both neurotics and psychotics may display exaggerated forms of behavior patterns (described earlier in this chapter). Neurosis is considered a relatively mild personality disturbance that usually does not incapacitate the individual or demand his hospitalization. Psychosis is a very severe personality disturbance that may necessitate hospitalization. The differences between neurotic behavior and psychotic behavior are not always clear-cut, but the following may serve as an acceptable guide:

1. Psychosis is more severe and implies greater personality disorganization.
2. Psychotics are often dangerous to themselves or others and may destroy property; neurotics rarely are dangerous in these ways.
3. Psychotics usually need hospitalization both for care and for protection; neurotics can usually get along without special care and without hospitalization.

4. Psychotics rarely recognize that they are emotionally ill, but neurotics are often aware of their symptoms, even though they cannot change their neurotic behavior.
5. Psychotics may show intellectual deterioration, but neurotics can function at or near their normal intellectual level.
6. Psychotics are out of touch with reality in some way; neurotics can differentiate reality from nonreality, although they are unable to control the aspects of their own behavior that are affected by their neuroses.
7. Neurotics are much more likely to respond to psychotherapy than are psychotics.
8. Psychotics often exhibit delusions and hallucinations; neurotics do not.

Differentiating meaningful categories of neurotic and psychotic disorders turns out to be a much more difficult task than it might seem. Three important questions require consideration.

First, should there be categories? Some people argue that placing people in pigeonholes destroys their individuality and causes others to view them only in terms of their categories. Moreover, people do not behave exactly the way the categories suggest, and different professional observers often end up disagreeing about which category a particular person fits into. But without using some kind of classification system, communication becomes impossibly difficult (think of the communication problems that would arise if none of the departments in your college had a name).

Second, if categories are worth developing, on what should they be based? On the symptoms of the disturbed person? On the severity of the disorder? On the preferred method of treatment? On the future course of the disorder? On the causes of the difficulty?

The third question is obvious: once you have decided the bases for the classification system, what categories do you use? The American Psychiatric Association (1968) has decided that classification systems are valuable, that they should be based on symptoms (which undoubtedly are related to severity, treatment, future course, and causes), and that it would be helpful if everyone used the same system. The following discussion is based on the system devised by psychiatrists and accepted by most psychologists.

NEUROSIS

Neurosis refers to relatively mild personality disturbances, chiefly characterized by anxiety. This anxiety is sometimes expressed openly, but it is often controlled by the individual and expressed only indirectly through neurotic behavior (American Psychiatric Association, 1968). Although neurotic persons can get along without hospitalization or constant supervision, they do exhibit symptoms that interfere with effective functioning.

The major categories of neurotic behavior include *anxiety neurosis, hysterical neurosis, phobic neurosis, obsessive-compulsive neurosis, depressive neurosis, neurasthenic neurosis, depersonalization neurosis,* and *hypochondriacal neurosis* (American Psychiatric Association, 1968). However, keep in mind that people do not fall neatly into these pigeonholes. Not only do many individuals display symptoms from more than one category, but symptoms do not remain static—disturbed people change their behavior patterns just as all others do.

ANXIETY NEUROSIS

Anxiety is a fear of something vague, uncertain, or nonexistent. A person suffering from **anxiety neurosis** feels great fear or anxiety with no apparent immediate cause. Bodily changes such as rapid heartbeat and extreme perspiration often accompany these feelings of anxiety. Both the subjective feelings and the bodily changes, which are influenced less by the external environment than by the emotional state of the individual, are likely to become chronic in a person suffering from neurotic anxiety reaction.

HYSTERICAL NEUROSIS

In **hysterical neurosis,** the individual suffers the loss of some motor, sensory, memory, consciousness, or identity capability. The two forms of hysterical neurosis are **conversion type** and **dissociative type.** The former refers to the loss of sensory or motor functioning without apparent physical damage. A person is said to suffer from hysterical neurosis–conversion type when he cannot see, but no damage has occurred to his eyes, brain, or nervous system. Medical treatment is often useless, because no organic problem is present. This kind of neurosis should be differentiated from *psychosomatic illness* and from *malingering.* The former is a real physical illness caused by emotional stress; the latter refers to the act of purposely faking some type of medical problem. In hysterical neurosis no bodily changes are found, and no conscious faking is involved. Despite the lack of actual organic symptoms, however, the hysterical symptoms appear to be real and do share certain characteristics with normal medical problems.

A young auto mechanic had caught his hand in a vise and severely injured the nerve. However, after the hand had completely healed medically, he was still unable to move it or to be sensitive to any sensation from the wrist to the fingers—even a needle jab elicited no response. The physician decided that a psychiatrist should examine the mechanic.

The psychiatrist quickly diagnosed the problem as *glove anesthesia*, probably a hysterical response to some form of anxiety and stress. That it had no organic basis was obvious because the anatomical structure of the wrist and hand would not permit that particular region to be incapable of function. But the diagnosis was easier than the treatment.

The therapist learned that the mechanic hated his work in general and his job and employer in particular, but he had a wife and two young children to support, and auto mechanics was the only field that permitted him to earn a reasonable living. He was caught in a double bind, and the generous company sick-leave policy and disability insurance permitted him to remain away from work and still draw his salary.

Over a period of weeks the psychiatrist did enable the mechanic to understand what he was doing, and the paralysis disappeared. Within ten days after returning to work, however, the mechanic was fired from his job when, while being bawled out for getting grease on a new Cadillac, he threw a pair of pliers at his boss.

The second type of hysterical neurosis, dissociative behavior, can itself be further subdivided. The **multiple personality,** a very rare occurrence in real life, is popular in fiction. This disorder refers to the condition in which one person exhibits two or more distinctly different personalities. Often Personality B is aware of Personality A, but the latter does not recognize the existence of the former.

Another dissociative symptom is **amnesia,** also very popular with writers of fiction. Amnesia is the total or partial blocking of memories concerning certain past events or periods of time. It is usually assumed to result from emotional stress working through the mechanism of repression. When this memory blocking occurs over an extended period of time, the condition is termed a **fugue state.** Some fugue victims will actually begin a new life with a new identity, although such cases are rare.

PHOBIC NEUROSIS

From time to time a person will exhibit a dread or morbid fear of some object, person, or situation. This morbid fear, or **phobia,** is much stronger than the situation normally calls for. Perhaps you occasionally feel a little uncomfortable in a small elevator, but the person with claustrophobia (fear of enclosed places) might perspire, shake, or even faint in the elevator. Whatever produces the **phobic neurosis** is often interpreted as a symbolic substitute for the real cause of fear and anxiety.

OBSESSIVE-COMPULSIVE NEUROSIS

In the famous sleepwalking scene in Shakespeare's *Macbeth,* Lady Macbeth, some time after her husband has killed the king, wanders through the halls of the castle muttering "Out, out, damned spot!" She is attempting, symbolically, to rub her hands clean of the blood of the king, whose murder she encouraged, but she cannot do so. Lady Macbeth is obsessed with the idea that she has the king's blood still on her, and she feels compelled to continue rubbing and cleaning her hands. The **obsession** is the idea, and the **compulsion** is the behavior. Obsessions and compulsions are usually considered "a single . . . behavior pattern" (English & English, 1958).

In **obsessive-compulsive neurosis,** a person's thinking is dominated by a feeling, image, or idea—he is obsessed by it. The compulsive behavior is an attempt to cope with the obsession through some ritualistic act, which seems to be a symbolic attempt to ward off the "evil." The compulsive behavior often seems irrational not only to observers but to the person himself.

> Rocky Prater went to college only because of pressure from his older brother. Unfortunately, he got into several courses he hated, so that the entire schoolday seemed difficult and dull. Shortly before midterms, Rocky developed the obsession that he was forgetting to set his alarm clock. He would wake up in the middle of the night with the terrible feeling that the alarm was not set, but it always was. Still, he compulsively continued to go through this alarm-checking ritual at least once every night and often more frequently.
>
> Finally his counselor helped him realize that his obsession resulted from his conflicting desires to (a) avoid class and (b) get there on time. After his talk with the counselor, Rocky's obsessive-compulsive behavior began to fade away.

Rocky was certainly not seriously neurotic, in spite of his exhibiting this particular obsessive-compulsive behavior pattern. As a matter of fact, his specific symptom is not unusual in college students. Rocky's case is an excellent example of how a normal person can have one non-normal pattern of behavior that interferes only slightly with day-to-day effectiveness. What other examples of obsessive-compulsive behavior have you observed?

DEPRESSIVE NEUROSIS

We have all had the feeling that nothing is going the way it should, that life offers little fun or pleasure, and that the future appears bleak. But when a person maintains such attitudes constantly and far in excess of what conditions justify, his symptoms are those of **depressive neurosis.**

NEURASTHENIC NEUROSIS

The person suffering from **neurasthenic neurosis** feels constantly fatigued and lacking in energy. However, the fact that you feel overwhelmingly tired the moment you begin to study does not mean that you are neurotic.

DEPERSONALIZATION NEUROSIS

Sometimes a person feels that the world is unreal—that he is not himself, not part of his body, not in his environment, not a person. He is depersonalized. In **depersonalization neurosis,** this feeling would occur quite often, be fairly severe, and be mildly incapacitating.

HYPOCHONDRIACAL NEUROSIS

The walking medicine cabinet is a well-known, much-laughed-at figure. The person suffering from **hypochondriacal neurosis** is always involved with his health, his real or feared illnesses, and his physicians and medicines. Although his fears are not delusions in the psychotic sense, he is unable to rid himself of these feelings, regardless of medical advice. The hypochondriac often wanders from physician to physician.

Before you worry too much about seeing yourself in these descriptions of neuroses, recall the plight of Webley R. Confused.

PSYCHOSIS

By and large, humans can deal with stress well enough to avoid becoming psychologically incapacitated. Occasionally they use neurotic defenses to cope with the stress in their lives. Sometimes, however, for reasons not fully understood, the person under stress will not use neurotic defenses but will respond by losing touch with reality—that is, by becoming psychotic. A psychosis can be either organic or functional.

Much mental disturbance results from **organic psychosis.** This term refers to behavior disorders induced directly by brain damage, such as brain tumors, syphilis of the brain, brain injuries, lack of blood supply to the brain, or chemical changes affecting the brain. Organic psychosis often takes the form of **chronic brain syndrome,** which cannot be reversed through psychotherapy or other environmental changes, although its impact may sometimes by lessened. There are two major types of chronic brain syndrome: **senile psychosis,** which sometimes affects the elderly, is brain change that produces behavior disorder, memory loss, and confusion; the second type is brain change resulting from overuse of alcohol (Morgan & King, 1966).

FIGURE 10–3. The real world becomes too painful, and the person retreats into a world he has created for himself. Photograph by Lehman J. Pinckney.

Functional psychosis occurs when the stress in the environment becomes greater than the person can tolerate and overwhelms his defense mechanisms. The real world becomes too painful, and the person retreats into a world he has created for himself, where he has learned he can avoid the extreme discomfort of the stress. This does not imply, by any means, that psychotic people are happy. The general opinion of ex-patients and of professionals working with the mentally disturbed is that they are extremely unhappy, fearful, anxious, suspicious, and— for the most part—unable to enjoy work, human relationships, or anything else, no matter how they might appear to a casual observer.

Individual differences in the cause, symptoms, and future prognosis remain vitally important. Even with organic disorders, the picture of the disturbance is affected not only by the particular kind of brain damage, but also by the unique history and present life circumstances of the victim. A consideration of both biochemical and environmental factors is necessary for a full understanding of mental disorder.

The major categories of psychotic behavior include *schizophrenia, affective disorders,* and *paranoid states* (American Psychiatric Association, 1968).

SCHIZOPHRENIA

Schizophrenia is the most common classification of psychosis, although whether the term refers to a single disorder or a group of related but still different disorders is still uncertain. In reading the following description, based on the American Psychiatric Association system (1968), continue to keep in mind that people rarely fit neatly into categories—either they show symptoms that are not consistent with a given category, or their symptoms change over time, so that what seems to describe them today is less accurate next month.

The person suffering from **simple schizophrenia** shows a loss of interests, loss of ambition, emotional indifference, and withdrawal from social relations (Coleman, 1964). Situations that would arouse deep emotional feeling in a normal person receive only a casual shrug. This schizophrenic copes with stress by withdrawing from most of the world, but he often remains sufficiently adjusted to avoid hospitalization.

Perhaps the most dramatic form of mental disorder is **paranoid schizophrenia.** This schizophrenic has bizarre delusions (false beliefs) and frequent hallucinations (false perceptions). His behavior is often aggressively hostile and extremely unusual, and he will almost inevitably come to the attention of the authorities.

Barney Hauser came from a very strict, devoutly religious family and had been brought up with a strong sense of the horrible price a person pays for sin—whether actual or fantasized. During his senior year in high school, his parents decided to divorce. Shortly after they separated, Barney had a dream that recurred frequently in later weeks. In the dream Barney was told that he was a re-creation of Jesus Christ and that "the Son of God would be thrown out of the House of God."

As the dream was repeated again and again, he came to believe it was true, and he thought of a way to test the dream's truth. In the poorest section of his city was an old church called the "House of God." Since this was the phrase that turned up in his dream, Barney visited the minister of this church to ask his advice. The minister quickly realized how disturbed Barney was and asked him to leave, but Barney refused and began to pound on the desk in his excitement. The noise brought some men from the store next door, and they held Barney while the minister called the police. Barney was taken from the church to the nearest psychiatric hospital. However, the entire occurrence only confirmed his dream: the Son of God (Barney Hauser) was being thrown out of the House of God.

Barney's experience shows how hallucinations (the voice in his dreams) and delusions (the belief that he was the re-creation of Jesus) form a pattern of behavior of the mentally disturbed. A person is considered to have paranoid delusions when he feels people are always talking about him, plotting against him, trying to kill him, or asking him to conquer the universe.

The person suffering from **catatonic schizophrenia** may spend days, weeks, or longer in an apparent stupor. If his hands are placed on his head, they may remain there for hours (try it for a few minutes). He needs to be dressed, bathed, and fed. In spite of his apparent withdrawal, the catatonic is often very much aware of what is going on, and his passive behavior occasionally changes into violence, probably accompanied by hallucinations and delusions.

Confused, immature, and often silly, the person with **hebephrenic schizophrenia** has strange ideas and responds inappropriately to emotional situations. He uses words incorrectly and sometimes makes up his own. The hebephrenic frequently regresses to childish behavior.

AFFECTIVE DISORDERS

Affective disorders refer to major disruptions in mood. A person with an affective disorder may exhibit extreme depression or extreme elation, often accompanied by delusions and hallucinations. Some patients alternate between a depressed state and an elated or **manic** state. In between the two moods such a patient may function normally in the community for months or even years. This condition is termed **manic-depressive psychosis, circular type.**

Most manic-depressive patients, however, display only manic or only depressed symptoms. The manic is, in varying degrees, joyful, boisterous, and excited; he claims that everything in the world is just wonderful. He talks rapidly and constantly and is very optimistic, although these attitudes may be interpreted as camouflage for low self-esteem.

The depressed patient is just the opposite. If he is inactive, sad, pessimistic, and prone to delusions about being dead or rotting away, he is suffering from **retarded depression.** If, on the other hand, his depression involves much activity, rapid walking, and talk about how terrible he is, the symptoms describe **agitated depression** (White, 1964). Both types display considerable self-hatred and frequently discuss suicide.

One other type of affective disorder deserves mention. **Involutional melancholia** is depression characterized by worry, anxiety, agitation, and severe insomnia. It typically occurs between the ages of 45 and 55 in women and between 50 and 60 in men. Impending old age and concern regarding loss of vitality and sexuality are believed to be causal factors.

PARANOID STATES

Paranoid (as opposed to paranoid schizophrenic) persons develop a system of delusions that is consistent, seems to make good sense, and is often persuasive to others. The delusional system often centers around persecution or grandeur, but the rest of the individual's behavior seems relatively normal. Some paranoids have hallucinations, but they do not discuss them because they know they will not be believed. The condition is relatively rare.

> Peter Beschwan, a competent engineer, was fired from his job with a missile-research company. The reason for his dismissal was a book outlining a new theory of aerodynamics that he had written and had published at his own expense. When the company's senior engineers read the book, they expressed great doubt that Peter had any idea of what he was talking about, and they felt that his statement that his theory "outshone both Einstein and Newton" was—to say the least—a little farfetched.
>
> When Peter learned that he was being fired, he immediately sent a letter to the company president in New York City; he received a brief, unsatisfactory answer. Then he wrote protests to several top state officials, including the attorney general and the governor. His letters were so well written and made so much sense to anyone who did not understand the technical problems involved that one state senator demanded a legislative investigation of the missile company for incompetence in the use of tax funds for research. At that point Peter wrote a follow-up letter to the senator to thank him for his interest. In it he included the revelation that the suicide of a well-known nightclub singer had actually been murder: she had spoken up for him after her performance one evening, and Peter's employer had ordered her killed.

In every other respect Peter remained a competent, well-functioning individual. He had no hallucinations, got along well with his fellow employees on his new job, was a good husband and father, and lived a sensible and rather conservative life. As long as the topic of his book and his old job is avoided, you would never know he had any psychotic symptoms. Even if he did tell you about his troubles, you might be inclined to believe him—at least until he told you about the nightclub singer.

The American Psychiatric Association classification system is much more extensive than that outlined here. For example, it also describes personality disorders, which are "maladaptive patterns of behavior" but not so extreme as neurotic or psychotic symptoms. Among these are the paranoid personality, the explosive personality, the hysterical personality, and the inadequate personality. You can undoubtedly figure out the symptoms for yourself. Another example is **psychotic depression,** which refers to severe and disruptive depression, but with origins in the immediate environment rather than in some form of chronic instability.

SOME THOUGHT ABOUT TERMINOLOGY

Did it occur to you that the term **mental illness** was applied only to circumstances in which an organic basis was assumed? Although you are likely to read in newspapers and magazines that you are up-to-date when you view "crazy" people as mentally ill, many psychologists are reluctant to use the term. One common feeling is that the word *ill* implies that the origins of the disorder are biochemical or anatomical and that, therefore, the most effective treatment must be under medical auspices and involve medication. Psychologists often believe that the most significant causes of functional disorders are environmental stress and faulty social learning (Albee, 1969). If so, then looking at these disorders as problems in learning to adapt and learning to cope makes better sense than viewing them as illness.

Moving away from the medical model of mental disorders also moves us away from physicians to psychologists and teachers, from medical settings to home and community settings, from medication to relearning, from professionals and experts to people seen every day.

Thomas Szasz, a well-known psychiatrist, carries the argument even further. He insists that what others call mental illness is really only a disagreement in how to live and how to view the world (1961). For example, if you believe (like Barney Hauser) that God has visited you and given you instructions about something, those who would call you psychotic are only disagreeing with your perceptions and your values. Two centuries ago people would not have considered you mentally ill, because their values were different then. Perhaps God really did speak to you—how can anyone prove beyond a shadow of a doubt that He did not? Furthermore, Szasz feels that diagnosing someone as mentally ill and trying to get that person into treatment or, failing that, into a mental hospital is to punish him for his views, so that the so-called mentally ill person has fewer rights than an alleged felon.

Although few psychologists and psychiatrists accept Szasz' views as he expresses them, this psychiatrist has had a strong impact on the thinking of many people. The use of classification, the tendency to respond to people as ill because we label them ill, the recognition that previous practices have often deprived mentally disturbed persons of their rights—all these awarenesses have been brought into prominence by Szasz and others who think similarly.

SUMMARY OF IMPORTANT IDEAS

1. Normal behavior falls within a wide range of possibilities, and it varies with cultures.

2. Basically, a normal person is one who knows the difference between what is real and what is not, who does not use defense mechanisms to excess, and whose behavior is not dominated by excessively rigid, irrational, or self-defeating actions.

3. Faulty adjustment becomes more obvious as the stress in a situation increases, and the resulting behavior becomes more confused and disorganized, more rigid, and more (apparently) irrational.

4. Genetic factors can probably influence mental disorders by producing a predisposition to mental disturbance and by helping determine the type of disorder that will develop.

5. The two major classifications of severe emotional disturbance are *neurosis* and *psychosis*. Among the many differences between them are the following: neuroses are milder, less likely to require hospitalization, and more amenable to psychotherapy than psychoses.

6. Among the symptoms of neurosis are extreme anxiety, defective sensory or motor functioning without organic cause, dissociation, extreme fears or phobias, obsessive-compulsive behavior, and chronic depression.

7. Among the symptoms of psychosis are hallucinations, delusions, inappropriate emotional responses, withdrawal from social relationships, feelings of persecution and other paranoid feelings, physical immobility, regression to earlier stages of development, extreme depression, and extreme elation.

8. There is very likely a biochemical basis to all psychosis. However, the disturbances that are directly induced by brain damage are referred to as *organic*

disorders; those that are triggered by environmental stress are termed *functional disorders.*

9. The major categories of psychosis are schizophrenia, affective disorders, and paranoid states. Each of these terms, however, encompasses many kinds of behavior.

DEVELOPMENT
OF HUMAN
BEHAVIOR

PART 3

11 A View of the Beginning

The previous chapters have provided a basis for studying the development of human behavior. Psychologists and others emphasize the study of the early years of life because they are strongly convinced that experiences during this time leave an indelible mark on responses to situations in later years — even though an accurate memory of the early experiences may be lacking.

What is your earliest memory? How old were you? Only rarely do people recall anything prior to their second birthday (and often not before their third or fourth); yet psychologists insist that experiences during the earliest years of life probably have a greater effect on later behavior patterns than do experiences at any other time in the life-span. Even though the infant and young child face a limited range of situations and lack a conscious memory of what occurs, the first two or three years of life are tremendously important. The mature personality is largely the product of early parent-child relationships, early experiences, and the interaction between these factors and the genetic qualities the infant inherits.

THE PRENATAL EXPERIENCE/THE BIRTH PROCESS

A newborn infant has already had a history of roughly nine months of existence. Although his brain and senses were not well developed during that period, his condition was still influenced by the health of his mother and by what is termed the **intrauterine environment.** Thus his later appearance, intelligence, and behavior *may* be affected by what occurs between conception and birth.

PRENATAL INFLUENCES ON LATER BEHAVIOR

Women who maintain an adequate diet during pregnancy are more likely than poorly nourished women to give birth to healthy babies, and the birth itself and the recovery are much easier for them (Ebbs, Tisdall, & Scott, 1942). Although being undernourished is certainly harmful for the mother and the fetus, "eating enough for two" is not the proper alternative. Moderate amounts of food, with particular attention to a well-balanced diet, undoubtedly are most effective. In countries where pregnant women cannot receive adequate food and medical care, many infants die during the **prenatal** period.

When the mother contracts certain illnesses during her pregnancy, the future health, intelligence, and physical condition of the infant may be adversely affected. These illnesses include German measles, or rubella (during the first three or four months of pregnancy), syphilis, tuberculosis, and some strains of influenza (Montagu, 1958). Physical illness of the pregnant woman is not the only condition that may affect the fetus. Such environmental factors as irradiation and restricted oxygen supply "can substantially alter the course of development" (Telford & Sawrey, 1968), particularly if they occur at the stage when the fetus is most susceptible. There appear to be critical stages in fetal development: if the fetus is subjected to certain influences at the proper critical period, harm may occur; if the same influence occurs later, the harm will be diminished or nonexistent.

Women who are unhappy about being pregnant appear to have more problems during pregnancy, more medical difficulties at delivery, and less well-adjusted children in subsequent years (Engström, Geijerstam, Holmberg, & Uhrus, 1964; Wallin & Riley, 1950). Although it is not known how the unhappiness of the pregnant woman is related to future problems, it is probable that the anxiety or anger felt by the mother might cause a physiological change that affects the future infant. Another possibility is that women who are unhappy about being pregnant are more careless in taking proper care of themselves. They may ignore good nutrition, not get adequate rest, pay no attention to an illness, or not bother with prenatal medical examinations. And, inevitably, women who do not like the idea of being pregnant will probably resent the child after he arrives and will treat him in a way that leads to adjustment problems later.

Increased drug usage by women of childbearing age brings up the issue of whether their infants are also affected. Comparing these infants with those of non-drug-taking mothers is meaningless, since the women on drugs, especially if addicted, do not receive equivalent health care and nutrition during their pregnancy. One San Francisco psychiatrist stated ". . . if the mother is addicted, the child is also addicted. Heroin crosses the barrier, crosses the placenta, and goes from the mother's blood stream to the child's. When it is born, the child goes through the classic syndrome called cold turkey, goes into narcotic withdrawal.

This is true of methadone too" (Drews, 1972). Whether the effects are lasting or just temporary is not yet known.

Other maternal factors that may disrupt the normal development of the fetus include heavy drinking, which usually reduces the likelihood of a healthy diet, and smoking, which seems related to low birth weight and prematurity (Lowe, 1959). Incompatible blood types in the two parents can also result in impaired fetal development.

THE BIRTH PROCESS

A century ago the birth process was a time of danger to the health and life of both the new infant and the mother, and the proportion of both who died was quite high. Improved maternal health, hospital conditions, and general medical care have been major factors in producing an amazing drop in the death rate at

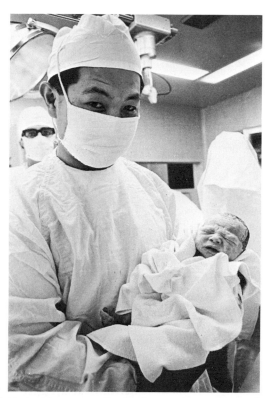

FIGURE 11-1. The supposedly "just-born" infants you see in the movies are actually several weeks old. Infants look more like this one immediately after birth. Photograph courtesy of UCLA.

birth and during the neonatal period. Unfortunately these improvements have not been distributed evenly throughout this country, and infant mortality is about twice as high for nonwhites as for whites.

A distressing outcome of this progress has been the much-publicized **population explosion,** contended by some to be among the biggest problems facing the last third of the twentieth century. Can you explain the significance of this term and its relationship to reduced infant mortality? What other recent technological, scientific, or social changes have affected the population explosion?

An increasing number of expectant mothers follow a program of **natural childbirth,** based on physical exercise and the development of emotionally healthy attitudes toward pregnancy and childbirth (for example, Dick-Read, 1960). Some mothers prefer not to be anesthetized during the birth process, if possible, because they wish to witness the birth of their infant; fathers are often permitted in the delivery room for these births. Physicians and hospitals usually do their best to discourage this kind of parental participation in the actual birth process, because they claim that their task becomes more difficult and, sometimes, more dangerous. Some expectant mothers have the kinds of attitudes that make natural childbirth a very rich, worthwhile experience. Other women are undoubtedly better off adhering to the more traditional approaches.

EARLY DEVELOPMENT

"To be honest, I didn't really enjoy my son until he was about a year old — that's when he began to have a real personality." In spite of a common belief that all babies are alike, definite individual differences are evident at birth.

Even during the first two or three days of life, infants display considerable differences in responding to noise and other stimuli (Schachter, Bickman, Schachter, Jameson, Litachy, & Williams, 1966). Subsequent observations during the first few months show differences in motor behavior (movements), reactions to frustration, and readiness to smile (Diamond, 1957). Some infants are generally more responsive to their environment and more easily stimulated by what goes on around them. These personality differences occur so early and with so little opportunity for learning that they seem to be at least partly the result of inherited factors.

THE FIRST TWO WEEKS OF LIFE

The infant in the first two or three weeks of life is called a **neonate.** In the first two or three days of life, neonates have little awareness of their environment. Although their senses are reasonably well developed at birth, they lack the capacity for interpreting the stimuli they receive.

Recent studies have shown that the neonate has a greater capacity to respond to his environment than had previously been assumed. He reacts to flashing lights, he differentiates colors, he moves his eyes to follow a light, he has a fairly well-developed sense of smell, and he responds to touch (Hartup & Yonas, 1971). Neonates are also sensitive to taste, heat, cold, and loss of balance (Mussen, Conger, & Kagan, 1969). In addition, evidence exists that neonates can be quieted by having someone speak to them (O'Doherty, 1968); they can even learn to turn their head to get milk (Siqueland, 1968).

An infant's early movement is largely mass activity. That is, his entire body will move in response to stimulation of one part of the body. Neonates can suck

FIGURE 11–2. Motor development in children. Adapted from Shirley (1933); by permission of the University of Minnesota Press.

and swallow, which allows them to take food, but these actions are **reflexes** that occur automatically, without learning. Motor behavior, such as grasping, crawling, and walking, develops more slowly than sensory abilities and varies considerably from child to child. Figure 11–2 shows the average age at which certain behavior is first observed, but it is perfectly normal for children to develop much later or much earlier than these averages.

The neonate sleeps about two-thirds of the time but—as parents learn to their dismay—will wake up every few hours crying to be fed. Slowly, as his body grows larger, he can take more food at a time and will need to eat less frequently. Crying and other forms of agitation can be soothed not only through feeding, but also by gentle rocking, pleasant sounds, or a sweetened pacifier, even as early as the second or third day of life. Some babies can be comforted more easily than others; they also differ as to the stimulus that works the best (Birns, Blank, & Bridger, 1966).

AS BABIES MATURE AND DEVELOP

Physical, social, emotional, and intellectual changes are probably greater during the first two years of life than during any other two-year period. In the first year alone, body weight approximately triples, the first tooth normally appears, sitting alone and walking with help take place, familiar people are recognized and strangers are feared, and a vocabulary of words is understood (and perhaps a few words are spoken).

By the end of the second year, language has developed from the initial cooing and babbling into a small speaking vocabulary and a substantial understanding vocabulary. Words are used with comprehension, and the baby is beginning to put them together into phrases, although it is not until about age 2½ that phrases and sentences become common (Lenneberg, 1967).

As babies mature and develop, they become increasingly social creatures, and their parents and others in the environment respond to them in kind. Although a baby's first smile may be relief at passing gas and his first "ma-ma" may occur because he likes the sound, these examples of behavior produce responses from others that interact dynamically with the awareness, feelings, and behavior of the infant. Slowly he learns the meaning of words, of expressions, of voice tones, and of the presence or absence of a particular individual. And slowly he learns how to behave in order to produce a desired change in the people and things (bottle, pacifier, rattle, Daddy's eyeglasses) that are meaningful in his life.

The effects of parental stimulation during these early months are frequently underestimated. One study found that even 5-month-old infants were measurably

FIGURE 11–3.   During the first two years of life, an amazing amount of motor development and learning occur. Photograph by Lehman J. Pinckney.

more active and attentive if their mothers spent time playing with them and providing other types of interaction (Kagan, 1968). Studies of this nature raise some fascinating practical questions. For instance, infants seem to recognize strangers around 5 or 6 months but display fear of them between 7 and 9 months (Bronson, 1968). This observation suggests that introducing a parent substitute at this age may lead to some difficulty, but it is not known whether the difficulty would have a permanent impact.

The question of the effects of early experiences needs further study. How seriously will the behavior of a 12-year-old boy be affected by having received little stimulation during the first year of life? Is there a particular age at which certain kinds of stimulation should occur in order to have maximum effect? If stimulation is lacking at a certain age, can it be compensated for later? One study showed that monkeys that were raised in isolation (that is, without either parents or playmates) exhibited great fear when they were placed with other monkeys for the first time. Those that had been isolated for a relatively brief time eventually learned normal behavior patterns, but those that had experienced longer periods of isolation were never fully able to compensate. In later years they displayed many forms of antisocial behavior, including violence (Harlow & Harlow, 1967).

CHILD-REARING METHODS AND PERSONALITY

Psychologists believe that experiences during the first few years of life are vitally important in shaping the entire personality. As a result, they have spent much time and effort exploring the methods parents use to rear their children and the various parent-child relationships that result. Some of the specific aspects that have been studied include early feeding experiences, early toilet-training experiences, and early sex-behavior training.

These experiences are important for several reasons: (1) Early experiences set the stage for later expectations. (2) Since early experiences have not been contradicted by other experiences, they may have greater and more lasting impact. (3) The child's attitudes toward himself begin to develop at a very early age. (4) Early experiences may affect later unconscious motivation.

Attitudes of parents toward children may be described in many ways, but the two dimensions most frequently indicated in research and in theories are: (1) warmth (or acceptance) versus hostility (or rejection), and (2) control (or restrictiveness) versus permissiveness (or independence) (Maccoby, 1964). It is generally assumed that these two factors, rather than the specific techniques of child rearing, are of primary importance. Thus, in the discussion that follows, we must consider the behavior of individual parents according to the degree of warmth they show and the degree of independence they allow their children.

Warmth and acceptance are assumed to be more effective than hostility and rejection in bringing children up to be happy, healthy adults. Warmth does not mean a smothering kind of affection that restricts the infant's opportunities to explore or to begin to take the initiative for his own behavior. Sometimes such a display of warmth is not really acceptance but is an attempt by the parent to compensate for strong unconscious feelings of rejection.

The second dimension is more complex, and experts disagree about how much control or permissiveness is best. Much of the difference in opinion is based on the questions "best for what?" and "best for whom?" If having obedient children is extremely important, parents would be well advised to be rather restrictive; if obedience is low on the priority list, greater permissiveness is probably in order. Also, parents and children differ. Some parents are uncomfortable in providing too much independence for their children; some children require more limits on their behavior than others, not because they are "naughty" but because they have greater needs for order and deference. Within the same family, one child can be left on his own without fear for his safety, but another child is reluctant to wander too far from his mother.

In a comparison of Russian and American child-rearing methods, Bronfenbrenner (1970) found that the Russians were more restrictive. They were much more likely to hug, kiss, and cuddle their babies, as well as to hold them tightly and give them little chance to move about on their own. Japanese parents also hold their infants more than American parents do and, like the Russians, are reluctant to let them out of their sight. Whenever a Japanese baby cries, someone in the family will pick him up and either find out what is troubling him or hold him and bounce him gently up and down until he stops.

EARLY FEEDING EXPERIENCES

For the infant, hunger needs and their satisfaction are among the most compelling forces in life. If the hunger need remains unsatisfied too long, he may develop fear or anxiety regarding his ability to obtain food. Children who have suffered severe hunger during their very early years have later been observed to stuff food into their pockets, even when the supply was plentiful. If early eating experiences are tense, uncomfortable occasions, the child may develop negative attitudes not only toward eating but also toward the individuals associated with these early events.

Breast feeding.   For years many physicians and psychologists have strongly advised women to breast-feed their babies if they are physically capable. Nonetheless, American mothers are less likely to nurse their infants than are mothers from most other societies (Whiting & Child, 1953). Social-class differences in nursing are also evident: in the 1930s, middle-class mothers were more likely than lower-class mothers to bottle-feed, but in the 1960s the tendency was reversed (Mussen et al., 1969). The behavior of middle-class mothers probably represents a response to prevailing theories of child rearing, whereas the behavior of lower-class mothers may be more dependent on finances.

Breast feeding does offer the advantages of allowing close physical contact between mother and child and of letting the child associate the warmth of his mother with the satisfaction of his hunger. It may also permit the mother to feel that she is performing a traditional female role. Disadvantages are also present; for example, the mother's schedule is extremely restricted, and her sleep is often interrupted. In the final analysis, recent research evidence indicates that the mother's attitude and affection toward the infant are more important than the specific feeding technique she uses. Therefore mothers are probably well advised to follow whatever practice they find most comfortable.

Weaning.   Eventually the young child must be removed from the breast or the bottle and taught to drink without sucking. According to the famous Dr. Spock (1957), most infants are ready to begin this step between 7 and 10 months,

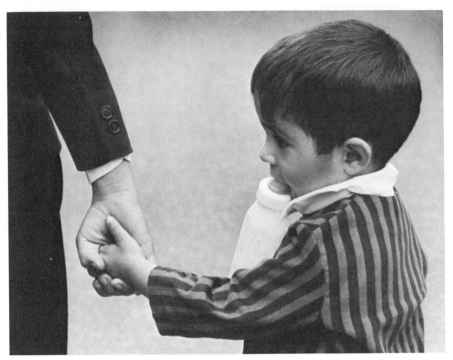

FIGURE 11-4. Eventually the young child must be weaned from the
bottle and taught to drink without sucking. Photograph by Liane Enkelis.

although they may begin taking sips from a cup as early as 5 months. Anthropological investigations of small, less developed societies show that **weaning** of the child from the breast typically begins between ages 2 and 3. Of 52 groups investigated, only the Marquesans weaned their children earlier than Americans (Whiting & Child, 1953).

Weaning should occur gradually, preferably by the elimination of one feeding at a time (Spock, 1957). An infant who is shifted suddenly from the breast or bottle to the cup may find the experience upsetting.

TOILET TRAINING

Primitive societies usually do not begin **toilet training** until the child is around 2, and the Bena of Africa may wait until he is 5 (Whiting & Child, 1953). American families, however, usually start much sooner; toilet training may begin as early as 5 months, and it is complete at about 18 months on the average (Sears, Maccoby, & Levin, 1957).

Some parents feel a flow of pride if they can toilet-train their child before he is 9 or 10 months old, even though pediatricians and psychologists discourage attempts at toilet training too early. Being toilet-trained demands a certain degree of maturation: the child must learn to associate the physical pressure within his body with the acts of elimination; he must also have sufficient muscle control to withhold the waste until he can get (or be taken) to the toilet. Many children will toilet-train themselves if left alone; when they are around 2 years of age, they wish to imitate their parents and their older friends or siblings. The later the training begins, the less time it takes (Sears et al., 1957).

It may seem strange that psychologists and pediatricians place so much stress on toilet training, but there is a good explanation. For the parents, toilet training is likely to be the first attempt to train their child; for the child, it often involves the first taste of real discipline and the first fear of disappointing the parents. Perhaps most serious, the child is often frustrated because he cannot please his parents by doing what they expect of him. He may thus develop a self-concept of inadequacy, which could generalize to other phases of living. Since toilet training, unlike other types of child training, continues for many weeks or even months, fear of possible failure in satisfying the parents can become extreme. The child may even come to feel that being toilet-trained is the most important thing in his life. His parents praise him when he is successful, scold him when he is unsuccessful, and discuss it constantly. Sometimes the child thinks that the valuable thing is the feces, not the act of getting to the toilet:

> Karen Reiter's parents placed great emphasis on toilet training, and they were very unhappy at Karen's slow learning. At 26 months, Karen was still making many mistakes, and the family did everything they could to get her trained. Karen was a sensitive child who wanted to please her parents but seemed unable to learn this particular trick.
> One evening, while the Reiters were entertaining three other couples for dinner, Karen called to her parents to ask if she could bring out "something to show you." Her father, thinking she wanted to show the guests her brand-new furry slippers, called back "Yes." Karen trooped out, her pajama pants around her knees, displaying the bowl from the "potty"—full.

Children may consciously or unconsciously resist their toilet training as a form of aggression against their parents. A child who is apparently trained but then suddenly wets or soils not only insults the training techniques of his parents, but also produces a job of cleaning up that parents usually abhor. **Enuresis** (bed-wetting), sometimes interpreted as aggression against the parents, is more frequent among children who receive very severe toilet training (Sears et al., 1957).

Parents who desire rapid toilet training often emphasize other forms of cleanliness and neatness (Sears et al., 1957). The child who fails in his toilet efforts is reminded how "dirty" he is. A few years later the same body parts will again become the center of attention as a place where modesty must be maintained. The demands for cleanliness and the demands for modesty interact to make that part of the body a forbidden, exciting, "dirty" area.

Perhaps you feel that the importance of early feeding and toilet-training experiences has been exaggerated in this chapter. If so, discuss these topics with friends who have young children. Regardless of their specific experiences, you will quickly see what an important part this early training played in the lives of the parents. (And you can imagine how important it was to their children, who had much less in the way of outside activities to distract them.)

SEX–BEHAVIOR TRAINING

Young children invariably locate their genital areas during the normal process of becoming familiar with the sight and feel of their own bodies. Exploring or handling the genitalia is likely to elicit punishment from parents, although most mental-health authorities would probably say "Ignore it."

Children frequently explore each other's bodies, perhaps while claiming to play "doctor" (although they usually hide their game from adults). Parents often oppose any sort of sexual activity among children; in one study over one-half of a group of mothers expressed definite opposition to sex play (Sears et al., 1957). Yet in some societies sex play among children is accepted as natural (Whiting & Child, 1953).

When punishment for sex play is severe, it may produce sexual-adjustment difficulties that work against future mental health. The early training of many American adults has created fear, anxiety, avoidance, and even impotence and frigidity in sex behavior and affection.

To convince their children to avoid any sex behavior, some parents make up stories or relate "facts" that are not accurate, such as "If you touch yourself there, you will get sick or go crazy." Statements of this nature may create an immediate sense of panic, as well as long-range fear and avoidance of all forms of sex. The usual types of sex exploration and manipulation in which children indulge are unlikely to be harmful, unless the children feel anxious or guilty because they have been persuaded that their activity is sinful and unclean.

Methods of child training are considered important by most societies, and the contemporary United States is certainly no exception. But if infants are fed, toilet-trained, and sex-trained as part of a pattern of basically loving and affectionate parent-child interactions, the specific training techniques probably are of secondary importance. What is of primary consequence is how early rearing af-

FIGURE 11–5. Modesty is not natural; it must be learned. Photograph by John G. Warford.

fects the development of the individual's self-concept and his relationships with the important people in his life.

SIGNIFICANT OTHERS AND THE SELF-CONCEPT

The self-concept develops through interaction with other people, beginning in infancy. A young child's judgment of himself can be only a reflection of how he feels others are judging him, and those "others" who have a particularly great impact are referred to as **significant others.** For most infants and young children, significant others are the parents, and it is through their parents' eyes that children evaluate and picture themselves. In other words, significant others form a sort of psychological mirror (Cooley, 1902; Sullivan, 1953). The child looks to his parents to learn who and what he is, and what he sees reflected back forms his picture of himself.

Thus, if the child feels that his parents love him, he will think he deserves this love; if he feels his parents think him stupid, he will believe it of himself. He is not able to judge himself or them but tends to accept their viewpoint of himself (and of much else in the world) as right and proper. If his parents have treated him well or cruelly, paid attention to him or ignored him, shown him love or shown him nothing but abuse, he can only feel he deserved it. He has no other basis for comparison at his age.

> Elaine Lander's parents were well into their forties when she was born, and her sister and brother were both in high school. She was, by any definition, an unwanted child. Her mother, a private secretary to a business executive, quickly hired a housekeeper to care for her and returned to work. Her father was irritated with having to worry about diapers and babysitters again, especially when he was working unusually hard to save money for his older children's college education. Whenever either parent had to feed or change or otherwise handle Elaine, they did it as quickly as possible, not really caring whether she was bounced around a little in the process. They rarely bothered to give her that extra attention and affection that babies need.
>
> Both parents constantly referred to her as a "damned nuisance." They had no sympathy for her crying and little interest in how she developed, other than making certain that she received good physical care. As Elaine grew older, she began to recognize how her parents felt about her. When she played make-believe games, she would yell at herself "You're a bad girl, Elaine, and a nuisance and a damned and a not-hurry-up. You're an icky."
>
> She matured into a quiet, reserved, fearful girl who was constantly apologizing for bothering others. She was afraid to approach anyone for friendship, since she viewed herself as unworthy of friendship. Her parents had rejected her attempts at gaining their love, and she feared similar rejection from others. She later became a successful and popular nursery-school teacher.

As a very young child, Elaine accepted her parents' view of her as valid. She was unable to say to herself "I'm really a very good person, but my parents are too busy to notice me." All she could feel was "If my parents—who are my world—do not notice me, then I am not worth noticing." By the time she was mature enough to evaluate herself with greater objectivity, her self-concept and her behavior patterns were well formed, and change was extremely difficult. Why do you think she was able to succeed as a nursery-school teacher?

To make matters worse, children who feel unaccepted often behave in ways that irritate others. They may be so hungry for people to accept them that they are unable to disagree or to turn down a request for a favor, and they gain a reputation for being weak. Or, they may react in just the opposite way: having been unable to trust the significant others in their lives, they are unable to trust or whole-heartedly like anyone else; since others will usually respond to being disliked by disliking in return, these persons' self-concepts of inadequacy are made to appear true.

As the child matures, he is constantly coming into contact with other people who may influence his self-concept. They respond to his appearance, intelligence, verbal ability, temperament, or friendliness. Being treated by others as an attractive, intelligent, capable individual will encourage a corresponding self-concept. If this self-concept agrees with the very early self-concept developed through the parents, the child is likely to mature into a well-adjusted adult. On the other hand, being considered by others as an unclean, unintelligent, lazy person can create a corresponding self-concept. Even if the parent-child relationship is healthy, the negative reactions of later contacts with other people can partially undo the good the parents have accomplished. If—and this is more serious—the parent-child relationship was not good, later negative experiences will reinforce and perhaps make worse the already negative self-concept.

In any case, it would appear that changing the self-concept in a direction that contradicts the early learning from significant others becomes increasingly difficult as the person grows older. This is why psychologists place such great emphasis on the importance of early parent-child relationships: they set the stage for the child's entire life.

SIGNIFICANT INFLUENCES OF SIGNIFICANT OTHERS

Significant others influence the lives of children in other ways besides the development of the self-concept. First, they serve as models for behavior. Regardless of what parents tell children, the examples set by the parents are vitally important. When parents who swear insist that their children not swear, they are not really saying that swearing is wrong—they are saying swearing is wrong if someone is around to punish you for it or if you are a child. Second, parents provide most of the rewards and punishments in the early lives of their children. It is their smile or frown, their gift or slap, their love or rejection that means the most to the child. Later in life other people also become important, but the parents are the most influential figures in the first few years, and they usually remain so.

DEVELOPMENT OF LOVE

Significant others are associated with warmth, love, and affection, as well as with the satisfaction of the infant's hunger, thirst, and temperature-regulation needs. When the parents are not there, discomfort remains; when they are there,

FIGURE 11–6.   Significant others serve as models for behavior. Photograph by Liane Enkelis.

discomfort ceases. When the parents are not there, love and affection are missing; when they are there, love and affection are present. Thus the presence of parents is associated with the presence of those things that are important.

Because they are associated with such important satisfactions, the parents become valued for themselves. Just as some people like money for the sake of money rather than for what it will buy, infants come to love their parents for themselves rather than just as bringers of good things. This is the beginning of true love and affection.

Psychologists and psychiatrists have emphasized in many ways the importance of love and affection for infants, but a series of studies conducted over the past several years has captured the imagination of both laymen and professionals. Although this research has been carried out with monkeys rather than people, the implications for humans are obvious.

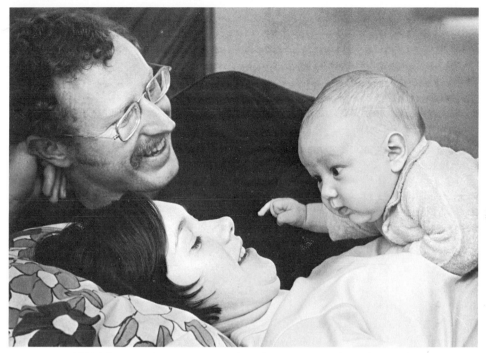

FIGURE 11–7. In most cases, when the parents are there, love and affection are present. Photograph by Lehman J. Pinckney.

Two "monkey mothers" were constructed, identical to each other except that one had a wire body and the other's body was made of sponge rubber and covered with terry cloth. Baby monkeys showed a strong preference for the terry-cloth mother, even when they were fed by a bottle inserted through the wire mother. When frightened, the animals would run for the soft, cuddly mother (Harlow, 1958). The soft mother offered a type of reassurance that may be compared with the physical affection the human mother offers her child. Later the monkeys that had been raised without normal mothers were themselves unable to perform adequately as mothers (Harlow & Harlow, 1962a). This result indicates that inadequate mothering will affect not only the children but even later generations.

Perhaps the major implication of these studies is that physical contact and cuddling are important for the proper development of infants and young children. Some people feel they have discharged their obligations as parents if they satisfy the physical needs of the child. But much evidence has been gathered suggesting that this minimal care provides only minimal benefits for the children. Again we face the double-barreled question: is inadequate physical contact a major factor in development, and, if so, can those children who lacked sufficient cuddling make up for it later? Since we cannot go back in time, can we do anything to make up for lost time?

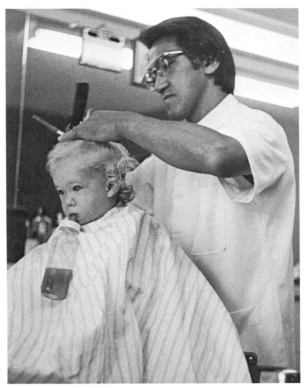

FIGURE 11–8. Physical contact with familiar and comfortable things is a source of stability at a time of anxiety. Photograph by Michael Parker.

Later research on "monkey love" brought out additional information. Baby monkeys who had spent their early days with a headless cloth mother-surrogate panicked when the psychologists finally attached the head. One monkey solved the problem by twisting the head off and rolling it into the corner. Another demonstration showed a preference for a rocking, as opposed to a stationary, cloth mother, up until about six months of age. Even warmed and cooled mothers were created, and the monkeys showed a preference for the former. When the warm mother was initially provided for several weeks, followed by a period during which the warm and cold mothers alternated, the baby clung to the warm mother and ignored the cold one. However, when the cold mother was presented for the initial extended time, followed by successive warm and cold mothers on successive days, the infant monkey never established the level of physical contact to either mother that was shown in the warm-mother-first situation. And, finally, when the warm-mother-first monkey was frightened, it ran away from its cold mother and huddled in the corner of the cage (Harlow & Suomi, 1970).

In spite of the danger of generalizing from animal behavior to human behavior, these studies contain rich insights that essentially bear out what we have come to believe about people. First, finding that a familiar and — if we can use the word — loved mother has suddenly undergone drastic change is extremely distressing, at least at certain ages, and the infant will do whatever he can to regain his original mother. Second, gentle movement and physical warmth encourage close contact. Third, initial relationships with a comfortable (warm) mother enable the infant to live through a siege with a cold mother; however, initial relationships that are cold make subsequent healthy relationships with warm mothers difficult. (Please don't lose sight of the use of the word *warm* as referring to physical, not psychological, warmth. Of course, some generalizing is undoubtedly appropriate.)

Offering a child love — not only physical affection but emotional warmth — is a great help in establishing a later healthy personality. The child develops the self-concept "I am lovable," which leads to feelings of adequacy and self-worth. You may recall that the needs for love and for self-esteem must be reasonably satisfied before an individual can become concerned with self-actualization.

Love can be abused, however. Some parents use their love to keep their children tied to them; others manipulate children to achieve what they themselves were unable to achieve, regardless of the inclination of the children; still other parents compete with each other through their children. You may question whether these parents actually do love their children, which involves us in a very tricky definitional problem. What are your feelings?

SEPARATION FROM SIGNIFICANT OTHERS

Often a parent must leave his child. The absence may be permanent, such as through death or some divorces; or it may be temporary, as when a parent is very ill, takes a long business trip, or is in the military or in prison. If the absence occurs before the child is 4 or 5 months old, his awareness of the world is probably not well enough developed to cause him to be upset. After this very early age, however, the infant has established enough rich associations with his parents that their extended absence can be very disturbing.

When a significant other leaves, the child may suffer **separation anxiety.** He senses that the source of love and satisfactions has left him, and he becomes fearful. A child who wakes up in the middle of the night and finds a strange babysitter instead of his parents will become very frightened or upset. Of course, if the child knows the babysitter and has expected her to be there, his fear will be negligible. Even a schoolchild who comes home after school to find his mother unexpectedly away is likely to be frightened.

When a child whose mother died before he was 5 reaches maturity, he is more likely than average to be emotionally disturbed or to be delinquent, unless an adequate replacement can be found or the father can do a good job of compensating. Types of separation other than death also lead to increased chances of later emotional problems (Barry & Lindemann, 1960).

Being separated from a parent produces emotional upset in two major ways: (1) The child has lost an important person on whom he depended for many satisfactions, and the loss, which is reflected in great excitement and confusion in the home, is very disturbing. (2) A home with only one parent is often less stable because of pressures of money, the decreased time the remaining parent has available to spend with the child, and other factors. If the separation is caused by death, the child may become confused about the meaning of death and its effect on him; children often think of death as a punishment, and they may become afraid that they, too, will die soon.

Separation anxiety has also been observed in children who entered a hospital or other institution when they were between 15 and 30 months of age, especially when circumstances allowed little or no contact with their parents. Their reactions involved three stages: (1) *protest,* when they showed active distress, crying, and eager searching; (2) *despair,* when they became withdrawn and inactive; and (3) *detachment,* when they seemed to have recovered from despair but in fact attempted to avoid emotional involvements with people (Bowlby, 1960).

Since infants and young children in hospitals and institutions often receive little personal attention and no affection from the busy nursing and institutional staffs, they lose their spirit and enjoyment of life. Even when given good physical care and diet, children in institutions develop more slowly and have a higher mortality rate than children raised in private homes. They are also more likely to have later behavior problems and to show apathy (Spitz, 1949).

> Roberta lost both her parents when she was 18 months old and was
> placed in an institution. A year later she was a tense, tearful child who fought

constantly with others and could not adjust to the nursery school the institution supported. At that point she was referred to the institution's psychological clinic. For several months she met twice a week with one of the psychologists there and did nothing but play; the psychologist gave his full attention to Roberta, sometimes playing with her, sometimes just watching as she played. At the end of ten weeks, both Roberta's housemother and her nursery-school teacher commented spontaneously that her behavior had improved greatly.

IS IT HOPELESS?

How pessimistic it must all seem. In reading much of this and the previous chapters, you may have thought back over your own life. If you received love, developed self-esteem, had pride, did not suffer the loss of a significant other, everything is all right. But what if you did not fare that well? Is your future hopeless?

The initial answer is a resounding "No!" followed by "but you may have to work harder." In psychology we rarely if ever talk in terms of *everyone;* rather, our research and theories usually refer to trends and tendencies. So the first reason for our saying "No" is that you may be one of the many exceptions.

Second, you need not feel that your early life leaves no room for change in later years. Personal growth and dynamic change are possible throughout the lifespan. Even the final facing of one's own death may lead to growth, as ironic as that may sound (Zinker & Fink, 1966).

Third, you are entitled to believe that you yourself can cause meaningful change in your own life. As important as early environment is, it is not insurmountable. The very greatness and extreme creativity of some persons appear to be a direct outgrowth of painfully difficult early years.

Fourth, resources for help are available. Your initial source of aid is probably the love and trust of your close friends and your family. You also have access to professional helpers, such as psychotherapists and some clergymen, family physicians, teachers, and counselors.

If the experience of this course becomes a self-fulfilling prophecy leading you to depression and failure, then whatever facts you have learned along the line will have little meaning. The insights you gain during this course should help you free yourself of some of the limitations placed on you by your previous life history and permit you to develop and mature throughout your life-span. How has taking the course affected you so far?

SUMMARY OF IMPORTANT IDEAS

1. The physical condition of the expectant mother affects the well-being of her future child; her emotional state *may* also have an influence.

2. At birth infants differ in motor behavior, activity level, and responsiveness to noise.

3. At birth infants have a minimal awareness of their environment, although their sensory apparatus appears adequately developed. Development is rapid in the first few months.

4. The degree of warmth and autonomy provided by the parents, rather than specific child-rearing techniques, seems to have primary influence on the child's later behavior and adjustment.

5. Breast feeding is considered, *on the whole,* superior to bottle feeding, but parental love and affection are far more important than the method of feeding.

6. Child-rearing practices in the United States are more severe than in most preliterate societies.

7. Toilet-training methods are important to the development of children, largely because parents place so much emphasis on control.

8. A young child's evaluation of himself reflects the reactions of others toward him; the most important of these others, usually the parents, are called *significant others.*

9. Young children accept the views that significant others have of them, usually without criticism or evaluation.

10. The child's love for his parents develops from the satisfaction they provide him, which includes satisfaction of his biological needs in combination with warmth, affection, and autonomy.

11. When a significant other leaves, the child may exhibit signs of emotional disruption and separation anxiety.

12. Children whose home background did not provide the optimal advantages may need to expend greater effort at adjustment when they mature.

12 The Developing Child

Chapter 11 focused largely on the biological, psychological, and social origins of human behavior, with emphasis on the first two years of life. This chapter extends these concerns both in time and in space; it continues with the chronology of child development and also shows the child beginning to recognize the world beyond his parents.

Life is not a series of time categories but a continuing flow that we describe in time periods for convenience. The total human personality and all aspects of this personality develop and change continuously throughout the life-span. Personality development is most remarkable during the childhood years and is determined largely by the parent-child relationship.

THE PARENT-CHILD RELATIONSHIP

The satisfaction that a child feels with himself, his life, and the world around him often reflects the satisfaction felt by his parents. Parents who are happy in their marriage, in their work, in their social relationships, and in their general approach to life seem to be good parents. Those who are bitter, frustrated, and unfriendly often allow their unhappiness to interfere with their relationships with their children.

The mother who was unable to have the concert career she had desired pushes her daughter into seeking a concert career.

The father who dislikes his wife and distrusts women in general convinces his son that women are to be exploited.

The father who is a failure at work is a tyrant in his own home, the only place where anyone listens to him.

The mother who is unhappy in her marriage to a cold, aloof husband turns all her attention to her son, whom she coddles and overprotects.

Unhappy and poorly adjusted children do not inevitably result from unhappy parents, and happy parents do not inevitably have happy children — but it generally does work out that way. Among the many factors related to healthy parent-child relationships are (1) the parents' ability to allow the children freedom and responsibility, (2) the children's opportunity to express their feelings, (3) the degree to which the children have been aided in self-actualization, and (4) parental methods of controlling or disciplining behavior.

ALLOWING FREEDOM AND RESPONSIBILITY

Freedom and responsibility go together. Children need to receive an increasing amount of freedom and responsibility as they mature, so that they will be accustomed to independence when they begin college, move away from home, or take their first job. Parents who overprotect their child, for whatever reason, are not preparing him adequately for adult life. Children need to be allowed to grow up and to leave home, without feeling that they are hurting their parents. (In some šocieties grown children would not wish to leave their parents, but we are here concerned with the mainstream of Western culture.)

Parents face a major dilemma. On the one hand, children have definite limitations, and they will inevitably fail at certain tasks and make incorrect decisions. On the other hand, in order to mature into self-sufficient adults, children need to try difficult tasks and make difficult decisions. An adult may "know better" than the child, but the child has to find out for himself much of the time; an adult may "do it better," but the child wants to do it himself.

Danny, at 12 months, refused to take any food that he could not get to his mouth through his own efforts, and this included ice cream, which he loved. His parents had to watch him go through strenuous effort and many spills in order to eat. It was hard on the floor, on his clothes, and on his parents, but Danny showed great pleasure in his achievements.

Lee's parents were in a hurry, and her father lifted her into the family car for a quick getaway. Lee protested loudly, scrambled out of the car, glared up at her father, and then pulled herself into the vehicle without help.

Children mature at different rates, and not all children of the same age will be sufficiently ready to take the same responsibilities or be given the same freedoms. One 10-year-old can be trusted to go shopping for his mother, but another cannot; 12-year-old Ted can be believed when he says his homework is completed, but 12-year-old Tom must be checked.

It seems logical that children who are prevented from taking appropriate responsibility and freedom will develop a self-concept of being inadequate: "My parents don't think I'm competent, so I guess I'm not." On the other hand, children who are pushed into responsibilities long before they are ready may feel that their parents are rejecting them; also, they are likely to fail at their tasks and as a result develop a self-concept of inadequacy. The most successful children seem to be those who are encouraged to take responsibility at appropriate age levels and whose parents can tolerate mistakes and misjudgments as part of the child's process of growing up.

Comments Children Can Get along Without

—You know I love you — look how much money I spend on you.
—Your brother likes to kiss me — he must love me more than you do.
—You're my child — you're supposed to love me and respect me.
—When I was your age, things weren't so easy.
—If I only had had the chances you kids get today. . . .
—Do you always have to do what the other kids are doing? If they all jumped off the Golden Gate (or Brooklyn or any other) Bridge, I suppose you'd jump off too.
—I used to love helping my mother around the house.
—When you get older, you'll think back to all the time you wasted.
—I don't know what's going to become of you when you get older.
—It took me a long time to realize that my parents knew what they were talking about, and I always regretted not paying attention to them sooner.
—Do you always have to spend your money on such trash?
—Is that any way to talk to your parents?
—I don't know why you can't do it — your sister always could.

COMMUNICATING FEELINGS

Parents have feelings, and so do children; both should have the right to express them. There are occasions when a mother is entitled to become angry with her child; there are times when children are entitled to express unhappiness with their parents' actions. If the basic relationship is good, and if the parents do not threaten to withdraw their love or administer violent physical punishment, an expression of anger may actually improve the situation. Children and parents can learn to respect the emotional expressions of each other if they are secure in their relationship.

Good communication consists of more than freedom to express feelings.

Ideas, wishes, plans, and activities also need to be communicated from parents to children and from children to parents. Some parents are always too busy to explain things, and others are always too busy to listen. Children do not need to be told everything that is going on or permitted complete conversational control — parents deserve privacy and a life of their own. But children are members of the family, and members of a group are entitled to be listened to and informed.

HELPING CHILDREN SELF-ACTUALIZE

Most parents wish to see their children make as much of their talents as they possibly can, whether the talents involve artistic, sales, administrative, technical, or social abilities. Parents are often less aware of their role in helping their child become more himself, which is also part of the child's process of self-actualization. Adults are frequently intent on bringing up their child to be as much like themselves as possible, regardless of how the child feels.

A consideration of Maslow's need hierarchy may be useful in discussing how parents can help their children self-actualize. Parents would never purposely deprive their children of adequate food or sleep, and lack of fulfillment of survival needs is seldom a problem in the United States. Nonetheless, parents may, often without realizing it, deny sufficient satisfaction of stimulation needs. By doing too much for a child, an unthinking adult may inadvertently stifle the child's need to explore and manipulate his environment.

Safety needs and love needs interact dynamically. Parents who show their child much love and affection are also providing him with a sense of security. A parental show of affection can rarely be an error, unless the love has strings attached or is so overwhelming that it smothers the child. "I'll love you if . . ." is not really giving love, but trading love. What husband would appreciate hearing his wife say "If you buy me a new dress, I'll love you"?

Some parents, because of their own upbringing, find it difficult to show physical affection or even other forms of love. Nonetheless, children seem to sense when they are loved and — also important — respected. To say that parents should respect their children does not mean that the children should be allowed to dominate their parents; rather, it means that the children should be treated as unique and worthwhile individuals, in spite of their immaturity. Even parents who provide lots of security and love do not always show their children this sort of respect. They may repeatedly communicate to their children how immature and dependent they are. By emphasizing the children's inadequacies, the parents may be robbing them of self-esteem.

How can parents take positive steps, over and above such general considerations as providing love and respect, to help their children self-actualize? There are innumerable answers to this question, of which the following are only a few:

1. Reading to children, even before they can understand all that is said, will expose them to the immense world of words and books. Children whose early contacts with books are happy ones are not so likely to find books and words a problem in school.

2. Children ask many questions, often foolish ones and sometimes impossible-to-answer ones. Asking questions is their way of learning about the world, and the adult who tries to answer them truthfully is reassuring and satisfying.

3. Children need to spend time with their parents and to do things together with them. Fathers in particular, since they are away from the home so much, can greatly enrich the father-child relationship by arranging some types of activities they can share with the children.

4. There comes a period for each child when he wants to learn to count or read or tell time, which marks an opportunity for the parents to encourage him

FIGURE 12–1. Children benefit from an appreciation of art. Photograph courtesy UCLA Extension: Arts and Humanities Division.

without pushing him. A warm, noncritical parental attitude of encouragement will probably do more good in the long run than any specific learning that may occur.

5. Children benefit from an appreciation not just of books, but also of art and music, of nature and science, of the behavior of machines and the behavior of people, of white-collar work and blue-collar work. The ability to appreciate a diversity of activities, interests, and people will help a child discover his own talents and respect the talents of others.

Self-actualization in children does not come about automatically when parents follow a rigid set of rules. Rather, it develops slowly when parents satisfy the more basic needs and provide an exciting and stimulating environment while respecting the child's individuality and his need to succeed in his own unique way.

PLACING LIMITS ON BEHAVIOR

When children are born, they do not know how society expects them to behave. Their parents take on the responsibility of placing limits on their behavior to make it acceptable. In different families, different sorts of limits will be established. One family will allow the child to play in mud; another will not. One family will keep the child out of the living room; another will give the child freedom to play in any room.

Once the limits are set, children appear to be better adjusted if the limits are enforced consistently. To discipline a child for throwing the jelly spoon at his sister on one occasion, but to laugh about it on another occasion, is an example of inconsistent limits on behavior. The child is uncertain about what is expected of him.

The methods used to keep behavior within limits are also important. Whereas punishment is probably the most common approach to maintaining limits, other methods are also available. Too much use of punishment merely draws attention to the forbidden act but does not reinforce the correct response.

Punishment has other dangers: it may cause the child to become angry with the parent for the punishment, instead of with himself for the improper act; it can induce frustration, which may lead to future aggressive behavior; it can become unnecessarily severe and cause undue pain or overly harsh restrictions.

Such arguments against punishment do not imply that it is never effective. The child may endanger himself by shoving a nail into an open socket, he may endanger others by ramming his tricycle into a playmate, or he may endanger property by twirling a large stick close to a breakable lamp. In each of these instances the adult may be able to reduce the danger in the child's behavior without resorting to punishment, but sometimes the unique demands of the situation require punishment. How would you, in each of these situations, change the behavior without the use of punishment?

Punishment does not eliminate the original learning but merely causes the person not to behave in a way that will elicit the punishment. Therefore, to change behavior, new learning is required. Suppose that a child who enjoys beating toy drums early Sunday morning is spanked. He has not, by virtue of being spanked, forgotten how to play the drums; neither has he ceased to enjoy playing the drums. What has happened is that he has stopped playing the drums out of fear of further punishment. The task of the parent is to find something for the child to do early Sunday morning to replace playing the drums—something he will enjoy. Therefore, when the child wakes up, he will no longer think about playing the drums, because Sunday morning now suggests to him playing cards or reading the comics. Eventually the child will forget all about playing the drums on Sunday morning (if you are lucky).

Interestingly, children may interpret parental lack of limits as an indication that the parents do not really care.

> "It was raining cats and dogs that day—I must have been about 9—and I asked my father if I should wear my rubbers. He told me to do what I thought was best. Well, I knew what was best, but I wanted him to tell me, because it seemed like he didn't really care. He wouldn't, so I went without my rubbers and caught a terrible cold. I hated my father for giving me that cold, and I hated him more because he reminded me that I had made the decision."

The maturation level of children is an important factor in the type of limits set on their behavior and the sort of enforcement used. Very young children do not understand language well enough to respond to "Don't!" Thus a mild slap on the hand may be called for. Of course, parents who take necessary precautions in childproofing their house will avoid many problems.

At certain ages children do not recognize the significance of what they are doing. They may spread jam on the tablecloth, shoot big brother's dart gun at the neighbor's baby, or curl up and sleep underneath Aunt Molly's car parked in the driveway. Sometimes they will hit another child as a release for their own frustrations. Constant punishment for acts they do not understand may be highly frustrating, especially for very active children. Still worse is disciplining a child for failing at something beyond his physical or intellectual powers to achieve. A child who is not ready to be toilet-trained or to memorize the alphabet will find punishment extremely frustrating, and it will be of little value in producing the desired behavior.

Considerable doubt exists about whether a spanking is more or less cruel than making the child miss a planned-for movie or keeping him in from playing.

"All right, so you admit it! You always admit it!
The question is when are you going to stop doing it?"

FIGURE 12–2.   Courtesy of Ed Fisher.

We do know, however, that a spanking in combination with reasoning works much better than a spanking by itself and that warm, loving mothers get better results from spanking than do cold, aloof mothers (Sears, Maccoby, & Levin, 1957). Studies of underdeveloped societies indicate that more theft occurs in groups that are very punitive than in groups that show great love toward their children, which implies that stealing may be a way to make up for not feeling loved (Bacon, Child, & Barry, 1963). In these instances at least, harsh physical punishment certainly did not lead to more responsible behavior.

Each parent has to work out a system of enforcing limits that is appropriate for his own personality, his child's personality, and the specific set of circumstances involved. Once again, the techniques are probably less important than what the parent communicates through his techniques: if he gets across the message of serious concern for the child's well-being, and if the punishment is not out of keeping for the act that was committed, the long-term effect will probably be better than if he is punishing because of his own needs or if the punishment is far too severe for the occasion.

Real parental love does not depend on whether the child eats his cereal, refrains from hitting his baby sister, or gets good grades in school. Parents who threaten to withdraw their love for any reason imply that that love is neither very strong nor very dependable; it is not given freely but must be earned. Such threats —like brutal physical punishment, which is used more to satisfy the parents than to discipline the child — may produce the immediate behavior desired but will also bring about long-range feelings of anxiety, resentment, and fear.

CHILDREN AFFECTING PARENTS

The parent-child interaction is extremely dynamic. Yet psychologists and others have long talked as though it were a one-way street, with the parent influencing the child but with the child having little effect on the parent. Thus, if the parent were tense, anxious, and punishing and if the child were aggressive, the assumption was made that tension, anxiety, and punitive behavior in a parent caused aggressive behavior in a child. Whereas this might well be the case, the opposite possibility also requires consideration: an aggressive child causes tension, anxiety, and a punishing attitude in his parents.

Other characteristics of the child will also have major effects on the way the parent feels about him: gender, physical attractiveness, healthiness, mischievousness, and so forth. One study showed that the temperamental differences in young children had a considerable effect on their parents and on how their parents, in turn, treated them (Thomas, Chess, & Birch, 1968).

> Josh Barry and his brother Seth are different in many ways. Josh is tall and large-boned with brown hair and a very light skin. He is charming and outgoing, argues constantly with his parents, is not studious, and displays a great deal of emotion. Seth is on the shy side, rarely disagrees with his parents (but gets what he wants more subtly), enjoys school, and shows little outward emotion. According to their parents, these basic characteristics have been evident since before the children could talk. Both parents are easily upset by noise, dislike any outburst of emotion, and insist that their children be highly successful in school.

Assuming the parents are correct in their recollections that the differences between the two boys (born a year apart) were observed very early in life, you can write up your own case history of these brothers.

DEVELOPMENT OF INTERNALIZED ATTITUDES

As the child matures, he begins to move away from the sphere of direct parental influence. Knowing this, parents try to teach their children, while they are still very young, behavior patterns and attitudes that they will follow the rest of their lives.

Before a child is 3, he has begun to develop a sense of what is considered right and what is considered wrong. At first this occurs without his questioning or knowing what he is doing. As his parents punish him for this and reward him for that, the child learns what is expected of him. He also learns from observing how his parents behave.

FIGURE 12–3.   The child learns from observing how his parents behave. Photograph by John G. Warford.

Since the significant others in a child's life are the world for him, he accepts their ideas and their behavior as correct. This acceptance leads to the process of **internalization,** through which the child takes on his parents' ideas and values as his own. When he is older, he will also internalize the ideas of others in his society; he will learn these ideas through his friends, through school, and through what he reads and hears and sees about him. However, in the beginning years the parents provide almost the only source of **values.**

The values that the child internalizes have a strong influence on his behavior, because his own sense of right and wrong, rather than fear of outside authority, controls his actions. This **value system,** through which a person approves or disapproves of his own actions, thoughts, and feelings, is the conscience.

To some extent the development of the conscience and of other internalized values is conscious. The child sees that his parents enjoy reading, so he picks up a book—even though he may hold it upside down. He internalizes the value that reading is "good" and "proper." However, the greater part of the process of acquiring conscience is **unconscious.** As a mother and daughter walk down the street, the mother spies a mangy stray dog and yanks her child away. Shortly afterward the girl wants to pet another dog, but her mother tells her not to because it is probably dirty. Slowly the child builds into her own belief system the value that dogs are to be avoided. She has internalized, or taken for herself, her mother's attitude toward dogs. Thereafter, when she wants to pet a dog, her conscience may tell her that it is wrong. These values will interact, in a dynamic fashion, with her personal experiences with dogs.

Internalization of values can be seen very clearly in young children:

> Bobby Regan, a bright 3-year-old, had been carefully taught not to color on the floor. One afternoon his mother heard loud shouts and slaps from Bobby's room. She raced in and saw him slapping his hand as hard as he could, shouting "No! Naughty! Don' do dat!" Then she saw that he had accidentally crayoned off the drawing paper and onto the floor.

SHAME AND GUILT

There are three basic reasons why an individual avoids doing something he would like to do and has the capability to do: (1) he recognizes that the punishment will be too great; (2) he experiences **shame,** the feeling that his family or country or some other valued group would disapprove of his actions; and (3) his conscience or internalized values will not let him—that is, he feels it is wrong, or feels **guilt.** In many situations all three feelings occur. For example, a student becomes so furious with his instructor that he wants to hit him, but he doesn't. Why? Because (1) he is afraid that he would be given a failing grade and probably expelled from school or even arrested; (2) he knows that his friends and family would be ashamed of his striking a 50-year-old man; and (3) he feels that such an action is simply wrong.

For most Americans and Europeans, internalized values and conscience are the major restraints against committing unethical and illegal acts. Americans will feel a sense of guilt when they do something to violate the conscience. Not only overt behavior but even thoughts and feelings may elicit guilt so disturbing that the individual will avoid the action, thought, or feeling that produced the guilt. You often realize that you could do something unethical or illegal with little chance of being punished; yet you behave honestly. The feeling of shame may enter into your decision, but the chances are that you wish to avoid the extreme discomfort caused by a guilty conscience.

In Japan and other parts of Asia the emphasis is not on guilt but on shame, especially on bringing shame to one's family (Benedict, 1946). Thus Japanese tend to be very polite to their friends and in their own homes because they wish to avoid shame. However, they may be very rude in crowded department stores and rush-hour subways, where no one can identify them and cause shame to occur. The American, who typically is more polite in public, is more likely than the Japanese to show rude behavior to family and friends.

In both **shame societies** and **guilt societies,** the family and the home are probably the greatest influences on behavior. The American conscience and the Japanese sense of shame will not develop adequately if they are not given encouragement by significant others. If children do not have respect or affection for their parents, they will not internalize parental attitudes (if American) or worry about bringing shame to the family name (if Japanese).

. Investigations have disclosed that American children with the strongest consciences are those who are brought up in families that use praise and reasoning rather than physical punishment. These children are shown warmth and acceptance by their parents and thus are more inclined to internalize the values of their parents while maintaining a positive self-concept. Children of warm and loving mothers are more likely to develop a healthy conscience than are children of cold and aloof mothers (Yarrow, Campbell, & Burton, 1968). Unfortunately, some parents may encourage their children to develop an unnecessarily strong conscience.

> Mary Fogarty was a physically affectionate mother, but she demanded a great deal from her children. Whenever one of them showed the slightest sign of misbehaving, Mary threatened to withdraw her love from him, and she would give extra attention to her other children. By being so affectionate, Mary gained the devotion of her children. She was then able to force them to meet her demands, since failure was punished by rejection. As the Fogarty children grew older, even thoughts of disobeying their mother caused anxiety and feelings of guilt.
>
> Jack Fogarty, Mary's oldest child, was especially afraid of his mother's disapproval and developed an exaggerated sense of guilt. On one occasion his teacher stated that someone had broken a classroom window during the lunch hour. Although Jack had been in the cafeteria with several of his friends during the entire lunch period, he felt compelled to explain to his teacher that

he had not been responsible — even though no one suggested that he had been. Another time a teacher announced that she had caught a student cheating on an examination. Again Jack, who had never been accused of the incident, needed to tell her he was not guilty.

Psychologists attempt to reduce these irrational or exaggerated guilt feelings through psychotherapy. Have you ever experienced guilt that was so strong you could not concentrate on your studies?

DEVELOPMENT OF AGGRESSIVENESS AND DEPENDENCY

All people have aggressive feelings, especially after a frustrating experience; similarly, all people sometimes feel the need to be dependent on others. Both aggressive behavior and dependent behavior are frequently punished when children exhibit them openly. The child who hits a playmate over the head with a metal truck is more likely to be punished than the child who never leaves his mother's side, but neither behavior is considered appropriate for a growing child.

Most healthy, normal children express some aggressive behavior. Parents who punish aggression, especially when the punishment is physical, seem to encourage further aggression. If the children are afraid to express their aggression directly, they may do so indirectly, perhaps through their play or their fantasies (Sears et al., 1957).

However, parents who completely overlook aggressive behavior do not reduce aggression either. One investigation revealed that the least aggressive children have parents who show a dislike for aggressive behavior and do not use physical punishment or extreme threats of punishment. The most aggressive children have parents who provoke aggressive behavior by using physical punishment and do not show any particular disapproval when their children are aggressive (Sears et al., 1957).

When a child is punished for aggressive behavior, he feels frustrated, and his own aggressive acts multiply. Similarly, when a child is punished for being dependent, he becomes more dependent, probably because of fears that his parents are rejecting him as an individual when they reject his attempts at being dependent. Research has verified that these relationships exist (McCord, McCord, & Verden, 1962; Sears et al., 1957).

Healthy dependency will make the child want to please his parents, so that he will internalize their values. Unhealthily dependent children have parents who are either rejecting and punitive or else **overprotective** (Sears et al., 1957). Children who are prevented from exploring the world while they are young, because their parents are either too fearful or too restrictive, may be afraid to explore later. Such children develop a self-concept of being dependent on their parents, rather than independent and self-sufficient. Children who feel loved and therefore secure develop a self-concept of being adequate and are not afraid to venture into the world at the proper time.

> Maureen, a very pretty 3-year-old whose parents both worked, was left with a full-time babysitter. The babysitter, a gentle, elderly woman, became very attached to the child and soon developed the need for Maureen to be dependent on her. She slept with Maureen when the child napped, refused to let her play at other children's homes, and even fed her, although Maureen could easily feed herself. Maureen did become dependent on the babysitter and soon internalized the self-concept that she was helpless—a self-concept the woman unknowingly encouraged.
>
> Not only was Maureen overprotected, but she was also overindulged. She was always able to get what she wanted by crying or throwing a tantrum. The babysitter was so afraid of losing the child's affection and so devoted to her that she frequently spent her own salary on gifts for the girl. Maureen made occasional attempts to break away by playing with other children, but the older woman hovered around, and the other children soon preferred to avoid this well-meaning but irritating supervision. When offered the alternative of a dish of ice cream with "the kids" or a walk to the store with the babysitter, Maureen would always choose to take the walk. (P.S. She got the ice cream anyway.)

RELATING TO OTHER CHILDREN

Although parents are the most meaningful significant others, other people become increasingly important to children as they grow older. Playmates and **siblings,** a term used to indicate both brothers and sisters, are among the most influential of these other people.

COMPETING FOR ATTENTION

The first child in the family has the full attention of his parents—until a sibling is born. Then he faces competition. All the aunts and uncles and grandparents and friends who used to tell 4-year-old Joey how cute he was now tell Joey how cute Lisa is. To top it all off, Joey's mother was taken away to the hospital, and Joey was shipped off to live with Grandmother. As soon as he returned, he was warned "Shut up, keep out of the way, and don't bother the baby."

After this introduction Joey is expected to show love, loyalty, devotion, and respect to the little creature that cries at all hours, cannot even talk, and is absolutely no fun to play with. Often the result is **sibling rivalry,** an intense and often hostile competition between two children in the same family.

To some extent older children can be prepared for the arrival of a new sibling.

> Leah, aged 2½, was well prepared for the birth of a new sibling. She felt the movement in her mother's tummy and even claimed "I have a baby in my tummy, too." She took great pride in becoming a big sister—a feeling her parents encouraged—and she was made to feel that the baby would be hers as much as her parents'. When the baby arrived, her parents made an extra fuss over Leah and depended on her help in various ways, such as for getting diapers out of the drawer and patting the baby's back when he needed to be burped.

> Jerry was 3½ when his sister was born. His parents talked about the coming baby and told Jerry he would love her and protect her. But when the baby arrived, Jerry was shushed, ignored, told to play outside, and rarely allowed to see her. When he did see his sister, he was instructed to kiss her and fuss over her. Within a few months, Jerry learned that the best attack was to pretend to show affection; while apparently kissing the baby, he would bite or pinch her. His parents punished him severely, and Jerry withdrew completely from his sister. In later years he had very little to do with her.

When the older child is not properly prepared for the new sibling and not allowed to play a part in the new infant's life, several reactions can occur: (1) active or subtle aggression directed against the baby; (2) increased attempts to gain attention from the parents, including—if necessary—naughty behavior, even though it may be punished; (3) attempts to get even with the parents; (4) withdrawal from the parents, to avoid the possibility of further emotional hurt; (5) **regression,** or a return to earlier forms of behavior such as bed-wetting, crying, or wanting a bottle.

Sibling rivalry can become intense and bitter, since the children are fighting for the attention of the most important people they know. Some parents make matters worse by comparing the children with each other: "Robert made good grades in school—why can't you?" "Mary Jean didn't wet her panties when she was 3."

Occasionally sibling rivalry is so intense that a grown child is afraid to leave home for fear that the remaining sibling will oust him from the good graces of the family. Most incidents of severe sibling rivalry cease after the children go to college or establish their own homes. By then the individuals have achieved a

FIGURE 12–4.   Relationships between brothers and sisters can be emotionally healthy. Photograph by P. C. Peri.

sense of personal adequacy without being so dependent on their parents. However, the effects do not always disappear.

PLAYMATES AND FRIENDS

Friendship among young children is usually limited to children in the immediate neighborhood and to children brought to visit by family friends. These **peer-group** friendships become more stable over the years until, by the third or fourth grade, a child may feel very uncomfortable leaving his friends and moving into a strange community (Hurlock, 1959).

Early social relationships may be very important for later adjustment. Generalizing from laboratory studies with monkeys, it appears that social relationships among those of the same age group grow stronger with maturation, but mother-child relationships weaken (Harlow & Harlow, 1967). These healthy social relationships are enriching and may partially compensate for inadequate parent-child relationships. Motherless monkeys who were allowed to play with one another showed normal social development, but comparable monkeys with no play opportunity were severely retarded socially (Harlow & Harlow, 1962b).

Children are not very subtle in their behavior. If they do not like someone, they will let him know it. The unpopular preschool child is described as one who "attacks vigorously, strikes frequently, or pushes and pulls." Other traits that lead to unpopularity include overdependence on adults, unwillingness to accept the routine of other children, and disrespect for the property of others (Hurlock, 1959).

In later childhood, playmates are usually of the same sex; social class, race, and religion also begin to influence friendships. Being accepted by a friendship group is important to people of all ages, and children are no exception.

PLAY IS MORE THAN FUN

Children's play is very important to proper development, although adults may think of it merely as a pleasant way for children to pass time. Play provides a child's initial experiences in entering into social relationships with others of the same age. At first children play by themselves. Soon they enjoy having another child around during their play. However, each child will play with his own things, by himself; the only contact between the two may be arguments when both want the same toy at the same time. This kind of play is known as **parallel play,** since the children are not interacting. Children begin to play with each other when they are about $2\frac{1}{2}$ or 3 (although, if one child is older, play may begin much earlier). Through such play they learn the need for sharing and for give-and-take.

Play also allows children to use their imaginations. They can travel to the zoo, take an airplane trip, or visit the planet Mars—all through the wonderful device of play. At the same time they can try out new roles by being Mommy or Daddy and thus experiment with their future behavior.

Children have many aggressive feelings that are not permitted direct expression but can be expressed through play. A young girl who is angry with her parents may gain some satisfaction by punishing a doll; a boy who has been spanked for breaking a dish can build a skyscraper of blocks and smash it to the floor.

Many other feelings besides aggression can be expressed through play. The little girl who is very attentive to her doll may be behaving as her mother has behaved with her, or she may be trying to compensate for a lack of maternal affection. (Can you suggest other interpretations?) She imagines herself as the doll and thus can receive from Mother (herself) the love she does not receive from her real mother.

Another benefit of play is that it leads to learning. This learning may take the

FIGURE 12–5.   Play provides exercise, excitement, and entertainment for children. Photograph by P. C. Peri.

form of new motor skills, such as hopping or skipping; increased verbal ability, which results from trying to communicate with others; or increased ability to understand and get along with others. Play gives children exercise, provides excitement, and is entertaining.

The attitude of adults can either contribute to or detract from the value and pleasure of play. To encourage appropriate play, adults should treat each individual child with respect, allow him freedom to make noise and get dirty (unless there are good reasons not to), enjoy the child's enjoyment, and provide him with toys that stimulate his imagination.

ALTRUISM AND THE NEED FOR ACHIEVEMENT

Altruism refers to behavior "intended to benefit another but which appear(s) to have a high cost to the (altruistic) person with little possibility of material or social reward" (Bryan & London, 1970, p. 200). You are altruistic when you donate money to a charity (especially if you do it anonymously), when you stop to help someone, when you go out of your way to drop a very casual friend at his home, when you lend someone money (especially if you know you will probably never see it again), when you give blood, or when you offer your time to work with a volunteer fire department or a tutoring program for ghetto children. Obviously you receive recognition for some of these altruistic gestures, but the recognition is not enough to make the job worth doing. The greatest reward for altruistic behavior is **psychic satisfaction** — that is, it makes you feel good to help someone else.

The **achievement need** refers to the desire to succeed or to accomplish something. People with a high need to achieve are usually ambitious, independent, and highly competitive. They prefer to take risks at achieving great success rather than to settle for security and average success (Rogers, 1969). Achievement needs may be satisfied through earning money, getting high grades, gaining high political office, climbing a previously unclimbed mountain, getting a lot of work done, or selling the most advertising for the campus newspaper.

On the surface, altruistic behavior and achieving behavior might seem to conflict, but this need not be the case. A person with a great need to achieve who is reasonably successful may take pleasure in giving his time, money, or energy for psychic satisfaction. If his need to achieve is too high, however, he will expend all his efforts in striving for success and pay little heed to altruistic behavior.

Both achievement and altruism are considered desirable by most people, although there is always someone to claim that chasing success or giving things away is only "for suckers." Also, parents and other significant others can increase achieving or altruistic behavior through their encouragement (Mussen et al., 1969; Bryan & London, 1970).

Not all kinds of achievement are rewarded. Boys may not be encouraged to achieve at sewing; Russian children are not encouraged to achieve if the achievement conflicts in any way with their being obedient (Bronfenbrenner, 1970); a college student may be pressured by his friends against getting too high an exam grade; a factory worker who far out-achieves the others on the production line is criticized as being a rate buster; competitive behavior is regarded negatively in many cultures.

Altruism is also seen as having a point beyond which people are not encouraged to go. Although in theory you may admire someone who gives up everything he owns to work with the poor, in practice you are likely to think he is foolish. How do you feel about the soldier who sacrifices his life to save his friend? What would you try to teach your own children to do in the following circumstances?

—A tough older child is beating up your child's friend, and there is no one in sight to call for help.

—Your child's friend has a broken leg, and his mother asks your child to come over two or three times a week to explain the homework; this means missing some enjoyable afternoon activities.

—An elderly woman asks your child to help her get on the right bus; if he waits with her, he will be late for school.

—Your child finds a letter in the street with an address but no stamp or return address; by holding it up to the light, he can see that there is money in the envelope.

Would you do the same things you would try to teach your child to do?

FIGURE 12–6. During the decade from ages 3 through 12, the child develops amazing motor skills and an awareness of complex social relationships. Photograph by Liane Enkelis.

OTHER KINDS OF DEVELOPMENT

Although our major focus has been on personality development and directly related matters such as parent-child relationships, internalized attitudes, and social interactions with peers, all these factors depend on other kinds of development. During the decade from ages 3 through 12, the child develops amazing motor skills. His body grows and his physical appearance changes. Intellectual progress is immense, not only in school learning but also in awareness of the world, of complex social relationships, of the significance of humor, and so forth. And each of these changes comes right back to interact with the kinds of development we have been discussing in detail.

SUMMARY OF IMPORTANT IDEAS

1. Adults who are satisfied with their own lives seem to be better parents. They are more likely to permit their children the proper balance of freedom and responsibility.

2. Many parents want to see their children self-actualize through optimum development of their talents. Unfortunately, not all parents are able to create the best environment for such development.

3. Certain limits need to be placed on the behavior of children. These limits should be enforced with consistency but with minimal punishment.

4. The child begins to develop a conscience when he is about 3 years old. He tends to accept the values and behavior of significant others as his own and to incorporate them into his conscience. This process is called internalization.

5. Inappropriate behavior is prevented by shame, by guilt or conscience, or by fear of punishment. Some cultures emphasize shame, and others maintain control through guilt.

6. An appropriate amount of conscience is more likely to be developed by children brought up in warm, loving homes. In some instances, conscience and resulting guilt feelings become unnecessarily self-punishing.

7. All people experience aggressive feelings and dependent feelings.

8. Sibling rivalry often develops between two children in the same family.

9. Social relationships with age peers are very important, even to young children. Such relationships can, to some extent, compensate for inadequate parent-child relationships.

10. Play enables children to learn to get along with others, to use their imaginations, to express many feelings indirectly, and to learn new motor and verbal skills.

11. Altruism and the need for achievement are two personality characteristics that develop during childhood.

13 The Adolescent Years

As the infant becomes a child and then an adolescent, his world becomes increasingly diverse. It is no longer limited to parents and a handful of significant others. Now he encounters a great variety of people who represent wide ranges of age, social class, belief systems, ethnic and religious backgrounds, motives, and goals. At the same time the individual becomes more and more responsible for making the decisions that affect his own life.

Adolescence seems to be a period of misunderstanding, with everyone insisting that *he* is the one being misunderstood. So much attention is given to the rebellion of teenagers that some of them probably feel they should rebel—whether they want to or not.

The decade between ages 12 and 21 is often considered a time of preparation for eventual maturity. Physically the individual attains full strength, maturity, and reproductive ability. Socially he accomplishes three major developmental tasks: (1) he moves from his parents' home and readies himself for becoming a parent in his own family, (2) he ceases to receive **nurture** and becomes capable of giving nurture himself, and (3) he learns to work and to love (Group for the Advancement of Psychiatry, 1968). By the end of this period the individual is expected to be ready to take his place as a self-sustaining member of the community.

The years of adolescence and the beginnings of young adulthood involve more than mere preparation and transition. Maturation results from a dynamic interaction of physical changes, personal changes, social changes, and changes in the environment. During this decade the individual awakens to the world around him and to his own sense of identity.

In a sense, the idea of adolescence as a distinct period in the life process is relatively new. Because of the extensive education demanded in the modern world, and because adolescents are no longer needed in the labor force, entrance into adult society is often postponed until a person is in his twenties. In past centuries the individual assumed adult responsibilities while still in his teens, often married before 20, and seldom lived beyond 50.

Even recently many **preliterate** (primitive) societies inducted the male child into official manhood at around age 13, when he became physically and sexually mature. Ceremonies of induction, known as **puberty rites,** often included painful rituals and demanded that the boy show his ability to fend for himself. At this time the boy was taught some of the tribal secrets, and he was thereafter considered in many ways to be an adult. (Why do you suppose the girls were usually ignored in this procedure?) In these societies the male moved directly from childhood to manhood without an intervening adolescence. Our society, however, recognizes adolescence as a separate phase. During this phase the person is especially aware of changes in the body, in the sense of individual identity, and in the form and meaning of social relationships, including sexual relationships.

THE CHANGING GROWTH PATTERN

The growth rate of children, which is very rapid during the very early years, tapers off until girls are about 10 and boys are about 12 (Tanner, 1961). At these ages a **growth spurt** occurs that lasts for about two or three years. Since this spurt begins sooner for girls, there is a period of a year or two when girls are taller than boys—the only time during the entire life-span when this is true.

PUBERTY

Before the end of the growth spurt, the child begins to enter **puberty,** the stage in his life when he becomes sexually mature. Most girls begin puberty, which is marked by the first menstrual period, between ages 12 and 14, although the range is from 10 to 17 (Cole & Hall, 1964). The determination of when puberty begins is less precise for boys, but it occurs about one year later than for girls.

Physiological changes accompanying puberty are well known. They include the growth of body hair and—primarily for boys—the growth of facial hair; changes in the contours of the body and the beginning of breast development for girls; the cracked voice for boys, which embarrasses them so frequently and which eventually matures into the adult male voice; and the beginning of menstrual bleeding for girls—at first irregularly and, later, every month.

AFTER PUBERTY

Physical growth tapers off slowly after puberty until, by the middle or late teens, the adolescent has reached his adult size. During this period the body-image is extremely important, and such concerns as being too tall (primarily for girls), too small (primarily for boys), too fat, or too thin are common. Another source of anxiety is adolescent acne, which causes more "maladjustments between parents and children, more general insecurity and feelings of inferiority, and greater (emotional) suffering . . ." than any other medical problem (Sulzberger & Zaidens, 1948). Unfortunately, no effective treatment for acne has been found, although proper health practices regarding rest, cleanliness, and diet are undoubtedly helpful.

Intellectual growth is also considerable during adolescence. Not only does the individual absorb a great deal of information and understanding, but his ability

FIGURE 13–1. With adolescence comes an increased ability to deal in abstract concepts. Photograph by Lehman J. Pinckney.

to deal in abstract concepts improves greatly. He is able to move away from what he observes and learns to deal with hypothetical propositions (for example, "If the gravitational pull of the moon is . . ." or "If my teacher thinks that I am . . . , then I had better . . ."). Intellectual stimulation is often welcomed during adolescence (Horrocks, 1969).

THE DEVELOPING SELF

Who are you? Not your name or your physical appearance or your family history but the *real* you — the you no one really knows, perhaps not even yourself. In other words, what is your **self?** Not your self-concept but your actual self.

A confusing question? Certainly, but a question that begins to have meaning during adolescence. According to one well-known psychoanalyst, the question of **identity** is the major "psychosocial crisis" that faces people between ages 12 and 21. To continue toward self-actualization, teenagers must — and usually do — overcome this crisis (Erikson, 1956).

How do you know when you are being yourself? As you behave, you become aware of your behavior and decide, partly consciously and partly unconsciously, whether the behavior represents "the real you" or not. When the behavior is not consistent with "the real you," you may feel "I am not myself." This feeling is upsetting and causes emotional discomfort. You may also be concerned about the effect you have on others when you are not yourself (Jourard, 1963).

People become unhappy when others treat them as though they had no identity. We refer to large, impersonal universities as factories, even though we recognize that their educational programs may be of high quality. You are probably pleased when someone remembers your name, because that signifies his awareness of your identity; you are an individual, apart from the thousands of other people he has met. People talk longingly of small towns, where everyone knows everyone else, because the individual has identity in these communities. The impersonality of large medical clinics, the use of numbers instead of names to identify people, the vast growth of computers, identical home designs — all are cited as examples of the loss of identity of the individual, regardless of their contributions to efficiency and the "good life."

In a world where many people complain about a lack of identity, it is not surprising that the adolescent is still seeking his. In his search he tries out new behavior patterns and new styles of living to see which ones are comfortable. For example, adolescents experiment with styles of handwriting, with variations in spelling their names, with an assortment of nicknames, with hairstyles and clothing styles, with speech mannerisms. The adolescent tries each of them on like a new pair of shoes, walks around a bit, and then decides whether it fits or not.

During the years of adolescence, young people also try out more important styles of behaving.

"It's some years ago, but I can still remember. One day I thought I'd be romantic and dashing, but that didn't work too well, so the next day I was the sweet-and-understanding type. That was better, but I still tried out a few others: I was the silent-and-in-emotional-pain type, the happy-go-lucky type, and the big-spender type. But each time I came back to the sweet-and-under-standing type. Even though I was aware of what I was doing, I kept feeling that I was really being myself. Today I don't try to be any type any more, but I guess that I still think of myself as more like the sweet-and-understanding type than anything else. Of course, I do know I'm not always either sweet or understanding."

Adolescents are strongly motivated to find out who they are and then to be-have consistently with what they feel that self to be. In attempting to learn who they are, adolescents and young adults have the added problem of trying to cope with a rapidly changing society. "Young people are . . . forced to make major deci-sions which will critically influence their lives, yet the increasing complexity of society has reduced assurances that their decisions will lead to [appropriate] goals" (Trent & Medsker, 1967). While trying to gain a sense of personal identity, teenagers need to have an awareness of their goals, which they can formulate only in terms of what they want to do in the future. Many in this age group feel be-wildered about why their life after high school graduation was not so satisfactory as they had anticipated, and they feel frustrated because of their powerlessness to produce any change (Trent & Medsker, 1967). They do not understand what they should do to make their future satisfying in such an uncertain world.

THE ADOLESCENT ROLE

Strange as it may seem, adolescents form a minority group that is the object of discrimination, prejudice, and segregation. And they respond, much as mem-bers of other minority groups, by forming their own society with its own rules and customs—a society that resembles the general society in most ways but in which some behaviors are distorted or exaggerated.

Adolescents in the United States are given no real place in the community. They are no longer satisfied with being children; yet adult opportunities, such as regular employment, sex and marriage, and independence and responsibility for their own behavior, are not available. They are reminded of their second-class citizenship by everything from restrictions on buying a bottle of beer to editorials in newspapers. Adults often consider them unstable, immature, and potentially violent. They are treated as being dependent and ineffective (Ausubel, 1954). Adults often feel that the only proper task for adolescents is to complete their education (Menninger, 1968), but even that accomplishment is not to help the adolescent self-actualize but to produce achievement and productivity that will help support the society run by adults (Kalish, 1969).

Three changes have taken place in the adolescent role over the past 60 years. First, teenagers have much more personal money. Although they may hold jobs and earn the money to make their own purchases, their earnings are no longer necessary for the well-being and support of the family. Second, since their schooling has been extended, few adolescents are in the labor force. Third, and perhaps because of the first two, the dependent role of the adolescent has been prolonged; he is well advanced in physical, sexual, and intellectual maturity before he can make his own decisions and lead his own life. Perhaps this kind of dependency provokes the adolescent to prove his maturity to himself and others by turning to violence and thrill seeking (Soskin, Duhl, & Leopold, 1968).

In years past, and in many parts of the world today, adolescents have been given a great deal of responsibility, from doing household chores to working side by side with adults in the field and the factory. These tasks were not just busy work but were essential for keeping the family going. In our country today we do not need to have adolescents take on these responsibilities, and we have deprived them of the feeling that they are making a real contribution. The Latter-Day Saints (Mormons) encourage their young people to participate in community responsibility; perhaps their low school dropout and delinquency rates are partly a result of their willingness to allow youths to assume a mature role.

A counterforce to these social changes that deprive the teenager of responsibility is the reduction of legal voting age from 21 to 18. As a result, the adolescent is recognized as having the ability and judgment to participate in a major decision-making process. His vote will count as much on election day as that of his father or mother. Whether the teenage vote will have a major influence on elections or whether, as when women were given the vote, they will vote as others in their family do, will not be certain until several elections have been held.

Perhaps adults overemphasize the differences between the teen culture and their own. For example, the social, political, religious, and other values of teenagers closely resemble those of their parents (Hyman, 1959; Troll, 1969). College women's values concerning political and social issues were found to be very much like those of their mothers and even their grandmothers, although each generation was a little farther to what is seen as the left than its predecessor (Kalish & Johnson, 1972). However, although each teenager resembles his own parents, the average teenager is more liberal than his parents (Kalish & Johnson, 1972). The difference in values, then, between the more liberal teenager and the average of his parents' *generation* is considerable, whereas the difference in values between the more conservative teenager and the average of his parents' generation is slight. If you can follow this logic, you will have some clues as to why the more liberal students are the most aggressive in condemning the views of their parents' *generation* while still being sympathetic with their own parents.

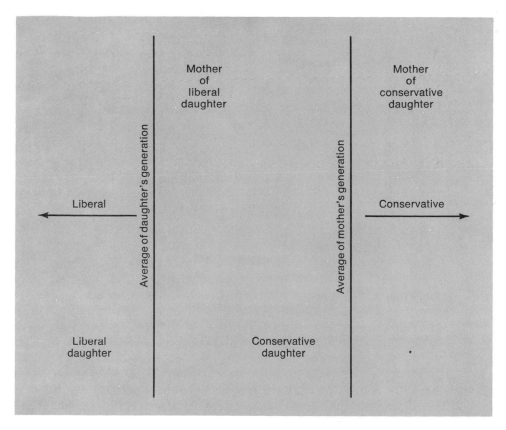

FIGURE 13–2.   The difference in values between the more liberal teenagers and the average of their parents' *generation* is considerable, whereas the difference in values between the more conservative teenagers and the average of their parents' generation is slight.

EMANCIPATION AND PRIMARY STATUS

As long as teenagers live with their parents and are dependent on them, they are identified as their parents' children. One author has described this position as **derived status,** because teenagers *derive* their *status* and identity directly from the status and identity of the parents, and because the parents are considered largely responsible for what the children do (Ausubel, 1954).

FIGURE 13–3.   One way to leave home. Photograph by Lehman J. Pinckney.

In their own culture, adolescents have **primary status.** Here the teenager is not known as Mrs. Johnson's boy but as Jack Johnson, who is responsible for his own behavior.

Although parents encourage their late-adolescent children to take responsibility and behave in a mature fashion, they often find it difficult to allow the children any decision-making power (Ausubel, 1954). The adult seems to be saying "I'll give you freedom and decision-making power when you prove to me that you're mature." The teen-ager responds "How can I prove I'm mature when you don't treat me as a responsible person?"

Sometimes, in an effort to emancipate themselves and establish primary status, teenagers will leave home against their parents' wishes. Boys may enlist in the military, and girls may get married; both, of course, can get work. Our society seems to perceive a married person or a working person as deserving primary status, and studies suggest that the main reason why teenagers work is to become more independent of parents (Boys' Clubs of America, 1960). Many college students become frustrated over remaining financially dependent on their parents while their friends are emancipating themselves through marriage and full-time jobs.

Not all adolescents seek emancipation. Freedom can be frightening, particularly for people whose physiological, security, and love needs are not adequately satisfied. To leave home and become established on your own demands giving up many of the comforts and satisfactions that you have been accustomed to. More than that, it demands that you make your own decisions and take responsibility for your own actions. Many people prefer to allow others to make decisions for them. If they leave home, they quickly find a person or an organization to tell them what to do and how to behave.

Slowly, however, the adolescent gains freedom from his parents and emerges into the community as a person in his own right—as a person with primary status. He no longer needs the teen culture for support. He can now take his place in the adult community and will very quickly become responsive to its demands.

Even after basic acceptance by the adult community, people seem to prefer to spend their time with their own age group. Perhaps they feel more comfortable with others who have lived through the same kinds of world experiences at the same general age (for example, being in high school during the height of the protest movement or being among the first to vote before age 21). Or perhaps their status in society, in terms of work, marriage, education, and so forth, is determined largely by age even after they become adults. Whatever the reasons, this tendency exists throughout the life-span for most people.

Some adolescents and college students face a more difficult task in their relationships with their parents. For them the problem is not how to become emancipated but how to deal with problem parents. All parents are, at various times, seen as problems by their children. But I am referring to adults who are too immature to take responsibility, who are too temperamental to hold a job, whose heavy drinking or sexual promiscuity or violent behavior gets them into constant trouble. These people's children face experiences that other children do not face: rarely having a meal set before them, finding a different man in their mother's bed every month, being severely beaten. These adolescents will become emancipated at an early age and with minimal conflicts (Ausubel, 1954). However, consider the other problems they may need to deal with.

FRIENDSHIPS

Since the peer group provides primary status and individual identity, acceptance by this group is vital to most teenagers. Unlike the adult who knows the limits of what he can do and still be socially acceptable, the adolescent is less sure of his identity and is not willing to risk a blunder that might cost him status in the age group that accepts him. Thus he is willing to accept pressures from his peers that he would vehemently reject from his parents. When he was young and his parents were the major significant others, he accepted their demands with little questioning. Now his friends are the primary source of satisfaction of his

FIGURE 13–4. The teenager's friends become a primary source of satisfaction for security, love, and esteem needs. Photograph by Lehman J. Pinckney.

security, love, and esteem needs, and the adolescent wants to do his best to see those needs continually satisfied.

When adults criticize the adolescent's friendship group, they are attacking the basis of his status and esteem, and he becomes very defensive (especially if he recognizes the adult comments as largely true, since this possibility is very damaging to his self-concept). In the long run, however, and with some obvious exceptions, the qualities that make an adolescent popular with his peer group and acceptable as a date are qualities that adults approve of.

All people have the potential to enter into warm and mutually rewarding friendships. The value of friendship is widely recognized, and most college students state that they would rather have a few close friends than a large circle of casual acquaintances.

Deep and sincere friendships are very satisfying, but they also present the possibility of loss. When you like someone, you place trust in him and become dependent on him in certain ways. If he disapproves of your behavior, you are more than normally upset; if he ignores you, moves away, or dies, you may feel you have been cheated, even though you recognize how unfair such a feeling is. You have invested a part of yourself in him, just as you invest money in a bank, and you count on some sort of return. If you get nothing in return or, worse, if the investment is destroyed, the emotional pain can be great. In any form of friendship, and especially in love and marriage, people take a chance on being hurt. To gain from a relationship, you must risk something. The emotionally healthy person has sufficient feelings of self-adequacy that he can take this risk. But some individuals may experience too much anxiety in risking a close friendship and are unable to trust anyone enough to give, or even to receive, in a close relationship. For example, foster children who are moved from home to home are often unable to trust others. In their experience, each time they allow themselves to like a new foster family, they are moved somewhere else.

BUILDING HEALTHY FRIENDSHIPS

Good friendships are based on many factors. Friends tend to be of the same racial, religious, social, and age groups; they tend to have similar intelligence and get similar grades; they tend to live or work near each other.

Friends also have similar needs, interests, reading habits, morals, and scores on personality tests (Ausubel, 1954; Banta & Hetherington, 1963; Izard, 1963). These factors enable people to satisfy each other's needs and to communicate with understanding—a condition just as important in healthy friendships as in good marriages. Thus in friendships, as in all healthy human relationships, the parties resemble each other in certain ways but also complement each other by satisfying each other's needs.

Carl Rogers, a well-known and highly respected psychologist, makes the following conclusions about self-awareness and friendship:

*It does not help, in the long run, to act like someone I am not.**

To pretend to be someone or to know something or to feel in some way that is not true to yourself builds neither friendship nor trust nor your own self-concept.

I find I am more effective when I can listen acceptingly to myself and can be myself.

People should try to understand how they really feel about others and not condemn themselves if these feelings are not what they "should be." If you are bored or irritated with someone, you should recognize how you feel and not be self-critical.

I have found it of enormous value when I can permit myself to understand another person.

Instead of trying to judge the words or behavior of another person critically, it is more valuable to try to understand why he does what he does.

I have found it enriching to open channels through which others can communicate their feelings to me.

People are often reluctant to discuss their real feelings for fear they will be laughed at or criticized. It is rewarding to allow someone to express his feelings to you, even if you disagree with him.

I have found it highly rewarding when I can accept another person.

It is not easy to accept another person for himself, without basing your acceptance on his race or his money or his beliefs or his age. Yet accepting someone along with his feelings and attitudes and values —even if they are different from yours—is rewarding.

The more I am aware of myself and others, the less I wish to rush in to "fix things."

In relationships with other people, you gain more by being yourself and trying to understand and accept others than by trying to change them (Rogers, 1961).

Healthy friendships are a source of satisfaction to both parties and help both parties become more complete and individual. Although friendships do place some restrictions on behavior, the overall result of a good friendship is that both individuals feel liked and respected and enjoy more, rather than less, freedom.

---

*The italicized statements are either directly quoted or slightly altered from Rogers' original statements.

POPULARITY

Every high school has one or more high-status crowds, consisting largely of the best-liked students and the student leaders. A study (Friesen, 1968) of more than 10,000 Canadian high school students, drawn from all over the nation, showed that friendliness is considered the primary qualification for getting into the leading crowd. Only a small fraction selected athletic ability as most important, but even that small fraction was nearly three times as large as the smaller fraction listing academic competence as most important. Not all studies have come to the same conclusion, however; Coleman (1961) found that boys considered athletic ability to be the major prerequisite for popularity.

BOY-GIRL RELATIONSHIPS

With the onset of puberty American adolescents become immersed in concerns over boy-girl relationships. Less than a decade ago a study of teenagers reported that dating began for most girls around age 14 and for most boys between a few months and a year later. By 17, nearly all adolescents were dating (Douvan & Adelson, 1966). And it appeared that dating was starting at younger and younger ages (Horrocks, 1969).

Then, in the late 1960s and early 1970s, a move away from previous forms of dating seemed to occur. Although the one-to-one date was not uncommon, both teenagers and college students began to spend more time in informal groups, without expecting everyone to be paired off. Even the word *dating* was used much less, and *going steady* was rarely heard, although many teenagers did in fact restrict their social life to only one person. Whether this trend is fairly permanent or only temporary is not yet known.

Being with friends of the opposite sex, whether on dates or in groups, is more than a way of spending time and having fun. It influences attitudes and behavior in many ways. Thus *going out together:*

. . . *affects the self-concept.* A girl knows she is well liked when she receives many calls to go out. Her self-concept develops accordingly. The boy will react similarly; if he finds girls are eager to be with him, his self-concept will be favorably affected.

. . . *is an indication of prestige and reputation.* Teenagers are judged not only by their own accomplishments but also by the popularity and accomplishments of those with whom they go out.

. . . *is an opportunity for learning.* The demands of married life in the United States and Canada are great because so much is expected of each partner. Both

FIGURE 13–5.   Being with friends of the opposite sex is a way of spending time and having fun, but it is also much more than that. Photograph
by Lehman J. Pinckney.

husbands and wives *expect* their mates to understand them, to be sensitive to
their needs, and to supply love, affection, and companionship. To deal with the
complexities of selecting the right spouse and living enjoyably with that person, a
great deal of experience and understanding are needed. Some of this occurs
through observing the relationship between the parents, but much can be learned
through the give-and-take of dating.

   . . . *allows young people to get to know many potential mates* in a very personal, informal situation, which in some ways is a preliminary to a permanent relationship. The teenager can test out certain behaviors, attitudes, and roles in a
relatively harmless arrangement. He can gain an understanding of the type of behavior that appeals to him in the opposite sex, and of what in his behavior appeals
to the opposite sex. In many societies, marriages are arranged and dating opportunities are limited or nonexistent, and the expectations each married person has
of his spouse are usually different from those of Americans. Talk to people from
other countries, and see if you can learn how different marital roles require different sorts of experience before marriage.

ATTITUDES TOWARD DATING

Many investigators have asked high school and college students to list the characteristics they consider most important in a date or future spouse. The lists are all a little different, but a 1956 University of Michigan study of qualities wanted in a date is still fairly typical. These students selected as most important being pleasant and cheerful, having a sense of humor, being a good sport, being natural, being considerate, and having a neat appearance (Blood, 1956). The same study also showed that men tended to overestimate how strongly the girls felt about their belonging to a fraternity, having money, dressing well, and being good dancers.

What are your motives for going out? Undoubtedly you have many, and they differ from those of your friends to some extent. There is reason to believe that men and women do not have the same primary motives in dating. Women seem more concerned about courtship, whereas men find recreation of greater importance (Skipper & Nass, 1966). Physical attractiveness and the possibility of sexual relations also play a major role. One research team arranged dates for college students on a chance basis and then obtained numerous personality and ability-test scores on all the students as well as an evaluation by outsiders of the physical attractiveness of each student. Later they asked each participant how much he liked his partner and whether he wanted another date. The *only* basis for approval found in this study was physical attractiveness: the more attractive the date, the more the person was liked (Walster, Aronson, Abrahams, & Rottmann, 1966). In surveys students do not express so much concern for physical attractiveness, but apparently the concern is there. The results of this study suggest definite limitations on some kinds of survey research—and also on computerized match-making.

GOING TOGETHER

Whether the arrangement is *going steady* (a formal agreement, perhaps involving an exchange of jewelry and an official announcement), *going steadily* (an informal agreement not to go out with others), or *going together* (spending most or all available time together), many students couple off with some feeling of long-term commitment to each other.

The difficulties of very intense relationships, regardless of what they are termed, include the possibility of getting bored with each other but being unable to break the habit, of moving into an overly demanding sex relationship, of limiting other social contacts, and of undergoing emotional strain from fear of breakups and suspected unfaithfulness. The biggest problem, however, is that of working into a marriage before the individuals are ready. As students move from early adolescence through the college years, the possibility of a relationship's becoming permanent increases.

Dating: Other Places and Other Times

Dating as practiced by most college students is a recent phenomenon that occurs mostly in the United States, Canada, and some European countries. The idea of a boy asking a girl to spend an unchaperoned evening with him was unknown a century ago. The couple might have gone for a Sunday afternoon walk, or they might have sneaked away from the community picnic to be together, but such activities are a far cry from present dating behavior.

In African, Asian, South American, and some European countries, going out "American style" is either virtually unknown or limited to a very small proportion of the population, usually the more wealthy and sophisticated. Even in those European countries where dating is common, group activities occur more frequently than the single date or double date, and going steady is usually avoided until the young people are in their late teens.

Chaperones are still very common in such places as the Philippines and Latin America. A young couple going to the movies is accompanied by an older relative or a trusted family friend. Sunday afternoon strolls are popular in many parts of the world, but parents may demand that even these walks be chaperoned, at least from a distance.

When a boy in Iraq wants to meet a girl he has seen, he must first ask his parents or a close friend to find out about the girl. Then he will try to arrange for his parents to call on the girl's parents and take him along or for the mutual friend to introduce them. Eventually he will be admitted to the girl's house without his parents, but the couple will never be left alone until they are engaged. In the meantime, they may be passing exciting love notes back and forth through a mutual friend or a servant.

A Japanese girl expressed what many students around the world probably feel: "I would like to be more free than I am, but I would not like to be free like American girls. They do too much with boys that is wrong. American parents are not strict enough with their daughters. And I know from talking to American students that their freedom does not make them any happier than we. No nice Japanese boy would marry a girl who behaved like an American girl."

SUMMARY OF IMPORTANT IDEAS

1. The decade from 12 through 21 is not only a transition from childhood to mature responsibility and opportunity but also a time of increased concern about the world and about a sense of personal identity.

2. Adolescence is not a distinct developmental period in all societies.

3. The growth spurt begins shortly before puberty. During and after puberty, many sex-related physiological changes occur.

4. After puberty, physiological growth slowly tapers off, but the importance of the body-image remains great.

5. Many adolescents are involved in a search for identity and a desire to understand *who* they are.

6. Adolescents are a minority group that is discriminated against; they have rejected the role of children but are not accepted as adults. Eventually they are emancipated and attain primary, rather than derived, status in the general community.

7. The importance of the peer group is that it is the only source of primary status for the adolescent.

8. The person with a healthy personality can give to and receive from friends.

9. High status and popularity in high school are determined by a variety of factors, usually including friendliness and, for boys, athletic ability.

10. The meaning of the term *dating* may be undergoing change, but boy-girl relationships are still of deep concern to American and Canadian adolescents.

14 The Student: In College and Out

The role of higher education has become increasingly important as knowledge and technology advance, and the role of the student in college has become increasingly difficult and demanding. For many students college provides freedom and responsibilities that are new, often exciting, and sometimes frightening. Unlike the high school student, the college student can drop out of school whenever he — or his college — sees fit. At the same time, his close, warm relationships with significant others have changed considerably, and love, sex, marriage, and work relationships move into the limelight.

Make the most of your capabilities! It's easy to say, but to do so takes more than good intentions — it demands that certain skills and knowledge be acquired. College not only provides an excellent source for obtaining some of these necessary skills and knowledge, but also offers new opportunities and helps develop interests and capabilities you may not have realized you had.

One way to evaluate the importance of higher education is to look at the attendance figures. In 1970 well over 6 million students were taking courses in the United States and another half million in Canada, with the number expected to continue to rise. Enrollment more than doubled between 1960 and 1970. The percentage increase is particularly dramatic in two-year colleges that award an Associate of Arts or comparable degree. About one-third of all colleges are two-year colleges, and new ones are still coming into existence.

Another, perhaps more pertinent, way to evaluate higher education is to determine whether colleges and universities are doing their job. This method requires a step back to examine what colleges and universities *should* be doing. Some immediate questions appear:

—What is the relative importance in a college education of job readiness, critical thinking, social awareness, and breadth or depth of knowledge?
—Do employers require a college degree because the education has meaning for the job or because such a requirement simplifies their hiring practices?
—Can everyone benefit from college, or should some individuals pursue their education through business colleges, technical institutes, art and drama schools, secretarial schools, and schools providing specialized programs for nurses, morticians, keypunch operators, and so on?

FIGURE 14–1. Can everyone benefit from college, or should some individuals pursue their education through technical institutes? Photograph courtesy of Litton Industries.

—Are some people better able to achieve their goals by not taking any post-high school educational or training program, other than on-the-job training? If so, who are these people?
—Should college-sponsored groups take stands on political and social issues,

or should these groups merely study the issues, leaving the political stands to off-campus organizations?

— Should college faculty encourage students to look critically at today's social institutions, with an eye to changing them, or should faculty provide all sides of every issue with equal enthusiasm, permitting the student to make his own selection from unbiased facts?

— Are today's mammoth institutions, with their thousands of students and extensive programs, truly the best fitted for the best education? If not, is there a practical way to change them? What options can be offered?

Many students complain that colleges are often not relevant to their needs, that they themselves do not have enough power in making decisions that affect their lives, and that colleges are being used to keep things from changing; simultaneously politicians, parents, taxpayers, and trustees often complain that colleges are overly concerned with the immediate social scene, that students have too much power in making decisions, and that colleges are unduly active in encouraging social change.

WHAT IS A COLLEGE?

Is a college just a group of buildings? Is it the students? The faculty? The administration? The spirit? Is it all these things together?

THE COMMUNITY OF SCHOLARS

Some people think of college as a community of scholars who come together to share their learning and to try to learn more. Students learn not only from the faculty, but also from other students; faculty members not only teach students, but also learn from students and from one another. Learning occurs formally, through the channels of textbooks, lectures, library assignments, audiovisual aids, teaching machines, and demonstrations. It also occurs informally, such as in conversing in a faculty office or over a cup of coffee, in hearing a faculty member or student talk of his original project or research, or in disagreeing so violently with a professor that you search for some additional information yourself (Kalish, 1969a).

In this community of scholars you can be like the gas tank of a car: you can sit back and let information be pumped into you, then run on it for a while, and eventually return for more. Or, you can be active in seeking information and understanding: you can go beyond the formal part of college education and enter into the spirit of the community by reading on your own, by seeking new ideas, by evaluating what is told to you and relating it to your own experiences, by questioning faculty members, by learning from other students, and by being alert to the meaning of your own experiences.

"I don't care whether I really understand Pragmatism or not— as long as I can pass the exam about it."

FIGURE 14–2.   Courtesy of Ed Fisher.

But is a college really a community of scholars? Should it be? College faculty have traditionally encouraged students to seek knowledge through their intellect, through knowledge, through the kinds of information that can be written down and communicated and tested for. However, some faculty and students now claim that feelings are more important than knowledge—that the accepted methods of teaching are worthless because they do not communicate the important insights that are available through personal experience or through mystical encounters. True understanding, they insist, is based on having experienced something yourself, not on having read about it in a book, and examinations cannot measure this true understanding (see Roszak, 1969). Other faculty and students question whether today's colleges can rightfully be considered communities of scholars or whether they are just places where people meet to earn money (the faculty) and credits (the students). What are your feelings?

STUDENTS VIEW THEIR COLLEGES

Although part-time students may remain in residence for several years, most colleges have an almost complete turnover in students every two or three or four years. A political speaker in 1972 who berated his college audience for having changed their minds since the 1968 campaign forgot that probably less than 10–20% of his listeners were in college in 1968. With this in mind, we can look at what "students" believe, with the realization that today's students are not tomorrow's students; rather, they are tomorrow's college graduates, young working people (or nonworking people), and young marrieds (or nonmarrieds).

In 1969, during the height of the college protest movement, a Gallup Poll (1970) showed that the lack of decision-making power, not the Vietnam War or civil rights, was the major complaint among students. But whereas students were overwhelmingly positive in their desire for greater say in running the colleges, the general public was equally strongly in opposition. While in college, the students questioned in this survey participated extensively in political protest, volunteered for community service, and chose teaching as their preferred future occupation by 3½ to 1 over their second-favorite choice (Gallup, 1970). By 1973 education had lost popularity, and students in unprecedented numbers were planning to study the environmental and health sciences and law.

Another study asked high school students what they wanted from a college education. The answers, from 640 middle-class teenagers, indicated that self-actualizing and financial considerations were equally preferred, although girls placed less emphasis on income (Johnstone & Rosenberg, 1968). The following were rated as "very important" reasons for going to college (first percentage indicates boys' responses; second percentage indicates girls' responses):

1. To discover a line of work that would really interest me (86%, 89%).
2. To prepare myself for a job with a really good salary (85%, 65%).
3. To learn more about subjects that really interest me (61%, 75%).
4. To meet new and interesting people (59%, 85%).
5. To develop my personality and become a more interesting person (59%, 83%).
6. To make my parents proud of me (58%, 61%).
7. To be stimulated by new ideas (44%, 73%).
8. To prepare myself to make a real contribution to mankind (38%, 54%).
9. To gain the social standing that comes from having a college degree (34%, 23%).

10. To take part in campus activities and social life (31%, 45%).
11. To get away from home and be on my own (30%, 34%).
12. To find a mate (27%, 29%).

Do you feel that students have changed since the late 1960s, when these surveys were taken?

In informal discussions students mention other reasons for college attendance, such as to avoid arguments with parents, to stay out of the military, to postpone getting a job, to have fun, and to do what all their friends are doing. Middle- and upper-class students receive strong parental pressures to attend college, although students from all social-class groups find that their parents encourage additional education.

Some students find college dull—just another obstacle to overcome before they can get a job. Others find excitement in the learning process: they see new potential in a creative approach to law enforcement, they watch their typing speed jump suddenly ahead, they gain new understanding of the principles of the stock market, they see new meaning in a poem or painting, or they achieve new insight into their own behavior.

WHO GOES TO COLLEGE AND WHO GRADUATES?

Not everyone goes to college, and, of those who do go, not everyone graduates. Going to college is associated with both academic ability and social class (Trent & Medsker, 1967). Social class seems to affect college attendance in several ways. Students from middle- and upper-class families have the money to go to college; their friends and relatives are going and probably assume they will also; they have already developed the value that college attendance is important; they are more likely to have attended a high school that prepared them for college; and their parents were much more likely to have encouraged them to continue their education. In essence, the basis for the motivation to attend college frequently comes from the family, and "aside from adequate intelligence, the factor most related to entrance and persistence in college is motivation . . . motivation is formed early in life, probably largely in response to parental influences and early school experiences" (Trent & Medsker, 1967).

A substantial number of extremely able high school students never enter college. The reasons are numerous: financial pressures, early marriage, desire for independence, lack of awareness of abilities, inadequate counseling, and a number of personality characteristics that make college seem inappropriate. A

FIGURE 14–3. Motivation to succeed in college is expressed, in part, by willingness to read. Photograph by John Odam.

person's definition of success is also relevant, since not all people define success in the same way.

SUCCEEDING IN COLLEGE

What is college success? How is it measured? Is it getting high grades? Getting a degree? Learning about the world? Obtaining job skills? Finding a marriage partner? The answer obviously varies from person to person. Just as the definition of a successful life varies, the definition of college success varies also. What is your measure of college success? How successful have you been, according to your definition? Research has shown that a college education is seen as "acquiring greater self-esteem and a feeling of personal power. Not acquiring an education is perceived as being quite a deflating experience" (Sinnett & Stone, 1964). Do you agree with these opinions?

Grades and Graduation: An International Comparison

Grades as measures of college achievement do not have the same meaning in all countries. In some European universities, grades are not given. Instead, students must pass lengthy, two- or three-day oral and written examinations to receive their diplomas. If the student fails these exams, which cover his entire course of study, he must wait six months or a year to try again.

In Japan, high school students are under tremendous pressure to get into good universities—much greater pressure than students in the United States. However, once they have been accepted, they worry less about grades, since almost no one leaves college because of low grades. College graduation occurs when the student has passed all his required courses and the necessary number of electives. If he fails a few courses along the way, no one cares much.

One Japanese student commented: "I think the American university system is cruel. It forces so much competition that students come to dislike each other. Our Japanese system is much better—students do not need to be afraid they will have to leave the university. When they have learned enough, they receive their degree. In the United States, if I take a very difficult course and get a D, the grade hurts my record, and no one cares if I learned anything from the course—it would have been better if I had not taken it. But in Japan, no one cares if I get a D, and I may learn a great deal."

In spite of her complaints, however, this Japanese student admitted that American university students study harder than Japanese students, although she felt Japanese high school students studied harder than Americans in order to get into college.

Each of these three systems—the American, the European, and the Japanese—has a method of determining whether a student has learned enough to deserve a diploma. Which one do you feel uses the most valid measurement system? How much tension is produced by each system?

As has been already mentioned, college success is based on a number of factors, including measured ability and motivation. One study (Trent & Medsker, 1967) investigated 10,000 high school graduates shortly before graduation and then again four years later. Although academic-ability test scores in high school clearly differentiated those who completed college from those who entered but dropped out, a very high proportion of students in the upper third in test scores did not complete college. Some undoubtedly returned to school later, but the study makes clear that more than ability is needed to finish college.

The best *single* method of predicting completion of college is to examine high school performance (Lavin, 1965), since the tasks to be accomplished in college are similar to those in high school. The second-best method of prediction is to examine scores on academic-ability tests (Reiter, 1964). The relationship between academic aptitude and college completion is not, however, a simple one. Other factors, such as personality and adjustment, attitudes and values, study methods, social activities, and parental influences, all interact dynamically to influence college success.

Personality and adjustment. Research results indicate that the successful student is more self-confident, more mature, more dependable, better able to overcome his personal problems, more efficient, and more realistic in his future goals than the unsuccessful student (Lavin, 1965; Taylor, 1964). He also has a higher need for achievement and is more curious and flexible (Lavin, 1965).

Personal-adjustment problems reduce study effectiveness, and the success or failure of poorly adjusted students often depends more on the method they use to deal with personal problems than on their academic aptitude (Malnig, 1964). Strong resistance to authority, inability to function independently, and inability to accept responsibility have all been associated with dropping out of college (Trent & Medsker, 1967).

Attitudes and values. The purpose of college as seen by the individual is related to college success. Students who see college primarily as a source of vocational training are much less likely to finish than those who emphasize general education (Trent & Medsker, 1967). Similarly, students who have a goal in college do better than those who do not (Wrenn & Crandall, 1941). These studies suggest that many students expect college to lead directly to job skills, and they are disappointed when they find so much emphasis on courses not directly related to jobs. Are these students in the wrong programs? Are they in the wrong colleges? Should they assume that their desires are inappropriate and go along with the demands of the college? Should the college assume that its demands are inappropriate and go along with the desires of the students? Here again we face the questions: Is college relevant to the student's needs of today and tomorrow? Who decides? What are the bases for the decision?

Although having a goal, even a very much desired one, does not ensure college success, the person with no goals at all has no real motivation to succeed. As one wise Indian philosopher said, "If you don't know where you are going, any road will take you there." However, goals set by parents and accepted without evaluation can be worse than no goals at all. Of course, many other goals (that is, many kinds of success) exist that are not met through college:

Susan Clay had wanted to be an actress since she was a little girl. After a year at Santa Monica City College, she dropped out to attend acting classes.

Marty Erikson thought an Air Force career would offer him the excitement he needed, as well as job security. He finished two years at the University of Maryland, enough to qualify him for flight school.

Phil Hernandez became increasingly involved with his work in the Spanish-speaking community. Eventually he left Miami Dade, hoping to return later, because he felt his community needed his services more than he needed an education.

Study methods.   The use of good study methods, although less important than attitudes toward college or motivation to succeed, is definitely related to finishing college (Brown & Holtzman, 1955).

Social activities.   One study showed that too much social life in college is more predictive of future dropping out than either financial problems or academic problems (Trent & Medsker, 1967). It is difficult to determine, however, whether the unduly active social life might not have resulted as much from low academic motivation as from high social motivation.

Parental influences.   Throughout this book the role of significant others has been emphasized. In appraising college completion, we again return to the importance of parents. Students who as high school seniors reported that their parents wanted them to attend college and often discussed college with them were much more likely to enter college and to finish (Trent & Medsker, 1967). Compared with college dropouts, those who completed college were more likely to seek occupational advice and general advice from their parents, which suggests that they had closer family relationships (Trent & Medsker, 1967).

Personality, attitudes, study methods, social activities, and parental influences are not isolated factors but are part of a total picture. Good study methods seldom occur in conjunction with poor attitudes, and a student suffering from anxiety may have difficulty concentrating on his studies. Success in college results from a combination of intellectual and personal elements.

DOES COLLEGE CHANGE A STUDENT?

What should happen to a student during the years he is in college? What does happen? We can probably assume that college graduates have learned a certain number of facts and concepts, but what else should they have learned? New ways of thinking? New ideas about society? New reactions to change?

During their years in college, students appear to become less dogmatic and prejudiced, less conservative, and more sensitive to artistic and other aesthetic experiences; they also become more likely to value independence and intellectual activities, whereas those who choose to work or marry at a very young age change little in their desire for independence or intellectual growth (Newcomb & Feldman, 1969; Trent & Medsker, 1967). College has also been shown to increase critical thinking ability and to decrease rigid and inflexible thinking (Lehmann, 1963).

Nonetheless, the characteristics a student has when he enters college have a greater influence on what he achieves than does the nature of the college itself (Astin & Panos, 1969). Little is known about why these changes occur or about why some students change in the directions just described, whereas others do not change or even change in the opposite direction.

NEW FREEDOMS AND RESPONSIBILITIES

As little as three months or even less may separate the high school senior from the college freshman, but the change in freedom and responsibility can be immense. Even for older students—housewives, military veterans, or working persons—major adjustment is required, since the kinds of regular demands they are used to are often lacking in the college routine. Each individual is responsible to himself.

In high school, parents and teachers keep a close eye on a student, but this supervision of academic activities and personal life diminishes considerably in college. Attendance in class is not always taken, and there is little, aside from his own planning and motivation, to keep a student from falling impossibly behind. The parent or supervisor will frequently check up on the child or employee, but the college instructor normally waits until the student approaches him before he offers help. And in some of the extremely large classes, the instructor may not even notice the absence or low performance of one student.

> In her first semester at junior college, Helene Gould signed up for an average load of courses and a heavy load of social activities. Although many of her professors did take attendance, her instructors in English and psychology did not bother. Her psychology professor stated at the first class meeting: "Attendance is strictly up to you. You're in college because you choose to be, and your success depends on your performance. If you decide something else is more important than class, that's up to you, but it's your obligation to make up what you missed." Since her English and psychology classes were held on Monday, Wednesday, and Friday afternoons, Helene found that cutting these classes gave her a great deal of free time. At first she cut only Friday classes, but then she began to cut Monday and Wednesday occasionally. Neither professor said anything to her, so she felt safe—especially since she had

low-C grades going into the finals. The ax fell when she received her final grades: a D in psychology and an F in English. She visited her psychology professor, tears in her eyes, and asked if she could do extra work to bring her grade up. He listened patiently but said "No." Then Helene told him it was his fault she had gotten the low grade, because, she said, "you should have insisted that everybody come to class every time."

Even the scheduling of classes places a great demand on students to organize themselves. After a high school schedule of five days a week from 8:30 A.M. to 3:00 P.M., the college schedule of 15 to 20 hours a week in class seems like "a breeze." Knowing that the week has many free hours reduces any sense of urgency, and assignments may be all too easily postponed.

The independence demanded by college is too much for some students, even though they live at home. Those who live in dormitories may have still more difficulty. They need to contend with all-night talk sessions (often valuable, always interesting, but rarely substitutes for study) and noisy roommates, and they have no one to remind them that work must be done. Some students thrive on such freedom; they work better and mature faster than when closely supervised. Others simply cannot manage this much freedom.

NEW SOCIAL RELATIONSHIPS

High school students are likely to share common interests and backgrounds, especially in urban and suburban communities, where large areas of similarly priced homes are found. But college students usually represent a wide variety of races, religions, social classes, and nationalities, so that any one student has an excellent opportunity to meet others from diverse backgrounds.

Some students have difficulty in being with those whose backgrounds are different and whose behavior may therefore not be so predictable. They may feel socially inadequate or fearful of making blunders, so they avoid stress by returning to more comfortable ground:

> Mel Peterson lived within a 20 minutes' drive of a good state college, and he decided to enter there, along with many of his old friends. However, Mel felt lost among the 16,000 students at the school. So, for his social life, he returned to his old high school, where he felt more comfortable. Being a college student gave him new prestige, and he was soon spending time with one of the most popular and attractive girls at the school. But the next year she also entered State, where she quickly found men more exciting than Mel. And Mel returned to his high school again. This continued for four years, until all his prestige and glamour were replaced by the reputation that he was simply someone who could not make the grade with college girls.

In a sense, Mel was unable to establish his identity as a college student. His behavior was obviously not in response to growth motives. He lacked self-esteem and feelings of security. Little growth can occur in a person who does nothing but repeat over and over again his earlier experiences.

The college student needs to gain a sense of identity as a student in both on-campus and off-campus relationships. Many parents and friends, unfamiliar with the actual situation at colleges, may have inaccurate perceptions of college students, and students find themselves treated in terms of stereotypes that may be upsetting and discouraging. For example:

> *Spoiled.* "Kids in my day didn't have it so good. College kids today have it easy—easy life, good job, lots of money. They don't know what real work is."
>
> *Wild.* "Boy, the things I've heard about you college people! I was just reading that every college man has at least two girls just aching for loving."
>
> *Snobbish.* "You guys aren't as good as you think you are. You're no better than anyone else, so don't put on airs with me."
>
> *Brilliant.* "I know how hard you have to study to stay in college. You must be really brilliant."
>
> *Hippie.* "All you college guys with beards and those girls with long hair and no makeup—nothing but oddballs."
>
> *Rich.* "I guess you have to have a lot of money to go to college."
>
> *Radical.* "You guys are mostly Commies, aren't you? Always yelling about peace and equal rights and stuff."

FIGURE 14–4. New social relationships become satisfying and foster personal growth and maturity. Photograph by Lehman J. Pinckney.

Only when an individual is secure in his identity as a college student can he interact effectively with those who maintain such misconceptions. Although the new social relationships on and off campus can be somewhat difficult at first, they eventually become more satisfying and foster personal growth and maturity.

CHALLENGES TO COLLEGE SUCCESS

Although students are expected to be much more independent in college than they were in high school, personal and academic growth may be limited by numerous factors. Among the most common of these are academic problems, social and emotional problems, financial difficulties, and health problems. These areas are not isolated but interact with one another. What is originally a financial problem may lead to a health problem, which, in turn, produces an achievement problem that subsequently aggravates the health problem.

Fortunately, many colleges are well equipped with sources of help for these problems. These sources include counseling facilities, faculty advisers, the library, and medical facilities.

ACADEMIC DIFFICULTIES

For many students the most difficult task in college is adjusting to the academic demands. Because of the grading system, particularly in large classes, some students will inevitably receive low grades. Poor grades, particularly for those accustomed to being among the better students, can lead to irrational, self-defeating behavior. The student blames everyone but himself, or he may feel inadequate and decide to give up. On the other hand, low grades affect some students like a cold shower on a sleepy person—the shock jolts them back to reality.

What alternatives does a student have when his academic achievement falls below par? If he does not understand where his difficulties are, his first step should normally be to see his instructors. If the instructors cannot help, the college counselor often can. Low grades may result from inadequate high school background, poor study methods, physical illness, insufficient motivation, personal problems, or lack of the necessary academic aptitude. College counselors, through tests and interviews, can usually determine the basis for the low grades.

If nothing seems to work, the student may need to re-evaluate his college goals. Perhaps he should shift from one major to another or from one college to another. Perhaps the answer is to quit college and enter business school or a hospital training program. In some instances it might be better to leave college with the idea of returning at a later time with a more realistic and mature set of goals.

However, any major change should be undertaken only after all other possibilities have been eliminated—that is, after the student has tried to study as hard as he can, after he has eliminated poor study methods, when he believes that personal or health or emotional problems are not producing his difficulties, and when he is certain that neither outside work nor social obligations are robbing him of needed time.

SOCIAL AND EMOTIONAL PROBLEMS

Life is not divided into neat, isolated compartments. Whatever affects one phase of living also affects every other phase. When a marriage is unhappy, the couple's job effectiveness may be reduced, their children may become anxious, and their physical health may even be disrupted. Similarly, an unhappy family situation, an unfaithful fiancée, or an undue amount of suspicion can all reduce study effectiveness and deprive the student of his ability to make optimum use of his potentials.

> Mike Minton's childhood had been secure and happy, but his father died when he was 12, and his mother eventually married a man of modest means with children of his own. The insurance money left by Mike's father gradually went to pay living expenses, although it had originally been earmarked for Mike's college education. In the meantime the relationship between Mike's mother and her new husband had deteriorated, and sometimes their arguments became so violent that blows were exchanged. At this point Mike began his freshman year as a community student at a junior college about an hour's drive from home.

Compared with the successful student, the underachiever tends to lack confidence and to be prone to depression; he shows signs of maladjustment rather openly, which indicates that he lacks control; he is less likely to have a good relationship with his parents or other authority figures, such as instructors; with other people, he tends to be withdrawn, uninterested, apathetic, and dependent. The low-achieving student may also be uncertain about his goals in college, or else he tends to set goals for himself that are beyond his level of ability (Taylor, 1964). With a few exceptions, students who are not living up to their potential in college tend to be the same ones who have difficulties in nonacademic areas. Since the individual's personal problems indicate that he has not adequately satisfied needs lower in the hierarchy, he is unable to make the most of the capacities he does have.

FINANCIAL PROBLEMS

The man with all the money he wants is a rarity anywhere in the world. In college, students with financial difficulties often seem to outnumber those without such difficulties. Some students find that their success — perhaps even their ability to remain in college — is threatened by money problems.

Moreover, college students prize their independence, which is curtailed when they are supported by funds from home. In order to be independent, some students reject family offers of support and take part-time jobs. Occasionally the work-plus-study load is more than the student can handle, and he must quit work, leave school, or risk physical illness.

Students whose living costs are greater than their available funds plus earnings from part-time work have several alternatives:

1. Scholarships and grants are available for students with good academic records or with a background of participation in campus activities.

2. Today's generation of college students may have an opportunity to obtain low-interest loans. The federal, state, and local governments, as well as banks and college authorities, have made funds available.

3. A compromise measure is to work full time and attend classes on a part-time basis. Although such a procedure postpones completion of college, it is usually better than carrying a full academic load while trying to hold a full-time job.

4. Often overlooked is the possibility of reducing expenses, which may be simpler than increasing earnings. In today's wealthy society people feel entitled to luxuries. However, certain items can be readily eliminated from the budget if necessary. Have you ever made out a budget and then kept a day-to-day expenditure log to see how to cut your expenses?

Students are often unaware of all the potential sources of financial help. Those who have extremely restricted financial support should seek advice from the campus scholarship and loan office, from a college counselor, or from some other adviser.

HEALTH PROBLEMS

Students are more likely to neglect their physical health than their automobiles, their appearance, or their social activities. Fatigue and poor diet are common on college campuses. Physical problems inevitably reduce study efficiency. Although obvious symptoms, such as a high fever or stomach cramps, usually receive attention, many students do not maintain a good day-to-day program of physical care.

The relationship between physical health and academic performance is not difficult to understand. For example, although a link between nutrition and performance has been established, many students eat large quantities of food containing very small quantities of food value. The lack of preventive medical and dental care may cause a minor difficulty to become a major one, perhaps involving the loss of an entire semester or quarter. Also, some medicines (such as cold pills) produce drowsiness or "highs," which are not conducive to good academic performance. And lack of sleep reduces effectiveness and increases irritability, restlessness, and inattention.

A good friend of mine learned about the effects of extreme fatigue when he and I were taking freshman economics together:

> The economics midterm was scheduled for 10:00 Wednesday morning, and Ralph Zeff closeted himself into a study room at 6:00 the evening before to begin reading the semester's assignments — which his active social life had previously prevented. Sixteen hours, 3 packs of cigarettes, 12 cups of black coffee, and 5 stay-awake pills later, Ralph walked into the classroom, satisfied with his all-night job of cramming. On my way out of the exam room, about ten minutes before the bell, I had to walk past Ralph's chair. I noticed that his head was resting on his left hand, which was also being used as an eye shield. Since I had already turned my paper in, I looked at Ralph's answers, and I was startled to see only about one-third of the questions completed. At that point I pulled his arm away from his forehead, and he woke up with a snort that caused everyone in the room to snicker.

IDENTITY AND PURPOSE

Few issues remain highly relevant throughout time. Most controversies arise, flourish, and then die away and are forgotten. Two questions, however, appear to plague college students of all eras. They are not always important to every student, and they are not always answerable; but they do occur, and they do require serious thought. These questions are "Who am I?" and "Why am I here?"

WHO AM I?

The adolescent wish to answer the question "Who am I?" often continues through the college years. Large, impersonal colleges with student identification numbers, interminable lines to wait in, computerized advising and grading, and huge classes may only intensify the confusion about identity. Because he is not treated as an individual, the student may become anxious about whether individuality still exists.

Even his role as a student is uncertain. In high school he had been high man on the totem pole—a graduating senior. He knew his way around, had many friends, and was proud of his future status as a college student. Three months later he is low man on the totem pole—a college freshman. He is new, does not know his way around, and is probably not especially proud of his status as freshman.

Perhaps more important, the college freshman does not know exactly how to act. He wants to behave like a college student and to have an identity as a college student, but he is a little unsure of what this means. I had the following experience as a freshman:

> During high school I had learned to smoke a pipe. I liked myself with it, and the girls I knew in high school seemed to admire it too. Knowing that college men smoked pipes, I was puffing around campus during my first week, rather pleased that I was able to present such a mature and scholarly picture: Young Man with Pipe. Then, at the local coffee shop one evening, I overheard one of the upperclassmen comment to his friend: "You know, you can always spot a freshman—they're the ones who smoke pipes." And they both laughed. I packed my pipes and tobacco away that evening and did not dig them up again for two years, when I was secure enough in my status not to fear being considered a freshman.

College studies may open new and exciting—sometimes even frightening—avenues for consideration. What is your relationship to God? To the universe? To nature? To other human beings? Here again the problem of identity becomes important. These are problems that cannot be answered in a lecture or through a textbook, but only through living and thinking and feeling and experiencing.

WHY AM I HERE?

The purpose of life is a philosophic question, but it affects behavior. There are many possible purposes of life, such as serving God, serving your fellow man, having a good time, being creative, becoming famous, becoming wealthy, aiding a worthwhile cause, or just plain living one's life. Although relatively few people make a decision like "The purpose of my life is so-and-so" and stick with it, the question often returns to haunt us, and this makes it a psychological question.

Have you ever had the feeling that there is no purpose in life and, therefore, nothing you do really matters? Or do you think of your parents, who worked so hard all their lives with so little enjoyment to show for it, and wonder what the purpose of their existence was? (They may never have worried about it, but you do.) Or do you contemplate the fate of your friend who died in combat or in an accident, before he had "really begun to live," and wonder what it means?

Some people can answer these questions to their own satisfaction without difficulty—they *know* that their purpose is to advance a particular cause or to create great music or to experience as much of life as possible—they are absorbed in what they are doing.

Commitment is also a major issue for some young people. Their concern is not so much "Who am I?" but "I know pretty well who I am—I am a worthy, unique individual, I have value, and I can love and be loved. Now, how can I put all these things together to make a contribution?" (after J. Geiwitz, personal communication).

THE ALIENATED, THE ACTIVISTS, AND THE SELF–SEARCHERS

For some people the difficulty in answering the question "Who am I?" goes far beyond their role as a college student. They feel alienated or separated from their society; they do not feel that they belong or are a part of their culture. They feel lonely and alone, even when they are with many other people.

One psychiatrist referred to three rebellions: the red, the black, and the green. The red rebellion is against the economic and political system; the black is against racism of all sorts; and the green rebellion is against today's style of living (L. J. West, cited in Kovach, 1971). As one young woman stated, "I don't want to rear my kids in the artificial, impersonal suburban environment that I grew up in" (Kovach, 1971, p. 6). These rebellions, or feelings of wanting to be removed from the general society, led to the hippie movement during the 1960s and to the settling of hundreds of rural and urban communes in the early 1970s.

Because these people wanted to drop out of the society they knew but could find no society they wished to drop in to, they have attempted to create their own societies by establishing communes. Each commune has its own special orientation. Some are founded on religious principles, whereas others are primarily atheistic; some encourage hard work, but others encourage as little work as possible; some have extremely free sexual codes, while others have more restrictive codes; some espouse active involvement in revolutionary plans, whereas others are intent only on avoiding people as much as possible; some tolerate a great deal of petty theft from the surrounding community, but others strongly condemn such action; some are on isolated rural farms, while others are in large houses in urban areas.

The hippie culture and the communes challenged the values of what they called the Establishment. The Establishment firmly believed that work, achieve-

FIGURE 14–5. The hippie culture of the late 1960s challenged the values of what they called the Establishment. Photograph courtesy of Columbia Broadcasting System.

ment, learning, competitiveness, productivity, and the nuclear family (parents and dependent children) were all important for society to function properly. The Establishment also resented the great sexual freedom that many hippies and communes displayed, as well as their use of illegal drugs. The commune members responded by asking why, if the Establishment values were so wonderful, its members depended so much on alcohol, aspirin, tobacco, tranquilizers, and antidepressant pills and why they found it so necessary to fight wars, maintain a large standing army, and have such a high crime rate.

The terms *hippie* and *Establishment* are seldom heard today, but they are part of the very recent history of the social movement of urban and rural communes. Whether the communes will provide a satisfactory answer to the feelings of alienation of many young people is still not known. Whether these communes will continue to be a part of the national scene or whether they will disappear as quickly as the term *hippie* is something you can evaluate yourself. One expert

(Haigh, 1967) has recommended absorption and involvement as solutions to the problem of alienation. Certainly the work demanded in many rural communes and the intense human relationships found in almost all communes foster such involvement and absorption.

A far more outspoken group of young people who are also seeking identity and purpose are the activists. Although some parallels can be drawn between commune members and activists, the latter are almost never alienated. They may be antagonistic to society and wish to change it, but they are too deeply absorbed in what they are doing to be alienated (exceptions, of course, exist).

The activist movement probably began partly as a result of the 1965 student participation in voter registration in the South and partly through the Free Speech Movement at the University of California at Berkeley. Anger was generated primarily at the U.S. position in the Vietnam War and at conditions in the urban ghettos.

*"Remember the good old days—when
it was just panty raids?"*

FIGURE 14–6.   Courtesy of Ed Fisher.

The activists picketed speakers, spoke out through publications and campus forums, and eventually became involved in violence (although it is difficult to determine how much of the violence was brought about by the students and how much by the authorities). Only a small portion of American college students have been activists; even where they are strongest, they probably never number over 10% of the student body at any one time. However, activists have influence out of proportion to their numbers, because they are vocal, because they represent the brighter, higher-achieving students (Block, Haan, & Smith, 1968), and because many of their views appeal to nonactive segments of the campus populations.

Who were the activists? First, they tended to come from families in which the father was a professional man or higher-level businessman. Second, both they and their parents tended not to have strong church affiliations or traditional religious beliefs. Third, they emphasized intellectual and artistic activities, service to others, and self-expression, and so did their parents. Fourth, they were above-average students (Flacks, 1967). They were more flexible, more objective, more independent, more imaginative, and—perhaps because of the pressures put on them—more tense and anxious (Trent & Craise, 1967).

What did the activists believe in? They did not seek more material goods for themselves. Many actually gave up material gain in order to help others live a better life (Keniston, 1967). Nor were they alienated from all Establishment values. In many ways, they believed in the traditional values expressed by the leaders of this country. One activist who later became a professional sociologist felt that the activists had eight major orientations:

1. They did not like to be bound by conventions; they wanted to feel free to "do their thing."
2. They opposed many forms of authority.
3. They emphasized the importance of everyone's participating in government, and they were particularly upset when some people were denied that opportunity.
4. They wanted to be flexible and resented rigid philosophies.
5. They were strongly opposed to hypocrisy and phoniness.
6. They felt that people should be a part of their community and be involved in their community.
7. They distrusted religious, legal, educational, and other institutions.
8. They rejected careers in the sciences and industry for careers in fields permitting self-expression, such as painting or movie production, and in fields allowing service to others, such as social work (Flacks, 1967).

Eventually some activists turned to violence, but others entered the electoral process. In some communities the student activists contributed greatly to the election of a particular congressman or city councilman. Occasionally the activist himself was elected to office.

Another group of people have sought to understand meaning and identity by looking within themselves. In asking the questions "Who am I?" and "Why am I here?" many students and nonstudents have found the search for the answers very compelling. Members of this movement wanted to learn more about who they were and why they were here; they looked to their own churches, to other religions, and often to Eastern religions for answers. Some turned to mysticism and astrology. Many who had tried psychedelic drugs at one time or another shifted their interest to biofeedback systems, hoping to achieve some of the same effects with less danger. While astronauts were exploring outer space, these persons claimed they wished to explore inner space—the world that was within their own head.

Meditation also became popular, and the magazines and newspapers that had exploited hippies, activists, and communes began to run articles on witches and astrology and Jesus freaks and alpha waves.

These three different responses to the problem of purpose and identity—alienation, activism, and self-searching—were not rigidly separate movements. Some people adhered to more than one at a time, or drifted back and forth from one to another, or were fringe members. Yet most students fell into none of these categories but continued to pursue more traditional goals—although not without being affected by the actions of these three groups and by the related social forces around them.

SUMMARY OF IMPORTANT IDEAS

1. From 1960 to 1970 the number of students pursuing higher education more than doubled, with an even more dramatic increase in two-year colleges.

2. A college may be looked on as a community of scholars who come together to share their learning and to try to learn more. However, the accuracy of this concept has been disputed.

3. Students feel that the primary value of college is related to future work and to opportunities to self-actualize.

4. Both entering college and completing college work are related to academic ability and motivation.

5. The best single predictor of college success is high school success; the second-best predictor is academic-ability test scores.

6. Also related to college completion are personality and adjustment, attitudes and values, study methods, social activities, and parental influences.

7. During college, students appear to become less dogmatic and prejudiced, less conservative, and more likely to value artistic experience and intellectual activities.

8. College requires that the student deal with freedom from supervision and with new social relationships.

9. Among the most common challenges to college success are academic difficulties, social and emotional problems, financial restrictions, and health problems.

10. College students often ask themselves the questions "Who am I?" and "Why am I here?"

11. In trying to answer these questions, some students become alienated from society, some take activist positions against society, and some turn their attention inward and become self-searching.

15 Adjusting to Relationships in Sex and Marriage

Awareness of sex relationships and contemplation of marriage occur in childhood and assume increasing importance with time. With the advent of puberty, the individual develops a concept of himself as a sexual being, and marriage (and its alternatives) attains new meanings. Both sex and marriage remain matters of major concern throughout adolescence and the years — even decades — that follow. In the middle and later years of life, although the physiological needs for sex may diminish and the social relationships of marriage have often stabilized, few matters lead to more concern, produce more problems, or permit more enjoyment and satisfaction than sex and marriage.

Throughout the history of the world, thoughtful parents have taken great pains that their children avoid inappropriate sexual relationships and that they enter into appropriate marriages. Many parents have themselves made these vital arrangements rather than leave the decisions to their children. Although these parents have generally sought a spouse their child could like or even come to love, family finances, family reputation, social class, religion, and various forms of bride payment, or dowry, have been the deciding factors in choosing mates.

Even today, in many parts of the world, marriages are arranged by parents, often without asking the prospective bride and groom for consent. Although Americans are frequently upset by this custom, our own high divorce rate has been cited by people of other nations as evidence that love marriages are not particularly successful.

Sex, marriage, and divorce are matters of immediate interest to every high school graduate. Today more than half the girls in this country are married before their twenty-first birthday (*Information Please Almanac,* 1966), and many are pregnant at the time of marriage. Half of all American men are married by the age of 23. Thus almost every college student has seen some of his friends marry — and perhaps divorce.

SEXUAL RELATIONSHIPS

Movies, novels, and other communications media have had a great deal to say about sexual enjoyment, both in and out of marriage — perhaps so much that some people begin to think that sex is what life is all about. Little doubt can exist that sexual desires are powerful motivating forces. Although society attempts to restrict sexual behavior to certain individuals and to certain conditions through laws, customs, internalized feelings of guilt, and fear of punishment, the sex drive has been too strong to be successfully limited. Men and women jeopardize marriages, careers, health, and stability in exchange for sexual satisfaction.

Nonetheless, sex is only one of numerous forces that motivate people, and most individuals either develop a satisfying sex life in ways that do not interfere with their other sources of personal fulfillment or else restrict their sexual activities to avoid endangering their other activities.

THE SOCIAL MEANINGS OF SEX

Having a sexual relationship satisfies a biologically based desire. But sex is much more complex than that. For example:

- Sex is a way of showing affection.
- Sex is a sign of maturity — an indication that one has entered the adult world.
- Sex is used to attain status and prestige.
- Sex behavior is seen as a sign that the individual is *really a man* (or, with lesser frequency, a woman).
- Sex can be used to express power over someone or to exploit someone.
- Sex can be used to manipulate, bribe, or gain favors from someone; or, it may be a payoff for favors given.
- Sex can be directly exchanged for cash.
- Sex can be used to entice someone into a deep commitment.

—Sex may be seen as a symbolic punishment aimed at absent persons, such as parents or a spouse: "How that person would suffer if he only knew what I'm doing now." "If I get pregnant, my parents will really be upset."

You can undoubtedly think of other motives. Men and women view the social meaning of sex differently, although there is speculation that these differences are diminishing. The meaning of sex also varies as a result of marital status and age; both laws and customs are more restrictive concerning the unmarried and the younger members of society (although the sex life of the elderly is often the source of jokes).

Although sexual enjoyment can enhance a good marriage, some individuals claim to have deep love, great affection, and a good marriage with only moderate or low enjoyment of sex. There are other ways of displaying affection, such as a touch on the arm, a smile, a look of understanding. In a healthy relationship these forms of affection are more common and, perhaps, more important than the strictly sexual expression.

SEX BEHAVIOR OF COLLEGE STUDENTS

Although some people believe that college students are sexually much more active than others, Kinsey (Kinsey, Pomeroy, & Martin, 1948; Kinsey, Pomeroy, Martin, & Gebhard, 1953) found that the sex experiences of college students were actually more limited than those of people outside college. Although Kinsey's data are more than two decades old, no one has attempted to duplicate his work, and we have no more recent study that is as careful, as thorough, and as complete. Kinsey also found that people from the middle class (which includes most students) were less likely to have been sexually intimate outside marriage than those from the lower class.

Almost all college students had kissed and necked at one time or another, and many had done so on numerous occasions. Petting (involving the breasts or genitals) was less common, but more than nine out of ten college men and women had done some petting by their twentieth birthday, with about one-third reaching complete sexual release through orgasm in this fashion.

In many instances, necking and petting do not lead to intercourse but consume enough time and allow enough excitement so that intercourse does not take place. Rather than hazard the risks of sexual intercourse, college men frequently indulge in mild lovemaking and then get release through masturbation at a later time. Although some people still believe that masturbation leads to mental disturbance, no evidence exists to support this assumption (except that guilt over masturbation can be emotionally disturbing). Almost all boys and many girls masturbate, so that it can hardly be considered strange or unnatural, and it is especially common among college students.

Another form of sexual release that prevails among adolescents is the sexual dream. Although the manifest content of the dream (what you "see") may or may not be sexual, the latent content (what the dream represents) will be. Eventually the dreamer, usually male, will have an orgasm (thus the expression "wet" dream), which may or may not wake him up. Both because of the sexual content of the dreams and because the orgasm produces wetness that is often thought to signify bed-wetting, uninformed adolescents are often very much distressed by this experience.

Codes of sex behavior among college students have apparently changed substantially since the late 1950s. On many campuses the kind of sex behavior that alarms parents and teachers has become so acceptable to students that it is no longer an issue. The evidence, however, is not completely clear. Some claims indicate that college students participate more freely and more frequently in intimate sexual relationships than they used to. Other claims indicate that the behavior has not changed — that sexual relationships have always been abundant — but that attitudes and values toward this behavior have changed. And some evidence still suggests that neither behavior nor attitudes have changed — people are simply talking more about them.

One pair of investigators (Bell & Chaskes, 1970), returning to a campus where the women had been surveyed ten years earlier regarding premarital sex behavior, found some changes between 1958 and 1968. The 1968 college woman was about twice as likely to have had premarital intercourse as her 1958 counterpart. She also expressed much less guilt, which implies a major change in attitudes and values.

Which came first: the decrease in guilt or the increase in sex behavior? Did the girls have more sexual affairs *because* they no longer felt guilty about them? Or did their attitudes toward sex change *after* their behavior changed, so that they could justify the behavior to themselves? Or has there really been any meaningful change at all? Results of one survey indicate that students themselves do not believe that their own standards for sex behavior differ much from those of their parents (Reiss, 1968).

If sex-behavior codes are changing, it means that factors inhibiting such behavior are disappearing, which may lead to increased sexual intimacies on college campuses. We then need to ask whether college students are setting the pace for the rest of the nation, merely following what others have established, or behaving relatively independently of what others are doing. We can also ask whether sex codes may be changing only in certain regions of the country or only in certain states or even only in certain communities.

Until very recently sexual relationships outside marriage — and to some extent even within marriage—have been inhibited for some people by the fear of pregnancy. Today, however, knowledge about contraceptive devices and their relative availability have considerably reduced this concern. Many parents, including some who strongly disapprove of premarital sexual relationships, inform their sons and daughters about "the pill" and "the loop" and encourage them to use these devices, at the same time trying to discourage their participation in the intimacies that call for such use. Although clinical studies suggest that no artificial contraceptive, even when used correctly, is 100% safe, student use of contraceptives has undoubtedly increased greatly during the past decade, in spite of the opposition of some religious, educational, and legal authorities.

Another factor that potentially inhibits intercourse is the prevalence of venereal disease. Only a few years ago assumed to be under control, gonorrhea and other strains of this illness have become a major health problem in this country. Although treatment is usually available, both ignorance and embarrassment often permit these conditions to be passed on before they come to the attention of health personnel.

Most observers agree that sexual relationships are more open now than in previous years, but it is still uncertain whether there is also an increase in casual sex behavior or whether, as one investigator stated, "Sexual intimacy . . . takes place in the context of a relationship that is serious . . ." (Katz, 1968). The evidence is obviously in conflict, partly because of inconsistent reports and partly because of our lack of knowledge about sex behavior 30 and 50 and 70 years ago.

A PSYCHOLOGICAL LOOK AT SEX

Each individual has internalized values regarding sex. Beginning with toilet training and modesty training, children learn to keep the genital area private and clean and touched as little as possible. Later they are taught that sex without love and affection is not appropriate. Although many people are fortunate in internalizing the value that sex in marriage is to be enjoyed, others have had early learning experiences and have faced parental and community attitudes that make difficult any sort of later sexual enjoyment without ensuing guilt and anxiety.

Evidence exists that once sex behavior is initiated, guilt does not inhibit continuation of that behavior. Apparently both males and females participate in sexual relationships that initially cause guilt, but they continue the activity until the guilt diminishes and then go on to more advanced sexual behavior until the guilt associated with that also decreases (Reiss, 1968). Thus guilt, although serving as an inhibiting force, does not eliminate sex activity.

Homosexual and other deviant relationships occur more often than is usually realized, although most of those who report homosexual experiences were involved only in isolated incidents. About 10% of the adult men in Kinsey's survey had maintained homosexual behavior over an extended period of time (Kinsey et al., 1948). (See Chapter 19.)

Other cultures differ from ours in their sexual attitudes. Some restrict sex so effectively that even sex in marriage is not enjoyed. Others teach that sex is a basic part of affection. Still others restrict nonmarital sex officially but allow it to occur unofficially: "Don't do it — but if you do, don't get caught." And a number of cultures allow premarital sex but demand complete faithfulness in marriage (Ford & Beach, 1951; Murdock, 1957).

Behavior in other cultures does not determine appropriate behavior for our culture. There are people who contend that complete sexual freedom would improve mental health. However, many circumstances having no relationship to sex contribute to our emotional problems (intense competition, need for status, uncertainty about social role, desire for material possessions). There is no real evidence that Americans would suddenly become mentally healthier if they became sexually free (Ausubel, 1954).

Those who cannot cope with their sex conflicts may have difficulties that originally arose from other sources, such as: (1) inadequate parent-child relationships, (2) poor marriage relationships between parents, (3) poor family attitudes toward sex, (4) personal-adjustment problems, (5) insufficient social-learning opportunities, (6) misleading sex education, and (7) extremely disturbing childhood or early-adolescent sex experiences. Such factors can lead to inadequacy in later sex relationships. Strangely enough, feelings of sexual inadequacy can lead both to withdrawal from sex relationships *and* to unusually strong desires for sex relationships. The person who is not secure in his own sexual adequacy often feels the need for sexual exploits to prove to himself and others that he is adequate.

SEX AND SELF-ACTUALIZATION

For some people, sex can be a thoroughly enjoyable, exciting event; for others, it is something that is moderately pleasurable; still others find it a task that they must endure in order to please someone else; and, of course, a few people find sex distasteful. For those whose enjoyment of sex falls short of their expectations, a program of instruction has been developed through the work of Masters and Johnson (1966, 1970). The financial cost is extremely high, but there is considerable testimony that the program has a high rate of success.

It may seem like "pushing the middle-class thing" to claim that sex is enhanced when love exists between the two people, but that has long been the general consensus. Not just the psychological satisfaction of sex, but the physiological excitement as well, is greater when love is involved (Maslow, 1970). Furthermore, "self-actualizing men and women tend on the whole not to seek sex for its own sake" (Maslow, 1970, p. 187). Sometimes these people report an experience so intense accompanying orgasm that they describe it as mystical; at other times sex provides fun and amusement or enjoyment of touching and caring for the other person. Self-actualizing people also find that sexual attractiveness is based less on physical appearance than on the personal qualities of the partner (Maslow, 1970).

Is marriage required for sex to be self-actualizing? Evidence is lacking. Undoubtedly marriage is necessary for persons who feel it is important or who have lingering guilt contemplating nonmarital sex (and this includes many people who do not realize it). You will need to decide for yourself whether sex outside marriage can be self-actualizing for you. Sexual behavior is a personal matter, a personal decision, and a personal responsibility. A mentally healthy individual is able to arrive at his own decision, to feel it is comfortable for him, and to have the strength of purpose to remain true to his values, in spite of pressures to change. Probably the pressures on the college student are more heavily weighted in the direction of sexual participation than sexual abstinence, since it is more difficult for college women (and *much* more difficult for college men) to tell others that they have never had a sex relationship than it is to say, or at least to imply, that they are somewhat experienced.

LOVE

Love is a word used to describe a multiplicity of relationships, from the schoolgirl's crush on her favorite movie idol to the passion of young lovers to the warmth and serenity of the love of the no-longer young. Psychologist Erich Fromm writes that mature love lets a person remain very much an individual and retain personal dignity and integrity; it also helps break through the loneliness and isolation that so many feel. Immature love, on the other hand, requires that the other person offer love first (for instance, the infant's love for his parent is immature) and that love be based on a need for the loved one. Mature love follows the principles "I am loved because I love" and "I need you because I love you"; immature love says "I love because I am loved" and "I love you because I need you" (Fromm, 1956).

Love, in the sense the term is used here, is not limited to relationships between two mature adults of the opposite sex. Love can occur between virtually any two people. However, love need not be "between." A person may love another without reciprocation; for instance, he may love his month-old son, a political or religious figure he has never met, or his mother who died as he was born.

Love should help both the person giving and the person receiving to grow and to be better able to become what they wish to become. Of course, love, like friendship, has obvious hazards in that it opens the giver to the possibilities of rejection by the loved one and loss of the loved one.

Consider the variety of situations to which the term *love* can be properly applied:

A parent and child may love each other, regardless of their ages, and the love may continue long after one of them has died. Under certain conditions an individual may feel love for a parent of whom he has little or no memory.

A husband and wife may retain a very deep love for each other throughout their lives. And, after one member of the couple dies, the surviving spouse may continue to love the deceased mate, even though he or she loves another person and remarries. There is no principle of human behavior that prevents a person from loving both living and deceased spouses.

Sometimes a man and woman, not married to each other, develop a friendship deep enough to be called love but without overt sex or romance. Sadly enough, complications can arise in such a relationship, especially if either is married to someone else or if the relationship encourages jealousy from those not included.

An individual may feel love for nonparental significant others, such as a grandmother, a maid, or a teacher. Children who spend a long period in a hospital may direct such feelings toward a doctor or nurse. You can undoubtedly think of other circumstances that would lead to a similar sort of love.

Have you ever really loved someone in a man-woman relationship? How did you feel? What is love? Love is usually defined as a very intense affection or liking for a person or, sometimes, a thing. However, like many other terms, *love* is correctly used in a variety of appropriate ways for a variety of circumstances. You can have endless (and often meaningless) debates as to whether Person Q loves Person U, because each debater is using *love* in a different sense, both probably equally correct.

As we use the term, for the most part, in this book, love is an emotion or feeling that may be expressed through overt behavior or may, for many reasons, be kept unexpressed or even repressed. Healthy mutual love is likely to increase over the months and years and to help both parties grow as individuals *and* as a couple. It begins with mutual respect, a strong feeling of affection, the desire to be together, and the willingness to make more of yourself for the sake of the other person *and* to help the other person make more of himself as well. To lead to marriage, love should also include physical attraction, but physical attraction often grows from love.

Can everyone love? Some researchers claim not. They feel that people who have never been loved themselves cannot feel love for others. It has also been said

FIGURE 15–1.   Have you ever loved someone in a mature man-woman relationship? Photograph by Lehman J. Pinckney.

that a person cannot love others unless he can accept himself and trust others (Blood, 1955). These statements emphasize the importance of early experiences and relationships with other people, particularly with significant others.

Not everyone who claims to love another person actually has feelings of love; the same is true of those who claim to love mankind. Sometimes the person who is able to love other persons is also better able to love mankind as a result; sometimes people who claim to love mankind give a very distinct impression that they really do not like many individuals.

RELATIONSHIPS THAT DESTROY

What is often called "love" can tear down an individual's self-concept instead of building it up. It can produce constant fear, anxiety, and pain, and it can lead to deficiency motivation instead of growth motivation. These things occur when love is rejected or in danger of being rejected, when it is too demanding, or when it is based on psychologically unhealthy needs. Such love would appear inconsistent with the healthy personality. We might even question whether the word *love* can properly be applied to such cases. Consider the following example:

> Joe Calvin came to Los Angeles with a high school diploma, an amazing memory, and a tremendous motivation to get rich and be able to forget his poverty-stricken, rural Texas background. Maria Kent came to Los Angeles with a college degree, a great sensitivity to the arts, and a desire to make good on her own without the help of her family's money and status. They met, were strongly attracted to each other, and married. But the mild disagreements they had had before their marriage flared into a constant state of bickering and arguing after the marriage. Maria admired Joe's energy and ambition, but she resented his lack of sympathy for the arts and his lack of patience. Joe liked the idea of having a wife who dressed well, knew the right people, and enjoyed art, but he resented the way she nagged him to go to museums and concerts with her.
>
> In her irritation, Maria began to criticize Joe for his manners, his speech errors, and his lack of education; she was particularly hostile when Joe's well-educated business associates and friends were with them. Joe reciprocated by withdrawing into his work. He explained that her clothes and other money demands forced him to expand his business and devote more time to it. As Joe withdrew into work, Maria withdrew into the community art league and a relief organization for American Indians. Tired of waiting until 9:00 for Joe to come home from work, Maria volunteered for evening activities, leaving Joe to return to an empty house. Joe so hated the empty house that he began to have his dinners downtown, and he came home only after several after-dinner drinks. At that point Maria announced that she had accepted a job offer to work with American Indians that would require her to be away from home several days at a time.

Here are two basically well-adjusted people who are unable to communicate with each other; each frustrates the other, and each frustration leads to a new aggressive response which, in turn, leads to a new frustration. Slowly each tears the other down, leaving a less adequate person who becomes less able to respond to his spouse's needs. Would you apply the term *love* to the Calvin marriage?

Love is an enriching, enhancing experience when it is mutual, when it involves healthy, growth-directed motives, when the people involved can communicate with each other, and when it produces healthy interdependency, but not over-dependency.

PRELUDES TO MARRIAGE/ALTERNATIVES TO MARRIAGE

For the past 50 years or so, a progression of stages has led up to marriage: dating, going steady, and engagement, each indicating increasing degrees of serious intent and commitment. The entire sequence has been termed courtship. However, society — like individual behavior — is dynamic and always changing. So are its rituals and customs attached to the period leading up to marriage. Today. although the majority of young people still go through the traditional sequence, many do not. They may go directly from a series of friendly social meetings (perhaps no longer called dates) into the equivalent of a short-term marriage (that is, living together with the understanding that the relationship probably will not end in marriage).

Virtually every society has rituals and customs surrounding the period of time leading up to the marriage (or any permanent relationship), even though the people of that society do not realize they have them. Whether the boy comes to the girl's house with flowers for her mother, or whether he comes to the girl's apartment with a suitcase and moves in, there are recognizable events that take place.

WITHOUT BENEFIT OF CLERGY

In the late 1960s new forms of sociosexual relationships began to receive attention. The most conspicuous of these evolved from the decision of young unmarried men and women to live together, either in small groups much like a family or as couples. Such relationships have always occurred; what was new was the openness with which these relationships were expressed. In one well-publicized case a student forced her university's administration to admit that her living, unmarried, with a young man was none of their business. Inevitably such relationships were roundly criticized by many community authorities, but the criticisms had little impact on the participants.

Initially treated with a combination of horror, amusement, anger, and fear, these couples are slowly being accepted by their parents and their more traditional friends. A 50-year-old woman who spent a year trying to pretend to her friends that her daughter was rooming with another girl now tells the same friends "My daughter and her old man are dropping by for the weekend." The employer who was once reluctant to invite his new assistant over for the evening because "he might bring that woman" now takes his wife to a party at the home of Mr. Jackson and Miss (or Ms.) Adams.

Although most unmarried couples feel their relationship is based on love and mutual respect, some admit to being together for convenience — but so would some married couples if they were to be honest. They prefer to remain uncommitted because they feel the world is unsettled and their own futures are uncertain. They also admit that they do not want to be tied down, to have legal demands for faithfulness forever, to feel unable to go their own ways later. The case could be made that their refusal to get married shows more respect for the marriage vows than that of people who get married with the idea that divorce can follow close behind.

Some of these couples do get married; most probably do not. Although acceptance has increased, criticism is still widespread. What future do these relationships have? Will the children feel a lack of stability in a home where there is not even the legal commitment of a marriage? After a time will the men move on to younger women, an option that fewer females have? Is the entire phenomenon transient, or will it become another acceptable option in the future?

Jenny was 23, divorced, and had a year-old boy. She had just entered a community college as a freshman, with the encouragement of an aunt who provided a few dollars for her support and of her welfare worker, who recognized that Jenny did not want to spend her whole life on welfare. Financially it was tight, but Jenny did some babysitting (not reported to her welfare worker) and managed to get by. She met several men her age and older on campus, but none appealed to her enough to persuade her to go out with them.

At the end of the quarter she found herself attracted to Marcus Waters, the young head of the child-care center where she left her son. She saw him for coffee after class a few times, and then he began to drive her home, since it was on his way. This led to a couple of dinners, a movie or two, and a series of informal evenings together, some at her apartment and some at his. They slept together the day Jenny finished her last final. They were affectionate with each other, they respected each other, and they were able to avoid any serious conflicts; but they did not love each other.

After about six weeks of a very close relationship, Marcus came over one Sunday afternoon and simply moved Jenny and her son into his apartment. They lived pretty much as a family for about 18 months. Although Jenny's social worker reluctantly had to cut off her welfare funds, Marcus earned a sufficient income for all three to live comfortably. Then Marcus took a job in another city, leaving Jenny and her son with enough of his furniture and kitchen things to get by. By this time she had finished her Associate of Arts degree and was able to get a job to support the apartment. They stayed in touch for about a year but never saw each other again.

Jenny made no attempt to follow Marcus because she realized that, as nice as he was, he had begun to feel tied down in the relationship. She always suspected that he took the job in order to have an excuse to leave her. Their relationship never grew or developed; it remained comfortable, steady, sensible — and dull. They became like "old marrieds" without ever having had the excitement of being "young marrieds." The relationship served its purpose for the two years it lasted, but to have continued it would have been a mistake.

SOME NEVER MARRY

Our society puts such a high value on matrimony that we are often critical of those who do not marry. Some choose not to marry because they are unwilling to share their lives or because they do not like any member of the opposite sex enough to live together as man and wife. Others just do not find the right person at the right time.

Although unmarried people certainly miss much of the enrichment a marriage can bring, they gain in other ways. They can spend much more of their money on themselves and have less financial concern regarding the future. They can do things and go places as they please and travel extensively if they want, without worrying about anyone else. Often they have warm relationships with relatives, married couples, or children, and they receive some of the enjoyment of marriage indirectly.

We often forget that certain people who do marry would have been better off to have avoided this relationship but were pressured into it by well-meaning family members and friends.

CONFLICTS PRIOR TO MARRIAGE

Many things happen to prevent marriages: personality problems and conflicts, loss of interest, a new man or woman appearing on the scene, and the possibility that the strong feelings of love and affection just do not last. One author (Merrill, 1959) has listed several other major causes of friction during the period leading up to the marriage: (1) difficulty with families, (2) difficulty with friends, (3) conventions, such as manners and dress, (4) conflicting values, (5) use of money, (6) religious differences, and (7) affection and sex.

Difficulty with families.   "I'm marrying you—not your family." This statement is very true, but families do come as part of the package. The influence of the family on a marriage is great—even if all the relatives live a thousand miles away or even if no relatives are still alive.

Parents may disapprove of a marriage for a variety of reasons. Many parents become so attached to their children that they hate the idea of giving them up. Some parents need to have a child around who depends on them so they can feel that they have a place in the world. Others have difficulty in accepting the fact that their child is mature enough to leave home. Still others have such high standards for their children—after all, the person your child marries reflects credit or discredit on you as well—that no one can possibly be good enough. Sometimes parents object to religious, social-class, or nationality differences. Although parents usually try to keep the happiness of their children in mind, the end result of their behavior does not necessarily promote that happiness.

However, parents can be correct. They can see the prospective mate more objectively. They know their child, and they may see trouble ahead. Particularly with teenage courtship and engagement, parents are anxious to avoid letting anything become permanent too quickly.

There is another excellent reason to learn about the family of your prospective mate: they are the significant others in the life of the person you are going to marry. A perceptive boy will learn a great deal about his girl by seeing the way her parents treat each other, by observing for himself the social and religious values in her home, and by looking for important little details. Do the parents bicker? Is her younger brother totally undisciplined? Are the parents gossips? Is the home always noisy? These behavior patterns provide indications of what might be expected later from the daughter. The emotional climate of your childhood home inevitably affects the later emotional climate of your adult home after marriage.

Difficulty with friends. Since it is rare to meet anyone and like *all* his friends, one member of an engaged couple will usually dislike at least a few friends of the partner. Sometimes, rather than dislike any individual friend, the girl may resent her fiance's spending so much time with "the boys," whereas he feels that her girl friends are "just a bunch of gossips."

Previous romances also intrude on the couple. The newly engaged girl may be very jealous of all the dates her fiance ever had, and his talking about them does not help matters, especially when the engagement is recent and both are insecure in their new roles. Neither does it help for either one to describe all previous dating relationships "because I want to be honest with you."

Adjusting to conventions. Everyone displays certain behaviors that others might find difficult to accept on a long-term basis. Many of these actions are merely habits or manners and are so unimportant that they cannot interfere with an otherwise healthy relationship, but they can become a great annoyance far out of proportion to their real importance. For example:

Claudia smokes two packs of cigarettes a day, and her fiance cannot tolerate the smell of tobacco.

Mac likes to sit on the front porch or walk to the corner drugstore in his undershirt. His fiancée finds this very irritating.

Jonathan's mother is an immaculate housekeeper, and he demands that everything be neatly in its place. He acts like a hurt little boy when things are not just so.

Marlene puts her hair up in curlers right after supper. Her fiance cannot stand women with their hair in curlers. He argues that it is unfair to a husband to have to spend most of his life staring at his wife's bare scalp, just so she can look attractive for strangers the next day.

The period before marriage enables two people to learn each other's manners and habits and determine whether their feelings of attraction are sufficient to overcome any irritations that may arise.

Conflicting values.   No two people have the exact same values, and two people may be happily married with very different values. When important values are in direct conflict, however, both the engagement and the eventual marriage are troubled. If the man demands peace and quiet and the girl prefers noise and loud parties, their values conflict; if the girl insists on owning a home and having a stable life but the man enjoys freedom from responsibility and wandering from town to town, their values conflict; if he favors leisure and she admires hard work and high achievement. . . .

The use of money.   How important is money? How should money be spent? In marriage there is the feeling that the money is jointly possessed. When it is spent, even though it was earned by the man, the woman feels *her* money is being spent. How much should be spent, how much should be saved, and how much should be used as a down payment on credit buying? In our society disagreements over money can become a major problem for couples.

Religious and ethnic differences.   Church affiliation and religious values can create two major types of courtship problems. First, you feel yourself a member of a particular religious group and have a sense of loyalty to that group. Therefore you are likely to want the person you marry to be a member of the same group and to be willing to bring up your children similarly. Second, as a member of a particular religious group, you tend to internalize the group's values, some of which may conflict with those of other groups (for example, attitudes on birth control, church attendance, eating habits, or religious education). Two people who differ widely on these and other matters may find religious values a barrier to a satisfactory marriage.

Interfaith marriages have consistently higher divorce rates than same-faith marriages (Gordon, 1964). When religious values and habits are different, the relationship can lack an important basis for sharing. Students themselves indicate that marrying outside their religious group would be more difficult than marrying outside their educational, nationality, or economic group (Gordon, 1964).

In spite of these potential problems, of a sample of 5400 college students drawn from 40 colleges across the country, only 8% indicated that they would "break off at once" if they fell in love with someone of another faith; nearly half would continue to date. Perhaps these reactions occurred because 40% of the students had already observed an intermarriage in the family, and only one in ten had never dated a person of another religion; one-third of the students implied that they dated people of other religions as often or more often than they dated people of their own religion (Gordon, 1964).

It has been claimed that people who enter into interfaith marriages are neurotic or are trying to throw over the values of their parents. Recent evidence, however, shows there is no difference in emotional health between those who had intermarried and those who had not (Sklare, 1964).

Many factors relate to the success of interfaith couples: the intensity of their identification with their church group, the attitudes of their community and their friends, the acceptance by their families, and—probably the most important—the similarity in their values and beliefs.

Major problems also arise when the couple come from different racial or ethnic backgrounds. Marriages between black and white, Mexican American and Anglo (or black) American, or Asian and non-Asian are examples of relationships that have far more than an average amount of stress and strain placed on them. You may wish to pursue this topic in class or on your own.

Affection and sex. See earlier discussion.

MARRIAGE

Marriage, for most people, represents the most important human relationship of their adult years. Only vocation can even begin to compete with the family in its impact on a person's life. The success and stability of marriage influence the emotional health of all concerned, especially the children, and as a result influence the vitality of the entire country.

In the United States we believe that the goal of marriage is to make the two partners happy: it should be a worthwhile, self-actualizing, enjoyable experience for the couple. Carrying on the family name or taking care of the parents in their old age or bringing a dowry is no longer important to most Americans. These values are quite different in other areas of the world.

WHO MARRIES WHOM?

What brings two people together so that they wish to marry? The immediate answer is *proximity;* that is, they live or work or go to church or do something near each other, so that the chances are high that they will meet frequently and have the opportunity to get to know each other.

FIGURE 15–2. What brings two people together so that they wish to marry? Photograph by Lehman J. Pinckney.

Husband and wife tend to be similar in numerous characteristics, such as race, religion, education, intelligence, social class, age, previous marital status (that is, divorced people tend to marry other divorced people), attitudes toward drinking, and number of children desired (Berelson & Steiner, 1964). Husband and wife also tend to have similar personality characteristics, although these similarities are not so consistent as those just cited. When people select the characteristics of an ideal mate, they select characteristics similar to their own (Prince & Baggaley, 1963). Thus the old idea that opposites attract is not upheld.

Among college students, women prefer to marry older men, and men prefer to marry younger women. In one study all the college women wanted to marry men with more or at least as much education as they had; the men preferred the women to have about the same amount of education as they themselves had (Goldsen, Rosenberg, Williams, & Suchman, 1960).

WHAT MAKES MARRIAGES SUCCESSFUL?

Successful marriage depends on many factors, some of which are far from being understood. Nonetheless, research into this matter has been extensive, and psychologists can predict with some success which marriages will be happy and which will be unhappy. In reading the rest of this chapter, keep in mind that, although evidence may show that being happily married is *related to* some factor, this relationship does not imply that a happy marriage is *caused by* that factor. Thus happily married people are less likely to be depressed than unhappily married people (Renne, 1970), but it is not certain that depression leads to marital dissatisfaction, since the cause and effect could be exactly reversed.

Background factors in happy marriages. Many childhood experiences are found to be related to later marital happiness. First, if you were brought up in a home with a happy marriage, you will have better chances of having a happy marriage; if you had a happy childhood, your chances will also be improved. Second, good relationships with parents produce later happy marriages. Third, children receiving firm discipline administered without undue harshness or frequency make better spouses. And, fourth, when parents are frank regarding sex and communicate healthy attitudes toward sex, their children seem to have happy marriages (Terman, 1938).

In addition, a happy marriage is more likely if the partners have finished high school or gone further, are happy on their jobs and with their leisure activities, and are physically healthy (Renne, 1970). Social relationships are similarly related to marital satisfaction. Happily married couples are more likely to see close friends and relatives frequently but are no more likely to join social, recreational, union, professional, or community organizations (Renne, 1970).

You have undoubtedly also heard that early marriages are less successful than later marriages. In one Midwestern city, 40% of those who had married before age 21 wished they had waited, compared with less than 10% of those married after 21 (Inselberg, 1961). The early life of the individual and his age at marriage are definite factors in his marital success; yet they are certainly not insurmountable barriers.

Personal factors in happy marriages.   Marital happiness is greater when both husband and wife come from emotionally stable families and are themselves emotionally stable (Burgess & Cottrell, 1939; Lippman, 1954). Other personality characteristics have been found to be related to happy marriages: (1) consideration for others, (2) willingness to yield rather than insistence on dominating, (3) pleasantness as a companion, (4) self-confidence, and (5) ability to accept emotional dependence (Burgess & Wallin, 1953).

Husband and wife need not share everything—indeed, there is merit in being apart from each other occasionally—but enjoying many of the same things can enrich a marriage. Liking the same movies, the same sports, or the same books adds a common bond, as does having similar religious, social, political, and child-rearing values. It is interesting to note that not only do husbands and wives often share political attitudes, but each also assumes that the other agrees with him more than he actually does (Byrne & Blaylock, 1963). That is, husbands and wives overestimate the degree to which their spouses think as they do.

To some extent each person re-creates in his marriage the marriage he lived with in his parents' home. He will behave much as the parent of his own sex behaved and will expect his mate to behave much as his other parent behaved.

> Marcia Sohn was the daughter of an aggressive woman who pushed her to "go with the right people" and "do the proper thing." Marcia's mother pushed her father also, until he was wealthy and terribly unhappy. As a child Marcia swore to herself that she would never push her own husband to become wealthy. Marcia eventually married a very pleasant man who enjoyed building up his business. Marcia did not push him to become wealthy, but she did push him to become better educated. He tried, but he decided he did not like college. Unlike Marcia's father, her husband refused to be bullied beyond a certain point, and he suggested a divorce. The couple decided to see a marriage counselor. Through his help, Marcia realized that she had been repeating the same pushing pattern that her mother had shown, except that she had pushed her husband to improve his education rather than to earn money.

Obviously the role behavior of children is not exactly the same as that of the parents. Nonetheless, since we assume that role behavior is learned, largely through identification and internalization, the behavior of parents becomes a vitally important influence on the role behavior of their children.

In the United States marital roles are relatively *egalitarian,* which means that the husband and wife share the power to make decisions and are considered fairly equal in the marriage. In many parts of the world, marriages are husband-dominated. College men are, perhaps understandably, less favorably disposed toward egalitarian marriages than are college women (Kalish, Maloney, & Arkoff,

1966). This does not mean that women and men always want the same things from each other. Women show more need for love, affection, sympathy, and understanding; men have a greater need for a mate who is neat and tidy, can adjust to routine, and is even-tempered and dependable (Langhorne & Secord, 1955). Thus the woman who needs affection and can be neat will probably be happiest with a man who needs neatness and can be affectionate.

Although wives claim that their husbands are dominant in the marriage, a great majority of these women state that they are equal or superior to their husbands in budgeting, deciding where to live, and making all decisions regarding the children. The husband is given greater credit for his financial responsibilities, mechanical ability, greater aggressiveness, and knowledge of politics (Mowrer, 1969).

The early years of marriage seem more difficult for the wife than for the husband, perhaps because her shift from student or working woman to wife causes more change in her role and in her feelings (Barry, 1970). Contrary to what many people assume, one investigation of couples who had been married different lengths of time found that the marital satisfaction of the wife decreased during the years she was having children and during their early years at home; it subsequently increased until shortly before her husband's retirement. The man, on the other hand, does not show this decrease, although he shares the increase in later satisfaction (Rollins & Feldman, 1970). These and other studies have led one expert (Barry, 1970) to conclude that a successful marriage depends on whether the husband's self-concept is good enough so that he can help his wife deal with her new role. If so, the early conflicts are more easily settled and mutual growth can occur; if not, antagonism may build that will eventually disrupt the marriage. It would appear that the wife suffers greater stress in the early stages of marriage, thus requiring the husband to provide understanding and emotional support.

BEHAVIOR IN MARRIAGE

When two people enter into marriage, they usually have extremely high ideals. In spite of good intentions, most newlyweds do not find adjusting to marriage easy, even when they know each other well, are well suited to each other, and come from stable homes.

During the first several months of marriage, many unanticipated difficulties may occur, until the couple finally work out reasonably healthy life patterns. Love and willingness to make an effort can help produce a successful marriage and encourage personal growth.

"But, Ma, it *is* traditional, kind of—the bride's
family gives the pot party"

FIGURE 15–3.   Courtesy of Ed Fisher.

How can you contribute to making your marriage successful? A few of the many possible ways are the following:

Recognizing the needs of the other.   Two people who have spent a great deal of time together under a variety of conditions should know each other very well. In a good marriage each party becomes increasingly sensitive to the needs of the other until, after a time, each can understand the partner's feelings, even without being told.

Learning to communicate.   Sharing thoughts and feelings is important in marriage. The strong, silent type may be romantic before marriage, but he can be a frustrating husband. Some men feel that expressing their fears and hopes is a sign of weakness, but the opposite is actually the case, since a man must feel secure in his masculinity in order to be able to express his feelings.

Communication is important on a day-to-day basis. When a problem arises, it is useful to be able to sit down and talk it out. A new husband who feels his wife is flirting too much may be reluctant to mention it directly, so he displaces his anger by sulking in the corner or criticizing his wife's dress. However, if he and his wife can discuss the problem, they will probably be able to resolve it. When a married couple lack the ability to communicate with each other, they lack an important quality that fosters marital stability and satisfaction.

Learning to compromise. The importance of compromise is stated so often that it may actually have become exaggerated. Some compromise is necessary, but we often learn that a little discussion and thinking will allow both husband and wife to have what they wish.

Willingness to compromise sometimes means a willingness to give in. In one study, partners who reported that they both gave in were happier than the ones who stated that one of them gave in all the time and the other never gave in (Renne, 1970). Apparently even winning all the battles—at least on the surface—does not make a married person as happy as when an effective compromise is reached.

Respecting privacy. Although communication is important, so is the opportunity for privacy. Married couples have the right to keep certain thoughts and feelings to themselves. A husband need not mention that he was unpopular back in high school; a wife may prefer to remain silent when a brief visit with an old boyfriend rekindles some flame. Each should encourage the other to talk freely about feelings and ideas, but each should also respect the need of the other for privacy. Physical privacy is just as necessary as psychological privacy. The opportunity to be alone on occasion is very important to many people.

Maintaining individuality. Marriage should not make two people into one but should make them more distinctly two. Married couples tend to share similar values, attitudes, behavior patterns, and styles of living, but this is no reason to apply pressure when similarity does not occur.

Expecting too much. In countries where marriages are arranged, the participants do not expect much companionship or affection from the marriage. The husband may expect his wife to maintain the home, care for the children, uphold the family reputation, be careful with his money, be pleasant to him, give some physical affection, and respect his family. The wife expects to be cared for, given an occasional luxury, treated with kindness, and allowed some pleasures.

In the United States expectations are much greater. Besides all the behaviors just mentioned, both husband and wife expect the other to be a social companion,

FIGURE 15-4. The wife is usually expected to care for the children.
Photograph by Lehman J. Pinckney.

share interests and values, participate in activities with mutual friends, be sexually
exciting, and be intellectually stimulating. Expectations, often including impossibly romantic notions, are frequently greater than can possibly be met. Although
husbands and wives in arranged marriages may receive less, they also expect
less. Thus less difference exists between achievement and aspiration, and frustrations are fewer. This factor, often overlooked in discussions of marital success
and failure, is undoubtedly a vitally important variable.

Marriage is probably the most rewarding and the most demanding relationship of adult life. Research has shown that successful marriages can, to an extent,
be predicted from a knowledge of background factors, childhood experiences,
personality, attitudes, and needs of each partner. Marital roles and marital role
expectations also influence the happiness of marriage. An awareness of the importance of certain types of behavior during the marriage may lead to the increased satisfaction of security, love, and esteem needs.

DIVORCE

The divorce rate has been climbing steadily since 1958, when it reached its lowest period since the high World War II divorce rates. By 1969 the rate was 50% higher than it had been a dozen years earlier (*Family Almanac*, 1972).

A high divorce rate may be inevitable in a culture that feels marriage is entered into primarily for the happiness of the two people involved, rather than for their families. If the happiness of the partners is the only consideration, then unhappiness would logically lead to dissolution of marriage.

Several factors are related to divorce. For example, it is more common among less educated people, among children of divorced parents, in interfaith marriages, among nonchurchgoers, for those with brief engagements, and for those who did not know each other well before the marriage (Berelson & Steiner, 1964; Merrill, 1959). Divorces are especially common among couples who were married in their teens. Of every 100 teenage marriages, 50 end in divorce within five years (Menninger, 1968). The high proportion of teenage brides who are pregnant undoubtedly contributes to the divorce rate. In one study nearly half the high school brides surveyed had been pregnant on their wedding day (Inselberg, 1961).

The real picture of divorce, however, is given not by statistics but by observing the individuals involved. The divorced couple are punished for whatever mistakes were made, and so are their children. These children face three difficult problems: (1) the months leading up to a divorce are usually full of tension and family disruption; (2) the process of the divorce is often upsetting for the children; and (3) it is difficult for the children to live with only one parent or with a stepparent and to see the other parent irregularly.

It has long been debated whether the child is better off if his parents divorce or if they continue to live together unhappily. The dispute cannot be settled, except for individual cases. One child may be happier living with only one parent, because family arguments are hurting him deeply; another child, whose parents conceal their unhappiness with each other, is probably better off if the marriage stays intact.

Understandably, but unfortunately, the emphasis of both the media and the professionals has been on how to decrease the divorce rate. When I was quoted in a newspaper article as saying that more effort should be given to enabling divorces to become successful, I received several letters arguing both sides of the issue. A successful divorce would be one in which both parties find a way to live that permits more self-esteem and more self-actualization than when they were living together; it would also be one in which any "innocent bystanders," such as children or elderly parents, are hurt as little as possible and perhaps even enriched in some way. This is not a matter of advocating divorce, but of trying to permit divorced people to avoid subsequent harm to themselves and others. There are individuals who are so angry when someone else is divorced that they feel the divorced person should suffer greatly for his actions.

Most divorced people do suffer. They suffer from guilt, because they feel they should have been able to save the marriage; they wonder whether they will be able to love someone else adequately or to be loved by someone else; they suffer from loneliness; and they suffer from the views others often have of divorced people as failures, as immoral, as inadequate. Such people need support in regaining lost self-esteem.

SUMMARY OF IMPORTANT IDEAS

1. Parents have always considered seeing their children properly married to be one of their most important responsibilities.

2. Sexual satisfaction involves more than the reduction of a biological need.

3. Evidence conflicts as to whether there has been a substantial increase in sexual behavior among college students or whether attitudes regarding sex are just more open than they were previously.

4. Internalized values regarding sex behavior begin to develop early in the life-span.

5. Sex can be self-actualizing when love is involved. However, the exact relationship of love and of marriage to sexual enjoyment is not at all clear.

6. The parent-child and husband-wife relationships are only two of many settings in which love can occur.

7. Not all love relationships, or relationships that claim to be based on love, are enhancing.

8. The normal progression leading to marriage has been, for the past 50 years, dating, going steady, engagement, and marriage. This appears to be changing. It is becoming more and more common for unmarried couples to live together.

9. Conflicts prior to marriage are based on difficulty with families, difficulty with friends, conventions, conflicting values, use of money, religious differences, and affection and sex.

10. Marriage leads to the most important human relationship of the adult years.

11. The success of a marriage is related to the marital success of the partners' parents, to the prospective couple's childhood happiness, and to other factors of their earlier years.

12. In marriage, husband and wife are encouraged to recognize each other's needs and to learn to communicate with each other.

13. Divorce rates have slowly been increasing. Unfortunately, so much stress has been placed on reducing divorce that very little is said about how to enable the members of the family to function effectively after the divorce.

16 Psychology of Adult Development

It may seem a little unfair to devote five chapters to a discussion of the first 25 years of life and only one chapter to the subsequent 50 or so years. However, principles of behavior do not change merely because a person grows older. Nonetheless, there are certain matters of particular concern in the middle and later years of life, and these will be discussed in this chapter.

Is being an adult a time of life or a state of mind? Do you work to earn adult status, or does it just happen? Obviously individuals differ greatly, and the demands of different cultures also vary. However, at least in the United States and Canada, some generalizations can be made.

The fight for emancipation from parents should now be over. Health is usually good. Vocational skills have been recently acquired, and some work experience has been obtained. Social relationships may be enjoyed with fewer restrictions. Awareness, alertness, and energy are near their peak, and the future seems limitless.

With these new freedoms come new responsibilities. The adult is expected to organize his own time, handle his own money, seek advice when he needs it, and enter into much more mature and demanding relationships. He is also fully responsible legally for his own actions and is expected to participate in the community and contribute to it.

And there are new frustrations. Competition is often demanding. Financial pressures sometimes appear never-ending. Relationships with the opposite sex that once seemed so exciting become stressful. Children prove a not-unmixed blessing. Initial job success becomes a pattern of ups and downs.

EVALUATING CHANGES RESULTING FROM AGE

Differences that result from age can be measured in two basic ways: first, by following the same group of people across a period of time and taking regular measurements; second, by comparing groups of different ages at the same time and assuming that differences between them result from aging.

Both approaches have limitations. The first approach, termed **longitudinal** research, requires much time to carry out. Also, it is greatly affected by what could be called accidents of history. For example, if we find that people who were tested in 1940 and again in 1970 show a change in attitudes toward religion, how can we know whether those attitudes changed because the individuals aged 30 years or because of specific events that took place between 1940 and 1970?

The alternate approach, the **cross-sectional** method, is also limited. Suppose you find that the young and the elderly differ in vocabulary, with the young getting higher test scores. You might hypothesize that vocabulary skills decrease with age. However, it is well known that the educational level of the elderly is far below that of the young, which could account for the differences. And how motivated are older people when they take tests? How much experience in being tested have they had? Thus, whether you are comparing vocabulary scores or attitude scores, it is very difficult to determine whether differences between age groups are caused by the process of getting old or by the fact that different age groups have had different life histories.

FROM YOUNG ADULT TO OLD

The early adult years still involve experimentation. The individual may experiment with his new emancipation from his parents, perhaps carrying freedom to excess one time, then being afraid to venture forth another time. He tests out relationships with the opposite sex, but with marriage more likely the purpose than in earlier years. He tries different jobs, lives in different houses, participates in different activities. From the great range of possible behavior patterns, he selects those that satisfy him the most.

As he moves into his thirties and forties, he gains a better idea of where he wants to go and where he is likely to be able to go. Although some people do make substantial changes in their life patterns after 30 or 35, most have settled into a type of routine that they will maintain until retirement age.

The decade between 40 and 50 "should be the peak period in life, not only for financial and social success but also for authority and prestige" (Hurlock,

1959). During this period the individual is still active, vigorous, and alert, and he has accumulated experience and knowledge. Identity, sex, emancipation, and purpose in life are no longer such bothersome problems. They have been replaced, however, by the need to come to grips with the reality that time is not infinite and that whatever is going to be accomplished during the lifetime must be accomplished fairly soon.

The hopes a person feels in his twenties must, for the most part, be realized by the time he is in his fifties, or they will never be realized. This decade demands a painful personal re-evaluation. Some of his friends have surpassed him and are much more successful than he; the expensive home he had hoped he would own may be as much a dream as ever; his children are not the geniuses he had always desired. Retirement suddenly becomes a concern, and his health may no longer be so good. His level of aspiration must be modified in terms of the present reality.

However, maturation and personal growth do not cease when a person reaches 21; they continue throughout his life-span. There will be times when he will feel the great satisfaction of knowing that he has made effective use of his capabilities—that he has accomplished his goals on a work project or in preparing his children to meet the world or by giving enjoyment to others.

Even in later years, happiness, satisfaction, and self-actualization can continue. People then have much to look back on and still have much to look ahead to. Some, of course, psychologically curl up and wait for death, but others use their later adult years to do the things they had always wanted to do but never had the time for. Their old age is rich and exciting, filled with warm, human relationships and stimulating activities.

CHANGING PATTERNS OF BEHAVIOR

Behavior changes during the years from childhood through maturity, and at each stage of development new roles become appropriate. Nonetheless, certain consistent patterns do carry over. The aggressive child is likely to mature into a competitive adult; the bright child becomes an intelligent adult.

One interesting study (Kagan & Moss, 1962) traced a group of individuals from infancy into the early adult years. The investigators found that the need for achievement among children between 6 and 10 predicted their actual achievement in their twenties; this was especially true for intellectual achievement. In the same study teenage boys who did not date or show other typical masculine interests seemed to avoid contact with the opposite sex ten years later. Children who displayed no aggression turned into adults who were afraid to express aggressive feelings, and boys who were aggressive and dominant became competitive as adults.

Another study followed adults from their engagement until nearly 20 years later. The religious values and vocational interests of this group changed relatively little although their attitudes toward marriage and child rearing did show change (Kelly, 1955).

Although general personality characteristics and underlying values are resistant to change, change nevertheless does occur. Caucasian women attending a South Carolina university were given an attitude test in 1935, and the same group was retested in 1965. The proportion of women who believed that blacks should have equal rights increased from 8% to 56%; those who believed that "militarism is necessary for proper defense and protection of individuals of our country" also increased by approximately the same amount (Capel, 1967). People's attitudes do change in time, probably because of changes in the attitudes of others and because of changing conditions in society.

Many studies have been conducted on behavior changes during the life-span. In essence, they show that, as people become older, they also become more cautious and restrained, less likely to need to be or want to be with other people, and less flexible (Riley, Foner, & Associates, 1968).

As might be expected, work patterns also change over the years. The older a worker is, the less likely he is to move from one job to another (up to retirement) and the more likely he is to feel satisfied with his job. Injuries and absenteeism remain about the same from the late teens through the mid-sixties (Riley et al., 1968). Of course, as people get older, they also tend to move out of the kinds of jobs that might lead to injuries and accidents, either into supervisory positions or into jobs that do not require heavy lifting or quick reactions.

CHANGING INTELLIGENCE

At one time it was believed that general intelligence did not improve after the early adolescent years, but recent research has suggested otherwise. Certain groups, such as those who go into more intellectually demanding jobs, increase their IQ scores, and their intelligence does not drop until they are well advanced in years (Bayley & Oden, 1955). Even then, the decrease in IQ-test scores may not occur for all people but only for those who are physically ill or have suffered strokes.

An individual's intelligence *relative to others of his age* shows considerable consistency over the years. Those who were more intelligent than average when they were young tend to remain above average in intelligence in their mature years (Bradway & Thompson, 1962). However, changes in intellectual functioning do occur over the years. After the rapid increase from infancy through childhood, the growth of intelligence slows down during the junior high school years. Then, in the late teens or early twenties, performance on *some types* of intellectual tasks ceases to change until the later years, when it begins to decline (Bayley, 1955).

The kinds of change in intellectual ability that occur with age will probably not be a surprise. For example, memory for recent events does diminish, but memory for events that occurred much earlier remains high. You may have had the experience of talking with an elderly person who recalls his childhood vividly but cannot remember what he said to you an hour ago; a similar pattern, although not so extreme, is often found with middle-aged people. Knowledge, on the other hand, shows little or no loss as people get older. For people whose work makes intellectual demands on them, abilities tend to remain high (reviewed in Horn, 1970).

PHYSICAL CHANGES AND PSYCHOLOGICAL REACTIONS

Between early adulthood and old age the body undergoes many slow changes. The hair thins out, especially for men, and the skin begins to develop wrinkles. Muscles tend to lose their tone, and an increase in weight is common. These changes, along with an increase in medical problems, usually do not make themselves felt until the person has approached or passed his middle forties, although they occur to different people at different ages.

During the late forties many women go through **menopause,** a period during which the menstrual flow becomes less and less frequent and eventually stops. Menopause signals the end of the woman's potential for childbearing but not for sexual enjoyment.

The impact of menopause is more emotional than physical, although many women describe disturbing physical symptoms also. Women often feel that they must be able to conceive to be truly feminine; thus, when they lose this ability, they feel they are also losing their femininity. Menopause is also a distinct and unavoidable sign of advancing age. These psychological problems, accentuated by physical discomfort, may produce feelings of depression and irritability.

The United States has been called a youth-centered society, because we place so much emphasis on looking and behaving youthfully. Age means the end of youth—of its health and energy and physical attractiveness, of its hopes and opportunities and status. People resist the idea that they are growing old. Many men and women attack the most obvious symptoms of age through cosmetics, hairpieces, diets, and a variety of special treatments. Others participate in activities that appear out of keeping with their maturity level, such as the mother who insists on being "one of the gang" at her 14-year-old's parties but refuses to spend time with her own age peers.

Although physical changes that come with age are rarely pleasing, people are certainly not equally bothered by them. Mature individuals who have built satisfying relationships and who have developed absorbing interests are likely to spend less time and energy worrying about physical changes. They are not so concerned about appearing youthful, since other, more exciting, ventures occupy their time. They find their work challenging and their family relationships rewarding; home, friends, and enjoyable leisure, perhaps combined with political work or artistic endeavors, keep them busy.

FAMILY RESPONSIBILITIES AND SATISFACTIONS

Your parents are likely to be the most significant others in your early development; your spouse and children will become vitally important to your adult years. Changes in your self-concept will depend to an appreciable extent on how these people look on you and respond to you. The parent who is loved and respected by his family becomes a more complete person; the parent who is not loved or respected by his family becomes a less complete person.

Having a marriage partner and children offers opportunities for growth but also adds demands and responsibilities. Your behavior, your health, your interpersonal relationships, and your happiness now affect not only you but others as well. You can help others grow and mature effectively, or you can contribute to their having unfulfilled safety and love needs. How can you best help your family grow and make the most of their capacities?

Being a parent, particularly for the first time, causes great concern for both husband and wife. They listen to advice, perhaps read books, and think back on what their own parents did that was right or wrong. Often they make great resolves about the wonderful things they will do with their children, but beneath everything is the question "Will I really be a good parent?" Some people undoubtedly are better parents than others, but new parents should realize that "there is no such thing as a professional parent. We are all amateurs . . ." (Adams, 1968).

THE PURPOSE OF CHILDREN

Do you want to have children? For what purpose? At first the idea of a purpose for having children may seem absurd, since it seems natural to want them. But throughout history children—especially male children—have had a very definite financial value: they helped on the farm, worked in the family store, or contributed to the support of the family through some other form of work, and they took care of elderly and disabled parents and relatives.

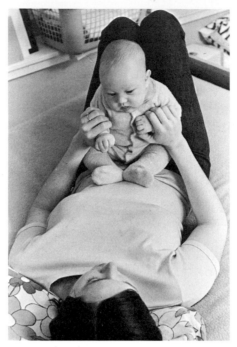

FIGURE 16–1. The best reason for having children may very well be
to enjoy them. Photograph by Lehman J. Pinckney.

Today, in the United States and in many other countries, children are needed
neither to work for the family nor to care for the parents in their old age. As a
matter of fact, having children is a great expense and responsibility. Nonetheless,
people continue to have children. Married couples without children are often
considered unfortunate, and those who do not want children may be looked on
as peculiar.

The best reason for having children may very well be to enjoy them—to
enjoy watching them grow and to enjoy helping them lead satisfying lives. Yet
many foreigners observe that American parents do not really seem to love and
enjoy their children—they worry about them, send them to college, protect them
with insurance, and use good measures to protect their mental and physical
health; but they just do not appear to enjoy them. Does this observation relate
to the often-heard comment that American parents push their children to grow
up too fast? Why have so many foreigners felt this way? Do you feel that American parents are able to enjoy their children?

PLANNING CHILDREN

Family planning is not exactly the same as birth control, although the two terms are used in similar situations. Birth control refers to preventing conception through the use of a variety of methods ranging from mechanical devices (the "loop," condoms) to oral medication (the "pill") to altered behavior (interrupting intercourse, restricting it to relatively safe periods). These approaches differ greatly in their effect on sexual enjoyment, their availability and cost, their ease of use, and their likelihood of effective protection.

Family planning involves the decision, made by prospective parents, to have a certain number of children spaced a certain number of years apart. They will probably use one or more of the birth-control methods to enable their plan to become a reality. Although as recently as the 1950s having three or four or even more children was seen as an indication of great love and warmth, reactions changed in the 1970s, when people began to talk about zero population growth. It was suggested that no one be permitted to have more than one or two children and that parents pay more, rather than less, income tax for each child. What are your feelings?

The more a person approves of birth control, the more he approves of abortion (Kalish, 1963). The new awareness of the population explosion, together with changing concepts of the role of women and the meaning of sexual behavior, led to decreased resistance to abortion as a means of controlling the population and freeing women from unwanted children. Although a few states have lenient abortion laws, by and large abortions are given only when the mother's life is otherwise endangered. Nonetheless, it has been estimated that more than a million abortions are performed in this country each year.

Today's Family, Compared with the Family of 60 Years Ago

—They live in cities and suburbs, not in small towns or on farms.
—They commute to work.
—They move frequently. (One out of five Americans moves each year.*)
—They seldom live in the same home with grandparents; they often do not even live in the same community.
—They are less likely to have lost a parent by death but more likely to have lived through parental divorce.
—Work is rarely a family affair.
—Education continues until the late teens or even later.
—The mother is more likely to be working or involved in social, political, or service activities.

Thus, at the very time that members of the family become most dependent on one another, the realities of our society force them apart because work and education no longer occur within the family.

---

* Metropolitan Life Insurance Company *Statistical Bulletin,* April 1966.

Some married couples do not want children; they do not wish to expend the time, money, and personal involvement required by parenthood. They can move around more easily and can devote full time and effort to careers or creative tasks that they find more fulfilling. Some adults do not particularly like caring for children, although they may be very fond of other people's youngsters. Although the traditions and values of our society place a certain amount of pressure on married couples to have children, some individuals recognize that—for them—the disadvantages of being childless are outweighed by the advantages.

FINANCIAL RESPONSIBILITIES

In our society finances are important. The ways in which you get money and the ways in which you spend it influence much of your behavior. What you buy and the conditions under which you buy things are determined not only by your income but also by your needs and self-concept.

Jack Valdez and Martin Keene were both recently married and in need of a refrigerator. Martin, after a little shopping, bought a refrigerator "on time," since he did not have the money to pay outright. The initial price of the refrigerator was $272, but he ended up paying $343 through extra charges for the time payments. Jack was more frugal. Through a newspaper advertisement he picked up a used refrigerator for $60 from a person who was moving. Then he put $25 a month into a savings account at 5% interest. Ten months later the $272 refrigerator was on sale for $222.95. Jack easily bought it for cash and then sold his old refrigerator for $50. By using a second-hand refrigerator for one year, Jack and his wife saved more than $100.

Jack's approach seems to make sense, but it does not take into account Martin's self-concept. Martin's self-esteem is based partly on his ability to buy things like a new refrigerator. Also, he feels that buying second-hand goods implies that he is not a good husband. He wants his wife to have the best he can possibly afford.

The same product is not worth the same amount to everyone. One couple give up new clothing in order to take a trip; another couple put a substantial portion of their income into the bank instead of buying a new automobile; a third couple prefer to eat at home unless they can go to an expensive restaurant.

What financial responsibilities does a husband have? What about a wife? How much of one's income should be put away against future old age, illness, or some catastrophe? What kinds of insurance should someone carry? What is a good investment: land? stocks? government bonds? Each of these questions can be answered only on an individual basis. How do you think you will answer them in ten years?

Money can buy money. When you borrow money or make a credit purchase, you are using money to buy money. Like anything else, buying money can prove very expensive. By the time the hidden costs are accounted for, you may be paying a true annual interest of 20% or more to borrow money. A simple 1½% per month charge is 18% per year; if there is a minimum interest or carrying-charge payment of 50¢, the rate may easily go over 20%. Credit is alluring, but it has been the downfall of many families.

USE OF LEISURE

What do you like to do in your spare time? Sleep? Watch television? Tinker with an automobile? Listen to music? Read? Talk? Play cards? The amount of leisure time available to the workingman has been increasing steadily over the years until, today, the average amount of leisure per workweek is three times what it was in 1850 (Kaplan, 1960), and the future will most likely see a continued reduction in work hours and increase in leisure time. You may see, during your lifetime, a standard three-day weekend, a seven-hour day, and a three-month vacation every ten years. If these changes occur, what will you do with your vastly increased leisure time?

Leisure can be used for relaxation or for exciting activities, but it is usually a change from the regular daily routine. A strenuous camping trip is just as much leisure as a week of loafing around the house. Surprisingly enough, a man who spends a week camping may return to work more refreshed than the man whose free week was just an overextended loafing weekend.

FIGURE 16–2. Leisure can be used for relaxation . . . or for exciting activities. Photographs by Lehman J. Pinckney.

Productive work as part of the American tradition can be traced back to our Puritan ancestors and the early days of Protestantism. Many Americans, perhaps without realizing it, look on work as "good" and loafing as "bad." In casual conversation you do not brag about how little you work but about how hard you work. The emphasis on productive work has become so much a part of the culture that you may find it difficult to relax without feeling you should be "doing something." Yet leisure, whether relaxing or exciting, can be just as fulfilling as work. As a matter of fact, people who use their leisure effectively are likely to be able to work harder and get more done in the long run—and will probably live longer.

Educators are often very unhappy with the amount of time people spend watching television. The family television set is turned on for an average of five hours a day, seven days a week—and even more than that in the winter (Bogart, 1962). Educators also point out that many programs that are thoroughly enjoyed by first-graders are also followed faithfully by their parents, which hardly speaks well for the maturity level of the programming.

Television is relaxing. It requires neither thinking nor bodily activity. As such, it has a definite appeal to people who want to be entertained without any effort. Watching television may help children from disadvantaged homes by exposing them to new speech patterns and vocabulary, but it does little for the child or adult who already has a stimulating home environment.

Claims are made that television reduces the time children would spend on more productive activities, but the evidence does not fully bear this out. Watching television cuts most deeply into such activities as listening to the radio, going to movies, and reading comic books. In England at least, television seemed to have little effect on other activities; both book sales and library use, which dropped just after television first appeared, increased as people ceased finding the novelty of the home screen exciting (Himmelweit, 1962).

Leisure activities are influenced by many factors, including personality, needs, interests, and the availability of time, facilities, and finances (Lehner & Kube, 1964). People fortunate enough to have the initiative find ways to spend their leisure time enjoyably and with profit to themselves. Others are bored with spare time and end up killing time in any way they can; some even use increased leisure time for working at a second job.

RESPONSIBLE TO WHOM?

The balance between what you do to fulfill your own needs and what you do to provide service for the community (*community* referring to both the local community and the greater society) varies from person to person. Some people are intent on satisfying their own needs to the virtual exclusion of considering the larger society; others sacrifice their own needs in order to serve the broader society; and still others feel that their own needs can best be met when they also serve the community.

What responsibilities do you feel to your community? To your nation? To the world? You are a part of each of these, and you expect each to offer you something. What do you wish to give in return? One great American, Horace Mann, stated: "Be ashamed to die until you have won some victory for humanity." Do you feel you have any responsibilities to win some victory for future generations?

The work and the responsibility of supporting our community are always divided unequally, with some people doing much more than others. Those willing to put forth the time and effort, however, may have the satisfaction of seeing the effects of their work.

People can no longer shut themselves off from the rest of the world. The opposite ends of the earth are just a fraction of a minute away by radio, a few hours by jet airplane, and—sad to say—not very far apart for intercontinental ballistic missiles. Your life may be deeply affected by a tribal feud in Iran, an impoverished economy in Indonesia, or a political fight in Ireland.

The well-adjusted person recognizes that he is a part of the world, and he wishes to have knowledge of it beyond the slogans of propagandists. This means that he needs to know something about the historical and cultural backgrounds of other nations, as well as of his own. He needs to try to understand how people around the world think and feel and develop self-concepts and aim at self-actualization. The reactions of a soldier in Laos or a politician in Gambia or a farmer in France can be understood only in terms of *his* background, *his* culture, and *his* individual development.

THE SELF-ACTUALIZING PERSON

You also have responsibilities to yourself and your family and close friends. These include the satisfaction of physiological, safety, love, and esteem needs. And, of course, self-actualization needs.

Self-actualization should be seen as a process, not a condition or state. A person cannot say "I am in a state of self-actualization," as he might say "I am in a state of good physical health." He would need to say "I am in the process of self-actualizing." The difference is important, since self-actualizing must be seen as something that you are experiencing, not as something that *is* and that you either have or do not have.

Abraham Maslow, in studying psychologically healthy, self-actualizing persons, decided that they differed from other people in 13 basic ways (Maslow,

1962).* (You may wish to review the earlier material on self-actualization in Chapter 3.)

1. Superior perception of reality.   The self-actualizing person does not have such strong prejudices or fears or rigidities that he must reinterpret the world to suit himself. People who constantly blame Communists or capitalists for all the troubles in the world are not accurately perceiving reality.

2. Increased acceptance of self, of others, and of nature.   Some people do not like themselves. They are overly critical and unforgiving regarding themselves. They do not think that they are worthwhile people. In addition, they are unduly critical and unforgiving of others and may also feel that people in general

FIGURE 16–3. Psychologically healthy persons can be spontaneous. Photograph by P. C. Peri.

*The headings are taken verbatim from Abraham Maslow, but the explanations are my interpretations of Maslow.

are just no good. The self-actualizing person recognizes that he and all other people have limitations but that he can nevertheless accept himself and others as worthwhile. Such acceptance does not rule out self-criticism; the person enjoys a basic self-confidence but employs self-criticism to produce changes rather than to induce a deadening depression.

3. Increased spontaneity. Psychologically healthy persons can be relaxed and spontaneous. They need not worry unnecessarily about what others think, and thus they can behave more naturally. "Spontaneity" does not mean that they violate the rights of others or that they enjoy shocking others, but that they can act impulsively and emotionally.

4. Increase in problem centering. Since self-actualizing persons are not overly concerned with personal problems and with satisfying status needs, they have the energy and the desire to deal with the particular problems or activities that strike them as challenging.

5. Increase in detachment and desire for privacy. These days there is so much emphasis on getting along with others that we often neglect the importance of privacy. The self-actualizing person enjoys privacy and the opportunity to concentrate on his own thoughts and ideas.

---

*A Buddhist Legend Clarifies the Healthy Personality**

Once the Enlightened One came upon a couple of young boys having a fist fight. One of them was on the ground, with the other sitting on him. When they saw Lord Buddha approaching, they both jumped up and stood apologetically before him. Lord Buddha asked the winner what caused him to knock his friend down. "He called me a liar," the boy said.

"Are you a liar?" asked Lord Buddha.

"No, sir" was the reply.

"Then why did you fight?" asked the Enlightened One. "You know, you are the best one to decide whether you really lied or not. If you did lie, you should thank your friend for bringing it to your attention. If you had not lied, you know that your friend was mistaken. In either case, there seems to be no cause for such temper. You certainly do not knock a person down when he greets you by calling you a handsome and wonderful fellow, do you? You either thank him, or tell him he is mistaken, but you do not hit him."

In this legend, Buddha shows that the healthy personality has enough self-acceptance not to be bothered when an accusation is untrue, and has enough acceptance of others not to become angry when a friend makes an error.

---

*From Chatterjee, M.N., *Society in the making.* Ann Arbor, Mich.: Edwards Brothers, 1942. P. 30.

6. Increased autonomy and resistance to being dominated by the culture. Self-actualizing persons can remain independent of the pressures around them. They can evaluate the world they live in without being blinded by the fact that they are living in it. They remain faithful to their own values and are not susceptible to the pressures of propaganda.

7. Greater freshness of appreciation and richness of emotional reaction. Self-actualizing people are not bored with life and do not need to run after new thrills. They can enjoy new experiences and see new elements in doing "the same old thing." They can find stimulation and pleasure in a conversation, a baby, or an old piece of driftwood.

8. Higher frequency of all-absorbing experiences.   From time to time some of us have an experience that is so enthralling, so exciting, and so absorbing that we virtually lose track of time and place. We are "taken out of ourselves." Self-actualizing people report this experience more often than others.

9. Increased feelings of brotherhood to man.   The phrase "brotherhood of man" is often used without real meaning. The emotionally healthy person truly understands this concept. It is not just that he has friends, but that he feels he is a part of all mankind. Whatever happens to any man happens to all men and thus happens to him.

10. Good relationships with others.   People with healthy personalities are able to have a few very close, meaningful relationships, although they may not necessarily be popular with a large group.

11. More democratic beliefs.   Self-actualizing individuals accept people for what they are, not for the labels (such as racial, religious, or vocational) attached to them. They believe every human is entitled to dignity and esteem.

12. Greatly increased creativity.   Several of the previously described characteristics indicate the creative abilities of the psychologically healthy person. He is not overly involved with his own problems; he can respond spontaneously; he is relatively free from domination by his surroundings. Therefore he can see new relationships and consider new ideas without being hampered by prejudices and rigidity.

13. More subtle sense of humor, which lacks hostility.   Self-actualizers find more humor in the world, but the humor is not at the expense of someone else. They do not find it funny when someone else is embarrassed or criticized.

They enjoy laughing with people, but not at people, and they do not look on personal misfortune as a cause for laughter. (This final factor is not listed with the others but appears elsewhere in Maslow's writing.)

ADDITIONAL CHARACTERISTICS OF THE SELF–ACTUALIZING PERSON

Abraham Maslow described the characteristics of the self-actualizing person that he had observed through his research. They by no means exhaust the list of possible characteristics of self-actualizing individuals. I will suggest a few more.

14. The ability to make decisions, to accept responsibility for decisions, and to face the consequences of decisions.   Too often people do not wish to make decisions, because decisions involve responsibility. Inevitably, some decisions will be wrong, but the psychologically healthy person can make decisions when called upon. Since he is problem centered, his decisions are, on the whole, based on objective evaluation, rather than on his own personal needs or anxieties.

15. Increased goal-directedness.   The self-actualizer is working toward goals, rather than just "living" without any idea of what he wishes to do or why. His goals may not please others—they may even be considered foolish—and he may not achieve all his goals, but his behavior is not random or aimless.

16. High integrity.   Integrity means being honest, not merely to the letter of the law of honesty and decency but also to the spirit. A person with a healthy personality has integrity himself and can accept others as having integrity.

17. Appropriate flexibility.   At times people must be able to change their attitudes and ways of thinking. Flexibility, or lack of rigidity, does not mean bowing to the slightest pressures; it means being willing to consider change when the circumstances have changed or the information available has changed.

18. High social consciousness.   Although the self-actualizing person is often detached and values privacy, he does not shut himself off from the world. He is willing to take a position on an issue, even though his position may be unpopular.

19. High social awareness.   Emotionally healthy people are aware of the effects they have on others. They respond to others as "complete and whole individuals" (Maslow, 1962). To them, other people are not objects or tools but humans.

20. High ability to give and to receive.   We all need to be able to give to others, both materially and in terms of our time, our energies, and our interest and concern. Since the self-actualizer recognizes the importance of giving, he realizes the importance of being a gracious receiver. To give without being able to receive is as degrading to others as receiving without being able to give.

21. Increased insight.   People are limited in the degree to which they can understand themselves, but the psychologically healthy person finds that, because he feels secure and accepted, not much interferes with his self-understanding.

The healthy, self-actualizing person is certainly not perfect. The characteristics just described are not what every self-actualizing person lives up to, but they are more descriptive of the self-actualizer than of others. You may think of qualities that have been omitted, or you may feel that some of the characteristics listed have been overestimated in importance.

ON BEING OLD

Patterns of behavior change during the later years of adult life, and the elderly person must adapt himself to new activities, new expectations, and new opportunities and limitations. Over the past few years interest in geriatrics (the treatment of the aged) and gerontology (the study of the aged) has increased greatly, until now a much better awareness exists about the elderly and their concerns.

The proportion of the American population aged 65 or over has been steadily increasing. In 1900 less than 5% of our population was in that age group, whereas 10% of the population is now over 65. Americans seem to fear old age and try to appear youthful. One famous Japanese author wrote: "The sharpest difference between America and Japan is the truly inept manner of growing old demonstrated by the Americans and Europeans. . . . The sight of an old woman, decked in a sleeveless, short-skirted dress of a pink-flowered material, her face powdered a dead white, on the skating rink . . . is not objectionable, I suppose—but I . . . would not wish my grandmother to look like that" (Mishima, 1964).

In our society the elderly person often feels that he is without a meaningful role. Because he is retired, he has no work role; because his children are grown and out of the house, his role as a parent has lost much of its importance; as his friends die, the attractiveness of developing new social roles diminishes. As a result, the older person is likely to disengage. *Disengagement* refers to a mutual withdrawal of the older person and of the community around him (Cumming &

Henry, 1961). The older person finds the community more difficult to deal with and less appealing, and the community finds the older person less valuable; thus they pull away from each other.

Disengagement is not necessarily harmful; for some people it actually provides a healthy basis for adjusting to old age. Reducing community involvements may be essential for some older persons in order to maintain the energy and the money necessary for other activities. Older persons require more time to do things and can accomplish fewer things during the waking day. Of course, older people vary as much as younger people; some 80-year-olds are still going strong, whereas some 65-year-olds have slowed down measurably. Also, behavior in old age is undoubtedly a continuation of earlier behavior, and the people who withdraw at 70 might well have given indications of withdrawal when they were 40.

By and large, however, the life satisfaction of older persons is greater when they are more involved and more absorbed in life. In a study of older people in five European countries and the United States, it was shown that the elderly of each nation exhibited some disengagement, although the pattern differed con-

FIGURE 16–4. By and large, the life satisfaction of older persons is greater when they are more involved and more absorbed in life. Photograph by Liane Enkelis.

siderably among countries and among groups within countries. However, results consistently showed that high activity is related to high life satisfaction (Havighurst, Munnichs, Neugarten, & Thomae, 1969).

The fear of anticipated dependency weighs as heavily on the older person as any other matter. "I do not want to be a burden on my children" is a frequent statement. In many parts of the world grown children expect to care for their elderly parents; in the United States, however, the desire to remain independent is strong in all age groups. Perhaps if more emphasis were placed on mastery (that is, the ability to control the environment and the self) and less on independence, problems would diminish. No one of any age is truly independent—we all depend on others all the time. However, since our country values independence so much, children internalize its importance. Then, when these children grow up and become elderly, they resent their own dependence as a sign of inadequacy (Kalish, 1967).

SOCIAL ISSUES FOR THE ELDERLY

The elderly face the same problems as anyone else, except the degree to which they are affected by these problems is often intensified by their age. Thus all age groups have financial difficulties; but more than half the elderly couples in the United States are living on less than $5000 a year, and half the elderly who are not part of a family unit are earning under $2000 (based on 1969 statistics prepared from the U. S. Census Bureau and taken from *Economics of Aging: Toward a Fuller Share in Abundance,* a report of the U. S. Senate Committee on Aging).

The elderly often have difficulty in finding adequate housing at a price they can afford. Although well over half of all older couples own their own homes, these are largely small, older homes in areas that have undergone major social and physical changes. Taxes and repairs make even these modest homes difficult to maintain. Yet many elderly would rather remain where they are, regardless of the condition of their home, than move to better accommodations in unfamiliar neighborhoods where they would have to begin all over in building social relationships.

Social relationships for retired people are more readily available if there are many other older people around. Although we hear claims that the elderly really need to be surrounded by the young, evidence exists that people in general do not establish many friendships outside their age group and that living near other retired persons offers a more fruitful opportunity to form social relationships (Rosow, 1967).

Those who move to retirement communities express slightly higher life satisfaction than those who remain in their own community. They are also likely to have more friends, but they tend to regret the lack of contact with children and grandchildren (Wilner, Walkley, Sherman, & Dodds, unpublished data, 1969).

Family relationships are more difficult to maintain. Sometimes, because adult children wish to help their elderly parents but are not willing to share living accommodations or otherwise change their own life-styles, relationships can become tense. Nonetheless, in spite of many disturbing exceptions, those elderly who have living children and grandchildren are usually in fairly close contact with them (Riley et al., 1968).

Retirement can be distressing. Income is reduced, social contacts and meaningful roles are lost, and time is no longer structured by the work schedule. However, for many people retirement is the beginning of a long and rich life. Social contacts once found on the job can be made through organizations, including—but not limited to—senior citizens' clubs. Many older people feel useful through helping out in political organizations, volunteering for work in hospitals and social agencies, and providing care for elderly persons who are unable to take care of themselves. One of the more innovative programs for the elderly is the Foster Grandparent plan. Through this plan young children in institutions (for example, the mentally retarded, crippled, or parentless) are assigned foster grandparents who spend several hours every week with them. Both the child and the older person are given a meaningful relationship, and the older person is provided a small income to supplement his social security pay. Research has shown that retirement is not a major morale problem for most persons with adequate incomes (Streib & Schneider, 1971).

CHANGES IN THE AGED

The elderly face many problems. Their changing physical appearance makes them less attractive in the eyes of the rest of society. They may begin to forget things quickly—even things told them a few minutes earlier; and personality and self-concept changes become evident. Just as the adolescent and the middle-aged person must learn new roles, the elderly also must learn new forms of behavior consistent with their age and situation.

Physical and intellectual changes. In old age, bodily changes begin to speed up. The senses of sight, hearing, taste, smell, touch, and balance become less sensitive. Fortunately in a way, the sense of pain also becomes less acute. Strength diminishes, and reaction time becomes longer, so that responses are sometimes slowed down (Birren, 1964).

Physical appearance changes in many ways. The skin becomes loose and wrinkled; the body shape changes; and hair continues to thin out and changes in color to gray and white. Resistance to disease diminishes, and the bones become harder and more brittle.

Some types of intellectual abilities (for example, those involving memory or perception) decrease in old age. Other capacities, such as the ability to accumulate knowledge and information, show little or no decrease. When severe decrements in intelligence do occur, they may be the result of physical illness rather than of normal aging.

Individual differences among the elderly are great. Their previous history of health, nutrition, and care affects their vitality; their mental health and eagerness to live are also thought to be factors. Heredity and luck undoubtedly are also important. When death comes, it seems to be without pain in most cases — at least according to the words of the dying themselves (Osler, 1911). (See Chapter 8 for further discussion of death and dying.)

Personality changes.   The needs of the elderly are not met nearly so well as the needs of younger people. One psychologist (Kuhlen, 1963) has suggested five sources of frustration that restrict the satisfaction of both deficiency motives and growth motives in the aged.

1. An age status that idealizes youth. Since the attributes of youth are so admired, the aged often feel unwanted. Their self-esteem suffers, and they feel frustration, to which they respond in many of the ways described in Chapter 9.

2. Pressures of time and money that lead to restriction of interests and activities. The elderly have limited earning potential and often live on pensions, social security, and gifts from their children. At the same time, since they do not know how long they will live, they are forced to be cautious with their expenditures so they can continue to support themselves.

The pressures of time operate differently for the aged. Since they recognize that the years ahead of them are limited, they may feel reluctant to begin any long-range projects. Some can no longer look forward to new accomplishments. The hopes and plans that have not yet been fulfilled may never be fulfilled.

3. Physiological changes that demand attention. Because of the increase in illness and the increased danger from accidents, the elderly become very much absorbed in their own physical problems. This absorption restricts their opportunities to be concerned with other people and other things, and they may gain the reputation of being complainers.

4. Technological changes that outdate their skills. The world is changing rapidly, and new inventions and processes emerge constantly. Younger people can learn and become accustomed to these new ways, but older people have less opportunity and less motivation to do so.

5. The feeling that there is less chance to move out of a frustrating situation. Change is more difficult for the elderly, and many of their unhappy life situations, they realize, will never be changed. The elderly recognize that their physical and intellectual abilities are diminishing and will not return.

SUCCESSFUL ADJUSTMENT

The picture of the aged just described is certainly not a pleasing one. Some aspects of it are inevitable, in spite of advances in the medical and social sciences. However, many elderly people remain very vital, productive, and active. What do you know about the lives of Albert Schweitzer, Herbert Hoover, Pablo Casals, Bernard Baruch, Mahatma Gandhi, George Bernard Shaw, Grandma Moses, Amos Alonzo Stagg, Robert Frost, Pablo Picasso, or Ruth Gordon? Think of elderly people you know who lead enjoyable and productive lives. What qualities do they have that enable them to live like that?

Successful adjustment to old age is partly the result of proper planning. Those who plan for retirement and who want to retire remain happier and healthier, and they also are busier; those who do not plan or do not want to retire become bored easily (Thompson, 1958; Thompson & Streib, 1958).

When should you begin planning for old age? The answer is "yesterday." Financial planning begun during the early adult years will increase the chances of financial comfort during the later years. Physical health in later years is partly the result of diet, exercise, and other patterns begun today. Having interests and activities in the early adult years may ensure being interested in life in the later years. Such activities as travel, reading, music, certain types of mechanical work, painting, woodcraft, camping, and fishing can be begun in early years and easily carried over into later years.

People whose entire existence is centered exclusively around their family or their work find they have nothing with which to occupy themselves when their children are grown and independent and the retirement period begins. They feel useless and bored.

Recently, increased attention has been given the aged. Community activity centers have been established. Physicians, psychotherapists, and social workers have become more responsive to their psychological and medical needs. Institutions for the elderly are becoming oriented toward keeping their patients active and involved in the world, rather than merely maintaining them as bed patients. Perhaps most important of all, there has been an increase in the demand that the elderly be able to live in dignity in pleasant surroundings, with ample opportunity for activities and warm, human relationships.

SUMMARY OF IMPORTANT IDEAS

1. Maturity demands increasing responsibility and offers new opportunity.
2. The life cycle provides an ever-changing pattern of demands, responsibilities, roles, activities, and problems.

3. Changes that occur as a function of age are measured by the longitudinal method and by the cross-sectional method.

4. Certain patterns of behavior and certain capabilities remain relatively consistent from childhood to maturity.

5. Changes in intellectual ability with age are of two types: one kind reaches a peak fairly early in adulthood and slowly diminishes; the other kind remains high until the very late years.

6. Family responsibilities are characteristic of the mature years. Among the most important are relating to one's spouse and children, dealing with money matters, and gaining full satisfaction from both work and leisure.

7. The self-actualizing person differs from others in many ways.

8. One in every ten Americans is 65 years old or older.

9. The elderly person often feels that he lacks a meaningful role in the community. Sometimes disengagement occurs, as the older person and the community move away from involvement with each other.

10. The elderly encounter many social and personal problems, including unpleasant changes in appearance, health, and social role. But proper planning can help make retirement a very rich period of life for those who have adequate income and health.

ENVIRON-MENTAL INFLUENCES ON HUMAN BEHAVIOR

PART 4

17 Behavior and the Physical Environment

Do you worry about being "kissing sweet"? Do you pull back when someone gets too close to you? Did you ever see anyone become upset when he found that his seat in class was taken by someone else—even though no seats were assigned? If any of these incidents strike a familiar chord, you have had some personal experience with the effects of the physical environment on behavior.

THE PHYSICAL ENVIRONMENT AND HUMAN BEHAVIOR: SOME APPARENT CONTRADICTIONS

Nothing illustrates the complexity of human behavior better than some apparent contradictions in the way behavior interacts with the physical environment. People are adaptable to their environment yet strangely rigid. Their behavior varies according to their culture and surroundings yet displays consistency from one setting to another. The behavior of one individual changes from situation to situation yet remains consistent through time. People can communicate across space and time yet are unable to understand those they love the most. Behavior results from the most subtle and intricate factors, both internal and external, yet is to some extent predictable.

ADAPTABLE YET RIGID

More than any other creature, the human can change his environment to please himself. Over the centuries he has learned to build structures and manufacture clothing to protect himself against extreme cold and to create air condi-

tioning to protect himself against extreme heat. He has devised medicines to prolong life and bombs to destroy life.

Man can live on the earth, under the earth, in the air, in outer space, on the
water, and under the water. He has obtained power from lower forms of animal
life, from water, from heat, and from splitting the atom. He can create clothing
out of chemicals, build computers that play chess, and send words and pictures
over thousands of miles in a matter of seconds. He can establish laws and customs
to control his own behavior, so that millions of people can live within a short
distance of one another without constant conflict.

In spite of his amazing ability to alter his environment to suit himself, man
displays disturbing signs of rigidity. Once he takes a stand on an issue, he is
extremely reluctant to admit he is wrong. He gives up his superstitions very
slowly, if at all, and he hesitates a long time before altering any of his more important values, even when the world around him is changing rapidly. He likes new
gadgets and appliances but has a difficult time accommodating himself to new
architectural styles or new teaching methods. He is much more adept at finding

FIGURE 17–1.   Man has developed amazing levels of technology. He is
less adept at using this technology for peaceful purposes. Photograph by
Lehman J. Pinckney.

ways to win wars than at finding ways to stop wars. Thus, although man has made immense strides in creating and adapting his physical world, he has been less successful with his personal and social world.

CHANGEABLE ACROSS SPACE AND TIME YET CONSISTENT

"There are only two indisputable truths in psychology," one professor remarked in his first psychology lecture. "The first is that people are similar, and the second is that people are different."

For example, every society has a family system of some sort, but the systems vary quite a bit. In the United States the family usually consists of a mother, father, and children, but the Tibetan woman may marry two brothers simultaneously (Peissel, 1965), and a married couple in Japan is likely to reside with the husband's parents and take care of them as long as they live.

Such emotions as love, anger, joy, and jealousy are known throughout the world; yet each society permits different ways of showing emotions, and the members of any given society may express emotions differently from one another. In France and Italy anger is often shown directly. In Japan anger may be expressed directly toward a child or a servant, but not toward an equal. Yet *some* Japanese express anger toward equals, and *some* Frenchmen and Italians are inhibited in showing anger.

Behavior varies not only because of societal influences, but also because of the immediate situation. A normally placid person may erupt with anger if his steak is overdone; the child who is talkative and socially aggressive at home hides behind his mother's chair when the family is visiting friends; the teacher who is normally patient with children becomes highly irritable after a sleepless night. Although the behavior of any one person is consistent (that is, reliable — see Chapter 2) to a substantial degree, it is also subject to change as the result of the specific situation. A balanced perspective between situational influences on behavior and enduring characteristics must be maintained.

EFFECTIVE IN COMMUNICATING YET INEFFECTIVE IN COMMUNICATING

Man is the only creature that can communicate effectively across time and space. A telephone call can connect a travel agent in Kansas City with a hotel manager in Calcutta; a radio enables people to communicate with an astronaut hundreds of miles in outer space; a television set allows a track fan in Vermont to watch an Olympic track meet in Germany.

Man can also send and receive communications across time. A technique has been developed that will determine the age of a rock; ancient scrolls have been found recently that report what life was like 2000 years ago; records of our present civilization have been buried, and civilizations in the future may uncover them and be able to understand the present era. Only man has the ability to send messages into the years ahead or to understand the messages left by people years and even centuries ago.

Despite man's achievements in communication, people often cannot communicate with those closest to them. Parents give their children great love and care, yet the children often find themselves unable to explain their deepest feelings to their parents. A wife wants desperately to tell her husband that she needs more of his attention, and a high school student wants to ask his parents to respect his privacy; but fear and inhibition prevent the expression of these feelings. Man has learned more about the scientific techniques of communicating across time and space than he has learned about communicating deep feelings to those he loves.

COMPLEX YET PREDICTABLE

No two individuals look or behave exactly alike—even identical twins are different. Each person combines physical appearance, personality, abilities, and attitudes in a unique fashion. Nonetheless, psychologists have found that, within limits, human behavior can be predicted. In spite of its complexity, behavior is not a complete mystery.

HUMAN ECOLOGY

The term **ecology** has recently become so popular in this country that it has almost lost its meaning. Everyone is suddenly an ecologist. You fix faucet leaks, use rubbish containers instead of throwing gum wrappers on the sidewalk, vote against a new electric power plant for your community, and advocate birth control—all in the name of ecology. Although the popularity of the term is recent, the concept of ecology has been around awhile. And, as you know, it does not mean saving water, avoiding litter, keeping the air clean, or reducing population pressures. Ecology is the study of the relationship between living organisms and their physical environment, especially those aspects of this relationship that permit the organism to adapt to the environment and, therefore, to survive. When the living organism is man and the environment under question is your own, the problems of ecology become very literally matters of life and death.

FIGURE 17–2. Problems of ecology become very literally matters of
life and death. Photograph by Lehman J. Pinckney.

The social problems of human ecology are well known. Some of the most
familiar are dangerous pollution of our atmosphere, our water, and our earth;
contamination of food; the upset of the ecological balance of animal life so that
species are destroyed, endangering in the long run not only those species but in
some instances our way of life as well; noise pollution from traffic, jet airplanes,
electric guitars, and so on; disposal of solid waste; exhaustion of natural resources; and the population explosion. Every one of these problems has a direct
impact on our present existence and presents the possibility of drastic change in
the no-longer-distant future.

Overcoming such ecological problems is fantastically difficult. Some will be
solved by improved technology; others will require extensive education programs
and the use of either persuasion or laws that are strictly enforced; still others
will cost millions—perhaps billions—of dollars to overcome. Nor are solutions
as clear-cut as some would like to believe. Some laws that have been proposed
would permit the government to determine who could have children and when;

other laws and regulations would force certain industrial plants to close down, thereby throwing thousands of people out of work and perhaps destroying entire communities; because of pollution and safety requirements, increased costs of, for example, driving an automobile might require that some families do without a car, which would provide a major hardship for many individuals.

Having outlined some of the major sociopolitical aspects of human ecology, we are going to shift our direction. Psychologists have made some initial explorations of human ecology—the impact on humans of their physical environment—and this will become our focus. In a sense, you could categorize much of psychology as being ecological, since many chapters of this book discuss the effects of the environment on human behavior. Such a global definition, however, can make an idea meaningless. Therefore we will give particular attention in this chapter to the influence of physical space on human behavior, with a brief look at noise and temperature.

PHYSICAL SPACE AND HUMAN BEHAVIOR

Psychologists have been so concerned with man's social environment (for example, family relationships, peer-group demands, attitudes of teachers and supervisors) that they have paid little attention to his physical environment. Psychological ecology is an attempt to understand how the physical environment interacts with the social environment to influence human behavior.

TERRITORIALITY

Both lower animals and humans establish personal claims to specific areas of space. Among humans, this occurs not only at the individual level but also at the level of the community or the nation. War is frequently an attempt by one nation to extend its spatial boundaries at the expense of another nation; fights between individuals occur when a property line is contested or two individuals or groups wish to occupy the same territory at the same time with conflicting needs (one wishes to picnic while the other wants to play softball, one wishes quiet while the other has a blaring portable radio, one wishes to make love and desires darkness and privacy while the other wishes to play cards and desires light and company).

Territoriality is the term applied to the way in which people (and other animals) perceive, use, and defend physical space and physical objects; territoriality in this sense requires that the individual look on the space or object as

FIGURE 17–3. The runner is a friend of the girl's. Otherwise she would object to his "invading her space." Photograph by P. C. Peri.

his—he feels possessive toward it (Altman, 1970). By extending the meaning only slightly, other people can be included along with objects and space.

On returning to the furnished cottage we were renting for the summer, we found that it had been broken into and burglarized. Very quickly we checked on our belongings and found they were all intact. Only things belonging to the landlord had been taken. Nonetheless, the feeling that someone had been in "our" house was extremely disturbing—"our" territory had been violated, "our" space had been disturbed. Our children were apparently more affected than we. And when we described the event to friends, we found they all seemed to sympathize greatly with our territoriality, and most of them had similar stories to tell.

Although the territoriality of wolves and dogs is limited primarily to physical space, which they stake out against intruders by urinating a boundary, people are often more tied to objects. You feel fully at home in your new apartment after your books, pictures, and furnishings arrive and are in place. These mark the space "yours." Recent efforts to permit older people residing in convalescent homes to bring their own pictures and knickknacks—perhaps even a favored chair or bureau—seem valuable in giving a feeling of comfort and hominess.

Sometimes an individual will relate to other people as though they belonged to him. If you as a man come too close, physically, to the wife of another man, you may well find that you have invaded his territory—even though the wife might not mind a bit. If you are a woman, you can arouse the same reactions in the wife through the same invasion of physical space. Ironically, in a sense, the intrusion into the physical is often seen as more threatening than the intrusion into the psychosocial realm. For example, a husband is likely to be more upset and angered by another man's being physically intimate with his wife on one occasion than by another man's having a very close social relationship over an extended period of time. (However, he is not likely to be overjoyed by either relationship.)

A study of territoriality was conducted with Navy personnel who volunteered for the task. Pairs of men were placed in one of two settings: either a single room or a connected pair of rooms. These rooms were small and furnished sparsely enough to provide adequate comfort but no recreational activities (not unlike a small submarine). Once in the rooms, half the pairs were told that they were to be there 4 days and the other half 20 days. Subsequently, without notifying the men, the investigators extended the study to 8 days for all groups.

In this research territoriality was measured by noting (observers could look into the rooms) how much time each man spent on his own furniture and his own side of the room (or in his own room) and how much time he "invaded" the territory of his partner. Some pairs of subjects could not stand the project and insisted that they be released; others remained until the end of the 8 days. In a comparison of the two groups, those who dropped out were, at the beginning of the study, much less territorial; that is, they interacted more with their partner without regard to whose property they were using or where they were; by the end these subjects were much more territorial. The same pattern was found for their level of stress and their social activities. Apparently the men who were able to deal with this kind of close human interaction (close in terms of physical space) were more able to anticipate future needs from the beginning, so that the increased time did not especially increase their stress and anxiety. Those who left the study had begun with undue optimism and had ended with extreme tension (Altman, Taylor, & Wheeler, 1971).

This study is intriguing from several points of view. First, it combines the laboratory method with the field study; that is, although the men were in a kind of laboratory, the setting was very much like what it would have been under natural conditions. Second, the results suggest that the uses of physical space affect different people far differently and that ability to plan the future and to adapt to the demands of present surroundings is of primary importance. Third, the findings have implications for a variety of settings in which physical space is at a premium, such as prisons, the military, college dormitories, and apartments in urban poverty areas.

CROWDING

As cities grow in population, many writers insist that the effects of crowding make life miserable. They claim that urban crowding produces "crime, war, riots, mental illness, and a host of other evils." They may be correct, but most of the available evidence comes from observations of lower forms of animals (Zlutnick & Altman, 1971). Although investigators have found more crime and mental illness in densely populated urban areas than in suburban or rural areas, they have not controlled for such causes as more poverty or poorer health-care facilities in the urban centers. It may well be that the bases of social breakdown in crowded urban centers have nothing to do with crowding.

What exactly is *crowding?* Obviously, crowding takes place when many people come together in a small space. But a summer camp with eight children and a counselor living in a small cabin involves a much different kind of crowding than a city tenement housing 800 people in 20 floors adjacent to four other similar buildings. A jammed bus or subway may cause totally different reactions than a jammed freeway. Other matters that need careful consideration are the length of time the crowding is going to continue and how the existing space is used. Children spend only a small amount of time in a crowded bunkhouse; crowding on a subway or freeway is also temporary; but an urban slum apartment dweller may not see the road to escape. A bleak, empty 12 × 12 room may cause totally different feelings to its inhabitants than would a nicely decorated room of the same size. In addition, the personality and previous experiences of the individuals who are being crowded undoubtedly affect their responses (Zlutnick & Altman, 1971).

Somehow it seems to make sense that crowding will influence behavior; thus, working in a densely populated area will be more difficult than working with ample room to spread out. Yet one study that placed groups of high school students in rooms of varying size (from amply large to very crowded) found that the density did not affect performance, at least under their experimental conditions (Freedman, Klevansky, & Ehrlich, 1971). Another project might explain these results. College students who were crowded together showed no behavior change, whether it was hot or cool. However, a group of young men, including many juvenile delinquents and prison parolees, displayed considerable aggressive behavior when crowded together under warm conditions, but not when the temperature was moderate (Rohles, 1967). Do you feel different in a crowded room than in a sparsely filled room? In what way? How crowded is crowded?

In analyzing the effects of crowdedness and population density, one author (Milgram, 1970) suggested six ways in which people deal with such an environment:

1. They give less time to each interaction.
2. Low-priority interactions are disregarded.
3. If one person suffers from too many demands, he attempts to shift his burden onto another person.
4. People find ways to block off some social interactions.
5. The emotional impact of relationships with others is diminished, producing only weak and relatively superficial interactions.
6. Special settings are created to handle some kinds of interactions (for example, welfare departments).

Do you think this analysis is accurate? Is it applicable to the crowded settings that you know?

PRIVACY

Privacy means being alone, but even being alone can have many different meanings. One author (Westin, 1967) has outlined four. First, you can have *solitude,* indicating that you are both physically alone *and* unobserved by others. Second, *intimacy* refers to being part of a very small group, perhaps only two or three, with otherwise complete solitude. Third, you have *anonymity,* even in public, if no one knows who you are or pays attention to you. Fourth, *reserve* occurs when you feel like being left alone and others respect your feelings, even though you may be at a party or with many people.

Although most people request privacy in living arrangements, privacy can also lead to loneliness. A comparison of hospital patients in private rooms with those in double rooms showed that the private-room patients showed more delusions and hallucinations and other forms of confusion (Wood, 1971). Many institutions, such as mental hospitals and convalescent homes, provide the resident with so much privacy that feelings of isolation result. These feelings can occur even if people are physically close to one another, since furniture arrangement and the opportunity for eye contact and conversation can be more important than merely occupying the same physical space. Unfortunately, moving furniture in an institution to encourage conversations and other social interactions is often frowned upon by staff members and even some residents (Sommer, 1970).

Violation of privacy (or intrusion into the territory of another) is a sign of power. The person whose space is violated can be degraded by loss of privacy. Reynolds (1972, in process), after arranging to enter a mental hospital as a sup-

FIGURE 17-4. Solitude: both physically alone and unobserved by others. Photograph by Lehman J. Pinckney.

posed suicide attempter, emphasized the importance of having been permitted to use the toilet unobserved, although classification as suicidal normally required constant supervision. His only privacy in the mental hospital occurred when he was physically on his bed, although he was still exposed to all sorts of visual observation (Westin's *reserve* situation).

AND OTHER MATTERS

Much more could be said about the uses of physical space. The distance between you and the person with whom you are speaking will largely control how loud your speech is; it will also influence what you talk about. Can you imagine telling your physician about some intimate medical problem from a distance of 10 feet away? Or suggesting to your companion that the party is dull and you want to leave—from across the room? (Of course, previous experience may have given you effective nonverbal communication skills.)

Ethnicity and other factors can also influence use of space. Even in a community where such groups are not in apparent conflict, you are likely to find different sections of town unofficially mapped off as "turf" belonging to a particular group. The groups may be blacks, Mexican Americans, and whites; they may be Irish Catholic and Polish Catholic; they may be Christian and Jewish. Each group permits the other group its physical space and assumes the understanding will be reciprocated. Perhaps within your high school or even your college, you will find physical space divided according to ethnicity or age, activity, or interest. In the cafeteria one table is almost always occupied by the highly sophisticated, well-dressed, middle-class blacks; another is home base for the white members of the football team and their girlfriends; a third table is used by members of the drama club and their friends; a fourth table is taken by married students or older students who have returned to college. This situation virtually parallels the relative willingness of the United States to allow China and Russia to control their part of the world, as long as they do not intrude into the territory the United States feels is its domain.

This entire topic is only now coming under psychological investigation. Much more information will be available in the near future.

NOISE AND TEMPERATURE

Noise control is becoming a political issue. There is no doubt that constant or intense noise is unpleasant. It wakes the sleeping, disturbs conversations, and — if frequent enough and bad enough — will do permanent damage to hearing. The effect of noise on performance depends on the kind of noise and the task that is being done. Noise can apparently increase the number of errors in some kinds of work, and it seems to cause people to become fatigued more quickly (Brown, Berrien, Russell, & Wells, 1966). Recent evidence seems quite clear that extremely loud, electronically magnified music does irreversible damage to the hearing of frequent listeners (and the players, too, although they sometimes stuff their ears with cotton) (Harris, 1972).

Temperature, humidity, and air movement all affect human behavior, but the research is unclear as to how far from the normal range these must be before performance is changed in a meaningful way. We certainly feel different when temperature is high, humidity is high, and air movement is minimal than we do when these factors are at comfortable levels. People visiting Hawaii often claim that they cannot do any work there, although there is no reason to assume lower levels of productivity for residents of that state than for residents of other states.

SOME FINAL THOUGHTS

We have just opened up the topic of the physical environment, and there are innumerable matters we have not even touched on. For example, how important is a view from your window? Does having an inside office, totally without windows, affect performance or feelings? Does having pictures on the wall make a home more pleasant for most people? What temperature is optimal for reading, and why are public schools and college classrooms so often overheated? To what degree do personality characteristics influence the relationship between physical space and social interactions? And, finally, back in the days when one bath a year was about average and the wealthy could camouflage the effects with perfume, when toothpaste and deodorants were unknown, do you think people avoided getting kissing close?

SUMMARY OF IMPORTANT IDEAS

1. People are adaptable to their environment yet rigid; their behavior varies according to their culture and surroundings yet displays consistency from one setting to another; behavior changes from situation to situation yet remains consistent through time; communication across time and space is often easier than communication with loved ones; behavior is complex yet predictable.

2. Ecology is the study of the relationship between living organisms and their physical environment, especially those aspects involving survival and adaptation.

3. Both humans and lower animals lay claim to areas of space, but humans are much more likely to lay similar claim to possessions.

4. The psychological effects of crowding are highly complex; research is just beginning.

5. Privacy has many meanings. You can have total solitude, and you can also be permitted privacy even though you are surrounded by others.

6. Many variables influence the use of space, including ethnic groups, interest groups, age groups, and so forth.

7. Noise and temperature also affect behavior, but little is understood about the specifics.

18 The Importance of Values

This look at values and attitudes may remind you of closely related materials on human needs, the development of the sex role, or the internalization of guilt. The emphasis in this chapter will be on how group identifications lead to the formation of values. Although the focus on values has been largely fostered by social psychologists, the topic is now under scrutiny by psychologists with a variety of interests.

What do you value? Life? Happiness? Freedom? Health? Money? Fun? Achievement? Travel? How much do you value each of these things? Do you value your religious beliefs enough to give up your life for them? Do you value a college degree enough to postpone purchasing a new automobile for two years?

WHAT ARE VALUES?

Values are *beliefs* about what are desirable and undesirable goals and about ways of reaching goals. In that case, what are beliefs? When you accept an idea, perceive a relationship, or take a principle for granted, on what *you* feel is adequate grounds, you hold a belief. "The world is round or very nearly round." Do you question this principle? Probably not. Why do you accept it? Your evidence is probably based on various kinds of authority. Also, it may "make sense." So you have a belief that the world is round (or very nearly so), even though you are unlikely ever to verify the roundness of the world through your own experience.

"Ty Cobb was a great ballplayer." You probably know about Cobb through the record books, through hearing others talk, or perhaps through some reading or a television documentary, but you never saw him play. Based on all these authorities, you believe that Cobb was a great star. You might develop the theory that Ty Cobb never existed, that he was created by the baseball owners to give the history of baseball some drama, that the pictures of him were faked, that the memories of those who claim to have seen him were erratic. But you are unlikely to go through these contortions — you will probably believe in Cobb's greatness.

"This book is dull." You perceive a relationship between your views of this book and your definition of dullness. I might argue with you, but you feel you have adequate grounds for this belief. I can argue that your belief is inaccurate, but I cannot argue that it is not your belief, since you will end up saying "I don't care — that's how I feel."

These examples have not been especially controversial, but many beliefs are. How would you react to the following beliefs? "Nixon is a great president." "No Communist can ever be trusted." "Women have been unfairly exploited by men for centuries." "A good soldier will obey any order given to him." "Jesus died for your sins." "'Shrinks' are all a little bit nutty themselves." "When the government ignores the common man, then the common man has an obligation to overturn that government — by force if necessary." (This discussion is based on Bem, 1970.)

In the previous paragraph the beliefs implied values, since concepts of good and bad entered into several of the statements. The makers of the statements are implying that they valued Nixon's characteristics, that they do not value Communism, that they value women, that they value the violent overthrow of the government under certain conditions.

Values serve as guides to action, they form the basis for attitudes, they structure the way we judge others and ourselves, and they provide a standard by which we try to influence others, such as our children (Rokeach, 1968). Also, values refer to beliefs that are maintained for long periods of time — they are not subject to sudden shifts. When you value something highly, you are strongly motivated by it. If you place a high value on money or new cars or grades, you will be strongly motivated to gain these goals.

People recognize their conscious values and can think about them and discuss them with others, but they also have values that influence their behavior without their conscious awareness. A person may value being considered good-looking without being aware that he has such a value. He may even deny that he values good looks; but the value would show through in his behavior, the way he dresses, the way he always asks whether others think he is good-looking, or the way he worries about the slightest mark on his face.

There are two basic kinds of values: (1) those related to your present conduct, such as honesty, courage, wealth, or intelligence, and (2) "ultimate concerns," such as religious salvation, freedom, equality, and peace. Each person has a hierarchy of values, with certain ones being more important than others. When the individual is faced with a conflict between producing wealth and being honest, he will normally express the value that is higher in the hierarchy.

VALUES AND BEHAVIOR

The values of any given person often conflict in ways that the value hierarchy cannot easily resolve. A soldier places high value on patriotism and being a hero, but he also wants to stay alive. A student values honesty, but he also wants the friendship of his roommate, who wants to copy from his exam paper. A coed seeks popularity, but not at the price of a series of affairs.

Value differences frequently lead to misunderstanding and disagreements between individuals. The student values "doing his own thing," but his parents value academic and vocational achievement. Recent research has shown that, of 12 "ultimate" values, policemen ranked freedom first and equality last, whereas unemployed blacks ranked equality first and freedom tenth (Rokeach, 1968). The conflict between police and unemployed blacks may be partially explained by their differing values. In terms of housing, for example, the policeman sees his freedom to sell his house to whomever he wishes as of primary importance; the black man views equal opportunity to buy as more important than the policeman's freedom to sell. Even when two people seem to agree on the verbal labels of what they value (for example, freedom, achievement, or equality), they may be far apart on what they believe constitutes an expression of that value. For example, freedom to carry a gun is most important to one person, and freedom of speech is primary for another.

Values shape behavior in many ways. The individual who places a high value on earning money will behave differently from the person who places a high value on being of service to other men. These two people will probably enter different vocational fields, vote for different political candidates, join different clubs, and try to teach their children different values.

People seek friends whose values are similar to theirs. The college student who is satisfied with a C average usually makes friends among others with similar values; the political liberal or conservative becomes friendly more easily with others of similar political beliefs; the accounting major tends to have relatively more friends interested in business than in teaching. (There are many exceptions, but the tendency to select friends with similar values exists.)

Sometimes a person is not even aware that he joins groups and makes friends among those who generally accept his values. Some of you are proud of having

FIGURE 18-1.   Courtesy of Ed Fisher.

"all sorts of people" for friends. However, if you stop to think, you will usually find that most (not necessarily all) of your friends share many values with you. You are likely to have relatively similar values regarding such subjects as moral and immoral behavior, religion, politics, school, money, the meaning of freedom, the purpose of work, and the place of athletics on campus.

Values are not isolated but occur in patterns, which are often called value systems. For example, students who favor the principles in the Bill of Rights also show very little prejudice toward minority groups (Robin & Story, 1964). What other values would you guess these students held?

FORMING VALUES

IMPORTANT PEOPLE IN EARLY YEARS

Parents and other significant figures probably have the greatest influence on the formation of values and attitudes. First, they reward the attitudes and values they like, leaving the others unrewarded or perhaps punished; second, they pro-

FIGURE 18–2.   The values of parents are transmitted to their children. If
the relationship between parent and child is good, the values are probably
even more likely to be internalized by the child. Photograph by Lehman J.
Pinckney.

vide models that their children consciously and unconsciously copy; and third,
they live in such a way that the children internalize their values regarding education, God, humanity, or work. Since the child hears his parents' ideas and relatively little else in his first few years, he tends to internalize these ideas without
much conflict.

Even in later years children maintain much the same values as their parents.
With few exceptions, studies have shown that children's values and attitudes
resemble those of their parents in such areas as politics, economics, and religion
(Hyman, 1959; Kalish & Johnson, 1972; Troll, 1969).

However, children's values are not exact duplicates of their parents' values.
Adolescents and young adults will even rebel aggressively against their parents'
views, although this rebellion frequently disappears after they leave home, marry,
and achieve a sense of emancipation from their parents. Sometimes a child de-

velops such an intense dislike for his parents or their values that he will discard parental values permanently.

Values are also determined by the self-concept and by needs, both of which are, of course, greatly influenced by parents. People maintain values that are consistent with their self-concept and expressive of their personality characteristics. People who are rigid and inflexible tend to value cleanliness and orderliness, rather than casualness and informality. People who are anxious and fearful may prefer a strong, perhaps dictatorial, leader who they feel will protect them. If you conceive of yourself as studious and serious, you will probably place a high value on these characteristics.

DIRECT EXPERIENCES

Strangely enough, direct experiences are probably less important in affecting values than are the ideas internalized through parents, friends, and groups. People often find it so important to maintain their values that they do so even in the face of much contrary evidence. A devoutly religious student commented to an agnostic friend: "You don't really take your own experiences into consideration. If Jesus ever did appear to you in a real vision, you would probably put yourself in a mental hospital rather than admit He truly existed." The agnostic admitted that his friend was correct.

However, personal experiences can change values, as the following story illustrates:

> "One summer I joined the staff of a summer day camp in Gates Mills, a very wealthy community close to where I lived. I had been raised in an average sort of home, and I felt that these rich kids would give me a lot of trouble — I just *knew* they would be snobs. To make matters worse, most of the other counselors were also from wealthy homes. Much to my surprise, this was the best bunch of kids I ever worked with. They were creative, interested in camp, bright, and reasonably well behaved. Of course, a similar camp in another wealthy community might have been altogether different, but I certainly changed my attitude about children from wealthy homes."

THE FRIENDSHIP GROUP

You tend to make friends with people whose values and interests are similar to yours. Once you have become friends, however, pressure is put on you to accept other values of the friendship group.

The values of your friends interact dynamically with your own personality and values and affect your value system; simultaneously, your values influence theirs. Parents, aware of this interaction, encourage their children to develop friendships with playmates whose values they approve of.

EDUCATION

The process of formal education affects values in many ways. Values are influenced by the books you read, the teachers you listen to, and the other students you meet. You learn about the values of other countries and of earlier periods in your own country. You study the values of the men who began the American Revolution, the French Revolution, the Russian Revolution, and the many South American and Asian revolutions. You learn from teachers who place a high value on being creative, from those who stress memorization, and from those who emphasize proper manners and good behavior.

The first year in college is often disturbing because you are told so many things that appear to contradict not only what you learned in high school but also other things you are learning in college. You are told that human behavior is determined by climate, body chemistry, love, hunger, traditions, society, money, religion—the professors cannot seem to get together. Are these professors actually disagreeing?

Temporary confusion regarding certain values may not be bad. As students form new values—often similar to the old ones but usually more carefully thought out—they may go through a period of confusion, but this experience frequently contributes to their maturity and self-understanding. The person who has never been confused has never had to think through what he believes in.

THE COMMUNITY

Every society, through its unique circumstances of history and geography, has developed its own values. Even two towns or two cities located an hour's drive apart may emphasize different values; people in one will work hard to provide money for an art museum, and residents of the other will work just as hard to raise funds for a ball park.

Values held by the general community need not be rigid; a variety of types of behavior may be allowed. Our society, for example, considers college success to be a positive value, but many people in our country do not feel that college is worthwhile. They are not put in jail or whipped, although they are punished in milder ways. Others in the community may criticize them, and they are likely to be turned down for jobs that require some college education.

The penalty for violating certain other values, however, is severe. In Texas in 1950 a white man bragged to me that he had slammed a bus window down on the hand of a black man who disobeyed the values of that community by sitting in the front section of the bus. In late 1971 a Catholic girl in Northern Ireland was planning to marry a British soldier during the conflict between the Irish Republican Army and the British military; she was kidnapped by members of the IRA, had her head shaved, and was tarred and feathered and left for the public to view. Community feelings become intense when certain values are violated.

A serious student of human behavior will wish to learn the historical origins of the values of the general community and of the subgroups within this general community. How did unions begin, how did they rise to power, and what are they like today? What is the recent history of the American Indian, and what is his life like today? How did free education begin, and how has it affected our country? Understanding such historical problems will help you understand the values and feelings of the older union member, the American Indian, and the schoolteacher who is extremely dedicated to free education. In the same way, to understand the values of people in other countries, you need to understand their history and traditions.

WORK AND CO-WORKERS

Your vocation also affects your values and attitudes. You may be influenced by those with whom you work, by your supervisors, or by the management or union philosophy prevailing in your company.

In addition, the type of work itself influences attitudes. A policeman spends so much time with the least pleasant elements in society that he may develop the belief that people cannot be trusted. A minister, partly because of the respect people have for his position, is much more likely to see people at their best — even the same people whom the policeman sees at their worst. Thus the type of work you do and the work relationships you enter into help form some of your values.

Of course, both the policeman and the minister bring their own experiences and personalities to the situation. Each may have entered his vocational field to help people, but each has elected a different way of going about this job. The very values that prompt one person to become a representative of the law and another a representative of God will also affect the ways in which each looks on others and interprets their behavior. Your needs and attitudes draw you to certain types of work; the work influences the nature of your contacts with people, which is in turn interpreted through your unique personality. Your attitudes and values are affected accordingly.

VALUES AND SELF-ACTUALIZATION

Many psychologists and others, perhaps including your instructor, believe that values develop fairly directly from biological needs. They feel that, in the long run, all values can be explained through association with the early satisfaction of survival needs and subsequent reinforcement of responses by significant figures and other persons. Another group of psychologists and others, perhaps including your instructor, believes that values develop through the desire to satisfy stimulation needs and those needs that are higher on Maslow's hierarchy of needs (Chapter 3). This latter group associates values with meaning and goals that are not established simply through association with survival needs. Inevitably, if you are deprived of food, you will place an extremely high value on food. But even then some people who are truly hungry will not sacrifice meaning and integrity to obtain food.

> "When I was a social worker with the county, I often found people, especially the elderly, who refused to accept welfare, even though they qualified. I did my best to point out to them that they were entitled to this help, but they would reject my explanations. They obviously preferred to live on less rather than to look on themselves as welfare recipients. Unlike some of the social workers, who seemed to feel that a person's pride could go hang if it stood in the way of his getting a few dollars, I respected those people who really seemed to hold to this belief out of conviction.
>
> "A few years later I found myself working for a state assemblyman. In this role when I talked with persons eligible for welfare and told them that they were entitled to benefits and should take advantage of them, I met an entirely new response from some of the elderly. Now I was perceived as speaking with the voice of not only legal authority but also political authority. I represented a lawmaker, not county welfare. It was not that their pride crumbled, but that they were able to retain their pride while accepting welfare because a duly elected state lawmaker approved. I'm still not sure I have the whole thing figured out."

In his latter role the social worker was able to reach these elderly people by permitting them to behave consistently with their values, so that—even in their situations of acute financial need—they could feel that they were maintaining their self-esteem and were being themselves.

HOW VALUES CHANGE

Values and attitudes, like other elements in the personality, undergo continual change, even though these changes are often slight and occur slowly.

As your roles and self-concept change, your values change also. The adolescent may value popularity with his own group, whereas the adult values being liked by the boss. The worker places great value on his union until he becomes a supervisor, at which time his values emphasize the success of the company. The professor who now values hard work valued "living it up" as a student. A freshman girl does not place much value on avoiding a fellow with a "fast" reputation, but when the same girl becomes a mother and *her* daughter wants to date in the "fast" crowd, she finds she has a strongly negative attitude.

CHANGING THE VALUES OF OTHERS

It seems logical that a good sound argument would be sufficient to change someone's values. That is, assuming you had supreme powers of logic and a pile of evidence on *your* side, you should be able to convince any normal person that you are correct and that his values are wrong. Try it. It does not work very often.

Values and beliefs are closely related to needs and motives and are often learned very early in life. Attacking them with logic merely forces the person to try to defend them with logic. Soon he is so deeply involved in justifying his views that he finds arguments he had never even considered before. Often the best way to make certain a person *never* changes his values is to argue vociferously against them. Attacking strongly held values can cause them to be still more firmly maintained (Kelley & Volkart, 1952), often with the support of defense mechanisms.

However, values and attitudes can be changed. The professions of advertising and public relations are devoted to changing people's attitudes and their resulting behavior. Salesmen, teachers, ministers, and clinical psychologists also find that much of their working time is spent changing attitudes and values, including people's attitudes toward themselves (that is, their self-concepts).

Occasionally one dramatic event can alter an attitude or value. In one such case an English professor was drowning, and he swore to return to belief in his religion if he lived. He did live and became a devoutly religious man. More commonly, however, values change slowly, as the result of many things, and people who wish to persuade others must take this into account.

Thus advertisers establish continuous campaigns instead of just presenting an occasional advertisement; psychotherapists meet continually with their patients, not just once; ministers have learned that the overnight convert usually becomes a backslider (in spite of occasional real conversions like the one just described).

Changing people's values is only the first part of the story. Most frequently the purpose of producing such change is to alter behavior affected by the values. The political candidate wants to change voting behavior, or the teacher wants to change classroom behavior. A recent study shows how difficult the changing of behavior can be. A program was undertaken to alter the behavior of 109 street-gang boys. The professional staff used individual counseling, group work, and a variety of other approaches over an extended time period to help the boys learn to be fully independent, self-sufficient members of the community. The boys responded well through each step of the program until the time came to cut their contacts with the professionals. This step produced failure—and the more the workers increased their efforts, the worse the failures became (Caplan, 1968). Apparently the professional workers had succeeded in enabling the boys to adjust well to living with the protection of the professionals, but not to assume an independent role in the community.

Changing long-term behavior is a very difficult task, and behavioral scientists need to learn a great deal more about such planned intervention. To see how limited the effectiveness of attempts at change can be, you need only ask yourself how successful you and your friends have been in such comparatively insignificant behavior as stopping smoking, cutting down on calories, sticking to the study schedule you set up for yourself, or not losing your temper.

VALUE CHANGE AND NEEDS

Since values are closely related to needs, the self-concept, and other personality characteristics, value change can be produced by changing the needs or the self-concept. Although this change is difficult, it can occur.

Politicians attempt to persuade people that their election will satisfy the needs of the voters (that is, needs for better schools, lower taxes, better military protection, less air and water pollution—whatever the voters perceive as their needs). In the same fashion the values children hold regarding school may improve if the children overcome their fear of school or their feelings of inadequacy in school.

The success of attempts to change attitudes and values is partly the result of the personalities of those under pressure to change. At one interracial summer camp, some of the campers became more prejudiced by the end of their camp experience, but others became less prejudiced. Compared to the latter, those who became more prejudiced were more aggressive and more afraid of punishment yet also felt more picked on (Mussen, 1950). The same camp environment led some white children to learn more negative attitudes, depending on their personality and values.

Personality is related to value change in another way. People appear to have the need to believe that their values and their behavior are consistent; if something changes their behavior, they are also inclined to change their values accordingly. Thus two groups of people were paid to lie about some relatively unimportant matter to their friends. One group was paid $20 each, and the second group was paid only $1 each. A later inquiry found that those who had been paid the smaller amount of money had changed their attitudes somewhat regarding the matter they had lied about; they had, to some extent, come to believe what they had said. The other group did not change much at all. Apparently the higher-paid individuals could justify the lie by having received so much money. But the group that lied for so little money had behaved inconsistently—they could not justify having lied, so they altered their values to reduce the significance of the lie (Festinger, 1957). Perhaps you have had a similar experience. Have you ever purchased something you could not really afford and then tried to convince yourself that you had made a wise purchase? This pattern helps salesmen immeasurably, since people who buy things tend to justify their purchasing behavior and are not likely to return the goods, even if they did not get a good buy.

> In college Jack Trevor prided himself on wanting to be of service to humanity, particularly by using his writing talents to improve the conditions of the economically impoverished. But after graduation he found he could not make a living through freelance writing, so he took a job with a magazine that published stories emphasizing murder, lust, and crime. Five years later Jack had become editor of the magazine and was earning a substantial income. However, his values had changed. When he first began with the organization, he claimed he would only stay long enough to get himself started, because "this magazine really puts out trash." Now that he had given up his mission to help the poor, he justified his behavior by stating that the magazine was important because many poor people read it and received great enjoyment from it; therefore he was really providing an important and useful service to the poor. His values and attitudes had changed in order to become consistent with his actual behavior.

Value change does not necessarily precede behavior change. When conditions cause people to behave in certain ways, their attitudes and values may change in order to support their new behavior, much as Jack Trevor's values changed during his job with the magazine.

THE MEANING OF PREJUDICE

To have a **prejudice** is to make a "pre-judgment," or to make a judgment or hold an attitude before all the necessary information is available. Being prejudiced also implies that the attitude or feeling is held with some degree of emotion and cannot be readily altered.

Everyone holds prejudices that lead to either favorable or unfavorable reactions toward people, things, and ideas. You may be prejudiced against a western on television without even seeing the show. You may be prejudiced in favor of men who smoke pipes.

FIGURE 18-3. Prejudice and discrimination against students are not unusual but are seldom expressed quite so openly. Photograph by Lehman J. Pinckney.

Although everyone has prejudices, any particular prejudice is neither natural nor inevitable. As with any attitude, belief, or value, prejudices are learned largely through interaction with significant others and tend to fit in with personality needs and the self-concept. They are then reinforced by approval from friends and from the community, by personal experiences, and by reduction of anxiety. Also, like other values, prejudices are difficult to change. They resist logic because they satisfy needs that may be more important than logical consistency or because they were so effectively internalized that they are stronger than logic. Research has shown that people will have trouble with simple problems in logic if their prejudices become involved (Sells, 1936).

Many people are rigid in their thinking. They seem to say "Don't bother me with facts or new ideas—I know what's right." They are referred to as people with closed minds, because they are not willing to consider new information. People who are racially prejudiced tend to be more rigid in their thinking than people who are not. They have more difficulty in discarding old ways of thinking and trying new ways (Frenkel-Brunswik, 1949).

A person's prejudices against (or for) other people may make his thinking less effective. A man who is prejudiced against a particular newspaper may not believe something it publishes, even though it is obviously true; a person prejudiced against Italians may not recognize the important contributions made by Italians. To be prejudiced is to prejudge or judge in advance. If a judgment is made in advance of adequate information or understanding, its accuracy may be reduced.

STEREOTYPES

Prejudices may be based on **stereotypes.** A stereotype is a "rigid and oversimplified or biased perception" (English & English, 1958) that leads to rigid and oversimplified thinking. Even the origins of the word emphasize this meaning; the term comes from printing and refers to something that is difficult to change once it is set in type.

Most stereotypes are harmless and interfere only slightly with effective behavior. Since they are likely to change when the individual has broader experience with the group he is stereotyping, they merely signify restricted views of the world. However, some stereotypes are extremely resistant to change. Any exceptions are explained away as inadequate challenges to the general stereotype; any examples of the characteristic being stereotyped are shown as proof of the stereotype's validity.

Think of the stereotype "Blue-collar workers are racial bigots." Such claims, especially when made by college students who are stereotyped by the blue-collar workers as snobs, are perceived as unfair. They may anger blue-collar workers, who then feel that they must justify those practices that are seen as bigoted. This justification, which is an understandable defense of their policies and views, merely adds fuel to the fire. And the stereotype becomes a self-fulfilling prophecy.

A student whose father is a blue-collar worker, whether or not his father holds views that might be considered racially prejudiced, is likely to find his self-image harmed by the stereotype. In the same fashion the black or Mexican American or Irish Catholic students who have suffered from being stereotyped as dumb, as violent, and as extremely religious share certain *perceived* characteristics. In some fashion they need to be able to see themselves as unique individuals and to see their ethnic group as undeserving of the stereotype. Otherwise they may come to despise their ethnic group and to resent themselves for being members of the despised group.

My contention is *not* that common stereotypes have no kernel of truth; rather, it is that rigid, stereotyped, and prejudiced thinking may distort the accuracy of perceptions, hinder the effectiveness of learning, and provide an oversimplified and untrue picture of the world. Since under these circumstances a person "knows" certain things to be true when they actually are not, the effectiveness of efforts for achievement and self-actualization may be negated.

PREJUDICE, DISCRIMINATION, AND SEGREGATION

Prejudice is an attitude. **Discrimination** is a form of behavior that usually stems from prejudice. Discrimination refers to treating people unequally. Prejudice against women leads to discrimination against hiring women for certain jobs. Prejudice against adolescents leads to discrimination against them by some adults. Prejudice favoring well-behaved students leads teachers to discriminate in their favor by giving them better grades than they deserve. What groups do you discriminate for or against? Why?

Discrimination arises from prejudice and in turn increases prejudice. As children grow up observing women being discriminated against, they tend to internalize the value that women really are inferior, which thus leads to prejudice. Prejudices and discrimination interact dynamically.

Since attitudes and values, when deeply felt, resist change, it is almost impossible to alter already formed prejudices by passing laws. However, laws can affect discriminatory behavior, which in turn will help create situations in which prejudices may be more easily changed and in which prejudices will not be so effectively passed on from generation to generation. Would you prevent women from voting? Your great-grandparents did, but laws were eventually passed that gave women the vote and other forms of legal equality. There is a definite tendency to accept *what is* as being *what is right*. Few Americans wanted women to vote 80 years ago, but few Americans would deny women the right to vote today.

When prejudice and discrimination become severe, **segregation** often results. Segregation is the act of isolating members of certain groups. At various times in history the Jews in Europe were segregated and were not allowed to live anywhere except in small, overcrowded ghettos.

Groups may segregate themselves. People try to live near others whom they consider similar. This similarity may be based on race, religion, age, national origin, or social class. Self-segregation or "clannishness" may result from a dislike for others. It may also be caused by **in-group** preference, which occurs when members of a particular group feel more comfortable with others in their group and feel uncomfortable with those who are not members of their group. The elderly living in retirement communities are not prejudiced against younger people, but they may feel more comfortable and more accepted in a community of the elderly. Americans of Armenian origin often live close to one another, not because they dislike non-Armenians but because they want to share traditions and customs and because they are more comfortable in their own group. (For a good example of in-group preference, notice how faculty chaperones stick together at student dances.) When segregation results from prejudice, it cannot be considered primarily the result of in-group preference.

Is prejudice against ethnic groups appropriate? How about discrimination or segregation? What rights do you have to avoid members of certain groups if you wish? Would it be right for your club to blackball someone because his ancestors were born in Africa? In Greece? In Sweden? If you do not want a member of a particular group to live near you, what action is justified? Economic pressure? Social avoidance? Threatening telephone calls? Damage to his property? Physical violence? What are the financial costs of discrimination? What are the psychological costs to the victim of discrimination and to the discriminator?

> The Irish immigrants who settled in New England and New York during and shortly after the potato famine of the 1840s were the object of much prejudice and discrimination. They were accused of being drunks, of fighting, of ignoring laws, of neglecting education, of being involved in improper sex acts, and of being traitors to the United States (*Newsweek,* 1964). They could get jobs only as maids and unskilled laborers, and many employers refused to hire the Irish at all.
>
> As a result, the Irish clung together, rarely pursued higher education, and developed self-concepts somewhat similar to what they were told about themselves. Their frustrations eventually burst through during the 1870s with a group called the Molly Maguires. The Mollies "struck back with incredible savagery, total terror—murdering, dynamiting, burning, pulling out tongues and slicing off ears" (*Newsweek,* 1964). Of course, such behavior only increased the hatred and fear others had of the Irish.
>
> Over the years the Irish changed this image people had of them. As time passed, their position improved financially, educationally, and politically. Today the picture of the Irishman is substantially different. He is still seen as a strong person who will not back away from a fight, but he now is the hero, rather than the villain. The self-concept of the Irish has changed also, and the term "shanty Irish," common even 40 years ago, is rarely heard today. In 1960 a man of Irish descent was elected President of the United States. However, for nearly a century the Irish in the United States suffered prejudice and discrimination. The cost in money, in human suffering, and in progress for the country as a whole was tremendous.

A second example of the wastefulness of prejudice is the feelings expressed toward Americans of German ancestry during World War I and toward Americans of Japanese ancestry during World War II. In 1918 Americans of German background were subjected to many forms of name-calling and hatred and were accused of being sympathetic with the Germans, who were fighting the Americans at that time. During World War II Americans of Japanese ancestry met with an even more obvious form of prejudice and discrimination. It was more obvious for two reasons: first, it issued directly and officially from the U.S. government; and, second, although almost all Americans of Japanese ancestry were affected, almost none of German ancestry were similarly affected.

The Japanese Americans were removed from their homes on the West Coast and placed in what amounted to prison camps scattered around the country. They were often pressured into selling their property—usually at a fraction of its true value—giving up their businesses, and living under worse conditions than we often demanded of enemy prisoners. As one Nisei social worker stated, "I lived in the stable next to Sea Biscuit's for two months. Of course, they had only put one horse in that stable, but they put four Japanese into it."

Many groups have suffered from prejudice and discrimination in the United States. The following are just a few examples drawn from our history: union members, Americans of Mexican ancestry, policemen, blacks, Roman Catholics, Masons, Southern whites, Jews, soldiers, Socialists, poor people, American Indians, atheists, wealthy people, actors, Americans of Greek ancestry, Mormons.

Prejudice against racial and religious groups is not limited to the United States. Citizens of countries that are highly critical of prejudices in the United States display strong prejudices themselves, although usually they are not so violent or so well publicized as American ethnic prejudices. England, for example, has recently been the scene of considerable prejudice and discrimination against nonwhite people from the West Indies, Pakistan, and elsewhere. In India the Untouchables are still subjected to discrimination, although laws officially forbid it. Communist Russia has shown prejudices against both Jews and Christians, and Canadians of French origin claim that British Canadians discriminate against them.

Prejudice does not result from one simple cause but is brought about by a combination of several factors. Consider the problems of Teresa Guerra.

> Teresa was brought up by affectionate, loving parents who accepted the values of their homeland, Mexico, regarding the proper role for a woman: getting married and having children. Since Teresa had little contact with children outside the Mexican American community, she never questioned her future role. Also, since her parents were not especially concerned about their daughter's education, they gave Teresa no encouragement in her school achievement. Little English was spoken in the home, and English-language books and magazines were never available. As one of eight children, Teresa received relatively little time and attention from her parents, both of whom worked.
> However, one of Teresa's high school teachers felt that she had the

potential for college. Unfortunately, when the teacher spoke to the assistant principal, he checked Teresa's IQ scores (administered when she barely spoke English) and claimed that she "wasn't too bright—just like the rest of *them*." The teacher then spoke to the school counselor, but the counselor did not want to be bothered with anyone who could not go on to college, and he insisted that girls from that kind of background were hopeless.

The teacher persevered and decided to wait for the PTA open house to talk with Mr. and Mrs. Guerra. However, the Guerras both worked hard all day and had little energy or interest for visiting the school. Finally, in frustration, the teacher telephoned Mrs. Guerra to ask her to make an appointment. Mrs. Guerra was doubly embarrassed: she was reluctant to admit that she worked in a bar, and she was ashamed to meet with a well-dressed, well-spoken "Anglo" when her own dress and speech were so inadequate. Although she was pleased by the attention Teresa was receiving, she was afraid to ask her husband for help, since she was positive he would get angry with her for suggesting their daughter should go to college when none of their sons seemed to have such an inclination.

Mrs. Guerra made one appointment but did not arrive; she made another one and called to break it. She then said she would call the teacher for a third appointment, but she never did. The teacher finally decided that perhaps the assistant principal and the school counselor had been correct in their appraisal of Mexican Americans.

Prejudice and discrimination are obviously not limited to ethnic groups. Elsewhere in this book you have read about the difficulties that discrimination causes for women, teenagers, the elderly, people on low-status jobs, and people of lower social-class background. Prejudices regarding ethnic, age, social-class, sex, and vocational groups are found throughout the world and throughout history, although they are learned and are far from inevitable. Prejudice can be created by any one, or several, of many factors, and each specific prejudice fits into the general value system of the person holding the prejudice.

CONFORMITY AND OBEDIENCE

Conformity refers to behavior, attitudes, or judgments that are intended to live up to the expectations of a particular group; the behavior, attitude, or judgment may or may not be consistent with the values of the person who is conforming.

Two types of conformity have been described: conventional conformity and yielding conformity. *Conventional conformity* alludes to behaving similarly to others from a similar background. It refers to being conventional in behavior, or at least conventional in terms of the groups with which the person identifies.

"Damned radicals!"

FIGURE 18-4.   Courtesy of Ed Fisher.

Conventional conformity implies that the behavior occurs without being evaluated; it has been internalized. Examples would include dressing in the same style as the other students or accepting the belief that members of your preferred political party are more ethical than the party's opponents.

Yielding conformity involves giving in to immediate social pressure, or responding in a particular fashion even if the response is contradictory to one's personal values. Taking a particular stand on a political issue, while actually feeling otherwise, in order to be accepted by a social group is one example; pretending to agree with the philosophy of a work organization in spite of feeling quite different is another (Beloff, 1958).

Yielding conformity was exemplified by the study of the groups of students who were asked to judge the length of a line while the psychologist arranged to have other members of the judging groups falsify their judgments (see Chapter 5). Opposing demands to yield can produce a high level of worry or anxiety. Those who "called them as they saw them" indicated higher anxiety as measured by physiological changes (Bogdonoff, Klein, Estes, Shaw, & Back, 1961). In one demonstration a subject who disagreed with the group on every occasion (and was correct on every occasion) was dripping with perspiration by the end of the session. Remaining independent of conformity pressures to yield is neither psychologically, socially, nor physiologically easy, but it can be personally satisfying.

Use of the term *conformity* presents a problem, because people tend to apply it to behavior that they disapprove of; when they approve, they are more likely to use the term *persuasion*. Thursday's newspaper will editorialize that students conform too much; Friday's edition will complain that students do not do what they are told. The real complaint is not that students conform, but that they do not conform to the desires of the newspaper.

Conformity obstructs self-actualization, because the conformist is not expressing his own feelings or doing what he feels is correct. Rather, he is responding to the pressures of the social environment. The anticonformist who is rebelling against society is not self-actualizing either; like the conformist, he is responding to social pressures—only his response is negative instead of positive. The true individualist neither rebels nor gives in but acts according to his own values. He is himself and is able to develop his talents without fear that society does not admire or reward those talents sufficiently. But how does the observer decide who is an individualist and who is a conformist or anticonformist?

Recent research on obedience to authority has led to some extremely thought-provoking results. In one study (Milgram, 1965) the subject was directed by the experimenter to administer electric shocks to another person as punishment for making incorrect responses on a simple learning task. Each time the other person, who was supposedly strapped in a chair behind closed doors, made a wrong response, the subject was ordered to increase the intensity of the shock. This procedure continued until the person being shocked began to shriek and beg to have the project stopped, but the experimenter demanded that the subject continue. In about half the cases, and with a variety of types of subjects, the shocks were continued in spite of evidence that they were causing great pain and were perhaps having dangerous effects. The subjects appeared to continue administering the shocks (though with great hesitancy and unhappiness) largely because they were being ordered to do so—they were obedient.

In actuality, the person supposedly being shocked was an actor, and his entire role was faked. However, none of the subjects realized this, and many seemed willing, although tense and fearful, to extend the shocks as long as the experimenter ordered. What does this study imply about the possibility of countries being taken over by dictators? What does it suggest about the Nazi regime in Germany or the trial of American soldiers for the My Lai killings?

Obedience to an individual and conformity to a group have much in common. People whose needs for security, love, or esteem are inadequately met are probably more likely to give in to others or to accept uncritically the ideas of others. To be a true individualist is to accept ideas on a basis *you* feel is adequate and to think and behave as *you* feel is proper. You will take what others think into consideration, but you will not let it become the basis for your own thoughts and behavior.

SUMMARY OF IMPORTANT IDEAS

1. Values are beliefs about what constitutes worthwhile or unworthwhile goals and about methods of reaching goals.

2. Values may be consciously or unconsciously held and may conflict with one another.

3. Values shape behavior in many ways, such as through vocational selection, choice of friends, and leisure activities.

4. Values are formed through the internalization of parents' values and those of other significant figures, through reward and punishment by parents, and through imitation of parents.

5. In spite of the influence of parents, children's values are not exact duplicates of their parents' values.

6. Values are also influenced by personality, personal experiences, the friendship group and other groups, education, the community, and vocation.

7. Values can change, although the changes occur slowly.

8. Changing the values of others is a very difficult task.

9. Prejudices, or "pre-judgments," may be positive or negative.

10. Stereotypes are rigid or oversimplified perceptions that often lead to rigid and oversimplified thinking.

11. Prejudice is an attitude; discrimination is a form of behavior that often results from prejudice; segregation is an act of physical isolation that often results from prejudice and discrimination.

12. Prejudices are learned; although everyone has prejudices, there is no evidence that any particular prejudice is "normal" or inevitable.

13. Ethnic prejudices exist all over the world but differ in intensity and content.

14. No one factor can explain all types of prejudice.

15. Obedience and conformity have a great deal in common.

19 The Individual and His Groups

The previous chapter discussed social and personal values. Here we turn to the closely related topic of group membership. Group membership results in part from values and attitudes and in part from other characteristics. Similarly, values and attitudes develop in part as the result of the groups to which the individual belongs.

Man is a social being. He has developed an extremely complex network of groups, ranging from a small face-to-face group like the family to large impersonal groups like the political party or religious denomination. Even maleness or femaleness can constitute belonging to a group.

The groups you belong to have a major influence on your self-concept. People identify the success or failure of their groups as their own success or failure. When a member of your nationality or ethnic group wins a high office, when a graduate of your college gets a starring part in a television show, when a member of your church is arrested for hit-and-run driving, you gain a sense of pride or shame based on your sharing of group membership.

Elsewhere in this text we have discussed age groups, religious groups, marital groups, and vocational groups. This chapter will focus on sex groups, social-class groups, and ethnic groups.

MALES, FEMALES, AND SEX ROLES

Rex Harrison, in *My Fair Lady*, complained that women should be more like men. Some men complain that women are already too much like men. And many women complain that they don't want to be like men—they want to be like themselves. Differences between women and men in appearance, in physical strength, and in size are obvious and most certainly are based on genetics. But what about differences in aggressiveness, sexual desires, or nurturance (the desire to help others)? When we find sex differences in these characteristics, are they based on inherited qualities or early learning?

"What can I do, honey—it's three against one!"

FIGURE 19–1. Courtesy of Ed Fisher.

Research has not yet provided a conclusive answer, but many investigators believe that sex-related differences in personality and in intellectual abilities are virtually all the result of early learning experiences. These experiences are so subtle, so persistent, and so unquestioned that being male or female leads to different learning even during the first few months of life. The differences become so well entrenched that, by the time the child enters school, he already has a clearly differentiated **sex-role** behavior pattern.

Other investigators hold a different point of view. Although they admit that many differences between the sexes result from early learning experiences, they feel that—*at least to some extent*—some differences result from constitutional (biological) differences between the two sexes. Among the characteristics mentioned in this regard are dependency, aggressiveness, activity levels, and emotionality. (See Bardwick, 1971, for an excellent discussion of this topic.) This is not to say that all males are more independent, aggressive, and active and less emotional than all females; but *on the average* such differences do occur, and they are based in part on biological factors. This is a highly controversial issue, with many people responding to what they want to believe rather than to effective sources of information.

THE DEVELOPING SEX ROLE

From the very earliest years, boys and girls are treated differently. Children learn their sex almost as soon as they learn their names, and even $2\frac{1}{2}$-year-olds are aware of proper sex roles (Vener & Snyder, 1966). Boys and girls are dressed differently, given different toys to play with, and rewarded for different sorts of behavior. Young girls are presented with dolls and encouraged to hold them "as Mother holds baby sister"; young boys are given trucks and airplanes. Boys are often allowed to get dirty or to be noisy, but girls may be punished, if only by a hard look, for exactly the same behavior.

Little boys are provided with certain kinds of advantages in terms of developing later power and status. They are encouraged to venture out and explore the world; girls are encouraged to learn skills for future homemaking. Boys go unpunished for certain kinds of aggressive acts for which girls will receive punishment. Boys are permitted rough play, but girls are taught to be neat.

The older the child becomes, the more important it is to behave in ways considered proper for his sex; it also becomes more difficult, since the community often makes conflicting demands. Thus parents communicate the importance of high academic achievement to their sons, at the same time assuming that intellectual activity may be somewhat unmanly and that school might be restrictive. Girls, on the other hand, "are expected to . . . accept the schooling process, but they are assumed not to be capable of serious intellectual achievement." In addition, school success may be seen as much less important for girls than for boys (Stone & Church, 1968).

Look back on the kinds of behavior for which boys and girls are differentially rewarded. Roughness, aggressiveness, exploration, and academic achievement are all qualities that lead to success in the competitive world of work. The characteristics encouraged in girls cause them to provide extremely useful services for the men. This situation is very distressing for people who feel that women, having equal capabilities and deserving equal rights, should not be socialized to accept an inferior role.

FIGURE 19–2.   Sex-role behavior is learned, in part, from observing the parent of the same sex and behaving as he (she) does. Photograph by Lehman J. Pinckney.

Sex-role behavior is learned from three basic sources: (1) from observing the parent of the same sex as a model and behaving as he (she) does; (2) from internalizing that parent's values as they relate to sex role; and (3) from being rewarded by significant others (or sometimes other people) for appropriate behavior and punished—or at least unrewarded—for inappropriate behavior.

Contact with adults of both sexes is probably helpful in learning proper sex-role behavior. The girl, for example, needs a woman whom she can imitate and whose values she can internalize. She also needs a man, so she can observe how men treat women and how women respond to this type of treatment. If one parent is missing, the children may turn to other relatives, family friends, teachers, or other community members to learn their sex role.

When the wife completely dominates the husband, the children may not know whose behavior patterns to internalize—those of the strong mother or the weak father. The same problem occurs when one parent is very cold or hostile to the children and the other is warm and affectionate. The child of the same sex as the unpleasant parent does not want to be like that parent; yet, if he becomes like the admired or affectionate parent, he will internalize the attitudes and behavior of the opposite sex.

There seems little doubt that the best situation for proper sex-role development occurs when both parents are warm, have a good relationship with each other, provide a good parent-child relationship for their children, and express their sex roles in emotionally healthy ways. Whether only the traditional sex roles are emotionally healthy or whether only roles that eliminate sex-related differences are healthy is currently being debated. Perhaps, when the evidence is finally in, we will find that the specific nature of the sex role is less important than was previously assumed.

Of course, if—as some feel—differences between men and women are learned and are not really useful, the sex of the parent with whom the child identifies would be unimportant. On the other hand, if there are sex-related qualities that make it better to internalize the sex role of the same-sex parent, then confused sex identification is a meaningful concern.

OUTCOME AND ALTERNATIVES

There is no need to chronicle the ways in which women are victims of discrimination. Solid evidence is readily available that they have more difficulty in getting into graduate schools, that they suffer from job discrimination, and that their own desires to achieve success cause them conflict. A recent study of college students showed that the men seemed to have no difficulty in accepting their own desires to be successful and to achieve, but the women often backed away from trying to be successful or were confused as to whether vocational success was important to them (Horner, 1970). This situation reflects the early socialization of women to feel that vocational success is a violation of femininity and that success as a wife and mother is of primary importance.

The major issue is that women are so effectively socialized as very young children into accepting their roles that they do not question the adequacy of their less powerful, less achievement-oriented position. Because of this early socialization, they want to become wives and mothers, to serve their husbands, and to take pleasure from the success of their husbands and sons rather than from their own achievements. Three-fourths of a large sample of Chicago wives stated that the husband was the dominant person in their marriage, although roughly the same number credited themselves as making most of the decisions on budgeting and housing and having the most influence on the children (Mowrer, 1969).

Let's look at the way the argument goes.

—Men have more status.

—They also have more anxiety.

—No, being a woman and therefore unable to self-actualize adequately causes more anxiety; being confused as to whether housework and child rearing are the most important tasks in the world causes more anxiety.

—But women live longer, and the more affluent the nation, the greater the difference in life expectancy becomes.

—That does us no favor. It just leaves us more years of widowhood, and with reduced income at that.

—The jobs that most men have are tedious and uninspiring, and most men would retire immediately if they could afford it.

—I just want my chance to have equal opportunity at those dull jobs—to decide for myself instead of being told what I must do.

—You'll be competing for work with men whose wives are not working; whereas our home will have two income earners, another household will be on relief.

—Then let's divide all jobs in half, so that there are more jobs to go around, and no one will need to be out of work.

—But the children need you.

—They can get equally good care and even some professional teachers at the local child-care center.

—A mother's love is better than a professional's care.

—All right, then you and I will each work halftime, and our children will have both a mother's love and a father's.

—I'd like to, but jobs don't come in halves.

In our society and in most others, being a man is considered more desirable than being a woman, and more American girls would prefer to have been boys than boys would prefer to have been girls (Brown, 1957). This sex preference stems from the greater freedom, higher prestige, and more exciting lives that men seem to have.

Throughout the life-span, the role of a woman is rather restricted. She has less freedom to travel, to do things by herself, and even to use her education than does the male. Given the choice between educating the son or the daughter, most families still would select the son. Even though the American woman is now recognized as having a potential for maturity, competence, and stability equal to men, she is treated differently because of her sex role.

Some Comments about the Role of Arab Women
in the Middle East (Muhyi, 1959)

—Before marriage the Moslem girl is "expected to stay at home, to help with the housework and . . . the younger children, to obey her father, mother, brothers, and . . . older sisters."

—In the very traditional families, the girl studies primarily household arts; she may even wear a cloak and veil. She has little voice in the selection of her husband, although she may refuse a marriage.

—The wife is not supposed to protest against anything her husband does.
—Most of the modern and better-educated girls disapprove of dancing or going to movies with boys.

Many women have complained that their world is surrounded by the walls of the kitchen and is inhabited by creatures 3 feet high with runny noses. They may exaggerate the excitement in the lives of their husbands, but there seems to be no doubt that many women have been frustrated by the activities they are forced into. Volunteer work, an evening college class, a lecture series, PTA work, an art class—these things are not enough for some women, who may be skilled teachers, secretaries, nurses, or beauticians. They are certainly not enough for women who would have liked to become engineers, business executives, physicians, or electricians but were prohibited because of job discrimination against women.

Sexist prejudice and discrimination appear in innumerable little ways. To tell a woman she thinks like a man is a compliment; to tell a woman she drives like a man is also a compliment. How about the reverse? But you would not tell a man that he cooks like a woman or that he shows a woman's tenderness for children. You would say that he cooks an excellent dinner or that he shows an admirable gentleness with his children. Even at the time of marriage, the woman is looked on as lucky and the man is looked on as having given up his independence.

Sex discrimination is found in the Bible; it is found in the Koran; it is found in the laws of our country, even though some were presumably made to protect women. Extremely active and vocal groups of women have joined together to demand changes in sexist laws and customs. But many unanswered questions arise: Whose responsibility is child rearing? How effective will child-care centers actually be? What will happen to women who enjoy the traditional feminine role? Will women also serve in the military on an equal basis? Is women's liberation a fad, a social movement, or a long-range trend? How do you feel?

THE WORKING WIFE

More and more women have joined the work force in our country, and this trend will undoubtedly continue. In 1969 about 37% of the entire labor force was female, and nearly 40% of all married women were working. Yet many married women who work suffer conflict over holding a job and not being at home.

There seem to be four major reasons why wives work: (1) to add money to the family bank account, (2) to satisfy needs for accomplishment and self-actualization, (3) to avoid child care (not necessarily children) and housework, and (4) to derive pleasure from the activities and relationships that occur on the job.

The woman who works to add money to the family bank account can do so if there are no major child-care expenses. However, working mothers often far overestimate the amount of money their work will add to family income because they underestimate the additional expenses: federal and local income tax, transportation (which sometimes includes a second car), housework help, lunches, clothing, cleaning and laundry, babysitters or nursery school, more frequent trips to the beauty parlor, less time to shop at sales, and extra recreation required because of "working so hard."

If money is the only motive for her work, the wife is likely to feel guilty for taking time from her children and her home. However, if she dislikes taking care of children all day, or if she has a need to do something with her talents, she may consider the income as a bonus. In such instances, working may well make her a better wife and mother than would staying at home.

Because the traditional male role requires that he support his wife financially, and because her working may imply that he is unable to do so, the husband

*"Whatsamatter, Mac,—think my place is
in the home or somethin'?"*

FIGURE 19–3.   Courtesy of Ed Fisher.

of a working wife must have a healthy self-concept in order to make a good adjustment to his situation. He must be secure in his feelings of masculinity and not fearful of criticism about his wife's working. Rather than actually competing with men for jobs, most women enter fields that are not dominated by men; less than 10% of all women select business, law, medicine, or engineering for a desired future profession (Goldsen et al., 1960).

Some light has been shed on the effect working mothers have on their children, but the question is far from answered. One study showed that year-old infants whose mothers did not work were more emotional and more active but also more dependent on their mothers (Caldwell & Hersher, 1964). Among very intelligent children, those with working mothers are more likely to perform below their capacities in school (Frankel, 1964).

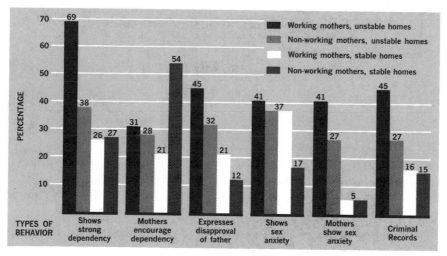

FIGURE 19–4. Effects of maternal employment and home stability on boys (McCord, McCord, & Thurber, 1963).

A more sophisticated study took into account not only working versus nonworking mothers but also stable versus unstable homes. The results indicate that the working mother in an unstable home had the most poorly adjusted children. However, the children of working mothers who provided stable homes were not much different from those of nonworking mothers (McCord, McCord, & Thurber, 1963). There is also evidence that the mother's attitude toward working or being a housewife is most important; that is, mothers who want to be house-wives and are housewives or who want to work and are working have good re-lationships with their children. Mothers at the office who would rather be at home and mothers at home who would rather be at the office have child-rearing prob-lems (Yarrow, Scott, deLeeuw, & Heinig, 1962).

HOMOSEXUALITY

Are homosexuals deviants? Are they queer? Sick? Perverted? Are they the victims of some biological imbalance? Have they learned faulty patterns of behavior? Are they normal people who, for a variety of reasons, have selected a life-style that antagonizes many people?

Both laws and social values are strongly opposed to **homosexuality** in the United States today. As a result, both male and female homosexuals are fearful of police interference with their activities and simultaneously may feel guilty for having participated in homosexual acts. Even a normal attraction, without sexual implications, to someone of your own sex may produce such guilt that an adult man finds it difficult to kiss his own father or embrace his own brother, although such affection is displayed freely in many nations of the world.

The difficulties of the homosexual do not stop with legal restrictions and social disapproval. Some psychologists and others claim that the homosexual, both male and female, has very low self-esteem and is unable to enter into satis-fying love relationships, even through homosexual "marriage" (Buxbaum, 1967). If homosexual behavior is actually an attempt to avoid the anxiety of a hetero-sexual relationship, then the behavior pattern obviously has rewarding elements, since it provides companionship and sexual release without involving the oppo-site sex.

Most people take the position that homosexual behavior is inappropriate and that homosexuals need help in altering their behavior. However, homosexu-ality is reported in societies throughout the world, some of which regard it with extreme tolerance (Ford & Beach, 1951).

In recent years many persons have openly admitted their homosexual activi-ties in an attempt to change the present customs and laws against their behavior. They contend that homosexuality is as natural and normal as heterosexuality, that they are not sick or inadequately socialized, and that they want to be per-mitted to follow their own sexual inclinations without fear of arrest, loss of jobs, or social ostracism.

On the other hand, some psychologists, psychiatrists, and others continue to insist that homosexuality results from sexual immaturity or improper sex-role identification. As a mental-health problem, it therefore merits a mental-health treatment, and various kinds of psychotherapeutic approaches have been used with homosexuals (Freedman, 1971).

One author sums up the research by stating that homosexuals are no more likely to be psychotic than are heterosexuals and that the very slight differences in incidence of neurosis among homosexuals could be explained by the extreme social pressure placed on them by the community. Furthermore, negative views of homosexuals are based on inaccurate stereotypes (Freedman, 1971). How do you look on homosexuality?

SOCIAL–CLASS GROUPS

In a democracy that emphasizes equality, as in the United States, the idea of **social class** is unpopular. After all, social class implies that there is a recognized hierarchy in which people are ranked according to respect and status. What does such ranking do to the idea that everyone is created equal and that no one is better than anyone else?

The answer is simple: social class is not a moral judgment but a description of how a person acts and how others react to him. As you move up in social class, you find an increase in income, education, influence, and status, among other things. This situation suggests that people in the higher-social-class groups are more fortunate or *better off* than others, but they are certainly not *better than* others.

Would you be pleased if your sister married a physician? What if she married a union carpenter? Or a bartender who just won $100,000 in a contest? How hard would you try to avoid a fist fight? Would you prefer to fight with words? Your answers will be based on values that are partly the result of social-class associations. No answer is right or wrong, except in relation to values.

A person's social class is evaluated primarily by his attitudes, values, and manners (Krech, Crutchfield & Ballachey, 1962). Other factors include his use of language, formal education, job status, income, neighborhood, family background, and even child-rearing techniques. Although we divide people into social-class groups (a very common division is upper class, middle class, working class, and lower class), these groups are not separated by distinct boundaries but are on a continuum. Neither do people *always* behave as a "typical person" of that class is expected to behave.

Most friendships, especially dating friendships, are between people of the same or similar social-class background (Hollingshead, 1949). The reasons are many: (1) people of the same social class tend to share the same interests and values; (2) they are likely to be at, or aspiring to, the same level on their jobs;

FIGURE 19-5. The kind of work an individual does is closely related
to his social class. Photograph by Lehman J. Pinckney.

(3) they live in the same neighborhoods and therefore attend the same schools;
(4) they often feel that a friendship with a person lower on the scale is not a good
idea; (5) they may also feel that people higher on the scale are snobbish.

As one interesting example of how social-class association affects behavior,
note Figure 19-6. A comparison of middle-class with working-class mothers
indicated that child-rearing practices differentiate the two groups. Obedience
and neatness are considered more important by working-class parents; dependa-
bility and self-control are stressed more by middle-class mothers. Middle-class
mothers also rely more on reasoning than do working-class mothers, and reasoning indirectly reinforces verbal behavior (Newson & Newson, 1967). Thus
middle-class children become accustomed to dealing with problems through
words and reasoning, whereas working-class children are more likely to receive
physical punishment or demands for obedience. Which group do you feel uses
more effective punishment? Which group do you feel follows more correct practices?

Another characteristic that distinguishes social-class groupings is attitude
toward physical aggression. Actual physical fighting is more common among

Belief	Preferred by Working Class	Preferred by Middle Class
Children should be toilet-trained casually.		x
Children should not play "Doctor" and other games involving nudity. Modesty is important.	x	
Masturbation and sex play with other children must be avoided.	x	
Children should be neat and clean.	x	
Spanking and other physical punishments are effective discipline methods.	x	
Threats of withdrawing love should be used in disciplining children.		x
Children must obey their parents.	x	
Children must be considerate of others.		x
Children should never talk back or show aggression toward parents.	x	
Children should not fight back or defend themselves against other children.		x
Both fathers and mothers should show children affection, including physical affection.		x
Children should be dependable and use self-control.		x
Children should be curious about things.		x
Parents should exert pressure for children to do as well as possible in school.	x	
Parents should exert pressure for children to complete all the schooling they are capable of.		x
Parents should use reason in handling children.		x

FIGURE 19–6.   Child-rearing methods among middle-class and working-class parents (abstracted from Kohn, 1959; Maccoby, Gibbs, et al., 1955; Newson & Newson, 1967; and Sears, Maccoby, & Levin, 1957).

lower-class children and adults; the middle class expresses aggressive feelings through words or other less direct methods. Does this mean that middle-class people are cowardly? Does it mean that lower-class people, who want to settle matters right away rather than wait and cool down (Schneider & Lysgaard, 1953), are tough?

EDUCATIONAL AND VOCATIONAL GOALS

Nowhere is the importance of social-class values better exemplified than in the pursuit of educational and vocational goals. Even the use of education as a means of achieving goals is a value acceptable primarily to the working class, middle class, and upper class. Lower-social-class people seldom consider education as proper *for themselves*. They may dream about being famous doctors or astronauts, but they rarely contemplate ways to achieve these goals.

To draw a parallel: you may feel that you could write a good movie script; you tell others how you feel, and you think a lot about it, but you never *do* anything about it. The whole business is just a hazy dream. It never occurs to you that books have been published about writing movie scripts or that courses are available in some colleges; you know you need an agent, but you do not know how to try to get one; you know nothing about instructions to the cameraman. So it all remains a dream, until you are about 50, when you begin to tell people "Oh, I could have written a movie script if I had wanted to, but I never had the time." Many children from the lower social class have the same hazy dream about college, because they understand very little about college and just assume that college is for other people.

Social class tends to be self-perpetuating from generation to generation. For example, lower-social-class parents do not know how to encourage education, but education is the best way for young people today to move up in social class. Since lower-class children, for a variety of reasons, do not do so well in school as children in the higher classes, they are not eligible for good jobs; thus their incomes are restricted, they live in lower-class neighborhoods, and they marry and have children who mature into the same pattern.

To accentuate the problem, lower-class people are less likely to internalize the value that immediate satisfactions should be sacrificed for long-range satisfactions (Gross, 1958). College education means sacrificing immediate income for a long-range better job; savings in the bank mean sacrificing immediate pleasures for a nicer home or investment or retirement security in the future; overtime work on the job means having less fun now but increases chances of promotion. College education, savings in the bank, and overtime work are all ways to move up the social-class ladder; but lower-class people may not recognize these ways as relevant, and they frequently ignore them.

School dropouts very definitely reflect social-class differences. Middle- and upper-class children rarely drop out of school. Not only do their parents encourage them more, but their teachers are also middle class and understand them and appreciate their problems more (Ausubel, 1954). The middle-class teacher and the middle-class student speak the same language. Also, lower-class children are more likely to want to see an immediate relationship between their schoolwork and their anticipated future job, which often does not appear to require an academic background. Middle- and upper-class children see more relationship between their future job success and job satisfaction and such courses as English or history. Lower-class children, not finding any meaning in education for them, tend to drop out of school.

Yet, in spite of this picture, some lower-social-class children break the pattern, get a good education or training, and obtain a job that is generally regarded as a working-class or middle-class position. These people have received help and encouragement from a teacher, a minister, a parent, or a family friend. Maybe they found something exciting in a book they read, or military service opened up a new world to them. Often no one knows what produced the motivation.

Of course, you might say "Lower-class people are lucky—they aren't worried about education or jobs. They're happy—maybe even better off than I am. Leave them alone." Or you might say "There's nothing wrong with these people—they're just lazy. They want to be poor and avoid responsibility. If they don't have the initiative to do something about themselves, I don't want to bother helping them." I disagree with both these points of view, but they should be discussed and understood.

SOCIAL–CLASS MOBILITY

The social-class structure is not permanently fixed. People constantly move up and down. Marriage offers one way to change social-class association, although merely marrying a person of another social class will not be sufficient; one's values and behavior must also change. Today, increased educational opportunities have enabled a great upward movement in social class.

The person who experiences **social-class mobility** has two types of problems. First, he is entering into social relationships with people whose values and manners he may not fully understand and who might have low regard for his background. Second, he is leaving an old group of friends whose resentment of his desertion might induce feelings of guilt. Many college students have had the experience of meeting an old high school friend who now seems to live in a totally different world.

The socially mobile person must adapt himself to the different manners, speech patterns, and values he encounters. Those who make the transition most successfully have begun to internalize the values of the new group even before they have moved into it (Krech et al., 1962). Socially mobile individuals who have difficulty internalizing these values often feel uncomfortable in the company of their new friends. To make matters worse, their children frequently take on the values of the new group very quickly and feel resentful that their parents are not truly of the group. The person moving down the social scale seems less happy and adjusted with his new role than does the person moving up (Douvan & Adelson, 1958); he even shows more racial prejudice (Adorno, Frenkel-Brunswik, Levinson, & Sanford, 1950). Although many people move along the social-class ladder with little or no problem, others pay a psychological penalty.

People usually internalize the values and behavior of parents, friends, family members, and neighbors. To some extent these values are also shared by others in the community, who, as a result, are assigned a particular status or class position by the community as a whole. Such values as vocational and educational goals and such behavior as methods of expressing aggressive feelings are indications of the class with which you identify. Social class should not imply a moral "good" or "bad" but a place in the status system of the community.

ETHNIC GROUPS

Numerous religious, racial, linguistic, and national-origin groups live in the United States. The term **ethnic group** is applied to a group whose members share one or more of these qualities. What ethnic groups do you belong to? Catholic? American of Irish ancestry? Black? Jewish? American Indian? American of Mexican ancestry? American of Armenian ancestry?

Ethnic-group identification affects personality for two basic reasons: first, different ethnic groups maintain somewhat different values, which are communicated to each new generation; and, second, people are evaluated partly in light of how their ethnic-group affiliations are perceived.

The self-concept, which depends so much on how you think others look upon you, is inevitably influenced by how you think others look upon the ethnic group to which you belong. If you associate yourself with an ethnic group commonly regarded as inferior and inadequate, your self-concept and resulting behavior will be affected. Perception of an ethnic group is often reflected in everyday expressions ("jew" him down), in laws (some states forbid marriages between people of certain differing ethnicities), in fiction and movies (how often do popular books or films show an American of Mexican ancestry as the handsome hero who wins the beautiful girl?), or in customs (many cities and towns have districts that exclude certain ethnic-group members as residents, without regard to their other characteristics). Under these circumstances, members of the particular group often internalize these attitudes as part of their self-concept.

Membership in an ethnic minority group may affect an individual's personality in six ways (Berelson & Steiner, 1964): (1) possible reduction in normal

FIGURE 19–7. Numerous racial, religious, and national-origin groups live in the United States. Photograph by P. C. Peri.

and casual contacts and communication with members of other groups; (2) increased importance of his own ethnic-group membership; (3) increased effort for acceptance by the majority group; (4) development of hostile and stereotyped attitudes toward other groups; (5) possible negative effect on self-esteem and self-concept; and (6) increased acceptance of violence if directed at the majority group.

Although during the greater part of the 1960s, black Americans were the only effectively vocal ethnic minority, by the end of that decade other groups were also demanding to be heard. These included the Spanish-speaking groups (Mexican Americans in the Southwest, Cubans in Florida, Puerto Ricans in the East), the Asian Americans (Japanese, Chinese, Korean, Hawaiian, Filipino, Samoan, and so forth), the native Americans, and eventually some of the white ethnic groups. Italians, Jews, and the many central European populations began to become better organized in demanding what they felt were their rights.

The black leader Martin Luther King said that, to understand someone, you had to "walk a mile in his shoes." The statement has great psychological validity and can be appropriately used to question the ability of any individual to write about any group when he has not "walked a mile in their shoes." Of course, if this policy were followed to the letter, I could not write anything about blacks, Mexican Americans, women, people with very high IQs, people with very low IQs, the mentally ill, the elderly, the dying, or the clergy. Perhaps each of these sections should have been written by a member of the groups being discussed; perhaps adolescents and college students should not be described by someone whose adolescence and college days are many years behind. What would be the advantages in following this principle? What would be the hazards?

THE SUBTLETIES OF DISCRIMINATION AND PREJUDICE

Ron Emerson, an electrical engineer in the aerospace industry, conferred with his black associate, Jake Woods, immediately after the failure of a project they had worked on for four months. Ron, who was white, was deeply depressed and said to Jake "Damn it, but things look black." And Jake came back without hesitation: "Oh, they aren't that good."

Paul Wang, a third-generation Chinese American, was arrested for breaking and entering along with eight other teenagers, a mixed group of blacks and whites. The judge let Paul off because "You come from a Chinese home, where the children are always honest. I know these other boys must have tricked you into going with them—probably because you're smart." Paul was furious because he was actually the leader of the gang, and the judge refused to give him credit for being that tough.

Bill Cannon, a black assistant principal of West High School, lived in a primarily white neighborhood. Bill also liked to garden, and on Sundays he often worked in his front yard. Tired of having people who were driving through ask him how much he charged for gardening, he finally responded to one especially patronizing woman: "I don't charge a thing, but if I do a good job, the lady of the house lets me sleep with her."

Patricia Herrera was up at 6:00 in the morning to get her children ready for school and then caught a 7:15 bus to the suburbs, so she could get to the home of whomever she was working for that day by about 8:45. She would leave at 3:30 in the afternoon, which got her home at 5:00, in time to begin supper for the family. By the time everything was cleaned up and put away, it was about 8:00, and Mrs. Herrera would do a few odds and ends, such as ironing and sewing. She followed this schedule five or six days every week. Her employers, however, knew only that she worked less than seven hours, and, as one complained, "With a schedule that easy, I don't know why she doesn't go to night school to improve her terrible English."

At a small Catholic college some 30 miles from the city, a group of black, Mexican American, and Asian American students were picketing the administration for being insensitive to the needs of minority students. The demands of one of their leaders included a course in black studies to be required of all students on campus. Thirty miles away, in the city, a white student was suing a state college because he claimed he signed up for a black studies course and was harrassed by the teacher until he was forced to drop out, leaving only black students enrolled.

And then there is the bumper sticker "Custer died for your sins."

THE BLACK COMMUNITY

Of all ethnic groups in the United States today, the black Americans appear to be the most harshly treated (although American Indians probably have the lowest standard of living of any ethnic group). Consider some of the problems of the black person:

- Certain jobs are closed to him, regardless of ability and training; advancement is often slow or impossible.
- He is often refused the opportunity to rent or purchase a home that fits his family's needs and finances.
- Certain social relationships are not easily available.
- He has evidence that he does not receive equal treatment before the law.
- To be permitted to vote, he has had to fight through the courts; and when he tried to exercise his voting rights, he was often met with threats of violence.
- Many of the professionals supposedly helping him, such as teachers, policemen, and social workers, admit to prejudices against his ethnic group.
- Restaurants, hotels, and similar facilities frequently offer him inferior service or reject him altogether.
- Medical and educational facilities available to him are often much less adequate than those available to others.
- The educational system reminds him that his origins were in slavery and ignores the fact that the ancestors of most other Americans were poor, illiterate farmers 300 years ago.

Can you think of other problems faced by blacks? How would you deal with these problems? What forms of discrimination and prejudice do *you* face because of your ethnic background?

Black children gain an awareness of their ethnic identification, and to some extent their ethnic role, when they are as young as 3 or 4 (Clark & Clark, 1958). Many of their parents admit having difficulty explaining to their children what it means to be a black American (Pettigrew, 1964).

So many things occur to these children just because they are black that they develop different self-concepts than a nonblack ordinarily would. Some of them turn their resentment onto themselves: they resent being black and perhaps internalize the value that blacks are inferior. Others respond by withdrawing; they do not exert a maximum effort and seem to be saying "If they don't think I'm any good, they might be right. So I'm no good, and I won't work very hard at trying to be." Others do increase their efforts, but often with the frustration that being black means they must work harder to get the same things.

The family also suffers. The male is hired less frequently than others with equal qualifications and is fired with less reason. The black woman is often hired for such low wages that the family remains impoverished or financially marginal. Given the long history of disrupted family relationships (for example, the constant breakup of the family during slavery, the higher death rates for the young and middle-aged), it is remarkable that the black family has endured so well. Even the relative lack of black men (according to the 1970 census, there are fewer than 91 black males for every 100 black females, all ages combined) has not destroyed the integrity of the black community (Jackson, 1971).

Blacks have been criticized for their high rates of illegitimacy, divorce, cohabitation, and unemployment, as well as for permitting their children to be cared for through neighborhood rather than family resources. Today, with considerable amusement, many blacks have pointed out that whites and others "are patterning themselves after blacks, not the other way around" (Jackson, 1971, p. 34). Experiments in alternative methods of family structure are certainly going on in many communities, not only black communities.

Contrary to common belief, black men, compared with black women, earn higher salaries, are more likely to be employed, are more likely to have higher-level positions, are much more likely to be the head of the household, and are about as likely to have college degrees. Some of the common assumptions about the dominance of black women and the inadequate sex-role behavior of black men require re-evaluation.

The black militants.   For many years the black community consisted of two major socioeconomic groups: the elitists who had "made it" in terms of middle-class achievement and the survivalists who were struggling for food. The former group has grown rapidly in numbers, although it has remained a much smaller portion of the black community (perhaps 15–20%) than its counterpart is of the general community. Those struggling for survival are an estimated 40–45% of the black community. Whereas the elitists are frustrated because they have been unable to gain status equal to members of the general community, the survivalists have suffered frustration by simply not having sufficient money for a minimal standard of living (Cohen, 1968).

Recently a third group has made its weight felt: the *militants*. Unlike the elitists and the survivalists, the militants did not see integration with the white community as the answer to their problems. Rather, they demanded better conditions for and more control by the black community. They emphasized pride in being black—"Black is beautiful" became a slogan—and pride in black history and black art and other achievements. Moreover, they blamed white racism for their problems. Their success came about for several reasons: (1) Many poor people—about 25% of them black—realized that they were not to be included in the growing American affluence. (2) Peaceful demonstrations and sit-ins, although making some gains, did not achieve the desired goals quickly enough. (3) Hopes that had risen with the 1954 Supreme Court decision requiring integrated schooling and the subsequent passage of many civil rights laws were not being realized. (4) The violence that did occur in black communities brought the hatred of many whites into the open; conflict and suspicion became intense to the point at which both residents of the black communities and nonblacks venturing into them were tense and ready for fighting.

Much of what took place can undoubtedly be related to the self-concept of many of the blacks. For 300 years of their history in the United States, they had lived in a society that constantly communicated to them the feeling that being black was equivalent to being inferior. They were treated like children, and, as is so often the case under such circumstances, they frequently found themselves responding like children. Today, however, they are rejecting the idea that being black is inferior or that they need the kind of patronizing care that has been given to them. Thus the leaders of the black communities are insisting that they be permitted to direct their own affairs (for example, increased autonomy of local schools) and that they be neither ordered about nor patronized. Since until very recently the behavior of most blacks did not suggest the intensity of the anger many of them felt, large numbers of whites could not understand the new attitudes. Much of the change in mood can be understood in terms of the desire of blacks to develop a much more positive self-concept for themselves both as individuals and as members of an ethnic group.

As this new mood intensified, anger mounted and the demands of the militants became greater. Some of their demands were met (for example, black history courses in the schools and new jobs), but others were rejected or ignored. Frustration frequently leads to aggression, which often leads to renewed frustration, particularly for the victims of aggression.

The black middle class. The rapidly growing black middle class (that is, the elitists) maintain values and manners similar in most ways to others of the same class (Parker & Kleiner, 1964). Yet they frequently find themselves caught between two forces. On the one hand, their shared values with middle-class nonblacks and their understandable desires for financial and vocational success suggest that they identify with middle-class whites in wanting to retain the status quo. On the other hand, the discrimination that they often suffer and their identification with the black community pressure them into demanding increased privileges and opportunities for all blacks, which sometimes causes them to defend highly aggressive or even violent actions that they would ordinarily not accept.

To make matters even more difficult, the long-time emphasis on racial integration began to be replaced by demands for equality of opportunity but without integration, at least by some black community leaders. The middle-class black often lived in an integrated area, worked next to middle-class whites, and was welcome in the homes of middle-class nonblacks. Under some circumstances he has been pressured to reduce the extent of his informal contacts with whites. As is so often the case, it is difficult to determine whether this situation is a temporary fad or a long-term trend.

Some people feel that the elitists, or even the survivalists, have so many advantages over the Russians or the Chinese that they should not complain. However, blacks do not develop their self-concepts and self-esteem in comparison with Russians or Chinese, but in comparison with other Americans. The past ten years have seen greatly increased opportunities for blacks, resulting from changes in laws and changes in people, but have seen little change in the black standard of living as compared with the white.

THE SPANISH–SPEAKING COMMUNITIES

The U.S. population includes several groups with recent origins in Spanish-speaking areas. These include Americans of Cuban and Mexican ancestry, most of whom live in Florida and the Southwestern states from Texas to California, the extremely large Puerto Rican community in New York City and elsewhere, and substantial numbers of immigrants from Central and South America.

Apparently black militancy has proven contagious, for members of the Mexican American community are also speaking out and demanding increased opportunities and a greater decision-making role for themselves. Although he shares certain social and financial difficulties with the black American, the American of Spanish-speaking background has been brought up in a home that emphasizes somewhat different values.

The family structure in Mexico stresses (1) father domination of the family and general masculine superiority; (2) strict discipline for children; (3) distinct separation of sex roles; and (4) strict obedience to authority figures (Ramirez, 1967). A comparison of Mexican American and Anglo college students—all of them middle class and all Catholic—showed that students tended to agree with the values of their country of origin, except for attitudes regarding masculine superiority and separation of sex roles. The continuing obedience to authority may explain why the Mexican American community did not enter the fight for civil rights as early as the black Americans did (Ramirez, 1967).

In addition to the strong family structure, two of the realities of the Mexican—and undoubtedly the Mexican American—community are the power and meaningfulness of the Catholic Church and the significance of poverty. Although Mexico is not a poor nation when compared with the world community, by virtue of bordering on the United States it suffers from relative deprivation, in spite of recent forward movement. Mexican Americans, for the most part, have limited education, few job skills, and a lack of understanding about how the bureaucracy of the United States operates—all this made worse by the fact that many lack facility in English.

The extreme diversity of Spanish-speaking communities makes it very dangerous to attempt generalities. Even among the Americans of Mexican background, those living in New Mexico may be descendants of settlers who arrived 200 or more years ago, whereas in the Los Angeles barrio the chances are greater that the person you speak with has been in the country for only 20 or 30 years or is a recent arrival. Similarly, the younger Mexican American may refer to himself as a Chicano, whereas his elders still wince at the term.

WHITE ETHNIC GROUPS

"The (white) ethnic American is sick of being stereotyped as a racist and dullard by phony white liberals, pseudo black militants, and patronizing bureaucrats. He pays the bill for every major government program and gets little or nothing in way of return. He himself is the victim of class prejudice" (quoted in *New York Times,* June 17, 1970, p. 49). These words express the feelings of many Americans of diverse national origins—people who maintain a sense of ethnic identity with groups that are not normally seen as minority, perhaps because they belong to the overall group of white.

In many towns and cities in the United States and Canada, areas ranging from a couple of blocks to a couple of square miles are densely populated by specific white ethnic groups from such diverse lands of origin as the Ukraine, Finland, Lithuania, Ireland, Italy, or Armenia (long since disappeared as a nation but still represented by people identifying themselves as Armenians). (Another white ethnic group is the Jews, also identified as a people, rather than with a land, but differing in values from the other groups being discussed). A high percentage of these white ethnic groups emphasize anti-Communism, hard work, strong discipline, and obedience to the law. They tend to be blue-collar workers, with some mixture of professionals and those at the managerial level. They often maintain traditional ideas regarding sex roles and sex behavior, long hair, and pornography. And they feel strongly that the emphasis on the nonwhite ethnic groups has interfered with their rights to live in their own neighborhoods, to attend their own neighborhood schools, and to hold their traditional jobs. How do you feel about their complaints?

ASIAN AMERICANS

Asian Americans come in as many shapes, sizes, and colors and have as many languages, customs, and religions as do white Americans, in spite of their relatively small number. They are Catholic, Buddhist, Hindu, Protestant, Confucian; they are first-generation, second-generation, third-generation, fourth-generation; they are farmers, businessmen, auto mechanics, teachers, physicians, day laborers; they are large with broad features and dark hair and skin, like the Samoans, or they are small with delicate features and dark hair and skin, like the Filipinos, or they are medium with medium features and dark hair and light skin, like the Chinese. And like the French and Germans, the Norwegians and Swedes, or the British and Irish, they have been at war with each other—back in their homelands—for centuries.

In the present vying of ethnic groups for attention, the Asian American groups (they are not one group but several groups who work together to compensate for small numbers) feel that their voices are hardly heard. Furthermore, when they do find a listener, the usual reaction is that Asian Americans are so advanced over other nonwhite minorities in education, jobs, and family cohesiveness that, whatever their ethnic problems are, they are simply not important.

In terms of economics, the Japanese, Chinese, and Korean groups have been very successful in overcoming the sometimes violent prejudices they encountered in North America. Nonetheless, their poor—and there are many—suffer not only from limited financial resources, but from a language barrier and from a lack of understanding of Western culture, its values and its bureaucracy. The experiences of the Japanese Americans with the relocation centers (concentration camps, as many of them called them) during World War II left many of them with amazingly little bitterness—and with a willingness to ignore the bitterness they did have in an effort to succeed in the United States.

The particular problem shared by the various Asian American groups is that of retaining their own ethnic values and identification without being excluded from opportunities offered to everyone. Because they are such a small minority, Asian Americans find it difficult to influence the local school systems or television programming. Many Asian American leaders fear that some of the cherished values of their ethnic groups that are not found in North America will disappear over time.

Perhaps the Asian American leaders are not eager to retain all the values from their countries of origin. They probably wish to keep the close family ties and the responsibility the young people feel for caring for their elders, but they probably would not wish to continue requiring that the daughters-in-law (and especially the wife of the oldest son) show extreme deference to their parents-in-law, as they do in Japan and China. They undoubtedly wish to maintain their present very low divorce rate, but it is dubious that many would seek to reinstitute arranged marriages.

The Asian Americans also have their elitists and their survivalists. Today their militants are beginning to make an impact.

AND SO FORTH

Our comments concerning the Asian Americans — and, to a lesser extent, the Spanish-speaking and black Americans — are frequently true of other ethnic groups. The French-speaking residents of Quebec Province in Canada and some of the New England states share with the non-English-speaking Filipino farm laborer in California a major difficulty in communicating his needs to some of his employers and his government officials; however, the power of the French in Quebec is so much greater than the power of the Filipinos in California that the comparisons cannot be carried too far.

The parallels involve the desire to retain ethnic identity — including ethnic foods, language, family structure, religion — without sacrificing equality. All ethnic groups, white and nonwhite, talk about the need for the social institutions of this country to provide options, rather than to try to turn out each person in the image of middle-class white America.

Discrimination, prejudice, anger, manipulation, exploitation, segregation — none of these are one-way streets. Although women, members of nonwhite ethnic minorities, and the elderly are especially punished by such treatment, these same persons are often on the giving side as much as the receiving side. You may wish to discuss whether this chapter has discriminated in favor of the normally discriminated-against groups or whether the position I have taken is still too pro-Establishment.

SUMMARY OF IMPORTANT IDEAS

1. People have developed an extremely complex network of groups.
2. Although many differences obviously exist between men and women, difficulties arise in trying to decide which are predominantly the result of biological factors and which are the result of social learning. Since many differences stem from the heredity-environment interaction, the task is very complicated.
3. Sex roles are developed at a very early age.
4. Boys tend to be rewarded for behavior that will make them aggressive and achievement oriented; girls are rewarded for behavior that encourages providing service.

5. The proportion of women who work is steadily increasing.

6. Whether homosexuals deserve punishment, need psychotherapeutic treatment, or should be left alone is the basis for a heated debate.

7. Social-class identification is important in determining behavior. A person's social class is influenced by his income, his ancestors, his job, and his education, but the criteria used most by psychologists are behavior, values, and manners.

8. Educational and vocational goals are related to social-class identification.

9. Social-class identification tends to be self-perpetuating, although people do show both upward and downward mobility.

10. Ethnic-group membership affects personality in two key ways: by influencing attitudes and values through internalization, and by producing an evaluation of the individual as a reflection of his ethnic group.

11. Discrimination and prejudice are often expressed very subtly.

12. Of all ethnic groups, the blacks probably receive the harshest treatment, although native Americans have the lowest standard of living.

13. The black militant has emerged as a force in the black community.

14. A major concern of many ethnic groups, including the various Spanish-speaking and Asian American peoples, is how to retain the positive and important values of their own tradition while still functioning as equals in North American culture.

20 Religion: Personal Belief and Social Force

This chapter has been included for two reasons. First, since everyone has had some form of personal experience with religious groups and religious values, they provide a framework for the study of groups and values in general. Second, I feel that religious groups and religious values are underestimated as forces both in this country and in the world in general. Before evaluating my assertion, study the numerous definitions of the term religious *given below so that you can interpret the term in its broadest sense.*

". . . only human beings are religious. Things are not, nor animals. . . . However much we may be related to animals, we are not related in religion." Throughout history religious feelings and religious institutions have helped shape individual behavior. Whether an individual supports some form of Judeo-Christian religion or whether he considers himself opposed to formal religion, it would be difficult to disagree with our opening quotation, by Dr. Don H. Gross (cited in Moberg, 1971).

The concern of this chapter is not to evaluate the validity of religious values or the adequacy of religious groups but to discuss such psychological matters as the development of religious values, the religious beliefs and problems of college students, and the relationship between religion and mental health.

WHAT IS "BEING RELIGIOUS"?

To find a universally agreed-upon definition of religion is impossible. The definition most commonly accepted by Americans would undoubtedly resemble that in Webster's *Intercollegiate Dictionary* (Fifth edition): "the service and ad-

FIGURE 20–1. Do you need to believe that angels are really little children with wings in order to find beauty in this statue? Photograph by Lehman J. Pinckney.

oration of God or a god, as expressed in forms of worship" or "an awareness or conviction of the existence of a supreme being, arousing reverence, love, gratitude, the will to obey and serve, and the like." Other types of definitions are also possible; for example, religion might be considered man's relationship to other men, man's method of explaining the unknown, man's ultimate concern (that is, whatever he is primarily concerned with or whatever he would be willing to die for), or man's ethical and moral guidelines.

Each person has a set of values and beliefs that affect his feelings about and behavior toward a supreme being, his relationships with people, his definition of his ultimate concern, and his method of explaining the unknown. These values may be described as sacred, such as those involving belief in an all-good, all-powerful God, in an afterlife, and in church ritual and prayer. Or, they may be described as secular, such as those involved in improving relationships among men, helping achieve peace, and fostering physical and emotional health. The values may be strictly followed or frequently violated, relatively stable or in a state of change, carefully thought out or learned from parents and never questioned. They may motivate the individual to join a religious group or to remain apart from all religious groups, to mature and use his capabilities or to become narrow and limit his thinking.

Belief in God?	Yes	*Belief in the Devil?*	Yes
United States	98%	Greece	67%
Greece	96	United States	60
Austria	85	Norway	38
Switzerland	84	Netherlands	29
Finland	83	Finland	26
W. Germany	81	Switzerland	25
Netherlands	79	W. Germany	25
Great Britain	77	Austria	23
France	73	Great Britain	21
Norway	73	Sweden	21
Sweden	60	France	17

Belief in Hell?	Yes	*Belief in Life after Death?*	Yes
United States	65%	United States	73%
Greece	62	Greece	57
Norway	36	Finland	55
Finland	29	Norway	54
Netherlands	28	Netherlands	50
Austria	26	Switzerland	50
Switzerland	25	W. Germany	41
W. Germany	25	Great Britain	38
Great Britain	23	Austria	38
France	22	Sweden	38
Sweden	17	France	35

FIGURE 20–2. A Gallup Poll of religious beliefs in the United States and ten European nations found that Americans adhere most strongly to traditional beliefs (published in the *Los Angeles Times,* December 28, 1968, p. 19).

When you ask someone if he is religious, what are you really asking him? Would you be satisfied with the response "Oh, I'm very religious—every noon I lie down under the tree in our backyard and offer prayers to Frodo"? Or "I am most certainly religious—I only wish I could have been alive during the Crusades to prove my devotion by killing infidels"? These statements are less exaggerated than you might assume.

A person can be religious in certain ways and not at all religious in other ways, depending on the dimensions of religiosity you accept. One approach (Glock & Stark, 1965) outlines five such dimensions: (1) religious experiences and feelings, such as the feeling of being "one with God" or the feeling of religious peace or the experience of fear of God; (2) religious beliefs, including belief in the existence of God, in the effectiveness of prayer, and in the immortality of the human soul; (3) religious practices, such as going to church, praying, or watching services on television; (4) religious knowledge, primarily concerning the history of religion, scriptures, and the basic assumptions of religious faith; and (5) consequences of religion, or the ways in which religion enters into day-to-day living and affects the individual's relationships with other people and with his environment. Although the chances are that a person with strong religious beliefs will also attend some related kind of religious services and will know a great deal about his religion, these relationships do not always occur. One college student may be very knowledgeable about the Bible because of childhood learning but may have discarded his earlier beliefs; another may have had deep personal religious experiences that brought him close to God yet believe that studying religious history or the Bible is worthless.

ALTERNATIVES TO TRADITIONAL RELIGION

You may have the impression, from our previous discussion, that only those who believe in the traditional views and practices of the Judeo-Christian world are to be considered religious. This is totally untrue, although a great deal of writing, talking, and thinking follows this assumption. You may have extremely strong beliefs concerning the nature of "true" religion; or, you may feel that each individual determines truth for himself.

The most obvious alternatives to Judeo-Christian religion are the other well-known religions, such as Islam, Buddhism, Hinduism, and other non-Western sects. We could also consider as religious atheism and agnosticism, both of which often include religious feelings and experiences (of being "one with mankind" instead of with God or of experiencing fear of nature instead of fear of God), beliefs, practices (drawing strength from beauty, human relationships, and nature, rather than from God), and consequences on daily behavior. Atheism, agnosticism, nonbelief, or whatever term you might prefer (they each have slightly different meanings)—all are valid alternatives to the traditional belief systems. The history of the United States and Europe has always included groups who have rejected the religious views of the majority.

EASTERN RELIGIONS AND WESTERN HUMANISM

The impact of non-Western religions in this country is fairly recent. Except for the influence of Islam on the Black Muslims, the religions of East Asia—especially Buddhism—are probably of greatest consequence. What has brought many Westerners to look to the Eastern religions? Some observers suggest that the Eastern emphasis on personal peace and meditation is most appealing. Others feel it is an outgrowth of American rebellion against authority, which would include religious authority; thus the individual leaves his childhood religion and seeks another kind of religion. A third possibility is the Eastern emphasis on avoiding competition.

Side by side with the growth of interest in non-Western religions has come renewed interest in the humanistic movement. The humanist tends to focus on relationships with other people, rather than relationships with God. He is concerned with the quality of life on earth, not with an afterlife. The humanist emphasizes the individuality of each person. He strives to be creative. He accepts responsibility for his own actions without trying to blame society or his parents. He believes that the individual can make a choice, rather than have his behavior determined for him by early learning or by religious forces. The concept of self-actualization is very basic to humanism.

All Christians do not believe in the same things or behave in the same ways. Neither do all Catholics, Jews, Baptists, Methodists, or Adventists. Therefore those Americans and Canadians who espouse atheism or agnosticism, an Eastern religion, or humanism should not be expected to think alike or behave alike. The humanist will be as consistent or inconsistent as the Presbyterian; the agnostic can be just as warm and cordial—or cold and angry—as the Lutheran; the student studying Zen Buddhism may get just as high on marijuana as the Jew or Catholic will get on alcohol.

BEHAVIOR OF NONBELIEVERS

"People who don't believe in God are lucky—they can do anything they please, and they don't have to worry about being punished."

"People who don't believe in God are in a miserable state—they must always be scared that something terrible will happen to them when they die."

The difference in behavior between believers and nonbelievers is much less than many people think. Nonbelievers neither do anything they please nor are fearful that something terrible will happen. The nonbeliever is not without problems, since he has taken an unpopular position and may be criticized for his views. However, there is no reason to believe that his emotional health or self-actualization suffers for not believing in God.

Although evidence does establish that the churchgoer drinks and smokes less than the nonchurchgoer, the churchgoer does not seem to be more honest (Goldsen et al., 1960) or more concerned with the value of human life and of mankind (Kirkpatrick, 1949). As a matter of fact, although those who attend church regularly seem less racially prejudiced than those who attend sporadically, nonchurchgoers have less prejudice than either of these other two groups (Allport & Ross, 1967). Those persons who are firmly committed to Christian ethics are less racially and religiously prejudiced. However, commitment to Christian ethics does not appear to be related to such factors as church attendance (Stark & Glock, 1968).

More important than the frequency of church attendance is the meaning of religion to the person. The studies just cited reveal that those who *live* their religion are much less ethnically prejudiced than those who *use* their religion. The former group consists of sincere, devout, concerned people. The latter includes people who use religion to advance their personal security, their status in the community, or their social contacts. Apparently, individuals who use religion for personal advancement have developed a set of values that cause them to reject people who differ from them, but those who live their religion tend to accept the concepts of brotherhood and love of mankind (Allport & Ross, 1967).

The nonbeliever often maintains humanistic values instead of the church-oriented values of his more religious peers. He usually believes that the present life is the only one he will ever have; thus he may feel under more pressure to produce a high quality of life for himself and for others while on earth, since he is not consoled by the thought that the next life will compensate for whatever he and others do not have during this life.

DEVELOPING RELIGIOUS BELIEFS

People learn religious beliefs and values, as they learn all beliefs and values, primarily through interaction with significant others. The school, the general community, and the mass media also have an effect. The unique personality of the individual is another obvious influence on the system of values he evolves.

IN CHILDHOOD AND ADOLESCENCE

Young children usually internalize the religious values of their parents and other significant figures in their environment. They almost always attend the church selected for them by their parents—usually without much question. Children tend to look on God as a person and accept literal interpretations of what they are told. One little girl who had been told "God is in you" was afraid He would leave when she had her tonsils removed. For young children, prayer is very self-centered and primarily an expression of wishes for things such as candy or toys. By age 11 or 12, prayer is associated with morals and ethics, and children ask for peace and human betterment (Long, Elkind, & Spilka, 1967). In essence, the child's concept of prayer, like many of his other concepts, develops from a vague idea to a concrete expression to an abstract concept.

In adolescence, questioning of certain aspects of religion begins. This questioning may also involve criticism, although criticism tends to be leveled at ceremonies and rituals, rather than at basic beliefs. Undoubtedly many adolescents (and many adults) never see religion as anything more than rituals and ceremonies. Doubting and questioning do not necessarily indicate loss of faith and

"Well, you were the one who said we shouldn't force religion on them—that they'd find it for themselves."

FIGURE 20–3. Courtesy of Ed Fisher.

can actually be a sign of maturity, since the childish concepts of God may need revision (Hurlock, 1959).

A study of religious experiences of ninth-graders had interesting results. When asked "When do you feel closest to God?" most of the respondents referred to some activity related to the church, but many reported having had this feeling at a time when they were alone. The personal experiences that made them feel "especially close to God" occurred most frequently when they themselves or a close friend or relative had narrowly escaped death or injury; the second most common situation was again when the student was alone (Elkind & Elkind, 1962). The importance of privacy and solitude in the religious feelings of these students is significant.

Toward the end of high school and during the years immediately following, young people increase their religious criticisms and doubts (Kuhlen & Arnold, 1944). Although this stage is often interpreted as a period of antireligious feelings, young people in the 16–25 age range are rarely atheistic or agnostic unless their parents are. Their criticisms of religion probably stem from a combination of two factors: first, they are seeking to understand their religious values better and must test them in discussions, or even arguments, with others; and, second, they are made unhappy by some of the behavior they observe in people who are, or claim to be, religious. Numerous studies have shown that 80–90% of high school students surveyed believe in a personal God and that a large proportion also accept the ideas of a Christian afterlife, of the value of prayer, and of the need for ritual and ceremony (for example, Kuhlen & Arnold, 1944; Remmers & Radler, 1957).

The changes in adolescent religious attitudes that occur with age seem to be in the following directions: (1) from a literal interpretation of the Bible to a symbolic interpretation; (2) from an almost complete acceptance of religious rituals, prayers, and ceremonies to some doubt; (3) from a strong belief that only one's own religion is correct to a feeling that all religions have something to offer; (4) from a virtually total belief in the existence of God to some questioning (Kuhlen & Arnold, 1944).

Church attendance in adolescence typically drops off. Although part of this decrease may be due to religious doubts, most of it probably results from reduced family demands for attendance. Many parents insist that their young children go to church but are more lenient with their teenagers.

IN YOUNG ADULTHOOD

Studies of the religious views of young adults, both in college and out, have led to several generalizations. First, young people are sincerely—sometimes almost desperately—trying to make sense out of religion and their religious beliefs. Second, youth are strongly influenced by both parents and the surrounding culture regarding religious values; their rebellion against the religious views of their own parents may be exaggerated. Third, adults probably overestimate the anxiety young people feel about sex and family matters but underestimate their concern regarding faith, values, and life goals. Fourth, information concerning religion and involvement in religious activities often have little carryover into day-to-day living. Fifth, adults frequently interpret the questions and doubts of young people incorrectly, assuming that they represent "hedging" and "drifting" rather than honest concern (Havighurst & Keating, 1971).

From time to time religious movements appear to gain strength among young people. Some years ago the Youth for Christ movement was believed by many people to suggest a major return of young people to traditional religion. More recently the "Jesus freaks" have been viewed in somewhat the same light. The hippie movement of the late 1960s has also been seen by some observers as a return to basic Christian values. The exact meaning of these movements is uncertain, but the general trend seems to be — at least for the moment — very much away from acceptance of traditional views and traditional rituals (Parker, 1971).

IN MATURITY AND OLD AGE

The man who is 20 years old today has lived through a world quite different from that of the person who was 20 years old in 1953 or the person who will be 20 in 1993. It would be strange if they had identical values concerning religion. Parents of the present generation of college students should not expect their children to agree with them any more than the next generation will agree with this one.

Once the person is married and away from his parents' home, antagonisms to parental values often fade away. By the time his own children begin to arrive, and especially when they reach Sunday-School age, he is likely to join a church again. Thus, from age 35 on, religious activity and traditional beliefs increase (Argyle, 1959). Religious conflicts tend to disappear during these middle years, and church attendance is high.

As people move from middle age to old age, they state that religion becomes more important to them and that they hold their religious beliefs more firmly, even though their church attendance and church activities diminish (Moberg, 1971). This apparent inconsistency is caused by health problems and transportation difficulties, as well as by the orientation of most church programs toward satisfying the needs of children, adolescents, and young adults, rather than the elderly. Although many churches and religious groups have established programs for the elderly, including housing, recreation, and opportunities to serve as volunteers, many experts in the field feel that clergymen should exert more effort in meeting the needs of older persons (Moberg, 1971).

FIGURE 20-4. As people move from middle age to old age, they state that religion becomes more important to them. Photograph by John G. Warford.

RELIGIOUS BELIEFS OF COLLEGE STUDENTS

Religious beliefs of college students vary greatly from school to school. In some colleges almost all students attend church; at other schools only a small fraction will go to church. About one in four college students attends church regularly, and about one in four does not attend at all. Attendance increases after graduation (Jacob, 1957).

One large study (Trent & Medsker, 1967) investigated the attitudes of many high school graduates and then requestioned the subjects four years later. Those who completed college were more likely to reject religious faith (13%) than were those who went directly to work (4%). At the same time, workers were much more likely than college graduates to state that religion had become more important to them during the four-year period under study. In general, college students seemed to move away from traditional religious values, particularly when compared with nonstudents.

Another major study investigated the religious attitudes of 4600 male college students, primarily in East Coast colleges. Although this group is not really typical of the rest of the country (for example, mostly nonchurch schools were included), their responses are worth considering. Half of these students accepted the traditional view of God, fewer than 20% discarded the idea of God, and most of this latter group said they believed in man, in science, or in natural law. Over 25% believed in "a power greater than myself which some people call God and some people call Nature." Only 1% claimed to be actual atheists (Goldsen et al., 1960). Those students who practiced their religion were more likely to feel that cheating was wrong but were also more likely to agree with the statement "If everyone else cheats, why shouldn't I?" They were less likely to be nonconformists and to believe that others should be allowed to express nonconforming ideas.

The results of two more recent surveys support the preceding data, but with some qualifications. *Newsweek*'s campus poll indicated that three out of four college students believed in God but that "in many cases the belief was highly tenuous." Also, almost 40% of all students interviewed felt that their college experiences had caused them to question their faith (*Newsweek*, 1965). In 1970 a Gallup Poll of students at 55 colleges asked "Do you think organized religion is a relevant part of your life at the present time or not?" Only 42% of the group said it was relevant; 58% indicated no relevance for them in organized religion (Gallup Poll, May 28, 1970, *Los Angeles Times*).

Putting these studies together with other information, a picture emerges of religious values among college students. By and large they believe very firmly in the traditional God; when they do not, they are either uncertain or have accepted science, man, or nature as their "ultimate concern." In later years many of them will slowly move back to the values they internalized in their earlier years and will undoubtedly join some church group, probably the same one their parents belong to or one slightly less traditional in its views. A small portion will retain agnostic or atheistic beliefs into maturity and throughout their lives.

In spite of the evidence that college students tend to move away from the traditional religious beliefs and rituals of earlier generations, they are not necessarily less concerned with many of the most important religious issues. They are still seeking meaning in life, still trying to understand the relationship of man to his universe and to other men, still searching for guidelines that they can live by, and, very often, still willing to seek answers through mystical practices. In spite of the importance of science today, many students feel that science cannot provide answers to vital questions of meaning, and they look to other authorities.

SOME RELIGIOUS PROBLEMS OF COLLEGE STUDENTS

Religious conflicts occur throughout life, but the period between the middle teens and the middle twenties is often considered the most difficult, perhaps because so many people begin to ponder the more complex problems of life at this point. The religious problems of college students include confronting the science-versus-religion controversy, learning about other religions, defining the place of religious freedom, considering the purpose of life, and understanding the meaning of death.

Science and religion.   Scientific and technical achievements have become so important in our world today that some people claim they have been made a substitute for religion. In addition, *certain* scientific findings appear to conflict with *certain* beliefs held by *some* religious groups. For example, the scientific assumption that the world is millions of years old conflicts with the belief that it is only a few thousand years old.

Nonetheless, the vast proportion of scientific findings do not conflict with the religious beliefs of any group. However, scientific thinking and religious thinking each demand different sorts of faith: scientific thinking demands a faith in the scientific method and the potential ability of man to comprehend the universe, and traditional religious thinking demands faith in an unseen supreme being.

Students are taught to think scientifically, to demand to see results, to insist on observing variables, and to be able to predict what will happen if compound A is added to compound J. Such learning may cause them to distrust thinking that does not operate scientifically and to cast aside traditional religious beliefs because they cannot be tested scientifically. Thus the beliefs of science and religion do not conflict, but the methods do. These same students, however, recognize that not all decisions require scientific proof (for example, political beliefs or the choice of a movie for Saturday night).

The religions of others.   Many students receive little or no religious training before college; others receive good training in their own religion but learn nothing of other philosophies or customs. In either instance college life can be upsetting, partially because courses discuss different religious ideas and partially because contact with students of other religious backgrounds is often inevitable.

> John Holdren grew up in a small town where people believed the theory of evolution to be the work of the devil. The state constitution restricted the way evolution could be taught, and his entire childhood was spent with people of similar religious values. "I even felt a little brave when my Boy Scout troop visited a Catholic church once a year."
>
> Will Gilberg was raised in a section of a large city where almost all his

neighbors were Jewish, and well over 80% of his high school was Jewish. He had never had a non-Jewish close friend.

When John and Will were assigned as roommates at college, they liked each other, but with reservations. John was astounded that anyone in the United States could deny the divinity of Jesus without being struck dead on the spot, and Will was dismayed that anyone in the United States could deny the truth of evolution. John began to worry that Will would not go to heaven, and Will began to worry that John was really anti-Semitic. John's religion taught him that drinking was sinful, and Will's religion included wine in its ceremonies.

Both took a philosophy course taught by a visiting professor from India. Since they had both always taken their own religious views for granted, learning how Christianity and Judaism looked to a scholar from Asia was very disconcerting. John firmly believed that Jesus walked on water, and Will firmly believed that the state of Israel could do no wrong; yet both were shaken when they realized how strange such ideas sounded to a person from a totally different culture.

The place of religious freedom. When asked directly how they felt about religious freedom, over 90% of the students surveyed expressed their belief in "unrestricted freedom to practice one's own religion." However, nearly 25% felt that religions preaching "unwholesome ideas" should be suppressed—a direct contradiction of the first belief. Another 17% were uncertain (Goldsen et al., 1960).

Not only students but adults of all ages are uncertain about how much religious freedom they wish to allow. When asked directly, they always favor religious freedom. However, notice that in the above survey fully 40% of the students refused to support the idea that all religious ideas should be expressed. They did not really favor complete religious freedom, but only freedom for those religions that did not make them unhappy. Are there any religions whose freedom you might not approve of?

The purpose of life. College students are sometimes disturbed by the question "What is the purpose of life?" They have heard the explanations of others — that the purpose of life is to serve God, or to serve one's fellowmen, or to enjoy life, or to be successful, or to serve one's country. But many students come to doubt that any of these purposes is their purpose of life; yet they cannot find an adequate substitute.

These students may go through a period of confusion and even depression. Life has no purpose; life seems vacant and meaningless. By reading, talking, and thinking, *they begin* to formulate what they feel to be the purpose in life. This formulation is not static and is likely to continue to develop and change during their mature years, but the confusion and depression that they may have felt as students will probably not recur.

The meaning of death.   Although the life expectancy of college students is many decades, and although their death rate is very low, they are still very much aware of death and concerned about what it means for them. Most major religions offer an explanation of why death occurs and what happens to the self (or the soul) after death. Some college students, however, reject the traditional concepts of the soul and the afterlife and claim that the end of life on earth also marks the end of existence of the self anywhere. Religious explanations of the meaning of death and existence after death offer comfort to many people, who thereby no longer have to face the prospect of nonexistence. Those who cannot accept these religious explanations need to work out some other fashion of coping with the reality of death.

RELIGION AND MENTAL HEALTH

Like other values, religious values can offer opportunities for growth and increased self-esteem and stability, or they can lead to intense conflict and limit the possibilities for growth motivation. Also, a church group may be warm, friendly, and emotionally satisfying or cold, demanding, and emotionally punishing. The degree to which any individual finds religious conflicts upsetting undoubtedly relates to his general emotional stability. Among the most important elements of religion in its relationship to healthy adjustment are faith, rituals, guilt, and church affiliation.

ON HAVING FAITH

An individual can have faith in any one of many religious value systems or in some combination of several. He may have faith that God exists or that no God exists, that the soul goes to heaven or hell after death or that neither the soul nor heaven and hell are real, that prayers are answered or that prayers are a waste of time. He may place more faith in science and technology than in the traditional religious values. When you view the behavior of peoples throughout the world, you can see that some have more faith in an ideology, such as democracy or Communism, or in money or power than in a personal God.

Faith implies acceptance of a system of religious beliefs based on what the individual feels is sufficient evidence or authority. Faith can be supported by logic, but it does not depend on logic. You have faith when you say "I don't know exactly why, but I feel that my concept of a supreme being is correct — I just know it is." Or you might have faith in the accuracy of a particular authority, such as the Bible, your parents, a minister, a philosopher, or a friend. Perhaps you believe you have come to your religious values through a process of reasoning; in that case, you have faith in your ability to understand religious ideas with your own reason.

A person cannot consciously decide to have faith. Faith can occur in many ways, but it does not occur through saying "I think I'd better get faith." Faith is a set of beliefs and values and is acquired just as other values are.

A person's specific religious values are probably less important to his healthy adjustment than the degree to which those values are consistent with his daily behavior and acceptable in the surrounding society. Opposing the standards of one's group can cause stress; also, behaving inconsistently with the self-concept can produce conflict and guilt. For example, the person who firmly believes that cursing is wrong but curses anyway will suffer conflict between his values and his behavior. He may eventually change his behavior, alter his values, or justify swearing in some fashion, but he will be motivated to reduce the tension-producing feeling of conflict.

A few people maintain religious values that are helpful neither for healthy adjustment nor for self-actualization. They may interpret their religion — often incorrectly — as unforgiving. They may have an "evil" thought and feel they have committed a terrible wrong; or they may feel that their religion requires that all who disagree with it be eliminated, with violence if necessary. Those faiths that are unforgiving, that demand an impossible level of "pure thinking," or that encourage disrespect or violence are not conducive to healthy emotional development.

ON RITUALS

Rituals are important or meaningless, depending on your religious feelings and your previous experiences with those rituals. Certain rituals are beautiful and add richness to life. For example, many non-Catholics can enjoy the color and excitement of a Roman Catholic High Mass. Others, such as the Catholic ritual of kneeling before entering and leaving the church pew, may be very meaningful to a Catholic but have little significance to a non-Catholic.

One anonymous psychologist once stated: "We need myths to live by in a technologically controlled existence." He was referring to the importance of heroes, legends, history — people and events that can serve as models, that have greatness, that produce excitement and romance. Otherwise, technology makes

FIGURE 20–5. Rituals are important or meaningless, enriching or tedious, beautiful or depressing, depending on your feelings and previous experiences. Photograph by Liane Enkelis.

everything cut and dried, sensible — and dull. Rituals and myths give people a sense of the greatness and beauty of their history. How do you feel about rituals?

Students who are searching for religious values are very much aware of inconsistencies. They are looking for meaning in religion, and they criticize rituals that seem impractical or so automatic that they appear meaningless. Also, students live in the present and often have little patience with the past; rituals usually have evolved over many years — perhaps centuries — and have meanings that are often traditional rather than contemporary.

Rituals become very familiar and may be comforting and satisfying, particularly in times of stress. They frequently occur in a group setting and give the participants a feeling of belonging to the group and a way of expressing their associations. On the other hand, a ritual can become a meaningless chore or habit that people continue to perform because of some vaguely felt belief that ignoring it will bring bad luck. When neglect of this type of ritual causes guilt and anxiety, the ritual is not only meaningless but potentially harmful emotionally.

ON RELIGION AND GUILT

Religious beliefs can contribute to both increased and decreased feelings of guilt and anxiety. Religion creates guilt when it is interpreted as overly demanding and overly punishing. When a young child fears that he will go to hell because he sneaked a candy bar from the drugstore, and when he wakes up shrieking from a nightmare of burning in hell, the guilt has progressed too far. When a college student cannot sleep at night because he fears he will be punished by God for harboring some slight religious doubt, anxiety has progressed too far. Religion sets up standards for behavior and feelings, but most religious leaders are aware that not all people can maintain those standards at all times.

People who cannot live up to their religious standards often feel the need to be forgiven. They may turn to prayer, to contemplation, or to such devices as the confessional. Not only can these methods be used to reduce the guilt and anxiety brought about by religious standards, but they can occasionally reduce guilt that originated in areas having little or nothing to do with religion.

Religious beliefs exert a great influence on behavior through inducing or reducing guilt and anxiety. Do you think that the feeling of having been forgiven can go as far in reducing guilt as to encourage irresponsible behavior?

ON CHURCH AFFILIATION

Motivation for church attendance varies. Some people go to church because they think it impresses their friends and neighbors; others have been persuaded that it aids peace of mind; still others attend with the vague feeling that they can "stay on the good side of God, just in case there is a God." A few people go to church to make business contacts or social contacts, to see who else is there, or to look the minister over.

Nonetheless, most church attendance is probably motivated by a sincere desire to join with a community of others to express deeply felt spiritual beliefs. In this seemingly impersonal world, many people feel alone and vulnerable. Church membership not only gives spiritual satisfaction, but also provides the important feeling of belonging to a group that has similar beliefs and performs similar rituals. For some, unfortunately, church affiliation leads to such extreme loyalties that they look down on or discriminate against other churches and their members.

Today religious leaders and theologians are giving increased thought to the future of organized religion. Many clergymen have decided that their spiritual guidance is needed more outside their church than within; others have left their religious groups altogether. Some church leaders are calling for a return to the "old-fashioned" beliefs and practices, whereas others insist that people must seek their own truths and their own salvation. At the same time that so much ferment is occurring within church groups, more and more people are looking within themselves for understanding. Where are you looking to find answers to the problems of meaning and of the spirit that concern you most?

SUMMARY OF IMPORTANT IDEAS

1. There are many possible definitions of religion: "the service and adoration of God or a god, as expressed in forms of worship"; man's relationship to other men; man's method of explaining the unknown; man's ultimate concern.

2. Religiosity is not a single characteristic but consists of several interrelated dimensions.

3. There are many alternatives to traditional Judeo-Christian practices and beliefs, including Eastern religions and Western humanistic thought.

4. The difference in day-to-day behavior between believers and nonbelievers in traditional Western religion is less than many people assume.

5. Young children usually internalize the religious values of their parents and other significant figures. They rarely resist their parents' requests regarding prayer, church attendance, or ritual adherence.

6. Adolescents feel close to God in situations involving privacy and solitude.

7. During adolescence religious values undergo some change: a diminishing acceptance of the Bible in literal terms, some doubts concerning ritual and prayer, more tolerance for other beliefs, and some questioning of the existence of God.

8. Religious values and activities continue to change after adolescence. In middle age, religious conflict seems to disappear; in old age, beliefs are held more firmly, although religious activities diminish.

9. Most college students believe in God, although some define their belief as being in "a power greater than myself that some people call God and some people call nature."

10. College students face certain religious problems, including confronting the conflict between science and religion, learning about the religious beliefs of others, deciding on the place of religious freedom, determining the purpose of life, and thinking about the meaning of death.

11. Religion affects mental health through both religious values and religious

group membership; either factor may lead to better emotional health or may precipitate mental-health problems.

12. The degree to which a person's life is consistent with his religious values probably contributes to his mental health.

13. A religious ritual is important or meaningless, depending on the individual's feelings, his previous experiences, and the context in which the ritual is conducted. College students often attack rituals because they seem to lack contemporary meaning.

14. Religious values may either increase or relieve guilt feelings.

21 Career Planning and the World of Work

This chapter carries the student from his present role to one of the most important of his future ones: the work role. Actually, this entire book could have been oriented around work, since work and careers are related to needs and personality, to abilities and testing of abilities, to the meaning of success, and to the process of self-actualization. Perception, learning, problem solving, and language are basic to work. And, as you well know, your ability to deal effectively with your sexual and marital relationships and your responsibilities to your neighborhood, your ethnic group, and your family all interact with your effectiveness on the job.

What career field are you planning to enter? Why? How much do you know about this field? Do you know what is required to enter the field? Are you familiar with the nature of the work? The working conditions? The opportunities for advancement? In what ways will the work satisfy your needs? We can assume your chosen field will earn you enough money to pay for food and shelter, but will it help you satisfy your security or self-esteem needs? Will it offer you the possibility for self-actualization?

Answers to these questions cannot be given on the spot, but they are very important to career planning and subsequent satisfactions during the adult years. After all, for better than two-thirds of your lifetime and for more than one-third of your waking hours, you will be engaged in activities related to producing income. Except for the retired, the disabled, and the housewife (whose working hours may be longer than her husband's), almost all adults work for financial return. Your career and your vocational success and satisfaction are highly significant in many ways. Inevitably, your job determines your income and thus affects your standard of living. Your job is also a measure of your status and that of your family—a status only partially related to income. For example, a teenager complained to "Dear Abby" that her parents were pressuring her to break up with her boyfriend only because his father was a garbage collector, although the incomes of the two families seemed comparable (*Los Angeles Times,* December 31, 1965).

Your job reflects your educational level, your past achievements and future prospects, your values and attitudes, your self-concept, and—at least for some people—your means of personal growth and self-actualization.

CAREERS: CHOICES AND DECISIONS

Perhaps the only decision you need to make immediately concerning your future career is the degree to which you will plan the direction you are going and the degree to which you will permit luck and circumstances to control your destiny. A decision that must be made at a later time—and this decision will probably change many times in your work life—is the relative importance to you of several competing values. Your future career will require some of the following choices:

- How much emphasis should you place on immediate income as opposed to long-range income?
- How do you divide your time *and* energy *and* emotional involvement among work, play, family relationships (with parents, spouse, children), creative activities, reading for pleasure, and various ways of improving your future opportunities?
- How much loyalty do you feel to your employer? How much to gaining your own ends?
- How much loyalty do you feel to your fellow workers? To your immediate supervisor? To those you supervise?
- How important is it to you to rise to the top or near the top of your work organization? Do you leave a company at which you have made a successful beginning as soon as a better offer comes along? Do you leave for more fun? More money? More independence?

To some degree, your answers to these questions will depend on your feelings regarding the meaning of work. If you feel, as many do, that working is honorable and that not working is a sign of moral weakness, then work is likely to absorb a great deal of your time and energy. If you feel that a job is primarily a way of getting the money you need to do what you want, your efforts will probably be less. If you feel that work is challenging or fun, then you will probably put in extra effort without even realizing what you are doing.

Although college and various forms of specialized training can increase your chances of getting the kind of job you want, formal education does not *make* the job challenging. Similarly, enjoyment of a job, like enjoyment of a relationship with another person, cannot be seen as the responsibility of the employer, the supervisor, or "the system" — it is the responsibility of the individual.

Occupation	Rank Order of Occupation in Regard to		
	Competence	Altruism	Truthfulness
Physician	1	2	1
Dentist	2	5 (tie)	3
Lawyer	3	9	9
Judge	4	5 (tie)	4
Professor	5	8	6
Psychologist	6	3	5
Clergyman	7	1	2
Psychiatrist	8 (tie)	4	7
Executive	8 (tie)	18	13
Plumber	10	14	12
TV Repairman	11	15	15
Schoolteacher	12	7	8
Auto mechanic	13	16 (tie)	17
U. S. Army general	14	12	14
TV news reporter	15	11	11
Law-enforcement official	16	10	10
Newspaper columnist	17	13	16
Labor-union official	18	16 (tie)	18
Politician	19	19	19
Used-car salesman	20	20	20

FIGURE 21–1.   Attitudes toward selected occupations, based on ratings by 296 university students and 100 nonstudents (adapted from Rotter & Stein, 1971).

CAREERS AND MEANING

A common complaint about work is that it lacks *meaning*. Some people move from job to job, always without real satisfaction, because none of their jobs have meaning for them. They are alienated from their work. When we discussed marriage, we suggested that one of the major difficulties in marriage today is that people expect too much from a human relationship. The same probably holds true of careers and jobs.

Victor Arsounian decided to become a male nurse, in spite of teasing from some of his friends, because he felt that a nurse could provide meaningful services for people on an individual basis. Once in the field, however, he realized that he could reach only a few people of the many people who needed care. He took some additional training, worked very hard, and was quickly promoted to a supervisory position. Even this job proved frustrating, however, because the handful of nurses who worked under him still reached only a fraction of the patients and because some of his employees found him too demanding and requested transfer to another unit. By this time Victor had saved a modest amount of money, and he decided to buy a convalescent-care facility. He received some backing from a wealthy friend, borrowed heavily from the bank, and purchased a home that was on the market. He immediately had to hire a director of nursing, since his time was consumed by management responsibilities. His home now has 90 patients and 40 employees. He is running a good institution, but he still has the feeling that he has never been meaningful in the way he had wanted to be when he first began.

Victor Arsounian has been meaningful to hundreds of people, primarily the elderly, during the few years he has been in charge of his home, but he wants to feel that he can have an impact on thousands or hundreds of thousands. A handful of people have that kind of impact, but most do not. On the other hand, certain individuals bring meaning with them to whatever they are doing. Through cheerfulness, concern for others, and a willingness to become involved with other people without trying to make decisions for them, they are able to be meaningful on almost any job. Perhaps a nurse or a fireman is able to see immediate evidence of his work efforts more easily than a shoe salesman or a television repairman; but if you have ever bought a pair of shoes that were too tight or had a television repairman overcharge you for a simple job, you will understand how meaningful competence and human decency are for these kinds of positions.

In career planning, then, you will need to decide what you find meaningful and how you can bring personal meaning to the work you are doing.

CAREERS AND SUCCESS

Each person defines success for himself and then determines how he is going to move toward what he sees as success. Obviously his definition will be influenced by the feelings of his family, his friends, and his surrounding society; also, he may change his definition as he goes along, since experience and self-evaluation may indicate that the meaning of success *to him* has changed.

How do you define success for yourself today? Some people seek the satisfaction of knowing that a job has been well done or that they have overcome some sort of challenge. Maslow (1967) feels that high success occurs when there is a kind of natural harmony between the individual and his job, much like a perfect love affair; for such people their work becomes so much a part of them that they cannot conceive of themselves without it.

Others feel that success comes from money or fame or prestige. Still others consider themselves successful if they can be creative or test out new ideas or be of service to humanity or gain power. And there are those who feel good when they have worked hard—and those who feel good when they have done as little work as possible. Success means different things to different people, depending on their individual needs.

JOBS, CAREERS, AND SATISFACTION

Peter Drucker, a well-known management consultant, stated that job satisfaction depends less on a person's specific aptitudes than on having a job for which he is temperamentally suited (Drucker, 1968). Drucker suggests that the job seeker ask himself four questions:

1. Do I want security and a work routine I can depend on, or do I want challenge and creative opportunity but with a high chance of failure?
2. Do I want a large organization, or do I prefer a smaller organization?
3. Do I wish to start at the bottom and work my way up slowly but on a firm base, or do I want to begin much higher up and risk falling off?
4. Do I want to specialize, to become an expert in a small area, or do I want to be a generalist, to have breadth rather than depth?

These questions become particularly important in light of the fact that recent graduates often find their first postgraduate jobs a great disappointment. According to one study (Schein, 1968), at least half the men surveyed left their first jobs within a brief period of time. The frustrations met by these men were numerous. One of the biggest shocks was finding out that their ideas were usually rejected or ignored, even when they were specifically asked to come up with an idea and regardless of the value of the idea. They had just not learned enough about the human side of business and industry, and they expected their supervisors to respond in terms of business logic, rather than in terms of their own personal needs and biases. These new graduates also underestimated the resentment they aroused in management, who saw them as overly ambitious, impatient, immature, and inexperienced. The fact that they were often better educated than their supervisors merely added fuel to the fire (Schein, 1968).

Note the factors in Figure 21–2 that were considered most important in determining job satisfaction and those that led to dissatisfaction. The former related to what the person does, and the latter referred to the job environment (Herzberg, 1968). Apparently the opportunity for self-actualization makes a job

Factors Leading to *Job Satisfaction*	*Factors Leading to* *Job Dissatisfaction*
1. Achievement	1. Company policy and administration
2. Recognition for achievement	2. Supervision
3. Nature of work	3. Salary
4. Opportunity to take responsibility	4. Interpersonal relations
5. Opportunity for advancement	5. Working conditions

FIGURE 21–2. Determinants of job satisfaction and dissatisfaction of engineers and accountants (Herzberg, 1968).

worthwhile, whereas a restriction of the work environment makes a job unpleasant. In an article that carefully reviewed existing research on job satisfaction, two psychologists (Zander & Quinn, 1962) found that job satisfaction was primarily based on the opportunity for self-actualization and decision-making, satisfying relationships with co-workers and supervisors, and perception of self-adequacy through pay, status, and recognition.

Job satisfaction is important not only to the worker but also to his employer. Substantial evidence exists that employees with high job satisfaction are less likely to leave for another position and less likely to be absent from work (Vroom, 1969); they also have fewer accidents (Brayfield & Crockett, 1955). However, job satisfaction is not *always* related to job performance (Vroom, 1969), although there is a tendency in that direction.

> Marcy Waters was an attractive young secretary in the college business office. She was cheerful, warm, lively, and friendly. She was also extremely talkative, and she seemed to have a legion of friends from all departments who dropped in often to talk with her. Any student who came by with a problem received her immediate attention, even if she knew little or nothing about the matter; any rumor about a student, staff member, or instructor was immediately passed on to the next person Marcy saw. Marcy thoroughly enjoyed her job, and everyone thoroughly enjoyed Marcy—but she rarely did any work.

When members of a work group are cohesive and get along well with one another, the nature of the group helps determine how productive each individual will be. If the group's major values seem to be work and productivity, the performance of most of the group members will be high. On the other hand, if the group members have little regard for the goals of the management or if they are so cohesive that they spend most of their time being social, little will be done. In addition, a new member to the work group will face strong pressures to keep his output from being higher than the group average.

Management personnel have become very much aware of the importance of job satisfaction. At one time the emphasis in business and industry was to simplify jobs as much as possible so they could be done quickly and easily and without much thought. However, this simplification made the jobs dull and unchallenging for many workers, and both production and turnover changed for the worse. As a consequence, **job enrichment** has begun. Job enrichment gives workers considerably more responsibility, a wider range of tasks, and more opportunity to make decisions; it also produces jobs with higher skill-level demands (Hulin & Blood, 1968).

Job success and job satisfaction can support an already healthy self-concept or can bolster low self-esteem. They can lead to great satisfaction, the feeling of accomplishment, and self-actualization. Lack of job success and low job satisfaction can have just the opposite effects.

KNOWING YOURSELF

How well do you know yourself? What should you know about yourself when you begin your career planning? Does it matter whether you are aggressive or shy, adept with your hands or clumsy, interested in earning lots of money or in helping others? Of course it matters. Some of the more important personal characteristics in career planning include interests, needs, values, personality, abilities, education, environmental pressures, and characteristics such as sex, age, and ethnic background.

INTERESTS, NEEDS, VALUES, AND PERSONALITY CHARACTERISTICS

If you are interested in your work, if the tasks you perform help satisfy your needs, if the purpose and methods of your organization are consistent with your values, and if your personality characteristics are appropriate for the work, then you are very likely to be successful on the job. You will readily spend extra time on the job, and the time will pass quickly. You will not say to yourself, when you get up in the morning, "Nuts—another day of work. I'll sure be glad when it's over."

Unfortunately, some people are not interested in their work or satisfied with what they do or with the organization they work for. Their work bores them. They spend each day looking forward to going home; each week, looking forward to the weekend; each year, living for their vacation.

Why do some people end up in a career they dislike? Perhaps they lacked the training or competence to do what they wanted; or, they misjudged their own interests and personal attributes; some might have wrongly estimated the degree to which they valued money or status or working conditions; others have simply yielded to the demands of family and friends. Inevitably there are those who never really planned their careers but suddenly found themselves in a job before they ever stopped to figure it out.

Each individual has a unique pattern of interests, needs, values, and personality characteristics. Any one pattern is appropriate for certain careers but not for others. Police applicants, for example, have higher than average needs for achievement, dominance, and exhibitionism; they are also very masculine but not especially interested in independence (Matarazzo, Allen, Saslow, & Wiens, 1964).

One investigation (Astin & Nichols, 1964) tried to determine what basic factors relate to career choice. The investigators found that a person's selection of a vocational field depends largely on the degree of importance he places on the following: (1) having a good self-concept (desire to be popular, emotionally stable, or influential); (2) being personally comfortable; (3) enjoying artistic and creative tasks; (4) desiring prestige; (5) enjoying scientific and technical tasks; (6) being able to help others and to become personally mature. Students majoring in business placed above-average value on personal comfort; clergymen stressed the value of helping others; both nurses and secretaries indicated above-average value on both personal comfort and helping others. How much importance do you attribute to each of these six values?

ABILITIES

As a result of the dynamic interplay between heredity and environment, each person develops a unique pattern of abilities and potential abilities. Since different careers emphasize different ability patterns, an effective career plan tries to match the abilities of the individual to the requirements of the field. Both automobile salesmen and bank managers need to have good verbal ability, but the automobile salesman should have a different type of persuasive ability. Both carpentry and nursing require only a minimal level of ability with numbers, but the carpenter must be able to turn a blueprint into reality, and the nurse must be able to deal with sick patients.

How successful are you in maintaining good relationships with other people? Almost every job depends to some extent on this ability, and some jobs—like that of a salesman, social worker, minister, or union organizer—depend greatly on human-relations skills. However, much more than an ability and interest in getting along with people must be considered in planning a career, as the following hypothetical case illustrates.

Evelyn Darcieux came to the counselor's office to discuss her career plans. "I don't have much of an idea of what I want to do, except that I want to work with people." The counselor grinned and said: "Okay, if that's all you care about, you could be a missionary in Africa or a policewoman on the narcotics squad or a lifeguard or a nursery-school teacher. All these jobs involve the ability to work with people." Evelyn laughed, and the counselor continued: "Of course, the most important thing is to decide what kind of relationship you want with what kind of people. Very few of us have the ability to get along with all people under all conditions. Do you want to be in charge of people or work under people? Do you think you have the ability to persuade others or to learn to see through others when they try to persuade you? Do you have the ability to make decisions and risk being unpopular? Or do you prefer to carry through someone else's decisions? Does your ability extend to all age groups equally? Does it include normal people, emotionally disturbed people, or lawbreakers? Do you prefer a few people at a time or many? The same people every day or

FIGURE 21–3. What kinds of relationships, with what kinds of people, do you want in a job? Photograph courtesy of Los Angeles Society of Crippled Children.

new people all the time?" Evelyn cut in as the counselor paused a moment, "I'd better think about it some more."

When she returned a week later, she had given the matter a great deal of thought. "I think I know what I want, although of course I may change my mind later. But I think I want to work with adults—normal people. I'd like to work with the same people, rather than different ones; and I want to be in charge of people, even if I do become unpopular. Also, I'd prefer to have close relationships with a few people, rather than casual relationships with a large number."

Can you suggest some vocations that would meet Evelyn's criteria? Each individual has job-related abilities, but, like Evelyn, many people need help in relating their abilities to vocational fields.

EDUCATION AND TRAINING

Although many organizations give some on-the-job training, schools and colleges are responsible for teaching most job skills. Traditionally, colleges and universities trained managerial and professional personnel, and high school marked the end of training for everyone else. Today junior colleges supply a stream of students not only to four-year colleges but also directly into the job market.

ENVIRONMENTAL PRESSURES

Career planning is strongly influenced by several sources of environmental pressures, including family and friends. These pressures often operate unconsciously because they stem from values the student internalized before he entered college.

The son of a soldier killed in the Korean War has internalized the value that a professional Army career is dignified and worthy.

A young girl watches her mother wait tables in a restaurant and internalizes her mother's beliefs that office work is far preferable.

A young father, together with his son, spends hours working happily to keep the family car clean, efficient, and comfortable. The son grows up feeling that being an auto mechanic would be getting paid for having fun.

Pressures may be more obvious, as when a father offers his son a new sports car if he will study accounting or a girl's parents refuse to finance her college education if she majors in journalism. Friends can also influence vocational choice. A person whose friends are all entering college is reluctant to admit that he has no intention of going. If everybody in a group of college women expects to become a career girl, the one member who is interested only in marriage and a home may feel inadequate.

SEX, AGE, AND ETHNIC BACKGROUND

In certain vocational fields success does not depend only on ability—or even on ability plus luck plus pull. Other factors, often having little or nothing to do with ability, are related to getting jobs and must be considered in career planning. These factors include sex, age, race, religion, and nationality.

FIGURE 21–4. Some jobs are closed to women because of sex discrimination. Exclusion from other jobs is based on work-related factors. Could a woman do this work? Photograph by Lehman J. Pinckney.

Sex. In the United States certain vocational fields are looked on as being largely or strictly for men; these include engineering, medicine,* physics, con-

* In Russia, however, more than half the physicians are women.

struction work, radio announcing, and many factory jobs. Other careers, such as elementary school teaching, nursing, and many secretarial jobs, are considered most appropriate for women. People can, of course, enter careers traditionally associated with the opposite sex, although they may face discrimination both in receiving training and in getting jobs.

Age.　Some positions are closed to those who are too young, and others are closed to those who are too old. Even looking too young may be a problem. A competent personnel interviewer had difficulty getting a job because he looked much younger than his 26 years; personnel directors felt that prospective workers would take him for a teenager and be resentful.

Ethnic background.　Members of certain groups find work unusually difficult to obtain, even when they have the necessary qualifications. The black American is probably the most severely punished by job discrimination, but Americans of Mexican, Puerto Rican, Italian, Greek, and Asian ancestry also meet frequent hiring and promotion problems. Jews, Catholics, and native Americans have similarly suffered from job discrimination.

Even highly qualified members of some of these ethnic groups have trouble in getting jobs, and even more trouble in being promoted. Recently, however, some employers have gone out of their way to hire people of non-Anglo backgrounds. Initially such hiring took the form of adding one minority-group person, placing him conspicuously for visitors to see, and then returning to old hiring practices. And often the person hired had high-level training. Slowly, however, some employers became aware that nondiscriminatory hiring had to be accomplished at all ability levels, and a few organizations even instituted affirmative-action programs, making special efforts to hire and promote minority-group members (and women) to help equalize the previous imbalance. Federal and state laws have been passed to outlaw discrimination in hiring based on sex, age, or ethnic background, but the success of these laws is still to be determined.

Other characteristics.　Additional individual characteristics that enter into career planning include physical health and stamina, appearance and size, sensory acuity (such as good vision and hearing), citizenship, criminal record, ownership of a driver's license, and present marital status. By and large, you can evaluate the relevance of these characteristics to your own career choices.

To plan a career, an individual should know about himself and about the variety of career possibilities. He needs to consider his own unique pattern of background, personality, and abilities and to relate these to what various vocational fields offer and require.

KNOWING ABOUT THE JOB

So far our discussion has emphasized the qualities of the job holder, but a careful consideration of the characteristics of the job and the job market is also essential. Do you have a clear picture of the field you intend to enter? What are its requirements? What does it offer you? Some of the more important considerations in evaluating a career field include the job market, job requirements, job description, working conditions, advancement opportunities, income and other material benefits, social status of the job, and opportunities for personal growth and satisfaction. Keep in mind that you may be well suited for more than one vocational field. How would you prepare under such circumstances?

Even a good career plan loses some value if a student does not know how to look for a job. Many unnecessary frustrations can be eliminated by a carefully planned and conducted job search.

1. Begin to search for a position at least eight to ten weeks before graduation.
2. Use all available sources: classified advertisements, government job listings, friends and relatives, and college and other placement bureaus.
3. Apply to several organizations.
4. Be prepared to wait; personnel decisions may take several weeks.
5. Have references all lined up.
6. Have a well-executed biographical outline mimeographed; these outlines can be left with references, enclosed in letters to prospective employers, used to supplement application forms, and sent to friends to keep an eye out for you.
7. For job interviews, dress appropriately, be relaxed, and do not try too hard to impress the interviewer; honesty is the best policy.

THE JOB MARKET

Our country is a dynamically changing nation. Entire vocational fields are born and disappear each decade. Automation is eliminating certain careers while creating new ones. The funeral director, the kindergarten teacher, the commercial artist, the policeman, and the receptionist are all likely to be around for a while; but miners, railroad firemen, dock workers, and certain types of white-collar workers are going the way of the blacksmith.

Not all job fields are equally crowded. At any given time certain career areas have an overabundance of qualified people while other fields suffer shortages. Also, the job market in your community may differ from the job market 100 or 1000 miles away. Because of the changing nature of the job market, train-

FIGURE 21-5. Entire vocational fields are born one decade . . . and disappear the next. Photographs by Liane Enkelis.

ing and education beyond high school become important in providing career flexibility, so that you can move easily from one field to a related one. Without a doubt, your career plan is made more effective by a careful consideration of the job market, both present and future and both local and national.

THE JOB REQUIREMENTS

Different vocations have different requirements. Experience, education, human-relations skills, and good language abilities are merely a few of the many types of demands that must be met to succeed in certain vocational fields.

Job requirements must be known before any career plan can be established. Many students talk casually about becoming dentists or atomic physicists — only to learn to their dismay that these careers demand seven, eight, or more years of college. Others decide to become electricians or television stagehands and do not find out soon enough that they must enter highly selective unions.

Standards in many vocational fields are being upgraded. Sixty years ago teachers and social workers did not even need a high school diploma in many states; today most such positions demand a minimum of a college degree. The nurse, pharmacist, funeral director, librarian, and military officer have all seen their fields tighten requirements for entrance. Some states now demand that barbers, policemen, and real-estate salesmen pass written examinations.

Earlier it was stated that career planning demands an awareness of personal characteristics. Job requirements are the other side of the coin, and the career plan should attempt to match personal characteristics with job requirements. (You may prefer to consider job requirements as pertaining not only to getting a position, but also to success and satisfaction on the job.)

THE JOB DESCRIPTION

What, precisely, will you be doing on your eventual job? Strangely enough, many students do not bother to investigate this matter carefully. It sounds romantic to be an FBI agent, but what does he do on a typical day? Some girls think nurses spend all their time helping kindly old women and unhappy little children, but what do nurses actually do? The work of an airplane pilot or a reporter may seem exciting, but is it really?

Exactly what tasks does your chosen career call for? Will you sell to people? Buy from people? Give orders? Take orders? Make decisions? Carry out the decisions of others? Use a pencil? A lathe? A typewriter? Be subject to stress? To time pressures? Sit behind a desk? Work outside? Travel around the country? Around the city? The things you do from day to day will be a major factor in your enjoyment of your career. Too often people allow the image of their job field to blind them to the importance of the daily routines.

WORK CONDITIONS AND OPPORTUNITIES

The characteristics of a particular job include physical and psychological working conditions, income and income potential, advancement opportunities, job status, and chances for self-actualization.

Working conditions. Working conditions, such as having a private office or personal secretary, being indoors or outdoors, and enjoying safety, cleanliness, and comfort, inevitably require consideration in career planning.

The forest ranger spends much time alone; the skilled automobile mechanic gets greasy; the beautician handles chemicals; the riveter works under noisy conditions (as does the nursery-school teacher); the stockbroker wears a business suit and sits in an office all day.

Literally hundreds of potential factors, ranging from the hours, the shift, and the travel requirements to the dirt, the temperature, and the smells, determine working conditions.

*"It's not so much the money that interests me, as
the chance to do the kind of work I'm fitted for."*

FIGURE 21–6.   Courtesy of Ed Fisher.

Income and income potential.   Some people have a great need for money
or the security of a good retirement plan and other benefits, but others are more
easily satisfied. One element of career planning is the evaluation of how the individual's needs would be satisfied by his probable income in certain fields.

Advancement opportunities.   Advancement can come by staying within a
career field or by changing to a related career field, by remaining with a company
or by moving to a different job. One plumber opens a plumbing-equipment shop
and becomes a businessman; then he sells his business and is appointed vice-
president of a firm that manufactures plumbing equipment. Another plumber
becomes increasingly successful, takes on several helpers, but remains a plumber
himself. Both have advanced.

Certain careers offer only limited advancement. Sometimes a position looks
good at first and offers a fairly good salary, but, after several years, the employee
realizes that he cannot advance and that he would have to take a large salary cut

if he changed jobs. These dead-end jobs are very frustrating, because a look into the future reflects an image of the present.

Social status.   When people are asked to rank jobs according to status, they do so with remarkable consistency (Deeg & Paterson, 1947), and the average rankings today are not much different from those of 30 years ago. One of the main reasons why students attend college is to be able to get a "better" job—that is, a job with better social status as well as higher income.

> Gene Machover had been working as a wholesale milk delivery man for 12 years. Unlike the door-to-door delivery man, who usually carries only two or three bottles at a time, Gene had to haul heavy cases of bottles. Considering his lack of job skills, the pay was good. But two things bothered Gene: (1) his income was remaining fairly constant and promotion was unlikely, since administrative positions were usually given to college graduates; and (2) his back was beginning to bother him. He began to look for a new career field and soon found a position representing a canned-goods producer. His job involved visiting food markets to see that his company's products were well displayed, introducing new products, and taking care of complaints. His initial income dropped by 30%, but Gene anticipated he could make that up over the years. In addition, he proudly listed other advantages: he drove a company car, he didn't have to get up at 4:30 in the morning, he could stay clean all day, and he had no heavy lifting to do. Also, his wife took pride in hanging white shirts on the clothesline instead of his uniform shirts.

Gene improved his working conditions, his advancement opportunities, and his job status, even though his income dropped temporarily. Evidence exists that higher-status positions lead to feelings of greater personal satisfaction (Hoppock, 1935).

Personal growth.   The purpose of career planning is to help the individual achieve satisfaction in his career. If the career choice is appropriate, the person should find the opportunity for personal growth and self-actualization. Work can be very satisfying when the individual is able to use his present talents and develop new ones, when he feels he is doing a good job, when he feels his work is benefiting others and that they appreciate him, when he can express himself through his work, when a challenge exists, and when the nature of the work is felt to reflect his "real" self.

When a person feels he is no longer improving, no longer learning, no longer finding new ways to do things, he begins to mark time. The workday becomes a time to be gotten through as quickly and easily as possible, and important satisfactions come primarily from sources outside work.

A person need not achieve something big in order to feel he is self-actualizing. Consider the following situation.

Bill Brock was a carpenter—perhaps not the most artistic or creative one around but nevertheless a good one. He undertook only what he was capable of doing, he worked every minute for which he was paid, and he cleaned up thoroughly before he left a job. Although the work he did for us was fairly simple, he approached it carefully and did it correctly, even though he had to change the design a careless friend had made for us. At each step he cautiously checked for something he might have overlooked before he went on. When something was not exactly right (a small knothole looking too conspicuous, a shelf fitting too loosely), he would go to any effort necessary to correct the error. And he spent an hour of his own time shopping to match a stain that had been weathered by the sun, so that the old and the new looked as though all had been finished at the same time. He had a six-week waiting list of customers, but he refused to hire an assistant because "I can't trust anybody but me."

No one ever commented on the work he did for us—it was hardly visible to anyone who did not make an effort to view it—but Bill Brock gave personal meaning to the entire project. And it was easy to see that his work was challenging, satisfying, and self-actualizing. Finding satisfaction may be more difficult for a person working on an assembly line or doing any repetitive task than for someone in the professions, the arts, or upper management, but personal growth is still possible.

DOING THE WORK

Just as each individual must define job success for himself, each supervisor and organization have special ideas about what kind of performance they want. Sometimes the job duties are not exactly what is officially called for. Thus, a secretary learns that she is expected to listen attentively as her boss complains about his ungrateful children; a salesman finds that every sale he makes requires a mountain of paperwork; a policeman realizes that he spends more time helping lost children and breaking up fights between husband and wife than in what he had thought was fighting crime. Every job has its official standards for job performance and its unspoken standards.

What makes a person successful on a job? Some of the factors leading to success are fairly obvious: intelligence, education and training, human-relations skills, appropriate personality, proper abilities, and effective career planning.

Personal and emotional stability are also related to job success. The work adjustment of a group of young employed people was found to be higher when their personality adjustment, tested some years earlier, was better (Havighurst, Bowman, Liddle, Matthews, & Pierce, 1962); moreover, anxiety seems to reduce work output (Hanes & Flippo, 1963). Various personality problems will affect job performance. The rigid person, although he might do well under normal conditions, may be unable to function in an unusual situation; an anxious person may communicate his worry to others; a fearful person may be afraid to make a decision.

In the long run, diligent workers receive the rewards. Ironically enough, when they are rewarded for hard work by being promoted to a managerial position, they find themselves working still harder. Professional and managerial personnel have much less free time than plant workers and office clerks (Lehner & Kube, 1964). However, the professional and managerial people enjoy their work more (Hoppock, 1935) and feel they accomplish more and self-actualize more, which may explain their willingness to work longer hours.

The role of the supervisor is more complex than many people realize. First of all, the supervisor must be able to perform many of the functions he supervises. A sales manager should be a reasonably good salesman; a charge nurse should have been a competent floor nurse. The supervisor must also make decisions and accept the blame when he is wrong. He must be able to get along with those whom he supervises and with those who supervise him. In addition, it is his task to communicate the messages of each group in the language of the other. For example, the superintendent of maintenance of a chain of banks may supervise 50 or 60 people, and he must communicate their feelings about their work and explain highly technical maintenance matters to the vice-president, who may know little about maintenance and may have had limited contact with the maintenance crew.

According to one expert (Blum, 1956), supervisors should base their actions on five principles:

1. *Fair evaluation of work.* Supervisors should give appropriate praise and criticism, taking care not to embarrass workers.
2. *Effective delegation of authority.* Supervisors must be able to know what tasks their subordinates can perform satisfactorily. Too many supervisors try to do too much themselves and do not know how to distribute work satisfactorily.
3. *Fair treatment for all.* All employees deserve equal treatment and need to be considered as worthy individuals.
4. *Availability to employees.* Supervisors should be available for employees to call on them and discuss appropriate matters with them.
5. *Employee participation in decision making.* Employees often respond better when they are allowed to participate in decision making, even if they are used in a strictly advisory capacity. If the decision affects the employees, their reactions to the decision are important and their help may be valuable.

Blum also suggests that the supervisor avoid the following: (1) taking advantage of his superior position; (2) pretending he knows things when he does not, especially regarding the tasks at hand; (3) interfering with an employee's work or looking over his shoulder too much; (4) showing favoritism or discrimination; (5) criticizing employees in public; (6) spending too much time and effort on minor details; (7) giving orders that conflict with previous orders or with orders of other supervisors; and (8) giving unnecessary orders (Blum, 1956).

Government and business organizations have learned that employees want to feel like a part of the company and to feel respected, unique, and important. A series of studies conducted 40 years ago showed that industrial production increased when employees felt they were meaningful to the success of the company. Later studies showed that feeling a part of the company did even more to improve production than did financial rewards (Roethlisberger & Dickson, 1939).

These realizations created new problems, as well as increased success, for supervisors. They needed to recognize that financial rewards and various threats are not necessarily effective in improving production or reducing absenteeism. Supervisors today are encouraged to be sensitive to the feelings, the frustrations, and the needs of those they supervise. Although maintaining such sensitivity is not an easy task, it can pay rich rewards.

Being a supervisor carries prestige, opportunity for further advancement, and increased income, as well as more problems and more opportunities for satisfaction and self-actualization. Unfortunately, as many people learn to their dismay, the qualifications of a good supervisor are different from those of a good worker.

GETTING THE INFORMATION

For effective career planning, the student must have information both about himself and about the various vocational fields. Information sources for the latter are readily available, but learning about yourself is much more difficult and gives rise to some interesting problems.

INFORMATION ABOUT THE JOB SEEKER

Learning about yourself is difficult for several reasons: (1) Psychologists can measure some human characteristics with reasonable accuracy, but they have not been so successful in measuring personality attributes such as motivation to succeed on the job or ability to make sound decisions. (2) People often resist accepting their limitations or admitting their inadequacies. (3) People tend to interpret information about themselves in a favorable light. (4) Even when much information is available, it is not always known how this information about the individual relates to vocational fields.

Many colleges provide counseling facilities, where trained personnel can aid you in understanding yourself. In addition, the instructor of this course can probably give you help or can refer you to someone who can. Whether self-evaluation is done through a counseling center or in class, the individual will have to take into account his interests, his aptitudes and previous achievements, and his needs and personality.

FIGURE 21–7. How would you go about gathering information on surveying as a career? Photograph by Lehman J. Pinckney.

INFORMATION ABOUT VOCATIONAL FIELDS

Many publications describe jobs and career fields. The college counselor or public library may have files of occupational information, including books, pamphlets, and even films discussing various careers. These sources give the income potential, educational requirements, advancement opportunities, work description, and other information relevant to specific careers. Much occupational information, however, paints an unduly attractive picture of the specified career and underestimates its disadvantages.

Good sources of occupational information include people currently in the field, people who have recently left that field, and college counselors, who usually have a large fund of information available.

Information regarding job availability can be gathered from the following sources.

Newspaper classified ads. Most newspapers have extensive listings of available jobs. By reading these listings for several months before graduation, the student can gain some insight about the type of position he might like.

Employment agencies. The United States Employment Service has branches in all major cities in the country. The USES makes job arrangements without cost and frequently maintains extensive job listings. Private agencies, however, will charge a fee either to the employer or to the employee. Reputable agencies make this charge only if the person takes the job. Since the better private agencies often get job listings that are not available to the USES, their services are useful.

Government civil service listings. The proportion of city, county, state, and federal government jobs has been increasing steadily over the years. Some of these positions require competitive written examinations, but others do not. Lists of available jobs, job requirements, and examination dates can be obtained through the proper authorities.

Personal contacts. An amazingly large number of jobs are obtained through personal contacts. You hear of a friend who has been promoted, and the company needs to fill his position; your father's old Army friend is assistant manager of a furniture store, and you are interested in retailing and can fulfill the job requirements.

Personal initiative. Sending a direct letter to the personnel director of an organization or making a personal call are very appropriate methods of job hunting.

Preparing for a future career is certainly one of the major purposes of a college education in the United States today. Colleges provide training in skills necessary for jobs and increase understanding and appreciation of others, of ourselves, and of the world around us—all of which may indirectly affect future job performance. Careers can be planned haphazardly, they can result from a string of accidents, or they can be planned in a thoughtful, organized way. The characteristics of both the individual and the career field must be considered in such planning.

SUMMARY OF IMPORTANT IDEAS

1. Except for housewives, the disabled, and the retired, almost all adults work for financial return.

2. Choice of a career and subsequent job success and satisfaction are highly significant in many ways.

3. Job success and job satisfaction are important to the adequacy of the self-concept and the enjoyment of life.

4. Students and others often lack the necessary information and understanding for career planning.

5. For an effective career plan, the individual should be able to evaluate his interests, needs, values, personality, and abilities. He should also be aware of how his educational level, age, health, and other characteristics affect his career potential.

6. The individual planning his career also needs to be informed about the characteristics of the job and of the job market.

7. Job fields differ in their requirements and in their opportunities for advancement.

8. Vocational selection necessitates an awareness of the day-to-day demands of the job (that is, the job characteristics) as well as such factors as income and fringe benefits, working conditions, advancement opportunities, and the opportunity for satisfaction and personal growth.

9. Career plans should carefully consider the individual's temperament and personality needs. Finding a job with challenge and the opportunity for self-expression and personal responsibility is often important.

10. Job success is defined differently by different people. For some, supervisory responsibility is a sign of success, but supervision requires capabilities often not demanded for the job being supervised.

11. Numerous sources of information are available regarding jobs: booklets, people in the field, college instructors, occupational-information files, and films. The student seeking a job who wishes to know more about himself can receive testing, counseling, and help with self-evaluation through the college counseling office or a comparable facility elsewhere.

22 Producing Change through Interventions

People are always trying to intervene in the affairs of others in order to produce change. These planned interventions range from trying through logical argument to get your friend to quit smoking to using psychotherapy with the mentally disturbed. The success of these methods is variable. We also attempt to change ourselves in a variety of ways. In every chapter of this book, we have discussed human behavior, and virtually every kind of human behavior is susceptible to planned change. We intervene in learning situations (schools, colleges), in sensing and perceiving (eyeglasses), with children (punishment, reward), teenagers (threats, bribes), with adults, in marriage (counseling), in education (teaching), in work (hiring, training), in values (television commercials, political campaigns), in religion (missionary programs), and on and on. In this chapter we will focus on interventions by oneself and by others to produce changes in mood and emotionality.

It has been claimed that the only certainties in life are death and taxes. Add another one: change. You change, others change, society changes, the environment changes, the world changes. Some of these changes are planned, and sometimes planned changes work. Many changes are not planned or are not what was expected when the plans were begun. A very stimulating book appeared in 1970 that caught the imaginations of many people. Entitled *Future Shock* (Toffler, 1970), the book suggested that changes were occurring too rapidly for people to adjust. These changes involve not only technology but also social relationships, the organization of business and government, and the outcomes of science (for example, increasingly long life, communication systems).

FIGURE 22-1.   Changes in styles come very quickly; so do changes in technology. Consider the stylistic and technological changes that have taken place in architecture since this building was constructed. Photograph by P. C. Peri.

Americans seem to be constantly in the process of changing everything — our houses, our spouses, our jobs, our furniture, our clothes, and our opinions. Foreign observers sometimes claim that we make a virtue of change, whether it improves things or not. Last year's exciting social cause is this year's dying fad and will be next year's ancient history. Try to recall the most exciting social issue of three years ago — the one change that you felt this nation could not exist without making.

Social causes are not the only circumstances that call for change. In recent years more emphasis has been placed on changing the individual himself so that he can feel more at home in the world, can relate more effectively to himself and to others, and can be himself and make more of his abilities (that is, self-actualize). Resources for such change range from a bottle of beer to long-term psychotherapy.

PRODUCING CHANGE THROUGH CHEMISTRY

When you hurt, physically or emotionally, it is simpler to take something in than to work something out. An aspirin, a tranquilizer, a couple of slugs of bourbon or a bottle of wine, a joint, some acid, hard drugs — all have the same purpose: they change your mood. The mood changer you choose is a function of your age, your income, and your attitudes regarding the law, the "system," the contemporary scene, and what you believe of what you read.

"I've quit smoking."

FIGURE 22-2. Courtesy of Ed Fisher.

ALCOHOL

Alcohol can be consumed in moderation with no permanent damage, although it can cause temporary loss of judgment, memory, self-criticism, awareness of environment (Block, 1970), and inhibitions (all very hazardous to automobile drivers). After sufficient time has elapsed, the alcohol is absorbed into the body, and normal behavior will resume. Since alcohol does stimulate the gastric juices, it is often used before meals both to increase hunger and to reduce the discomfort of some social interactions (Block, 1970).

Drinking is traditionally a symbol of the adult world and is forbidden to children and adolescents. The teenager who takes a beer or a glass of wine is also partaking of a symbol of the society into which he is soon going to enter. His self-concept may be bolstered by the changing picture of himself. Heavy drinkers in college were found to be less ambitious, less effective in planning and organizing, and less certain of their goals (Kukuk, 1960). Whether liquor was cause or effect, however, was not known.

Problem drinkers are more anxious and depressed than nonproblem drinkers. After a few drinks, their depression and anxiety leave, which may explain why they use alcohol as much as they do. However, these unpleasant feelings return if drinking becomes heavy (Williams, 1966). And persistent heavy drinking leads not only to difficulty in maintaining jobs and friends but also to cirrhosis of the liver and the possibility of alcoholism (Block, 1970).

"One drink is too many and one hundred is not enough." This expression, a basic assumption of the members of Alcoholics Anonymous, states the major problem of the true **alcoholic** (many very heavy drinkers are not alcoholics). Once he begins, the alcoholic cannot stop, and he finds it increasingly difficult to maintain effective behavior. Even after the initial problem that led to his alcoholism has disappeared, the history of heavy drinking and the probable loss of jobs, friends, money, and self-respect become major problems in themselves.

Whether alcoholism is a disease and should be treated medically, or whether it is the result of faulty social learning and inadequate relationships and should be treated with social and psychological techniques is not fully clear. Perhaps both aspects enter in, and perhaps both kinds of interventions are useful.

DRUGS

A **drug** is, very simply, any substance used as a medicine. Both the young and their parents can, with justification, accuse each other of using—and often abusing—drugs. The parents do so through diet pills, an amazing variety of headache and cold pills, tranquilizers, and—with a very slight stretch of the definition—alcohol, all of which affect mood and judgment. The young are more probably taking marijuana, other more powerful psychedelic drugs, or hard drugs. Although the most publicized concern is with the legal, moral, and health hazards of the illegal drugs, there is good reason to believe that middle-class, middle-aged drug users are also doing equal—perhaps greater—damage to themselves and society through their increasing dependency on pills and liquor. (Incidentally, I have omitted any discussion of tobacco.)

The history of drug use dates back at least 4000 years (Blum & Associates, 1969). (I will now restrict the term *drug* to such mood-changing substances as marijuana, heroin, opium, and so forth, unless otherwise indicated.) And drug usage is extensive throughout the world. According to California psychiatrist Joel Fort (in *Playboy*, February 1970, pp. 53–74), the World Health Organization estimates that there are 250 million marijuana users in the world, with roughly 5–8% of them in the United States. A 1972 government report estimated that between 15 and 20 million Americans had tried marijuana.

Numerous hallucinatory drugs are available on college campuses, but those eliciting the most controversy have been marijuana and lysergic acid diethylamide (LSD-25). More recently student attention has turned to hashish and a variety of other psychedelic drugs, such as peyote and THC, a derivative of marijuana. Initially drug users were relatively rare on campus, but increasing numbers began to "turn on." Some campus estimates and surveys have set the percentage of drug users as high as 40–50%. Usage among students at some high schools is believed to be equally high.

LSD. Those who take LSD experience strange, usually exciting, and occasionally terrifying perceptions and feelings. They claim to feel "at one with mankind" and "wish nothing but peace and brotherhood." Ordinary stimuli take on new and deeply significant meanings: "That apple might look like an ordinary apple to you, but to me it was the reddest, the sweetest, the loveliest apple I had ever tasted." Or, "The flower was reaching out to me, saying something to me." Obviously LSD affects the brain chemistry, although the particular mechanism is not fully understood.

Since legal sanctions were quickly applied to the sale, purchase, possession, and use of LSD, good research became difficult to accomplish. Nonetheless, over the years a few studies were conducted and reported. Two studies involving human subjects showed the possibility of temporary reduction of abilities involving visual perception and spatial orientation, as well as temporary reduction of abstract abilities. No generalized brain damage was shown. The investigators have emphasized that their research is only preliminary and that much more work will have to be done before they can draw more than highly tentative conclusions (McGlothlin, Arnold, & Freedman, 1969).

Whatever the research eventually establishes, some LSD users have had "bad trips," and a few have ended up in mental hospitals, usually for brief periods of time. Some individuals have committed acts of violence against themselves and others while under the influence of the drug. The use of LSD—and its publicity—has tapered off. Some of the reduction in LSD trips stems from the strict laws and severe punishments involved, but the fear of genetic damage is probably a more important factor.

Marijuana.   Marijuana produces much milder effects than any of the other drugs, and its potential for long-term harm has become a medical controversy. The American Medical Association and many other medical, legal, and law-enforcement groups have strongly condemned its consumption. But an AMA committee, although attacking its use, also attacked the penalties for violation of the marijuana laws as "harsh and unrealistic" (*Los Angeles Times,* June 20, 1968). In 1972 voters in California defeated a proposition to legalize the use of marijuana. Nonetheless, the measure was supported by one-third of the voters.

The issue of whether marijuana should be legalized—or at the very least whether the legal penalties for using it should be eliminated or reduced—hinges on several issues.

First, does marijuana produce dependency or addiction? It undoubtedly leads to psychological dependence, in that users come to like the mood that "pot" produces and seek opportunities to repeat the experience. Heavy users experience mild irritability when they stop using marijuana, but very few Americans are heavy users. It is not known whether withdrawal from marijuana is as difficult as it is from cigarettes or, for that matter, from frequent consumption of coffee. Two experts in the field, one a psychologist and the other a physician, state that "no physiologically addictive qualities" have been found in marijuana and that "no long-term physical effects of marijuana use have been demonstrated in this country, although more current studies are needed before this issue can be resolved. . ." (McGlothlin & West, 1968).

Second, does marijuana lead to crime, inappropriate behavior, or use of hard drugs? Of course, since the use of marijuana is itself a crime, marijuana leads to crime by definition. If we are talking about other crimes, the evidence is uncertain —studies have shown both positive and negative answers. Similar disagreements are found regarding the ability of marijuana to increase sexual desires and sex behavior; some investigators agree that marijuana use does increase sexual desire, but others state that use of marijuana reduces sexual appetites. Even the possibility that marijuana leads to taking other drugs, especially hard drugs, is not confirmed. It appears that marijuana users are more likely to investigate other psychedelic drugs than to move on to hard drugs.

Third, does marijuana improve creativity? This claim is also far from proven. Stranz (1971) reported the case of a student who was highly competent at composing modern music. Under the influence of marijuana, he composed an entire symphony that he knew was the best thing he had ever done—until the drug effects wore off, and he realized that his work was ridiculous.

Personality and attitude differences between users and nonusers of drugs do exist. Users have been found to be more insecure, more curious, less fearful about losing control, and more dissatisfied with themselves (Brehm & Back, 1968). Another study found drug users more involved in protests, more likely to read underground newspapers, more opposed to the administration in Washington, and more dissatisfied with the educational system and with their own educations (Suchman, 1968).

Good research into the long-range effects of marijuana on those who have recently begun to take it is not available. However, observations do suggest certain personality changes. Marijuana users appear more passive, more likely to turn inward, and less likely to be strongly motivated to achieve. Other changes include "apathy, loss of effectiveness, and diminished capacity or willingness to carry out complex long-term plans, endure frustration, concentrate for long periods, follow routines, or successfully master new material. Verbal facility is often impaired. . . . Such individuals exhibit greater introversion, become totally involved with the present at the expense of future goals, and demonstrate a strong tendency toward regressive, child-like magical thinking" (McGlothlin & West, 1968).

One study of adults who had used marijuana for several years obtained the following results. Of the 32 subjects, 28 stated that their driving competence was impaired due to perceptual distortion, speed distortion, slower reaction time, less alertness, and poorer judgment. Only 7 of the 32 reported long-term effects; 6 of these felt the effects were positive, but the seventh felt they were mixed (McGlothlin & West, 1968).

Another, very carefully conducted, research carried out in the laboratory showed that one-time use of marijuana probably causes some loss of ability on simple tests for nonusers, but regular users show virtually no intellectual or psychomotor change. The setting in which marijuana is taken, along with the user's attitudes and expectations, is probably a major determinant of the user's reactions. Both psychological and pharmacological influences of marijuana contribute to its effects on performance and on organic change (Weil, Zinberg, & Nelson, 1968).

In the past the use of marijuana and similar drugs has been associated primarily with low-income, unemployed persons. Today, however, users are largely young people, primarily from the middle class. Thousands of students have been arrested and many convicted on misdemeanor and felony charges as a result. This situation has intensified the resentment between the police and young people. Also, since those taking marijuana and other psychedelic drugs are, to a large extent, intelligent and critical students, much of the antidrug propaganda originating with the government, law-enforcement agencies, and some health authorities has been called into question. These sources have made enough inaccurate statements that many students reject anything they say. In time, a somewhat more honest and trusting climate may emerge, but suspicions are still widespread.

Even when a Commission established by President Nixon suggested major modifications in the laws governing marijuana, the President and many other decision makers refused to pay attention.

Drug addiction. Drug addiction, like alcoholism, is an immense national problem. Although estimates of the number of **drug addicts** in the United States and Canada are probably not accurate, it is safe to claim that hundreds of thousands of people of all ages are "hooked" on drugs.

Even more than alcohol, some narcotics create an extreme craving that can be satisfied only by more narcotics. Drugs, like alcohol, temporarily produce a wonderful feeling of well-being, but the same stressful world is there when the drug wears off. The world seems so much more pleasant to the person under the influence of drugs that the desire to escape the real world plus the habit-forming effects of the drug motivate continued use.

Often a person insists that he will have no trouble kicking the drug habit when he is ready, but the evidence does not bear this out. Those individuals who become addicted to narcotics find it unbelievably difficult to overcome their obsessive desire for more. Since most addicts do not have the funds to pay the high prices demanded by drug peddlers, they often turn to crime and prostitution for the money needed to satisfy their habits.

Treatment for both alcoholics and drug addicts has included psychotherapy, medication in a hospital setting, vocational rehabilitation, and membership in such organizations as Alcoholics Anonymous, Addicts Anonymous, and Synanon. Alcoholics seem more amenable to treatment than addicts, and Alcoholics Anonymous, with hundreds of chapters around the country, has had conspicuous success in helping alcoholics remain sober. AA's program includes social activities, regular meetings with explanations from members about how the organization has helped them remain sober, and—as one member phrased it—"a willingness to sit up all night and hold the hand of any member who has either had too much or thinks he will." Synanon provides large houses (the original one is in Santa Monica, California) where narcotic addicts and others live together in a relatively normal social setting and try to help one another overcome their addictions.

OTHER SOURCES OF CHANGE

Do you need to ingest chemicals to get high? Or do you have the power within you to make yourself high without chemicals? Recent answers to these questions would take us in two directions: first, to alpha-wave feedback and related kinds of input, and, second, to meditation.

Alpha-wave feedback consists of tuning in to your own brain waves. By adjusting an electronic apparatus to synchronize with your alpha waves (one of the many kinds of electrical waves sent off by the brain), you can listen to your alpha rhythms. Some persons report that the result is very similar to that of the more effective kinds of marijuana, but apparently without any danger. Eventually people become able to control their own brain waves, and they find this experience—with the feedback—very pleasurable (Kamiya, 1969).

People who are accustomed to meditation are also better able to influence their brain waves (Kamiya, 1969). There is no longer any doubt that individuals can affect their own body physiology through transcendental meditation (Wallace, 1970). More important, this phenomenon, which is probably similar to the practices of Zen monks, can be accomplished—after some training—with very little effort. Transcendental meditation is apparently highly relaxing, provides great satisfactions, permits people to feel they are "at one with themselves," and seems to have no possible harmful side effects. A Kansas physician reported that a yogi proved he could stop his heart for 17 seconds without passing out—a remarkable performance. The same physician, at the famous Menninger Clinic, has participated in helping people change the temperature of their own hands (which has medical value for certain conditions) merely by concentration (reported in *San Francisco Chronicle,* November 1, 1971, p. 4).

PRODUCING CHANGE THROUGH PROFESSIONAL HELP

The understatement of all time is "But nobody's perfect." Each of us reaches the point at which help from a professional source could enable us to cope more effectively with our life situation. Some individuals seek help only when their emotional distress is extreme or when neurosis or psychosis becomes so disabling that they are virtually required to look for help (see Chapter 10). Many others request attention well before their plight calls for drastic measures. And, increasingly, individuals with no particularly pressing problems are participating in programs that permit them to better understand themselves and their relationships with others.

Help for the troubled ranges from tranquilizers to psychotherapy to hospitalization. Sometimes psychological troubles are so closely related to social difficulties that environmental changes must occur before psychological progress is possible. A woman psychiatrist told me the following story.

"A nine-year-old boy was referred to me because he was unable to stay awake in class, and his teacher felt that psychological problems involving an absent father, a working mother, and five children living in poverty could be helped by seeing me. After three or four therapy sessions, I learned that the cause was obvious: rats! This child slept on the floor in a rat-infested tenement. He slept — or rather tried to sleep — on the floor because his mother used one small cot, and his three sisters slept on the one bed in the apartment. The boy was frightened of the rats that came sniffing around, threatening to bite him. As a psychiatrist I am accustomed to helping children who dream of rats, who fantasize rats, who talk about make-believe rats, who think they are like rats. But *real rats*!

"I called the city public-health department, only to learn that the apartment was owned by a member of the city council. After considerable pressure, county welfare gave another bed to the family, and ten weeks later the city required that a rat exterminator work on the building (but not on any of the surrounding buildings, some of which were also owned by the city councilman). As a result of the excitement and of the pressure of one young man in the city health department, one person found a happy ending — the boy now has a bed. However, my friend in the health department was transferred to another department where he would not have any contact with the public, and his replacement was notified to ignore any future reports I might make."

This psychiatrist almost made a common mistake in working with the child — that of assuming that all problems have a psychological basis. The opposite difficulty is also common — that of assuming that a person's troubles result from the stress of the immediate situation. Most problems probably stem from a combination of the two factors.

Producing change in someone else — even if he seems to want the change — is difficult. When a person seeks help for an emotional problem, he is trying to unlearn attitudes and feelings that took years to learn. These attitudes form part of his self-concept, are built into his defense mechanisms, and have greatly influenced his internalized values and social relationships. Thus, although a brief period of psychological help may make a person feel better and behave more effectively, any deep-seated problem may necessitate longer treatment. Fortunately, the improvement of day-to-day behavior through psychological methods does not always require a long time.

ENCOUNTERING THE SELF THROUGH GROUP ENCOUNTERS

The terms vary: encounter group, T group, sensitivity training, parent-effectiveness training. The process varies: some groups become very intense and encourage strong emotional displays, whereas others remain much more at the level of a discussion group; some are directed at family interactions, but others attempt to uncover deep personal feelings; some appear to encourage great freedom of expression, including sexual expression, whereas others are oriented toward dealing with the world as it is. The leaders vary: some are professional psychologists, psychiatrists, social workers, or clergymen, with years of training and experience; others have undertaken only a brief training course under a self-designated master.

But they share some common characteristics. First, they are all small (from 8 to 18 members) and relatively unstructured; the members can select their own goals and their own directions. Second, the leader's responsibility is to encourage the expression of both feelings and thoughts in the members (Rogers, 1967). Third, in this setting of little external structure and great personal freedom, the individual feels sufficiently comfortable to stop being defensive and to relate easily to others; his relationships will be based on honest feelings and personal encounters, rather than on the games and manipulation so common in many human relationships (Rogers, 1967).

Through such group encounter, with the members serving as semitherapists for one another and with the leader available to help or, as often stated, to facilitate, the members become better able to relate to one another and, subsequently, to people in general; they come to know themselves better and accept themselves for what they are and what they wish to be. These sessions are not for the emotionally disturbed—they are for people who are basically normal and adequate but wish to live more fully and enjoyably.

Through the acceptance and support of the group members, individuals become able to expose themselves—their uncertainties and fears and their feelings of guilt and inadequacy. Slowly their self-acceptance increases, although often only after great emotional anguish and, not infrequently, some shouting, arguing, and crying. These are encounters.

As you might imagine, encounter groups have their hazards. The most serious danger is that the experience can be very upsetting, and an individual who has been using defense mechanisms to deal reasonably successfully with his problems might have his "crutches" destroyed, which can result in much more serious symptoms. Group leaders are often unable to deal adequately with this problem, and what begins as a relatively harmless self-exploration can develop into a neurotic or even psychotic episode. Since people often seek out encounter groups in order to achieve a psychotherapeutic relationship, some participants are likely to have difficulties that are too much for such a group to handle.

In addition, there are problems of confidentiality—imagine coming home after an especially exhilarating session and not being able to tell anyone what happened, who said what, or who did what. Also, the group leaders are not always skilled enough to understand some of the dynamics of what is going on, and the group members are not always gentle with one another. Even well-trained psychotherapists often make errors, and many group leaders are minimally trained and lack supervised experience. Also, group leaders or members, carried away either by the excitement of the situation or by their own personal needs, may provoke fights, outbursts of temper or tears, or great displays of sexual and affectionate behavior. When skillfully used, these devices can lead to real depth of understanding, but they may have unhappy consequences when abused (Lakin, 1969). Another consideration arises from operant-learning theory. We know that behavior that is reinforced is more likely to be repeated. When group members shout or cry or talk about guilt-causing experiences, they are so rewarded and reinforced that they may try to outdo one another in admitting their guilt — and maybe even invent guilt that did not exist before.

Thousands — perhaps hundreds of thousands — of people have now participated in various kinds of encounter groups. The popularity of the groups and the feelings by most of the participants that they are valuable, along with the support of many highly competent psychologists and other professionals, suggest that — given appropriate settings — this form of psychotherapy is extremely useful. Nonetheless, as with any deeply personal relationship, they are not without hazards.

CRISIS INTERVENTION

Some sources of stress are largely situational. That is, a particular event or series of events produces a very high level of stress and may precipitate serious emotional disturbances unless handled immediately. Once the individual is gotten through the stressful period, he can function without help. Examples of such crises are the loss of a loved one through death, an impending divorce, serious illness in the family, major financial losses or a possible loss of job, or a vitally important decision or examination or task that is forthcoming.

To help alleviate these kinds of stress, crisis-intervention centers have been established around the country. A person with a problem can walk in or telephone in and receive immediate help, either from a professional or from a trained non-professional. Perhaps your campus has a *hot line,* which you can call to talk with someone about the stress you are living under. These hot lines become especially busy during final-exam periods.

The suicide-prevention centers established during the latter part of the 1960s were the forerunners of the crisis-intervention centers and hot lines. Suicide attempts are often perceived as a cry for help — and the centers have been set up to answer that call (Farberow & Shneidman, 1961). Often they receive calls from lonely and depressed people who are not suicidal; other calls come from drug users looking for a place to crash. Since anonymity is permitted by virtue of the telephone, these centers receive calls from people who do not wish to expose themselves to medical or legal authorities.

According to folklore, people who threaten suicide never actually kill themselves. This belief is completely untrue. Suicides, which rank tenth among causes of death in the United States and third among those of student age (Dublin, 1967), are often committed by exactly those people who have threatened to kill themselves.

FIGURE 22–3.   Suicide is the third-highest cause of death among those of student age. Photograph by Lehman J. Pinckney.

The person who attempts suicide is under great stress and may be emotionally disturbed. However, many, and perhaps most, attempts result from crises and will not be repeated if the crisis can be handled. The question is whether our society has the willingness to expand its time and money resources in trying to find ways to reduce these crises (for example, among lonely elderly men who see no future for themselves, or recent widows who have depended on their husbands, or students who feel the world holds no meaning for them).

1. *What do you think is the main reason why a person kills himself?*
   Serious physical illness 9%
   Insanity/mental illness 33%
   Psychological stress 26%
   Financial troubles 5%
   Troubles in love 5%
   Other/Don't know 22%

2. *How do you feel about persons who threaten to kill themselves but don't appear serious?*
   Angry 6%
   They should be serious or not act that way. 5%
   They need professional help. 17%
   They need to be punished. 1%
   They are looking for attention. 32%
   They are emotionally ill. 14%
   Sympathetic 15%
   Other/Don't know 10%

3. *If you knew someone was seriously considering suicide, whom would you contact for help?*
   Police 32%
   Clergy 18%
   Physician/Psychiatrist/Suicide-prevention center 20%
   Friend 5%
   Relative 16%
   Other/Don't know 9%

FIGURE 22–4. Responses of 434 residents of Los Angeles County to questions concerning suicide. The responses were roughly equally divided among black, Japanese, Mexican, and white Americans (Kalish & Reynolds, unpublished data).

PSYCHOTHERAPY

Psychotherapy is the process through which a person trained in psychological treatment techniques applies these techniques, using personal consultation, to help people learn to handle their problems more effectively. Psychotherapy is not limited to emotionally disturbed individuals but is frequently undertaken by normal people who feel that such help can be valuable to them. Although most psychotherapy involves one therapist and one client or patient, group psychotherapy has been shown to be effective also.

There are many theories of psychotherapy, and therapists argue over which is best. However, the different approaches have much in common:

1. Each theory involves a therapist who shows interest, trust, and respect for the client. The therapist may or may not offer obvious encouragement, but the

mere fact that he listens carefully and responds with understanding and patience is reassuring.

2. Each theory includes the opportunity for the client to express his feelings. In the therapy situation the client can usually discuss his most personal fears, desires, and hates and his most embarrassing and guilt-producing behaviors and fantasies. Once they are expressed by the client and accepted by the therapist, the client often feels less anxious, and his self-concept achieves a new sense of adequacy. We cannot express all these feelings to those we love or to a casual stranger, but we can reveal them to a person who shows he is interested in us and respects us.

3. Each theory encourages the client to increase his insight into his own feelings and motives. Although insight itself is no guarantee of an improved self-concept, insight in combination with the opportunity for self-expression and a healthy client-therapist relationship seems helpful. If the therapist tries to force the client to understand himself too quickly, the client may quit therapy. Insight must come gradually.

4. Each theory attempts to teach new forms of behavior, new attitudes, and new self-concepts, which are aimed at enabling the person to function more effectively in society and to recognize himself as an adequate and worthwhile individual.

The individual schools of therapy, in spite of sharing many basic characteristics, also differ in many respects. Some emphasize the need for lengthy treatment, and others try to provide treatment in a brief period of time. Some require that the therapist keep his own values divorced from his therapy, but others allow the therapist to include his values. Some regard the individual as a "patient" who needs to be "cured," and some regard him as a "client" who will effect his own improvement. Some insist that the person in therapy remain responsible for the pacing and the direction of the therapy; others give the therapist more freedom to control the sessions. Some include the use of psychological tests, and others reject these devices. Some assume that sex is usually the source of difficulty, but others emphasize the self-concept, personal identity and meaning, or inappropriate social learning.

More recently a form of psychotherapy has been developed that is based on operant-learning principles and the use of reinforcement. Called **behavior modification,** this approach has produced a storm of controversy. Behavior-modification therapists try to get the people they work with to relax their muscles as they think about matters that distress them. They begin with the least distressing stimuli related to the problem under attack, and the client dwells on this stimulus until he can be relaxed at the same time as he imagines the stimulus to be present —until it no longer produces anxiety and tension. Then the therapist goes on to a slightly more disturbing stimulus and repeats the process. This sequence is continued until the therapist has enabled the client to relax even while thinking about matters that were extremely upsetting on previous occasions. According to some criteria, this form of therapy has been shown by research to be more effective than the more traditional psychotherapeutic approaches (Eysenck, 1967). However, much more evidence needs to be accumulated before a final judgment is possible.

Another important aspect of behavior therapy is the use of reinforcement for appropriate behavior. Whenever the client does or says something that suggests he is behaving more effectively, the therapist rewards him often only with a smile or a word of approval—according to operant-learning techniques. Although a smile may not sound like much of a reward, approval by those we respect is very meaningful, and people respond to these slight reinforcements more readily than they often realize themselves. Think of the times when you watched a friend, a teacher, or an employer for the slightest sign of approval or disapproval; recall the hours that you have spent attempting to interpret a few words, a meaningful glance, or a pat on the arm from a person of the opposite sex whom you liked very much.

As the therapist reinforces certain statements and acts, he ignores others. The client repeats the reinforced statements more frequently and performs the reinforced acts more frequently. Eventually he learns to stop behaving inappropriately and to behave in ways that will satisfy growth needs. Behavior therapists are most concerned with the change of ongoing behavior and assume that underlying feelings will also change when the new forms of behavior are found to be more effective than the old. You may have noticed that there is little emphasis on insight, although the other three approaches held in common by most therapies are used.

Evidence on the effectiveness of behavior therapy is far from complete. Much research still needs to be done before anyone can decide whether behavior therapy is really better than the more traditional approaches, whether it really uses the same principles but without realizing it, or whether it works best only for those who feel more comfortable with it. In any event, its emphasis on producing fairly rapid change in behavior through rewards and reinforcement is compatible with community mental-health programs, whose main purpose is getting people to function effectively in the community as quickly as possible.

THE MENTAL-HEALTH MOVEMENT

The awareness that the community shares a responsibility for mental-health care and treatment is relatively recent. Up until 175 years ago, mental patients and others unable to care for themselves were housed under conditions as bad as those in the worst prisons of the time. At various periods in history they have been tortured and killed for being witches and helpers of the devil. Conditions in mental hospitals in the United States have slowly become better over the years, but even today many are overcrowded and understaffed.

Recent criticisms of mental hospitals have gone beyond their physical conditions. Many mental-health experts feel that the "hospital routine tends to reinforce (submissive) behavior and dependence. . ." (Bandura, 1967). These experts maintain that mental hospitals must be more than custodial institutions where patients can avoid some of the stresses of the community; the hospitals should prepare patients for a return to the community.

Part of this preparation for community living would involve reducing the hospital atmosphere in mental institutions. When you ask a physician to cure your stomach-ache, you usually follow his advice without much questioning, take the prescribed medicines, and assume you will feel better as a result. However, emotional problems do not readily respond to advice and medication. For functional mental disorders, the person in treatment needs to become personally active in the treatment process. Psychologists have advised that all treatment programs for mental disturbance, including hospitalization, offer the patient the opportunity to make decisions and to take responsibility for matters involving daily routine, personal freedom, and long-range plans. When they are placed under strict routines with no decision-making opportunities, mental patients realize that they are looked on as mentally ill and incapable of caring for themselves. And, "if people are expected to act crazy, most of them will" (Smith, 1968).

Much disturbed behavior results from learning, particularly learning aimed at avoiding stress and the anxiety that stress produces. If this is the case—and there are many who would disagree—then the way to alleviate the disturbed behavior is to arrange unlearning, relearning, and new learning opportunities. As one prominent psychologist has put it, "the institution developed to deal with these conditions may well be educational in nature" (Albee, 1968). Perhaps in the future psychological disorders will be treated in "learning centers" rather than hospitals or clinics, and those coming for help will not be looked on as patients who must receive help but as "responsible people who participate actively in developing their own potentialities" (Bandura, 1967).

Another trend in mental-health care is to move the caretakers out of the institutions or private offices and into the community. Personal problems do not occur in a vacuum—they occur in a social setting. The individual lives in a particular setting; therefore he must change in that setting. By bringing the treatment into the local community, the mental-health workers can become more familiar with what is actually going on (perhaps the child psychiatrist cited on page 437 would not have been so surprised by "real rats" had she spent more time in the child's community). Also, transportation difficulties are reduced, and the residents are more likely to see the mental-health center as their own; the center that they have to travel many miles to reach and that is housed in an expensive office may appear totally foreign to them.

Transferring mental-health facilities into the community would also:

—move patients away from old factory-like mental hospitals in isolated areas
    to smaller, community-based facilities;
—give patients as much freedom as possible to come and go;
—make it easier to enter hospitals voluntarily and to leave voluntarily;
—reduce the waiting time before treatment is available; and
—integrate the services for patients living in the facilities with services for
    outpatients (Smith, 1968).

Another type of arrangement provides institutional care on a part-time basis.
The patient may spend evenings or weekends in the hospital but work at a regular
job during the day; or, he may live at home but go to a mental-health center during the day (Wechsler, 1960).

Major problems still exist. First, it is very difficult to get help to all who could
profit from it. Many people will not use the help that is available, and others are
unaware that they can receive help or are unaware that they need help. Also,
mental-health facilities are not available in all communities.

Second, new ways of staffing the mental-health facilities are required, since
there are not enough professionals to go around and there is not enough money
to hire them, even if there were. This problem is being handled by hiring people
who have less formal training but whose personal sensitivity and awareness of the
community qualify them as *subprofessionals*. Frequently they are given a special
training course for their jobs. The use of subprofessionals has been accelerated
by the observation that mental patients and others who need help often respond
more successfully to help from people whose backgrounds are similar to their own
than they do to the help of professionals (Rioch, 1966). Thus well-educated
mental patients felt that the psychiatrists and psychologists were the most helpful to them, but less-educated patients stated that aides and fellow patients did the
most for them (Keith-Spiegel & Spiegel, 1967).

Third, the problems that exist in the community or in the family are not
necessarily going to disappear just because the individual has sought mental-
health help. The patient still has to be able to function in the community and with
the family. Involving the whole family in the program seems to be a partial answer, but it is only a beginning (Smith, 1968).

The trends in mental-health treatment have been summarized as follows:
(1) from emphasis on the person to emphasis on the person-in-the-environment;
(2) from facilities offering partial services to facilities offering comprehensive
services; (3) from complete domination by professionals to much involvement by
subprofessionals; (4) from simple custody to correction of the problem to prevention of the problem to enhancement and enrichment—that is, from doing nothing
to satisfying deficiency motives to satisfying growth motives (Arkoff, 1968).

DOES IT WORK?

In the final analysis, the cogent question is *does it work?* Does the therapy help? Do the community centers really improve things? Do suicide-prevention centers prevent suicide? These are among the most difficult and most fascinating questions in psychology. First, of course, you have to decide what you mean by *working*. One person may insist that psychotherapy is worthless unless it reduces the crime rate or the number of people in mental hospitals; another would agree that, if psychotherapy makes people feel better, it works. The arguments among psychologists as to whether psychotherapy works and, if so, what kinds work best are among the most heated in the profession.

FIGURE 22–5. Does our educational system work? Photograph by P. C. Peri.

The question "Does it work?" goes beyond psychotherapy. Does our educational system work? Does our family system work? Does college help? Is marriage good? Are American children properly socialized? Is it emotionally healthy to express your feelings? Or—perhaps more to the immediate point—is this book good? Is your course worth it? Should psychology and psychologists be dispensed with?

The answers to these questions can be tested only after you decide the meaning of *work, good, help, healthy,* and *worth.* If you wish to explore further, you will need to continue your study in psychology. You have only begun.

SUMMARY OF IMPORTANT IDEAS

1. People alter their self-concept and their behavior through drinking.

2. Moderate drinking appears to do little long-term harm, but heavy drinking has many unpleasant outcomes.

3. Any medicine is, technically speaking, a drug, but the drugs that are most in the news are those that are illegal and that alter mood and perception.

4. The debate over legalizing marijuana continues. Research on short-term effects of marijuana is now available, but there is none on long-term effects. However, some behavior patterns associated with long-term users include apathy, loss of motivation, and lack of effectiveness.

5. The drug addict, like the alcoholic, has a compulsive craving for his drug. Treatment of addicts and alcoholics is not especially successful.

6. More recent ways to gain the experiences associated with psychedelic drugs are through brain-wave feedback and through meditation.

7. At one time or another most people could use professional psychological help.

8. Encounter groups are very popular and appear to be valuable. However, they also involve serious hazards.

9. Crisis intervention and suicide prevention are attempts to work with persons undergoing immediate stress so that the long-term results will be reduced.

10. Psychotherapy is the process by which a person trained in psychological treatment techniques applies these techniques, using personal consultation, to help other people handle their problems more effectively.

11. Although many psychotherapeutic approaches share common principles, behavior-modification therapy is based on different principles.

12. The mental-health movement has made recent efforts to move from the large institution and the private office into the community, where the help is required.

13. Nonprofessional persons can be trained to provide high-level mental-health services under some circumstances.

14. The ultimate criterion *does it work?* is difficult to test.

Glossary*

Achievement: The present level of competence in performing a particular task.

Achievement need: Motivation to accomplish things well and quickly, to be successful in what is done, to overcome obstacles.

Adaptation: A change in the organism permitting it to cope with the demands of the environment; for example, sensory adaptation is a change in the sensory apparatus that permits it to cope with changes in the environment.

Affective disorders: A group of psychotic reactions characterized by inappropriate emotional response and mood.

Agitated depression: A type of affective disorder in which depression is marked by considerable, often rapid, movement.

Alcoholic: A compulsive drinker; an individual who cannot control his drinking. An alcoholic is *not* the same thing as a heavy drinker.

Alienation: The feeling of being isolated from the general community and from reference groups.

Altruism: Regard and concern for others, especially as opposed to regard and concern for oneself.

Amnesia: Lack of memory under circumstances in which normal forgetting is unlikely.

Anxiety: An unpleasant emotion, similar to fear, marked by a vague feeling that something unpleasant is going to occur in the future. Because of the vagueness of the cause, it is very difficult to overcome anxiety.

Anxiety neurosis: A form of neurosis in which the person is in a constant state of anxiety (*see* Anxiety).

Apathy: A withdrawal from emotional threat by retreating into a position of not caring, although the unconscious feeling may be that of caring very much. Sometimes used as a defense mechanism.

Approach-approach conflict: A conflict in which two positive goals are available, but the selection of one goal eliminates the possibility of selecting the other.

Approach-avoidance conflict: A conflict in which the same goal has both positive and negative features, so that it attracts and repels simultaneously.

Aptitude: The potential to gain competence, assuming that training and experience are available (*see* Achievement).

Attention: The active selection of and emphasis upon one aspect of the environment at a time; the relative limiting of what is responded to.

Auditory: Pertaining to hearing.

Avoidance-avoidance conflict: A conflict in which both alternative goals are repelling, and the individual has to select one or the other.

---

* In devising these definitions, I have relied heavily on *A Comprehensive Dictionary of Psychological and Psychoanalytical Terms*, by Horace B. and Ava C. English, published by Longmans, Green, 1958.

Behavior: The acts an organism performs; anything an organism does.

Behavior modification: Changing behavior through the use of the principles of operant learning.

Belief: An emotional acceptance of an idea or statement upon what the individual considers adequate grounds; the individual has not necessarily examined the bases for his beliefs, but may have accepted them without evaluation.

Biochemistry: The chemical basis for and functioning of plant and animal, including human, life.

Body-image: The image or picture an individual has of his physical appearance and physical body; may include clothing, hair style, deformities, and hidden scars.

Brightness: That quality of visual sensation that arises from the intensity of the light.

Case-history method: An intensive study of a single individual, utilizing a great variety of sources of information, such as school records, vocational evaluations, interviews, medical records, tests, and family history.

Catatonic schizophrenia: A form of schizophrenia marked by frequent apparent stupor; extreme excitement and activity are occasionally exhibited.

Chronic anxiety: An emotional state in which feelings of anxiety are continually present.

Chronic brain syndrome: A condition, frequently psychotic, that results from relatively permanent, largely irreversible damage to brain tissue.

Classical conditioning: A form of learning in which two stimuli are presented close together in time on numerous occasions until the response caused by one stimulus is also elicited by the second stimulus, although the latter originally did not produce this response.

Clinical psychologist: A psychologist who is involved with studying or treating individuals with mental illness or personal-adjustment problems.

Compulsion: That which forces a person to do something or feel or think something against his "will"; may contribute (as a ritual form used to ward off an obsessive thought) to the form of neurosis termed obsessive-compulsive reaction.

Concept formation: The abstraction of a common quality from several stimuli, or the generalization to a common quality from several stimuli; for example, the sky, your friend's eyes, the ink in your fountain pen, and your new sweater all share the common quality of *blue*.

Conflict: A type of stress produced when a person is motivated by two or more needs, in such a fashion that the satisfaction of one need is believed to mean the nonsatisfaction of another need, or that the satisfaction of one need is believed to involve unpleasant consequences.

Conformity: Behavior, including attitudes and judgments, that complies with the demands and expectations of a particular group; the behavior may or may not be consistent with the values of the person conforming.

Control group: A group of subjects, similar in every way possible to another group of subjects *except* that the latter group is treated in some predetermined fashion, so that any differences between the two groups after the experimental treatment can be tentatively assumed to result from the treatment conditions.

Conversion type: A form of hysterical neurosis in which the person displays such bodily symptoms as paralysis or sensory loss (blindness, deafness) without corresponding biochemical changes.

Cross-sectional: In research design, refers to the study of variables at one point in time (*see* Longitudinal).

Defense mechanism: An attitude or other form of behavior which is used by the individual—without his awareness—to maintain the adequacy of his self-concept.

Deficiency motivation: The process of satisfying needs for things the organism lacks. Hunger is a deficiency motive, but the desire (or need) to enjoy food is a growth motive (*see* Growth motivation).

Delusion: A false belief maintained in the face of overwhelming contrary evidence. A person may have the delusion that he is president of the world, that he is a great baseball player, or that his family is stealing all his money. Although these delusions indicate severe personality disturbance, less serious delusions can also occur.

Depersonalization neurosis: The feeling that one is not a person, that one is not alive.

Depressive neurosis: A form of neurosis in which depression is the major symptom.

Derived status: The position one has in the community as reflected from the status or accomplishments of a parent or other relative (*see* Primary status).

Discrimination: (1) In learning, the act of learning to recognize the difference between two stimuli and to respond accordingly; (2) in social psychology, the act of showing preference to one individual or group as opposed to another.

Displaced aggression: Redirected aggression, or hostile action directed away from the real cause of the aggressive or hostile feeling and onto another victim (*see* Scapegoat).

Displacement: The redirection of feelings, often anger or dislike, from the original cause usually to a less harmful person, object, or idea. The implication is that the person is prevented from directing his feelings toward the appropriate object. Occurs without awareness, and is often a defense mechanism.

Dissociative type: A form of hysterical neurosis in which the primary symptom is dissociation, that is, the separation of mental processes so that they cease to have the normal association between idea and emotion.

Distributed practice: Learning spaced out over a period of time, with intervening rest periods or periods of other activities; studying one hour each day for an examination would be an example.

Drug: Any substance used as a medicine. This term is often used in its more limited sense as referring to a narcotic—that is, a drug that affects awareness, decreases pain, or produces a stupor or a coma.

Drug addict: An individual who takes drugs compulsively; he has developed a strong need for a particular drug and may display bodily changes if deprived of it.

Dynamic: A condition implying change, in which a change affecting one aspect of the organism instigates other changes that may affect the initial change; for example, a gradual self-concept change, from submissive to moderately aggressive, will lead to new experiences that, in turn, may affect the direction of change in the self-concept.

Ecology: The study of the interrelationship between organisms and their environments.

Effector organs: The cells and structures with which the organism responds: muscles and glands.

Emotion: A feeling or state of arousal of the organism which stirs it to observable action or to internal change.

Enuresis: Bed-wetting that occurs well beyond the age at which the child can be expected to maintain control; the term can be applied to any uncontrolled act of urinating.

Esteem needs: Needs, as adapted from Abraham Maslow, for an individual to be respected by others and to respect himself.

Ethnic group: A group of individuals sharing a common language, religion, national origin, race, or cultural heritage.

Ethnic-group identification: The feeling of having membership in a particular ethnic group; association and affiliation with an ethnic group.

Experimental method: A research method in psychology and other fields. Implies a systematic approach in which one group of subjects is given one set of conditions and another group of subjects, another set; or in which the conditions are systematically varied to determine the effect of the change.

Exploratory need: The need of an individual, especially an infant or child, to examine his environment.

Extinction: In learning theory, the diminishing and eventual cessation of a response to its stimulus.

Fantasy: (1) An image that occurs as part of the thought process and that is fairly coherent; the image of a dream or daydream; (2) a type of withdrawal through daydreaming; sometimes a defense mechanism. The term may also be applied to a situation in which an individual purposely relives a previous action, rehearses a future action, or attempts some creative activity.

Feedback: A direct report regarding the effect of one's behavior on others or regarding the effectiveness of one's performance.

Forgetting: The inability to recall because of attention lack, disuse, or inability to make associations.

Fraternal twins: Twins, not necessarily similar in appearance and not necessarily of the same sex, resulting from two separately fertilized eggs.

Frustration: The unpleasant emotional state that results when a person's desired goal is blocked; caused by stress.

Fugue or fugue state: A lengthy period of amnesia or lack of recall for past events while previous learning of skills and other aspects of life are remembered. The person may wander from his home and live under another identity.

Functional psychosis: Mental illness caused by stress that exceeds the individual's stress tolerance; caused by environmental stress, as opposed to direct biochemical changes.

General-adaptation syndrome: A theory that physiological changes in the human body in response to stress occur in three stages: alarm reaction, resistance, and exhaustion.

Genetic: Pertaining to, or occurring as the result of, genes. Genes are elements that control many characteristics of the child and are transmitted from parents to child at the time of conception.

Growth motivation: The process of activating behavior as the result of satisfying the need to make use of one's capacities and talents (*see* Deficiency motivation).

Growth spurt: The relatively sudden increase in growth that occurs shortly before puberty.

Guilt: The feeling, giving rise to discomfort or anxiety, that one has violated moral principles.

Guilt society: A culture in which internalized values and conscience provide the major form of social control.

Hallucination: A perception that occurs without relevant stimuli but that is accepted as real.

Hebephrenic schizophrenia: A form of schizophrenia marked by silliness, giggling, and a general return to an earlier and immature condition.

Hereditary: Pertaining to the characteristics or influences that parents transmit biologically to their children at the time of conception.

Hierarchy of needs: As adapted from Abraham Maslow, a ranking of needs in terms of those that demand most immediate satisfaction; that is, the more basic needs are ranked lowest and are placed at the base of the hierarchy. They must be reasonably well satisfied before the individual can turn his attention to the next most basic set of needs.

Homosexual: An individual who prefers sex relationships with members of his own sex rather than with the opposite sex.

Hue: That quality of visual sensation, relating to color, that arises from the frequency of wavelength; the color itself.

Humanistic psychology: A range of approaches to the study of psychology and to the application of psychological principles; humanistic psychology tends to be holistic, man-centered, and approving of the individual himself as having power over his own destiny.

Hypochondriacal neurosis: The neurosis that involves a morbid concern about one's own health.

Hypothesis: A tentative explanation for an event, relationship, or other form of occurrence. Psychologists will frequently test hypotheses by collecting and analyzing relevant data.

Hysterical neurosis: A form of neurosis that is the result of conversion reaction (*see* Conversion reaction)—hysterical blindness, hysterical paralysis. Other meanings of this term are not relevant to this book.

Ideal self: The individual as he would like to be; the self the individual sees as the best "me" possible.

Identical twins: Twins, very similar in appearance and of the same sex, resulting from one fertilized egg.

Identification: Association or affiliation with a group or another person; acceptance as your own of the values and purposes of another person or group. Frequently used, without awareness, as a defense mechanism to improve the self-concept.

Identity: Although there are innumerable meanings for this word, only one is primarily relevant here: the awareness an individual has of himself as a unique individual; of how he relates to the rest of society; and of his place in society and in the world.

Illusion: A mistaken perception (*see* Delusion *and* Hallucination).

In-group: A group whose members have a strong need for association with each other and a strong need to exclude those not of the group.

Inherited predispositions: Tendencies to behave in particular ways or contract particular illnesses that parents transmit genetically to their children at conception.

Insight: (1) The understanding of your own motives and other mental processes; (2) the understanding of some meaning, process, pattern, or use.

Insight learning: The process through which the meaning, significance, pattern, or use of an object or situation becomes clear.

Intellectualization: An attempt to withdraw from the emotional impact of a conflict by approaching a problem in purely intellectual terms; usually a defense mechanism.

Intelligence: The ability to grasp abstract concepts and symbols, to learn and to solve problems, and to cope with new situations.

Internalization: The taking on of the values, attitudes, beliefs, ideas, wishes, and goals of another person as your own; the general cultural values are transmitted from parent to child in this fashion.

Internal senses: The senses *within* the body, for example, the senses of hunger and thirst.

Intolerance of ambiguity: A type of rigidity; an inability to deal with uncertainty; a need for clear-cut explanations.

Intrauterine environment: The environment of the individual within the mother's womb between conception and birth. The degree to which experiences and events in this environment affect later development is not well understood.

Involutional melancholia: A form of affective psychosis involving depression that occurs most commonly to people in their fifties.

Job enrichment: An increase in the variety of demands, tasks, and responsibilities of a job.

Kinesthetic sense: The sense that enables an individual to be aware of his movement through space.

Learning: A process that occurs whenever a relatively permanent change in behavior results from experience.

Level of aspiration: The degree of competence, learning, achievement, and so on, the individual anticipates attaining.

Longitudinal: In research design, refers to the study of variables as they change over a period of time (*see* Cross-sectional).

Loudness: The quality of sound that is determined by the amplitude of the sound wave.

Love needs: Needs, as adapted from Abraham Maslow, to feel the love, the warmth, and the affection of physical and emotional contact with others.

Manic: Pertaining to a condition, often found in the mentally ill, of great excitability and elation.

Manic-depressive psychosis, circular type: A form of affective disorder in which the person is highly excited and elated for a period, then highly depressed for a period; there may be a period of relative normality in between.

Massed practice: Learning that takes place continuously without rest or other occurrences interrupting. Frequently applied to study; cramming for an examination would be an example.

Maturation: Development; particularly those developmental changes that occur relatively inevitably in all normal members of the species provided with a relatively suitable environment. No special learning is required for maturation.

Menopause: The period during which a woman's menstrual cycle becomes irregular and eventually ceases, ending her ability to conceive. It usually occurs during the late forties or early fifties.

Mental illness: Behavior disorder or behavior maladjustment; a breakdown in adjustment that necessitates some form of professional help or hospitalization.

Motivation: The process of setting behavior into action because of a need.

Multiple approach-avoidance conflict: A conflict in which all alternatives include both positive and negative features.

Multiple personality: A form of dissociative reaction (neurosis) in which the individual maintains two or more distinct personalities, each of which appears separately at various times; an extremely rare condition.

Natural childbirth: A process through which a pregnant woman prepares herself, both physically and emotionally, for the birth of her child with minimum dependence upon anesthetics.

Need: A lack of something in the organism which, if present, would increase the satisfaction of the organism. There are numerous ways of classifying needs, including systems by Abraham Maslow and Henry Murray. Satisfying the need may be necessary to maintain existence, to provide stimulation, or to increase satisfactions.

Neonate: The infant between birth and about two or three weeks of age; a newly born infant.

Nervous system: The brain, the spinal cord, and the nerves.

Neurasthenic neurosis: The neurosis that involves feelings of chronic or frequent fatigue and weakness.

Neurosis: A relatively mild personality disturbance that does not incapacitate the individual or necessitate his hospitalization; the neurotic person remains in contact with reality.

Nonverbal communication: The transmission of a message without written or oral words, as through gestures or body movements.

Norm: A standard with which the performance of an individual can be compared. If, on a test of verbal ability, your score is compared to scores obtained by 1,000 entering freshmen, the 1,000 freshmen constitute the norm group.

Nurture: (1) The totality of environmental factors that influence an individual at any point in the life-span; (2) the providing of food, love, and care that permits an individual to develop.

Observational method: A research method for studying behavior; it consists of watching relevant occurrences either in person or with some mechanical aid such as a tape recorder. Controlled observations are carefully recorded in some objective fashion.

Obsession: An idea that seems to haunt a person, usually associated with dread or anxiety; may contribute to the form of neurosis termed obsessive-compulsive reaction.

Obsessive-compulsive-neurosis: The behavior pattern in which *obsessive* feelings elicit *compulsive* behavior, carried to the point of being a neurosis.

Operant learning: The form of learning in which the correct response to a stimulus is gradually selected out from among all potential responses.

Organic: Referring to the body and its anatomical and biochemical makeup, rather than to the surrounding environment, the self-concept, or the personality.

Organic psychosis: Mental illness caused by structural damage to the brain.

Overlearning: Learning in which practice goes beyond the point where the act can be performed with only the required degree of excellence; learning beyond the minimal level of adequacy, but without the implication that unnecessary learning has taken place.

Overprotective: Providing greater care than necessary, usually in reference to an infant or child; implies an unnecessary reduction in the opportunity of the individual to satisfy certain stimulation needs.

Parallel play: The play of very young children; each plays by himself in the presence of the other with only occasional interaction.

Paranoid: Marked by systematic, apparently logical, delusions. The person is often mentally disturbed but able to remain out of the hospital.

Paranoid schizophrenia: A form of schizophrenia characterized by unrealistic thinking, hallucinations, and delusions (especially of grandeur or persecution).

Peer group: A group consisting of one's equals. The term is usually used to refer to others of similar age, although it could also refer to equality of intelligence, competence, or social class.

Percentile: One of 99 scores that divide a group of scores into 100 equal parts. Thus, the student whose score is at the 53%ile (percentile) has received a higher score than 53% of those with whom he is being compared. (It does not mean he answered 53% of the questions correctly.)

Perception: The process through which the various sensations are interpreted and organized into meaningful patterns.

Personality: The dynamic organization of characteristic attributes leading to behavior and distinguishing one individual from other individuals. It refers to the total individual and includes needs, motives, methods of adjusting, temperament qualities, self-concept, role behaviors, attitudes and values, and abilities.

Phobia, phobic neurosis: A form of neurosis in which the person develops a dread, morbid, and exaggerated fear of something.

Physiological needs: Needs that result from lack of satisfaction of tissue requirements such as hunger, thirst, oxygen, rest, and sex. Physiological needs may demand satisfaction for survival or for stimulation.

Pitch: That characteristic of sound that is described as high or low; it is determined chiefly by vibrations.

Placebo: A medical preparation or experimental condition that does not physically affect the condition that it purports to affect; in essence, a "fake" in order to test the possible psychogenic elements of the situation.

Population explosion: A term applied to the rapid increase in population throughout the world, resulting primarily from the reduction in the death rate in general and infant mortality in particular.

Prejudice: An evaluation or belief, either positive or negative, developed without sufficient information or understanding and resistant to change. Prejudices about an individual often form as the result of the ethnic, religious, sex, age, or vocational group to which he belongs.

Preliterate: Being without a written language; usually applied by anthropologists to groups of people living under primitive conditions.

Prenatal: Pertaining to the period between conception and birth.

Primary status: The position one has in the community resulting from one's own worth and accomplishments, rather than the worth and accomplishments of a parent or other relative (*see* Derived status).

Probability: The likelihood that an event will occur.

Problem solving: The process of determining a proper solution for accomplishing a task; implies that some thinking is involved rather than only trial and error.

Projection: The process of attributing your own feelings, motives, or shortcomings to others. Occurs without conscious awareness, and is usually a defense mechanism.

Projective test: A psychological test, most frequently using ambiguous stimuli, that requires the subject to interpret the stimuli in light of his own feelings, experiences, and needs.

Propaganda: Actions or expressions of opinion deliberately designed to influence beliefs, values, attitudes, opinions, or behavior of others. Propaganda *may* have educational value, and education *may* have propaganda value.

Psychiatrist: A medical doctor whose primary concern is with mental illness and problems of personal adjustment.

Psychic satisfaction: Pleasure or enjoyment received for psychological or social reasons, as opposed to biological or financial reasons.

Psychoanalyst: An individual, usually a medical doctor, who studies and treats mental illness and personal-adjustment problems on the basis of Sigmund Freud's principles or some modification of these principles. A person must complete a carefully specified course of study to become a psychoanalyst.

Psychologist: An individual who studies behavior in order to understand, describe, predict, and influence this behavior; he uses research to lead both to theories of behavior and to effective practical applications directed at immediate and long-range problems. There are many types of psychologists.

Psychology: The discipline, field, or science that deals with behavior and the behaver (*see* Psychologist).

Psychosis: A relatively severe personality disturbance that often incapacitates the individual and may necessitate his hospitalization. The psychotic may lose contact with reality.

Psychosomatic: Pertaining to physical symptoms produced by biochemical changes initiated by emotional stress. Psychosomatic problems can do tissue damage, are often treatable through a combination of medical and psychiatric methods, and are not in the least imaginary.

Psychotherapy: The use of any psychological technique in helping an individual deal more effectively with personal or social problems; often restricted to trained psychotherapists operating in a situation in which they interact personally with the person or persons receiving the help.

Psychotic depression: A form of affective disorder marked by extreme depression and frequently precipitated by the immediate environment rather than by experiences in the early years of the victim's life.

Puberty: The period of human development during which the individual becomes sexually mature; usually between ages 12 and 14, but with wide variations.

Puberty rites: A ceremony, taking place around the time of puberty, that initiates the individual as a regular member of the community.

Questionnaire: A set of questions on a given topic or several topics to investigate beliefs, attitudes, preferences, actual or potential behavior, or other individual characteristics; it is usually readily scorable.

Rationalization: An attitude or other behavior that presents a plausible reason for something that would otherwise disrupt the self-concept. The individual is unaware of his purpose in using it; usually a defense mechanism.

Reaction formation: The establishment of a personality trait or behavior directly opposed to certain unconscious motives or feelings; usually a defense mechanism.

Receptor: A specialized part of the human or lower-animal organism sensitive to such forms of energy as light (for vision) or sound (for hearing); it changes this energy into a form that enables its impact to be transmitted to the brain.

Reference group: The people with whom an individual compares and judges himself.

Reflex: A simple action that occurs automatically and without the control of the individual, for example, the knee jerk in response to a tap or sneezing in response to having the nose tickled.

Regression: The return to an earlier form of behavior; sometimes a defense mechanism.

Reinforcement: The increasing of the probability that an indicated response will follow a given stimulus; the strengthening of the bond between stimulus and response through rewarding the correct response.

Relative deprivation, law of: The theory that a person's satisfaction or dissatisfaction will result from how much he has compared to how much he feels he should have (reflected by what he sees around him); thus, a poor Asian farmer feels less deprived than an American farmer because the latter is surrounded by wealth, but the former is surrounded by poverty.

Reliability: The consistency of a rating, test, or other psychological measurement. If you receive the exact same grade relative to others on every quiz or examination you take in your psychology course, your scores would be considered highly reliable (or dependable or consistent).

Repression: The process leading to being unaware of or being unable to recall something, as a defense against the anxiety or guilt that the awareness or recollection would produce; having such a strong need to be unaware or unable to recall that lack of awareness or recollection results. A defense mechanism.

Response: An instance of behavior that is stirred up or stimulated by an event, a situation, or other behavior.

Retarded depression: A type of affective disorder in which depression is marked by apathy, reduced movement, and lack of overt activity.

Reward: The satisfaction of a need in such a way as to increase the chance that the reward-eliciting behavior will occur the next time the need becomes motivating.

Role: The behavior expected of an individual who occupies a particular position in the social scheme; positions include age position, leadership position, vocational position, and innumerable others.

Safety needs: Needs, as adapted from Abraham Maslow, to feel safe and secure and not to fear physical violence or loss of property.

Sample: That part of a population that is used to represent the entire population.

Saturation: That quality of vision, relating to color, that determines the intensity of the stimulus, that is, a "strong" versus a "weak" color.

Scapegoat: The victim of displaced aggression; the person or thing that receives the displaced aggressive or hostile actions of another.

Schizophrenia: A group of psychotic reactions characterized by basic confusion regarding reality, by inappropriate emotional response, and by other forms of disturbed behavior.

Segregation: Forced separation of an individual from a group or of one group of individuals from another group. Often used in relationship to ethnic groups.

Self: All that constitutes an individual; the "real me" (*see* Self-concept). Some authors define this term in other ways.

Self-actualization: The process of making the most of your capabilities, developing your talents, and acting naturally or being yourself.

Self-concept: The idea an individual has of himself; what a person sees himself as. The similarity between self and self-concept varies from person to person.

Self-fulfilling prophecy: A statement about what will happen in the future that helps cause the predicted circumstance to occur; a student who predicts he might fail in a course may behave in such a fashion, because of his prophecy, that he does fail.

Senile psychosis: Mental illness affecting the aged, usually assumed to have at least some organic basis.

Sensation: That which occurs when some stimulus excites a receptor. Sensation has no meaning, except as it is interpreted by the organism.

Separation anxiety: The concern felt by a young child because of being apart from his parents; this concern is reflected in later life when people become unhappy at temporary or permanent separations from others.

Set: A readiness to act or react; it may be a readiness to move, a readiness to perceive, or a readiness to accept a thought or idea.

Sex role: The behavior expected of an individual because of his sex.

Shame: An unpleasant emotion produced by the feeling that others disapprove of your behavior or some other characteristic; there is some implication that the individual himself also disapproves of the behavior or other characteristic.

Shame society: A culture in which disapproval, ridicule, or criticism by others provides the major form of social control.

Sibling: The term used to refer to brother or sister, without regard to sex; your sibling may be either a sister or a brother.

Sibling rivalry: The competition between two or more children in the same family for the attention and approval of the parents or other significant figures; it occurs at all ages.

Significant others: Individuals who have an extremely important and continuing impact upon the development and behavior of an individual, especially of a child; the mother and father are most commonly significant others.

Simple schizophrenia: A form of schizophrenia marked by limited involvement with the external world and limited adequacy in interpersonal relationships.

Skin senses: The various senses associated with touch (for example, pressure, pain, warm, and cold).

Social class: A grouping of individuals sharing certain social characteristics that enable them to interact with each other as approximate equals. Your social class affects your social environment, which affects values and many types of behavior.

Social-class mobility: The ability to move from one social class to another; the ability to be accepted as a member of a social-class group other than that of birth.

Social psychologist: A psychologist whose primary interests are in the study of groups, of attitudes and beliefs, and of communication, and in general, of the effects upon behavior of the social environment and social interactions.

SQ3R: A method for improving learning and reducing forgetting in reading, especially in studying textbooks.

Stereotype: A rigid and oversimplified or biased perception or conception of an aspect of reality, especially of persons or social groups.

Stimulation needs: Those unlearned (although not uninfluenced by learning) needs that cause the individual to explore and manipulate his environment.

Stimulus: An object or event that stirs up or arouses behavior.

Stimulus generalization: The process through which the individual learns to respond to stimuli that resemble the stimulus originally eliciting the response.

Stress: A strong emotional force producing tension or discomfort.

Stress tolerance: The amount of stress an individual can withstand without exhibiting adjustment problems.

Suppression: A purposeful attempt to forget or ignore something; not a defense mechanism.

Survival needs: Those unlearned needs necessary to the maintenance of the life of the organism, for example, hunger, thirst, and sleep needs.

Tension: The feeling of emotional strain that results from stress, most often discomforting and motivating the organism toward its elimination.

Thinking: Judging, abstracting, reasoning, evaluating, recalling, imagining, anticipating, or performing a comparable intellectual task; does not include perceiving.

Threshold: The point at which a stimulus is just strong enough to cause a response.

Toilet training: The method through which the child learns to control his elimination processes until he can find a socially acceptable location for eliminating.

Trait (personality): A characteristic behavior pattern that differentiates people from each other.

Tranquilizer: A type of drug that reduces unpleasant emotional states such as anxiety and guilt and induces a feeling of calmness.

Transfer of training: The enhancement of or interference with learning a task due to having previously learned a similar task.

Trial: A single performance; a single attempt to respond properly to a stimulus.

Unconscious: Referring to the state of being unaware of what is occurring.

Unconscious motivation: The process of setting behavior into action because of a need or lack of something in the organism of which the person himself has no awareness.

Validity: The capacity of a test, rating, or other psychological measurement to measure what it is intended to measure. Your grade in psychology is valid to the extent that it measures how much you know about the material of the psychology course.

Value: A belief about what is good or bad. Each individual internalizes many values, which then may serve to motivate behavior. Values are often held without the individual's full awareness.

Value system: Several values related to each other and interdependent to some extent, so that a change in one value would probably produce at least a slight change in the others.

Variable: Anything that can change. In psychology, any attribute or property that changes as the result of another attribute, property, process, or event; for example, the variable *obedience* changes as the result of the event *spanking*.

Vestibular sense: The sense that enables an individual to maintain balance and to be aware of his position.

Visual: Pertaining to seeing.

Warm-up: A brief period of getting ready to do something during which the individual gains the proper set or readiness; derived from baseball.

Weaning: The process by which a child (or young lower animal) is taught to become accustomed to being without his mother's milk; the process by which any individual reduces his dependency upon a person or thing.

Withdrawal: An action or pattern of behavior in which an individual removes himself from a stressful situation in an attempt to reduce the feelings of tension or maintain a satisfactory self-concept.

Zygote: The cell, formed by the union of the male sperm and the female ovum, from which a new individual matures.

References

Abelson, P. H. LSD and marihuana. *Science,* 1968, **159,** 1189.

Adams, J. F. An introduction to understanding adolescence. In J. F. Adams (Ed.), *Understanding adolescence: Current developments in adolescent psychology.* Boston: Allyn and Bacon, 1968. Pp. 1–12.

Adorno, T. W., Frenkel-Brunswik, E., Levinson, D. J., & Sanford, R. N. *The authoritarian personality: Studies in prejudice.* New York: Harper & Row, 1950.

Albee, G. W. Conceptual models and manpower requirements in psychology. *American Psychologist,* 1968, **23,** 317–320.

Albee, G. W. Emerging concepts of mental illness and models of treatment: The psychological points of view. *American Journal of Psychiatry,* 1969, **125,** 870–876.

Allport, G. W. *The nature of prejudice.* Reading, Mass.: Addison-Wesley, 1954.

Allport, G. W., & Ross, J. M. Personal religious orientation and prejudice. *Journal of Personality and Social Psychology,* 1967, **5,** 432–443.

Alper, T. G., & Boring, E. G. Intelligence test scores of northern and southern white and Negro recruits in 1918. *Journal of Abnormal and Social Psychology,* 1944, **39,** 471–474.

Altman, I. Territorial behavior in humans: An analysis of the concept. In L. Pastalan & D. H. Carson (Eds.), *Spatial behavior of older people.* Ann Arbor: University of Michigan–Wayne State University, Institute of Gerontology, 1970. Pp. 1–24.

Altman, I., Taylor, D. A., & Wheeler, L. Ecological aspects of group behavior in social isolation. *Journal of Applied Social Psychology,* 1971, **1,** 76–100.

American Psychiatric Association. *Diagnostic and statistical manual of mental disorders.* (2nd ed.) Washington, D. C.: Author, 1968.

Anastasi, A. *Differential psychology.* (3rd ed.) New York: Macmillan, 1958.

Anderson, R. C. Educational psychology. *Annual Review of Psychology,* 1967, **18,** 129–164.

Argyle, M. *Religious behavior.* New York: Free Press, 1959.

Arkoff, A. *Adjustment and mental health.* New York: McGraw-Hill, 1968.

Asch, S. E. Effects of group pressure upon the modification and distortion of judgment. In H. S. Guetzkow (Ed.), *Groups, leadership, and men.* Pittsburgh: Carnegie Press, 1951. Pp. 177–190.

Astin, A. W., & Nichols, R. C. Life goals and vocational choice. *Journal of Applied Psychology,* 1964, **48,** 50–58.

Astin, A. W., & Panos, R. J. *Educational and vocational development of college students.* Washington, D.C.: American Council on Education, 1969.

Ausubel, D. P. *Theory and problems of adolescent development.* New York: Grune & Stratton, 1954.

Ax, A. F. The physiological differentiation between fear and anger in humans. *Psychosomatic Medicine,* 1953, **15,** 433–442.

Bacon, M. K., Child, I. L., & Barry, H. A cross-cultural study of correlates of crime. *Journal of Abnormal and Social Psychology,* 1963, **66,** 291–300.

Bandura, A. Behavioral psychotherapy. *Scientific American,* 1967, **216**(3), 78–86.

Bandura, A. *Principles of behavior modification.* New York: Holt, Rinehart, & Winston, 1969.

Banta, T. J., & Hetherington, M. Relations between needs of friends and fiancés. *Journal of Abnormal and Social Psychology,* 1963, **66,** 401–404.

Bardwick, J. M. *Psychology of women.* New York: Harper & Row, 1971.

Barrett, W. *Irrational man.* Garden City, N. Y.: Doubleday, 1958.

Barry, H., & Lindemann, E. Critical ages for maternal bereavement in psychoneurosis. *Psychosomatic Medicine,* 1960, **22,** 166–181.

Barry, W. A. Marriage research and conflict: An integrative review. *Psychological Bulletin,* 1970, **73,** 41–54.

Bayley, N. On the growth of intelligence. *American Psychologist,* 1955, **10,** 805–818.

Bayley, N., & Oden, M. H. The maintenance of intellectual ability in gifted adults. *Journal of Gerontology,* 1955, **10,** 91–107.

Beecher, H. K. Response to the Ingersoll lecture by a physician. *Harvard Theological Review,* 1969, **2,** 21–26.

Bell, R. R., & Chaskes, J. B. Premarital sexual experience among coeds, 1958–1968. *Journal of Marriage and the Family,* 1970, **32,** 81–84.

Beloff, H. Two forms of social conformity: Acquiescence and conventionality. *Journal of Abnormal and Social Psychology,* 1958, **56,** 99–103.

Bem, D. J. *Beliefs, attitudes, and human affairs.* Monterey, Calif.: Brooks/Cole, 1970.

Benedict, R. F. *The chrysanthemum and the sword.* Boston: Houghton Mifflin, 1946.

Bennett, E. L., Diamond, M., Krech, D., & Rosenzweig, M. R. Chemical and anatomical plasticity of the brain. *Science,* 1964, **146,** 610–619.

Berelson, B., & Steiner, G. A. *Human behavior: An inventory of scientific findings.* New York: Harcourt Brace Jovanovich, 1964.

Berkowitz, L. Impulse, aggression, and the gun. *Psychology Today,* 1968, **2**(4), 19–23.

Berscheid, E., & Walster, E. Beauty and the best. *Psychology Today,* 1972, **5**(10), 42–46.

Bexton, W. H., Heron, W., & Scott, T. H. Effects of decreased variation in the sensory environment. *Canadian Journal of Psychology,* 1954, **8,** 70–76.

Birns, B., Blank, M., & Bridger, W. H. The effectiveness of various soothing techniques on human neonates. *Psychosomatic Medicine,* 1966, **28,** 316–322.

Birren, J. E. *The psychology of aging.* Englewood Cliffs, N. J.: Prentice-Hall, 1964.

Birren, J. E., & Hess, R. D. Influences of biological, psychological, and social deprivations upon learning and performance. In *Perspectives on human deprivation: Biological, psychological, and sociological.* Washington, D. C.: Department of Health, Education and Welfare, 1968.

Block, J., & Thomas, H. Is satisfaction with self a measure of adjustment? *Journal of Abnormal and Social Psychology,* 1955, **51,** 254–259.

Block, J. H., Haan, N., & Smith, M. B. Activism and apathy in contemporary adolescents. In J. F. Adams (Ed.), *Understanding adolescence: Current developments in adolescent psychology.* Boston: Allyn and Bacon, 1968. Pp. 198–231.

Block, M. A. *Alcohol and alcoholism.* Belmont, Calif.: Wadsworth, 1970.

Blood, R. O., Jr. *Anticipating your marriage.* New York: Free Press, 1955.

Blood, R. O., Jr. Uniformities and diversities in campus dating preferences. *Marriage and Family Living,* 1956, **18,** 37–45.

Blum, M. L. *Industrial psychology and its social foundations.* (Rev. ed.) New York: Harper & Row, 1956.

Blum, R. H., & Associates. *Society and drugs.* San Francisco: Jossey-Bass, 1969.

Bogart, L. American television: A brief survey of research findings. *Journal of Social Issues,* 1962, **18**(2), 36–42.

Bogdonoff, M. D., Klein, R. F., Estes, E. H., Jr., Shaw, D. M., & Back, K. W. The modifying effect of conforming behavior upon lipid responses accompanying CNS arousal. *Clinical Research,* 1961, **9**, 135. (Also cited in D. Krech, R. S. Crutchfield, & E. L. Ballachey, *Individual in society.* New York: McGraw-Hill, 1962. P. 521).

Bowlby, J. Separation anxiety. *International Journal of Psychoanalysis,* 1960, **41**, 89–113.

Boys' Clubs of America. *Needs and interests of adolescent Boys' Club members.* Author, 1960.

Bradway, K. P., & Thompson, C. W. Intelligence at adulthood: A twenty-five-year follow-up. *Journal of Educational Psychology,* 1962, **53**, 1–14.

Brayfield, A. H., & Crockett, W. H. Employee attitudes and employee performance. *Psychological Bulletin,* 1955, **52**, 396–424.

Brehm, M. L., & Back, K. W. Self-image and attitude toward drugs. *Journal of Personality,* 1968, **36**, 299–314.

Bridges, K. M. B. Emotional development in early infancy. *Child Development,* 1932, **3**, 324–341.

Bronfenbrenner, U. *Two worlds of childhood: U. S. and U. S. S. R.* New York: Russell Sage, 1970.

Bronson, G. W. The fear of novelty. *Psychological Bulletin,* 1968, **69**, 350–358.

Brown, D. G. Masculinity-femininity development in children. *Journal of Consulting Psychology,* 1957, **21**, 197–202.

Brown, J. M., Berrien, F. K., Russell, D. L., & Wells, W. D. *Applied psychology.* New York: Macmillan, 1966.

Brown, W. F., & Holtzman, W. H. A study-attitudes questionnaire for predicting academic success. *Journal of Educational Psychology,* 1955, **46**, 75–84.

Bruner, J. S., & Goodman, C. C. Value and need as organizing factors in perception. *Journal of Abnormal and Social Psychology,* 1947, **13**, 33–44.

Bryan, J. H., & London, P. Altruistic behavior by children. *Psychological Bulletin,* 1970, **73**, 200–211.

Burgess, E. W., & Cottrell, L. S., Jr. *Predicting success or failure in marriage.* Englewood Cliffs, N. J.: Prentice-Hall, 1939.

Burgess, E. W., & Wallin, P. *Engagement and marriage.* Philadelphia: Lippincott, 1953.

Burt, C. The genetic determination of differences in intelligence: A study of monozygotic twins reared together and apart. *British Journal of Psychology,* 1966, **57**, 137–153.

Buxbaum, R. E. Homosexuality and love. *Journal of Religion and Health,* 1967, **6**, 17–32.

Byrne, D., & Blaylock, B. Similarity and assumed similarity of attitudes between husbands and wives. *Journal of Abnormal and Social Psychology,* 1963, **67**, 636–640.

Caldwell, B. M., & Hersher, L. Mother-infant interaction during the first year of life. *Merrill-Palmer Quarterly,* 1964, **10**, 119–128.

Calvin, A. D., & Holtzman, W. H. Adjustment to the discrepancy between self-concept and the inferred self. *Journal of Consulting Psychology,* 1953, **17**, 39–44.

Campbell, J. P. Personnel training and development. *Annual review of psychology,* 1971, **22**, 565–602.

Capel, W. C. Continuities and discontinuities in attitudes of the same persons measured through time. *Journal of Social Psychology,* 1967, **73**, 125–136.

Caplan, N. Treatment intervention and reciprocal interaction effects. *Journal of Social Issues,* 1968, **24**(1), 63–88.

Cates, J. Psychology's manpower: Report on the 1968 National Register of Scientific and Technical Personnel. *American Psychologist,* 1970, **25,** 254–263.

Cattell, R. B. Are I. Q. tests intelligent? *Psychology Today,* 1968, **1**(10), 56–62.

Chatterjee, M. N. *Society in the making.* Ann Arbor, Mich.: Edwards Brothers, 1942.

Clark, K. B., & Clark, M. P. Racial identification and preference in Negro children. In E. E. Maccoby, T. M. Newcomb, & E. L. Hartley (Eds.), *Readings in social psychology* (3rd ed.). New York: Holt, 1958. Pp. 602–611.

Cohen, N. The Negro and the American dream. *UCLA Alumni Magazine,* 1968, **42**(4), 5–9.

Cole, L., & Hall, I. N. *Psychology of adolescence.* (6th ed.) New York: Holt, Rinehart, and Winston, 1964.

Coleman, J. C. *Personality dynamics and effective behavior.* Glenview, Ill.: Scott, Foresman, 1960.

Coleman, J. C. *Abnormal psychology and modern life.* (3rd ed.) Glenview, Ill.: Scott, Foresman, 1964.

Coleman, J. S. *The adolescent society.* New York: Free Press, 1961.

Coleman, J. S., Mood, A. M., Campbell, E. O., et al. *Equality of educational opportunity.* Washington, D. C.: U. S. Office of Education, 1966.

Conrad, H. S., & Jones, H. E. A second study of familial resemblance in intelligence: Environmental and genetic implications of parent-child and sibling correlations in the total sample. *39th Yearbook, National Society for the Study of Education,* 1940, Part II, pp. 97–141.

Cooley, C. H. *The nature of human nature.* New York: Scribner's, 1902.

Cropley, A. J. *Creativity.* London: Longmans, Green, 1967.

Cumming, E., & Henry, W. E. *Growing old.* New York: Basic Books, 1961.

Dahlstrom, W. G. Personality. *Annual review of psychology,* 1970, **21,** 1–48.

Deeg, M. E., & Paterson, D. G. Changes in social status of occupations. *Occupations,* 1947, **25,** 205–208.

Dement, W. The effect of dream deprivation. *Science,* 1960, **131,** 1705–1707.

Diamond, S. *Personality and temperament.* New York: Harper, 1957.

Dick-Read, G. *Childbirth without fear: The principles and practice of natural childbirth.* (4th ed.) New York: Heinemann, 1960.

DiGiusto, E. L., Cairncross, K., & King, M. G. Hormonal influences on fear-motivated responses. *Psychological Bulletin,* 1971, **75,** 432–444.

Douvan, E., & Adelson, J. The psychodynamics of social mobility in adolescent boys. *Journal of Abnormal and Social Psychology,* 1958, **56,** 31–44.

Douvan, E. A., & Adelson, J. *The adolescent experience.* New York: Wiley, 1966.

Drewes, C. Unborn children of addicts: New study. *San Francisco Examiner & Chronicle,* January 30, 1972, Sunday Scene, p. 4.

Drucker, P. F. How to be an employee. *Psychology Today,* 1968, **1**(10), 63–65, 74.

Dublin, L. I. Suicide: A public health problem. In E. Shneidman (Ed.), *Essays in self-destruction.* New York: Science House, 1967. Pp. 251–257.

Ebbs, J. H., Tisdall, F. F., & Scott, W. A. The influence of prenatal diet on the mother and child. *The Milbank Memorial Fund Quarterly,* 1942, **20,** 35–36.

Edwards, A. L. *Edwards personal preference schedule.* New York: Psychological Corporation, 1954.

Elkind, D., & Elkind, S. Varieties of religious experience in young adolescents. *Journal for the Scientific Study of Religion,* 1962, **2,** 102–112.

English, H. B., & English, A. C. *A comprehensive dictionary of psychological and psychoanalytical terms: A guide to usage.* New York: McKay, 1958.

Engström, L., Geijerstam, G., Holmberg, N. G., & Uhrus, K. A prospective study of the relationship between psycho-social factors and course of pregnancy and delivery. *Journal of Psychosomatic Research,* 1964, **8,** 151–155.

Erikson, E. H. The problem of ego identity. *Journal of the American Psychoanalytic Association,* 1956, **4,** 56–121.

Eysenck, H. J. New ways in psychotherapy. *Psychology Today,* 1967, **1**(2), 39–47.

Farberow, N. L., & Shneidman, E. S. (Eds.) *The cry for help.* New York: McGraw-Hill, 1961.

Feifel, H. Attitudes toward death in some normal and mentally ill populations. In H. Feifel (Ed.), *The meaning of death.* New York: McGraw-Hill, 1959. Pp. 114–130.

Festinger, L. Motivations leading to social behavior. In M. Jones (Ed.), *Nebraska symposium on motivation,* 1954. Pp. 191–219.

Festinger, L. *A theory of cognitive dissonance.* Evanston, Ill.: Row, Peterson, 1957.

Flacks, R. The liberated generation: An exploration of the roots of student protest. *Journal of Social Issues,* 1967, **23**(3), 52–75.

Ford, C. S., & Beach, F. A. *Patterns of sexual behavior.* New York: Harper, 1951.

Foulkes, D. Theories of dream formation and recent studies of sleep consciousness. *Psychological Bulletin,* 1964, **62,** 236–247.

Frankel, E. Characteristics of working and non-working mothers among intellectually gifted high and low achievers. *Personnel and Guidance Journal,* 1964, **42,** 776–780.

Freedman, J. L., Klevansky, S., & Ehrlich, P. R. The effect of crowding on human task performance. *Journal of Applied Social Psychology,* 1971, **1,** 7–25.

Freedman, M. *Homosexuality and psychological functioning.* Monterey, Calif.: Brooks/Cole, 1971.

Freedman, M. B. The sexual behavior of American college women: An empirical study and an historical survey. *Merrill-Palmer Quarterly,* 1965, **11,** 38–48.

Frenkel-Brunswik, E. Intolerance of ambiguity as an emotional and perceptual personality variable. *Journal of Personality,* 1949, **18,** 108–143.

Friesen, D. Academic-athletic-popularity syndrome in the Canadian high school society. *Adolescence,* 1968, **3**(9), 39–52.

Fromm, E. *The art of loving.* New York: Harper, 1956.

Gallup, G. Student attitudes. In L. Freedman (Ed.), *Issues of the seventies.* Belmont, Calif.: Wadsworth, 1970. Pp. 270–280.

Garrison, K. C. Physiological changes in adolescence. In J. F. Adams (Ed.), *Understanding adolescence: Current developments in adolescent psychology.* Boston: Allyn and Bacon, 1968. Pp. 43–69.

Getzels, J. W., & Jackson, P. W. *Creativity and intelligence: Explorations with gifted students.* New York: Wiley, 1962.

Gibson, E. J., & Walk, R. D. The "visual cliff." *Scientific American,* 1960, **202,** 64–71.

Glaser, B. G., & Strauss, A. L. *Awareness of dying.* Chicago: Aldine, 1965.

Glock, C. Y., & Stark, R. *Religion and society in tension.* Chicago: Rand-McNally, 1965.

Gold, M. Juvenile delinquency as a symptom of alienation. *Journal of Social Issues,* 1969, **25**(2), 121–135.

Goldsen, R. K., Rosenberg, M., Williams, R. M., Jr., & Suchman, E. A. *What college students think.* Princeton, N. J.: Van Nostrand, 1960.

Goodenough, F. L. *Measurement of intelligence by drawings.* Chicago: World Book, 1926.

Goodnow, J. J. Effects of active handling, illustrated by uses for objects. *Child Development,* 1969, **40,** 201–212.

Gordon, A. I. *Intermarriage: Interfaith, interracial, interethnic.* Boston: Beacon Press, 1964.

Gorer, G. *Death, grief, and mourning.* Garden City, N. Y.: Doubleday, 1965.

Gross, E. *Work and society.* New York: Crowell, 1958.

Group for the Advancement of Psychiatry, Committee on Adolescence. *Normal adolescence.* New York: Scribner's, 1968.

Haigh, G. V. Psychotherapy as interpersonal encounter. In J. F. T. Bugental (Ed.), *Challenges of humanistic psychology.* New York: McGraw-Hill, 1967. Pp. 219–224.

Hanes, B., & Flippo, E. B. Anxiety and work output. *Journal of Industrial Engineering,* 1963, **14,** 244–248.

Harlow, H. F. The nature of love. *American Psychologist,* 1958, **13,** 673–685.

Harlow, H. F., & Harlow, M. K. The effect of rearing conditions on behavior. *Bulletin of the Menninger Clinic,* 1962, **26,** 213–224. (a)

Harlow, H. F., & Harlow, M. K. Social deprivation in monkeys. *Scientific American,* 1962, **207,** 136–146. (b)

Harlow, H. F., & Harlow, M. K. The young monkeys. *Psychology Today,* 1967, **1**(5), 40–47.

Harlow, H. F., Harlow, M. K., & Meyer, D. R. Learning motivated by a manipulation drive. *Journal of Experimental Psychology,* 1950, **40,** 228–234.

Harlow, H. F., & Suomi, S. J. Nature of love—simplified. *American Psychologist,* 1970, **25,** 161–168.

Harris, D. B. Work and the adolescent transition to maturity. *Teachers College Record,* 1961, **63,** 146–153.

Harris, F. R., Wolf, M. M., & Baer, D. M. Effects of adult social reinforcement on child behavior. *Young Children,* 1964, **20**(1), 8–17.

Harris, J. D. Audition. *Annual review of psychology,* 1972, **23,** 313–346.

Hartup, W. W., & Yonas, A. Developmental psychology. *Annual Review of Psychology,* 1971, **22,** 337–392.

Havemann, E., & West, P. S. *They went to college.* New York: Harcourt Brace Jovanovich, 1952.

Havighurst, R. J., Bowman, P. H., Liddle, G. P., Matthews, C. V., & Pierce, J. V. *Growing up in River City.* New York: Wiley, 1962.

Havighurst, R. J., & Keating, B. The religion of youth. In M. P. Strommen (Ed.), *Research on religious development.* New York: Hawthorn, 1971. Chap. 18.

Havighurst, R. J., Munnichs, J. M. A., Neugarten, B., & Thomae, H. *Adjustment to retirement: A cross-national study.* New York: Humanities Press, 1969.

Havighurst, R. J., Robinson, M. Z., & Dorr, M. The development of the ideal self in childhood and adolescence. *Journal of Educational Research,* 1946, **40,** 241–257.

Heron, W. The pathology of boredom. *Scientific American,* 1957, **196,** 52–56.

Herzberg, F. Motivation, morale, and money. *Psychology Today,* 1968, **1**(10), 42–45, 66–67.

Hilgard, E. R., & Atkinson, R. C. *Introduction to psychology.* (4th ed.) New York: Harcourt Brace Jovanovich, 1967.

Himmelweit, H. T. A theoretical framework for the consideration of the effects of television: A British report. *Journal of Social Issues,* 1962, **18**(2), 16–28.

Holland, J. C. Teaching psychology by a teaching machine program. Unpublished mimeographed report, 1960. (Cited in B. Berelson & G. A. Steiner, *Human behavior: An inventory of scientific findings.* New York: Harcourt Brace Jovanovich, 1964. P. 150.)

Hollingshead, A. B. *Elmtown's youth.* New York: Wiley, 1949.

Honzik, M. P. Developmental studies of parent-child resemblance in intelligence. *Child Development,* 1957, **28,** 215–228.

Hoppock, R. *Job satisfaction.* New York: Harper, 1935.

Horn, J. L. Organization of data on life-span development of human abilities. In L. R. Goulet & P. B. Baltes (Eds.), *Life-span developmental psychology: Research and theory.* New York: Academic Press, 1970. Pp. 424–466.

Horner, M. S. Femininity and successful achievement: A basic inconsistency. In J. M. Bardwick, E. Douvan, M. S. Horner, & D. Gutmann, *Feminine personality and conflict.* Monterey, Calif.: Brooks/Cole, 1970.

Horrocks, J. E. *The psychology of adolescence.* (3rd ed.) Boston: Houghton Mifflin, 1969.

Hovland, C. I. Human learning and retention. In S. S. Stevens (Ed.), *Handbook of experimental psychology.* New York: Wiley, 1951.

Hulin, C. L., & Blood, M. R. Job enlargement, individual differences, and worker responses. *Psychological Bulletin,* 1968, **69,** 41–45.

Hurlock, E. B. *Developmental psychology.* (2nd ed.) New York: McGraw-Hill, 1959.

Hyman, H. H. *Political socialization: A study in the psychology of political behavior.* New York: Free Press, 1959.

Inselberg, R. M. Social and psychological factors associated with high school marriages. *Journal of Home Economics,* 1961, **53,** 766–772.

Izard, C. E. Personality similarity and friendship: A follow-up study. *Journal of Abnormal and Social Psychology,* 1963, **66,** 598–600.

Jackson, J. J. But where are the men? *The Black Scholar,* 1971, **3,** 30–41.

Jacob, P. E. *Changing values in college: An exploratory study of the impact of college teaching.* New York: Harper & Row, 1957.

Janis, I. When fear is healthy. *Psychology Today,* 1968, **1**(11), 46–49, 60–61.

Janis, I. L., Mahl, G. F., Kagan, J., & Holt, R. R. *Personality: Dynamics, development, and assessment.* New York: Harcourt Brace Jovanovich, 1969.

Jessor, R., & Richardson, S. Psychosocial deprivation and personality development. In *Perspectives on human deprivation: Biological, psychological, and sociological.* Washington, D. C.: National Institute of Child Health and Human Development, Public Health Service, Department of Health, Education, and Welfare, 1968. Pp. 1–90.

Johnstone, J. W. C., & Rosenberg, L. Sociological observations on the privileged adolescent. In J. F. Adams (Ed.), *Understanding adolescence: Current developments in adolescent psychology.* Boston: Allyn and Bacon, 1968. Pp. 318–336.

Jourard, S. M. *Personal adjustment: An approach through the study of healthy personality.* (2nd ed.) New York: Macmillan, 1963.

Kagan, J. The many faces of response. *Psychology Today,* 1968, **1**(8), 22–27, 60.

Kagan, J., & Moss, H. A. *Birth to maturity: A study in psychological development.* New York: Wiley, 1962.

Kalish, R. A. Some variables in death attitudes. *Journal of Social Psychology,* 1963, **59,** 135–137.

Kalish, R. A. Of children and grandfathers: A speculative essay on dependency. *The Gerontologist,* 1967, **7,** 65–70.

Kalish, R. A. Suicide: An ethnic comparison in Hawaii. *Bulletin of Suicidology,* December 1968, pp. 37–43.

Kalish, R. A. *Making the most of college*. (2nd ed.) Monterey, Calif.: Brooks/Cole, 1969. (a)

Kalish, R. A. The old and the young: Generation gap allies. *The Gerontologist*, 1969, **9**, 83–89. (b)

Kalish, R. A., & Johnson, A. I. Value similarities and differences in three generations of women. *Journal of Marriage and the family*, 1972, **34**, 49–54.

Kalish, R. A., Maloney, M., & Arkoff, A. Cross-cultural comparisons of college student marital-role preferences. *Journal of Social Psychology*, 1966, **68**, 41–47.

Kalish, R. A., & Reynolds, D. K. Death and bereavement in a cross-ethnic context. Manuscript in process.

Kallmann, F. J. *Heredity in health and mental disorder*. New York: Norton, 1953.

Kamiya, J. Operant control of the EEG Alpha Rhythm and some of its reported effects on consciousness. In C. T. Tart (Ed.), *Altered states of consciousness*. New York: Wiley, 1969. Pp. 507–517.

Kaplan, M. *Leisure in America, a social inquiry*. New York: Wiley, 1960.

Katz, J. Quoted in the *Los Angeles Times*, Nov. 19, 1968, Section H, p. 6.

Keith-Spiegel, P., & Spiegel, D. Perceived helpfulness of others as a function of compatible intelligence levels. *Journal of Counseling Psychology*, 1967, **14**, 61–62.

Kelley, H. H., & Volkart, E. H. The resistance to change of group-anchored attitudes. *American Sociological Review*, 1952, **17**, 453–465.

Kelly, E. L. Consistency of the adult personality. *American Psychologist*, 1955, **10**, 659–681.

Keniston, K. The sources of student dissent. *Journal of Social Issues*, 1967, **23**(3), 108–137.

Keys, A. B., Brožek, J., Henschel, A., Michelsen, O., & Taylor, H. L. *The biology of human starvation*, Vol. 2. Minneapolis: University of Minnesota Press, 1950.

Killian, L. M. The significance of multiple-group membership in disaster. *American Journal of Sociology*, 1952, **57**, 309–314.

Kinsey, A. C., Pomeroy, W. B., & Martin, C. E. *Sexual behavior in the human male*. Philadelphia: Saunders, 1948.

Kinsey, A. C., Pomeroy, W. B., Martin, C. E., & Gebhard, P. H. *Sexual behavior in the human female*. Philadelphia: Saunders, 1953.

Kirkpatrick, C. Religion and humanitarianism: A study of institutional implications. *Psychological Monographs*, 1949, **63**.

Kohn, M. L. Social class and parental values. *American Journal of Sociology*, 1959, **64**, 337–351.

Kovach, B. Communes—The road to Utopia. *San Francisco Chronicle*, January 4, 1971, p. 6.

Krebs, D. L. Altruism—An examination of the concept and a review of the literature. *Psychological Bulletin*, 1970, **73**, 258–302.

Krech, D. The chemistry of learning. *Saturday Review*, Jan. 20, 1968, **51**, 48–50, 68.

Krech, D., Crutchfield, R. S., & Ballachey, E. L. *Individual in society*. New York: McGraw-Hill, 1962.

Kübler-Ross, E. *On death and dying*. New York: Macmillan, 1969.

Kuhlen, R. G. Motivational changes during the adult years. In R. G. Kuhlen (Ed.), *Psychological backgrounds of adult education*. Center for the Study of Liberal Education for Adults, 1963. (Also cited in J. E. Birren, *The psychology of aging*. Englewood Cliffs, N. J.: Prentice-Hall, 1964).

Kuhlen, R. G., & Arnold, M. Age differences in religious beliefs and problems during adolescence. *Journal of Genetic Psychology*, 1944, **65**, 291–300.

Kukuk, W. Traits of college drinkers. Unpublished master's thesis, 1960. (Also cited in H. C. Smith, *Personality adjustment*. New York: McGraw-Hill, 1961. P. 323).

Lakin, M. Some ethical issues in sensitivity training. *American Psychologist*, 1969, **24**, 923–928.

Langhorne, M. C., & Secord, P. F. Variations in marital needs with age, sex, marital status, and regional location. *Journal of Social Psychology*, 1955, **41**, 19–37.

Lavin, D. E. *The prediction of academic performance*. New York: Russell Sage, 1965.

Lazarus. R. S. *Patterns of adjustment and human effectiveness*. New York: McGraw-Hill, 1969.

Lehmann, I. J. Changes in critical thinking, attitudes, and values from freshman to senior years. *Journal of Educational Psychology*, 1963, **54**, 305–315.

Lehner, G. F. J., & Kube, E. *The dynamics of personal adjustment*. (2nd ed.) Englewood Cliffs, N. J.: Prentice-Hall, 1964.

Lenneberg, E. H. *Biological functions of language*. New York: Wiley, 1967.

Lenski, G. E. *The religious factor*. Garden City, N. Y.: Doubleday, 1961.

Levine, R., Chein, I., & Murphy, G. The relation of the intensity of a need to the amount of perceptual distortion: A preliminary report. *Journal of Psychology*, 1942, **13**, 283–293.

Lindemann, E. Symptomatology and management of acute grief. *American Journal of Psychiatry*, 1944, **101**, 141–148.

Lindsley, D., & Riesen, A. Biological substrates of development and behavior. *Perspectives on human deprivation: Biological, psychological, and sociological*. Washington, D. C.: Department of Health, Education and Welfare, 1968.

Lippman, H. S. Emotional factors in family breakdown. *American Journal of Orthopsychiatry*, 1954, **24**, 445–453.

Long, D., Elkind, D., & Spilka, B. The child's conception of prayer. *Journal for the Scientific Study of Religion*, 1967, **6**, 101–109.

Lowe, C. R. Effect of mothers' smoking habits on birth weight of their children. *British Medical Journal*, 1959, **2**, 673–676.

Maccoby, E. E. Developmental psychology. *Annual Review of Psychology*, 1964, **15**, 203–250.

Maccoby, E. E., Gibbs, P. K., & the staff of the Laboratory of Human Development, Harvard University. Methods of child-rearing in two social classes. In A. P. Coladarci (Ed.), *Educational psychology: A book of readings*. New York: Holt, 1955. Pp. 97–121.

Malnig, L. R. Anxiety and academic prediction. *Journal of Counseling Psychology*, 1964, **11**, 72–75.

Mann, R. D. A review of the relationships between personality and performance in small groups. *Psychological Bulletin*, 1959, **56**, 241–270.

Maslow, A. H. Deficiency motivation and growth motivation. In M. R. Jones (Ed.), *Nebraska symposium on motivation*. U. of Nebraska Press, 1955. Pp. 1–30.

Maslow, A. H. *Toward a psychology of being*. Princeton, N. J.: Van Nostrand, 1962.

Maslow, A. H. A theory of metamotivation: The biological rooting of the value-life. *Journal of Humanistic Psychology*, 1967, **5**, 93–127.

Maslow, A. H. *Motivation and personality*. (2nd ed.) New York: Harper & Row, 1970.

Masters, W. H., & Johnson, V. E. *Human sexual response*. Boston: Little, Brown, 1966.

Masters, W. H., & Johnson, V. E. *Human sexual inadequacy.* Boston: Little, Brown, 1970.

Matarazzo, J. D., Allen, B. V., Saslow, G., & Wiens, A. N. Characteristics of successful policemen and firemen applicants. *Journal of Applied Psychology,* 1964, **48,** 123–133.

McCain, G., & Segal, E. M. *The game of science.* Monterey, Calif.: Brooks/Cole, 1969.

McCord, J., McCord, W., & Thurber, E. Effects of maternal employment on lower-class boys. *Journal of Abnormal and Social Psychology,* 1963, **67,** 177–182.

McCord, W., McCord, J., & Verden, P. Familial and behavioral correlates of dependency in male children. *Child Development,* 1962, **33,** 313–326.

McGeoch, J. A., & Irion, A. L. *The psychology of human learning.* (2nd ed.) New York: McKay, 1952.

McGlothlin, W. H., Arnold, D. O., & Freedman, D. X. Organicity measures following repeated LSD ingestion. *Archives of General Psychiatry,* 1969, **21,** 704–709.

McGlothlin, W. H., & West, L. J. The marijuana problem: An overview. *American Journal of Psychiatry,* 1968, **125,** 370–378.

Mechanic, D. *Medical sociology.* New York: Free Press, 1968.

Mednick, S. A. Birth defects and schizophrenia. *Psychology Today,* 1971, **4**(11), 49–50, 80–81.

Mehrabian, A. Communication without words. *Psychology Today,* 1968, **2**(4), 53–55.

Menninger, R. What troubles our troubled youth? *Mental Hygiene,* 1968, **52,** 323–329.

Merrill, F. E. *Courtship and marriage.* New York: Holt, 1959.

Milgram, S. Some conditions of obedience and disobedience to authority. In I. D. Steiner & M. Fishbein (Eds.), *Current studies in social psychology.* New York: Holt, Rinehart, and Winston, 1965. Pp. 243–262.

Milgram, S. The experience of living in cities: A psychological analysis. *Science,* March 13, 1970.

Miller, G. A. The psycholinguists: On the new scientists of language. *Encounter,* 1964, **23,** 29–37.

Mishima, Y. Judging the U. S. giant. *Life,* Sept. 11, 1964, **57,** 81–84.

Moberg, D. O. *Spiritual well-being.* Background and Issues for the White House Conference on Aging. Washington, D. C.: U. S. Government Printing Office, 1971.

Montagu, M. F. A. Some environmental factors which may influence prenatal development. In J. M. Seidman (Ed.), *The child: A book of readings.* New York: Holt, Rinehart, and Winston, 1958. Pp. 42–50.

Morgan, C. T., & King, R. A. *Introduction to psychology.* (3rd ed.) New York: McGraw-Hill, 1966.

Mowrer, E. R. The differentiation of husband and wife roles. *Journal of Marriage and the Family,* 1969, **31,** 534–540.

Muhyi, I. A. Women in the Arab Middle East. *Journal of Social Issues,* 1959, **15**(3), 45–57.

Murdock, G. P. *Social structure.* New York: Macmillan, 1949.

Murdock, G. P. World ethnographic sample. *American Anthropologist,* 1957, **59,** 664–687.

Murray, H. A. *Explorations in personality.* New York: Oxford University Press, 1938.

Mussen, P. H. Some personality and social factors related to changes in children's attitudes toward Negroes. *Journal of Abnormal and Social Psychology,* 1950, **45,** 423–441.

Mussen, P. H., Conger, J. J., & Kagan, J. *Child development and personality.* (3rd ed.) New York: Harper & Row, 1969.

Newcomb, T. M., & Feldman, K. A. *The impact of college on students.* San Francisco: Jossey-Bass, 1969.

Newson, J., & Newson, E. *Some social differences in the process of child rearing.* Baltimore: Penguin Books, 1967.

Newsweek. Book review of A. H. Lewis, *Lament for the Molly Maguires* (New York: Harcourt Brace Jovanovich, 1964). Sept. 7, 1964, **64**, 85.

Newsweek. Campus '65. March 22, 1965, **65**, 43–63.

Nichols, R. C. Nature and nurture in adolescence. In J. F. Adams (Ed.), *Understanding adolescence: Current developments in adolescent psychology.* Boston: Allyn and Bacon, 1968. Pp. 101–127.

Noel, D. L. Group identification among Negroes: An empirical analysis. *Journal of Social Issues,* 1964, **20**(2), 71–84.

O'Doherty, N. A hearing test applicable to the crying newborn infant. *Developmental Medicine and Child Neurology,* 1968, **10**, 380–383.

Osborne, R. T., & Gregory, A. J. The inheritability of visualization, perceptual speed, and spatial orientation. *Perceptual Motor Skills,* 1966, **23**, 379–390.

Osgood, C. E. *Method and theory in experimental psychology.* New York: Oxford University Press, 1953.

Osler, W. To the editor of the *Spectator* (Nov. 4, 1911). In L. Farmer, *Doctor's legacy.* New York: Harper, 1955.

Pahnke, W. N. The psychedelic mystical experience in the human encounter with death. *Harvard Theological Review,* 1969, **2**, 1–21.

Parker, C. A. Changes in religious beliefs of college students. In M. P. Strommen (Ed.), *Research on religious development.* New York: Hawthorn, 1971. Chap. 19.

Parker, S., & Kleiner, R. Status position, mobility, and ethnic identification of the Negro. *Journal of Social Issues,* 1964, **20**(2), 85–102.

Parkes, C. M. Effects of bereavement on physical and mental health—A study of the medical record of widows. *British Medical Journal,* 1964, **2**, 274–279.

Pavlov, I. P. *Conditional reflexes.* (Trans. by G. V. Anrep.) New York: Oxford University Press, 1927.

Peissel, M. Mustang, remote realm in Nepal. *National Geographic,* Oct. 1965, **128**, 579–604.

Pettigrew, T. F. *A profile of the Negro American.* Princeton, N. J.: Van Nostrand, 1964.

Piers, E. V. Adolescent creativity. In J. F. Adams (Ed.), *Understanding adolescence: Current developments in adolescent psychology.* Boston: Allyn and Bacon, 1968. Pp. 159–182.

Powledge, F. *To change a child: A report on the Institute for Developmental Studies.* Chicago: Quadrangle Books, 1967.

Prince, A. J., & Baggaley, A. R. Personality variables and the ideal mate. *Family Life Coordinator,* 1963, **3**, 93–96.

Rahe, R. H., & Arthur, R. J. Life-change patterns surrounding illness experience. *Journal of Psychosomatic Research,* 1968, **11**, 341–345.

Ramirez, M. III. Identification with Mexican family values and authoritarianism in Mexican Americans. *Journal of Social Psychology,* 1967, **73**, 3–11.

Reiss, I. J. How and why America's sex standards are changing. *Trans-action,* 1968, **5**(4), 26–32.

Reiter, H. H. Prediction of college success from measures of anxiety, achievement motivation, and scholastic aptitude. *Psychological Reports,* 1964, **15**, 23–26.

Remmers, H. H., & Radler, D. H. *The American teenager.* Indianapolis: Bobbs-Merrill, 1957.

Renne, K. S. Correlates of dissatisfaction in marriage. *Journal of Marriage and the Family*, 1970, **32**, 54–67.

Reynolds, D. K. *Morita psychotherapy*. Doctoral dissertation, Department of Anthropology, UCLA, 1969.

Ribble, M. A. *The rights of infants: Early psychological needs and their satisfaction*. New York: Columbia University Press, 1943.

Riley, M. W., Foner, A., & Associates. *Aging and society. Volume I: An inventory of research findings*. New York: Russell Sage Foundation, 1968.

Rioch, M. J. Changing concepts in the training of psychotherapists. *Journal of Consulting Psychology*, 1966, **30**, 290–292.

Robin, S. S., & Story, F. Ideological consistency of college students: The Bill of Rights and attitudes toward minority groups. *Sociology and Social Research*, 1964, **48**, 187–196.

Robinson, F. P. *Effective study*. (Rev. ed.) New York: Harper, 1961.

Roethlisberger, F. J., & Dickson, W. J. *Management and the worker*. Cambridge, Mass.: Harvard University Press, 1939.

Rogers, C. R. This is me. In C. R. Rogers, *On becoming a person*. Boston: Houghton Mifflin, 1961. Pp. 3–27.

Rogers, C. R. The process of the basic encounter group. In J. F. T. Bugental (Ed.), *Challenges of humanistic psychology*. New York: McGraw-Hill, 1967. Chap. 28.

Rogers, D. *Child psychology*. Monterey, Calif.: Brooks/Cole, 1969.

Rohles, F. H., Jr. Environmental psychology: A bucket of worms. *Psychology Today*, 1967, **2**(1), 54–63.

Rokeach, M. *The open and closed mind*. New York: Basic Books, 1960.

Rokeach, M. A theory of organization and change within value-attitude systems. *Journal of Social Issues*, 1968, **24**(1), 13–33.

Rollins, B. C., & Feldman, H. Marital satisfaction over the family life cycle. *Journal of Marriage and the Family*, 1970, **32**, 20–28.

Rosenberg, L. A. Idealization of self and social adjustment. *Journal of Consulting Psychology*, 1962, **26**, 487.

Rosenfeld, A. The psycho-biology of violence. *Life*, June 21, 1968, **64**, 67–71.

Rosenthal, R., & Jacobson, L. *Pygmalion in the classroom: Teacher expectation and pupils' intellectual development*. New York: Holt, Rinehart, & Winston, 1968.

Rosow, I. *Social integration of the aged*. New York: Free Press, 1967.

Roszak, T. *The making of a counter culture*. Garden City, N. Y.: Doubleday, 1969.

Sanford, F. H., & Wrightsman, L. S. *Psychology: A scientific study of man*. (3rd ed.) Monterey, Calif.: Brooks/Cole, 1970.

Sanford, N. *Issues in personality theory*. San Francisco: Jossey-Bass, 1970.

Sarason, I. G., & Smith, R. E. Personality. *Annual review of psychology*, 1971, **22**, 393–446.

Saxton, L. *The individual, marriage, and the family*. Belmont, Calif.: Wadsworth, 1968.

Schachter, J., Bickman, L., Schachter, J. S., Jameson, J., Litachy, S., & Williams, T. A. Behavioral and physiologic reactivity in infants. *Mental Hygiene*, 1966, **50**, 516–521.

Schein, E. H. The first job dilemma. *Psychology Today*, 1968, **1**(10), 26–37.

Schneider, L., & Lysgaard, S. The deferred gratification pattern: A preliminary study. *American Sociological Review*, 1953, **18**, 142–149.

Sears, R. R., Maccoby, E. E., & Levin, H. *Patterns of child rearing*. New York: Harper & Row, 1957.

Sells, S. B. The atmosphere effect: An experimental study of reasoning. *Archives of Psychology*, 1936, No. 200.

Selyé, H. *The stress of life*. New York: McGraw-Hill, 1956.

Shirley, M. M. *The first two years: A study of 25 babies*. Vol. 2: *Intellectual development*. Minneapolis: University of Minnesota Press, 1933.

Siipola, E. M. A group study of some effects of preparatory sets. *Psychological Monographs*, 1935, **46**(210), 27–38.

Silberman, C. E. *Crisis in black and white*. New York: Random House, 1964.

Sinnett, E. R., & Stone, L. The meaning of a college education as revealed by the semantic differential. *Journal of Counseling Psychology*, 1964, **11**, 168–172.

Siqueland, E. R. Reinforcement patterns and extinction in human newborns. *Journal of Exceptional Child Psychology*, 1968, **6**, 431–442.

Skinner, B. F. *Science and human behavior*. New York: Macmillan, 1963.

Skinner, B. F. *Beyond freedom and dignity*. New York: Knopf, 1971.

Skipper, J. K., Jr., & Nass, G. Dating behavior: A framework for analysis and an illustration. *Journal of Marriage and the Family*, 1966, **28**, 412–420.

Sklare, M. Intermarriage and the Jewish future. *Commentary*, 1964, **37**, 46–52.

Skodak, M., & Skeels, H. M. A final follow-up study of one hundred adopted children. *Journal of Genetic Psychology*, 1949, **75**, 85–125.

Smith, M. B. The revolution in mental-health care—A "bold new approach." *Transaction*, 1968, **5**(5), 19–23.

Soffietti, J. P. Bilingualism and biculturalism. *Journal of Educational Psychology*, 1955, **46**, 222–227.

Sommer, R. Small group ecology in institutions for the elderly. In L. Pastalan & D. H. Carson (Eds.), *Spatial behavior of older people*. Ann Arbor: University of Michigan–Wayne State University, Institute of Gerontology, 1970. Pp. 24–39.

Soskin, W. F., Duhl, L. J., & Leopold, R. L. Socio-cultural dilemmas in the world of adolescence and youth. Cited in R. Menninger, What troubles our troubled youth? *Mental Hygiene*, 1968, **52**, 323–329.

Spence, D. P., Gordon, C. M., & Rabkin, J. Effects of rejection on psychogenic hunger. *Psychosomatic Medicine*, 1966, **28**, 27–33.

Spitz, R. A. The role of ecological factors in emotional development in infancy. *Child Development*, 1949, **20**, 145–156.

Spock, B. *The common sense book of baby and child care*. (Rev. ed.) New York: Pocket Books, 1957.

Stark, R., & Glock, C. Y. *American piety: The nature of religious commitment*. Berkeley and Los Angeles: University of California Press, 1968.

Stone, L. J., & Church, J. *Childhood and adolescence*. (2nd ed.) New York: Random House, 1968.

Stranz, I. Marijuana use of middle- and upper-class adult Americans. Doctoral dissertation, School of Public Health, UCLA, 1971.

Streib, G. F., & Schneider, C. J. *Retirement in American society*. Ithaca, N. Y.: Cornell University Press, 1971.

Suchman, E. A. The hang-loose ethic and the spirit of drug use. *Journal of Health and Social Behavior*, 1968, **9**, 146–155.

Sullivan, H. S. *Conceptions of modern psychiatry*. New York: Norton, 1953.

Sulzberger, M. B., & Zaidens, S. H. Psychogenic factors in dermatologic disorders. *Medical Clinics of North America*, 1948, **32**, 669–685.

Szasz, T. *The myth of mental illness*. New York: Harper & Row, 1961.

Tanner, J. M. *Education and physical growth*. London: University of London Press, 1961.

Taylor, R. A. Personality traits and discrepant achievement: A review. *Journal of Counseling Psychology*, 1964, **11**, 76–82.

Telford, C. W., & Sawrey, J. M. *Psychology: A concise introduction to the fundamentals of behavior.* Monterey, Calif.: Brooks/Cole, 1968.

Terman, L. *Psychological factors in marital happiness.* New York: McGraw-Hill, 1938.

Terman, L. M., & Oden, M. H. *The gifted group at mid-life: Genetic studies of genius,* Vol. 5. Stanford, Calif.: Stanford University Press, 1959.

Tharp, R. G. Psychological patterning in marriage. *Psychological Bulletin,* 1963, **60,** 97–117.

Thomas, A., Chess, S., & Birch, H. G. *Temperament and behavior disorders in children.* New York: New York University Press, 1968.

Thompson, H. Physical growth. In L. Carmichael (Ed.), *Manual of child psychology.* New York: Wiley, 1946. Pp. 255–294.

Thompson, W. E. Pre-retirement anticipation and adjustment in retirement. *Journal of Social Issues,* 1958, **14**(2), 35–45.

Thompson, W. E., & Streib, G. F. Situational determinants: Health and economic deprivation in retirement. *Journal of Social Issues,* 1958, **14**(2), 18–34.

Thorne, F. C. The incidence of nocturnal enuresis after age five. *American Journal of Psychiatry,* 1944, **100,** 686–689.

Toffler, A. *Future shock.* New York: Random House, 1970.

Trent, J. W., & Craise, J. L. Commitment and conformity in the American college. *Journal of Social Issues,* 1967, **23**(3), 34–51.

Trent, J. W., & Medsker, L. L. *Beyond high school.* Berkeley: University of California Press, 1967.

Troll, L. E. Similarities in values and other personality characteristics in college students and their parents. *Merrill-Palmer Quarterly,* 1969, **15,** 323–336.

Tyler, L. E. Human abilities. *Annual review of psychology,* 1972, **23,** 177–206.

United States Department of Labor, Bureau of Labor Statistics. *Retired couple's budget,* 1966.

Vener, A. M., & Snyder, C. A. The preschool child's awareness and anticipation of adult sex-roles. *Sociometry,* 1966, **29,** 159–168.

Voeks, V. *On becoming an educated person.* (2nd ed.) Philadelphia: Saunders, 1964.

Vroom, V. H. Industrial social psychology. In G. Lindzey & E. Aronson (Eds.), *The handbook of social psychology,* Vol. 5. Reading, Mass.: Addison-Wesley, 1969. Pp. 196–268.

Wallace, R. K. Physiological effects of transcendental meditation. *Science,* 1970, **167,** 1751–1754.

Wallas, G. *The art of thought.* New York: Harcourt, 1926.

Wallin, P. Cultural contradictions and sex roles: A repeat study. *American Sociological Review,* 1950, **15,** 288–293.

Wallin, P., & Riley, R. Reactions of mothers to pregnancy and adjustment of offspring in infancy. *American Journal of Orthopsychiatry,* 1950, **20,** 616–622.

Walster, E., Aronson, V., Abrahams, D., & Rottmann, L. Importance of physical attractiveness in dating behavior. *Journal of Personality and Social Psychology,* 1966, **4,** 508–516.

Wechsler, H. Halfway houses for former mental patients: A survey. *Journal of Social Issues,* 1960, **16**(2), 20–26.

Weil, A. T., Zinberg, N. E., & Nelson, J. M. Clinical and psychological effects of marihuana in man. *Science,* 1968, **162,** 1234–1242.

Wenger, M. A., Jones, F. N., & Jones, M. H. *Physiological psychology.* New York: Holt, Rinehart, & Winston, 1956.

Westin, A. *Privacy and freedom.* New York: Atheneum, 1967.

White, R. W. *The abnormal personality.* (3rd ed.) New York: Ronald Press, 1964.

Whiting, J. W. M., & Child, I. L. *Child training and personality: A cross-cultural study.* New Haven, Conn.: Yale University Press, 1953.

Williams, A. F. Social drinking, anxiety, and depression. *Journal of Personality and Social Psychology,* 1966, **3,** 689–693.

Williams, R. J. Biological approach to the study of personality. Paper presented at the University of California at Berkeley, 1960. (In E. A. Southwell & H. Feldman (Eds.), *Abnormal psychology: Readings in theory and research.* Monterey, Calif.: Brooks/Cole, 1969. Pp. 306–317.)

Wolfe, J. B. Effectiveness of token-rewards for chimpanzees. *Comparative Psychology Monographs,* 1936, **12**(60).

Wolfgang, M. E. Violence and human behavior. In F. F. Korten, S. W. Cook, & J. I. Lacey (Eds.), *Psychology and the problems of society.* Washington, D. C.: American Psychological Association, 1970. Pp. 309–326.

Wood, M. Clinical sensory deprivation: A comparative study of single and two bed room patients. Doctoral dissertation, School of Public Health, UCLA, 1971.

Wrenn, C. G., & Crandall, E. B. Behavior ratings and scholarship among college freshmen. *Journal of Educational Research,* 1941, **34,** 259–264.

Yarrow, M. R., Campbell, J. D., & Burton, R. V. *Child rearing: An inquiry into research and methods.* San Francisco: Jossey-Bass, 1968.

Yarrow, M. R., Scott, P., deLeeuw, L., & Heinig, C. Child-rearing in families of working and nonworking mothers. *Sociometry,* 1962, **25,** 122–140.

Zander, A., & Quinn, R. The social environment and mental health: A review of past research at the Institute for Social Research. *Journal of Social Issues,* 1962, **18**(3), 48–66.

Zborowski, M. *People in pain.* San Francisco: Jossey-Bass, 1969.

Zinker, J. C., & Fink, S. L. The possibility for psychological growth in a dying person. *Journal of General Psychology,* 1966, **74,** 185–199.

Zlutnick, S., & Altman, I. Crowding and human behavior. In J. F. Wohlwill & D. H. Carson (Eds.), *Behavioral science and the problems of our environment.* Washington, D. C.: American Psychological Association, 1971.

Index